The Evolution of Human Behavior:
Primate Models

A book in the Williams Press, Inc., Series

A grant from the E. A. Barvoets Fund
helped pay the costs of publishing this book.

SUNY Series in Primatology
EMIL MENZEL and RANDALL L. SUSMAN, *Editors*

All Royalties from the sale of this book will be donated to The Primate Conservation Appeal, established under the auspices of the International Primatological Society and the World Wildlife Fund-US, to assist in funding and implementing primate conservation projects.

Warren G. Kinzey, *Editor*

The Evolution of
Human Behavior:
Primate Models

1987

State University of New York Press

Published by
State University of New York Press, Albany

© 1987 State University of New York

For information, address State University of New York
Press, State University Plaza, Albany, N.Y., 12246

Library of Congress Cataloging in Publication Data

The Evolution of human behavior.

(SUNY series in primatology)
Papers presented at a symposium in Chicago at the
Eighty-second Annual Meeting of the American Anthropologi-
cal Association, Nov. 19, 1983, sponsored by the
American Association of Physical Anthropologists.
Bibliography: p.
Includes index.
1. Primates—Behavior—Congresses. 2. Primates—
Evolution—Congresses. 3. Social evolution—Congresses.
4. Behavior evolution—Congresses. 5. Human behavior—
Congresses. 6. Animal models in research—Congresses.
I. Kinzey, Warren G., 1935-   . II. American

10 9 8 7 6 5 4 3 2 1

Contents

Introduction   WARREN G. KINZEY   vii

I. Behavioral Innovations

1. **Gathering by Females:** The Chimpanzee Model Revisited and the Gathering Hypothesis
   NANCY M. TANNER   3
2. **Transportation of Resources:** Reconstructions of early hominid socioecology: a critique of primate models
   RICHARD POTTS   28

II. Primate-derived Models

3. **African Apes:** The significance of African apes for reconstructing human social evolution
   RICHARD W. WRANGHAM   51
4. **Chimpanzees:** Pygmy chimpanzees and common chimpanzees: models for the behavioral ecology of the earliest hominids
   RANDALL L. SUSMAN   72
5. **Baboons:** Baboon models and muddles
   SHIRLEY C. STRUM & WILLIAM MITCHELL   87
6. **Monogamous Primates:** A primate model for human mating systems
   WARREN G. KINZEY   105
7. **Howler Monkeys:** Diet, dimorphism, and demography: perspectives from howlers to hominids
   CAROLYN M. CROCKETT   115

III. Paleoecological Models

8. **Cytogenetic Methods:** Social and ecological aspects of primate cytogenetics
   JON MARKS   139

v

9. **Morpho-Physiological Analysis of Diets:** Species-specific dietary patterns in primates and human dietary adaptations
   ROBERT W. SUSSMAN   151

IV. Theoretical Issues

10. The reconstruction of hominid behavioral evolution through strategic modeling
    JOHN TOOBY AND IRVEN DEVORE   183

References   239

Contributors   288

Author Index   289

Subject Index   295

Introduction

Twenty-five years ago Sherry Washburn organized "The Social Life of Early Man," a Wenner-Gren conference aimed at reconstructing early hominid behavior. It was the first systematic attempt to put primate studies in the perspective of human evolution. Yet, field studies of the nonhuman primates were still in their infancy: François Bourliere wrote at that time, "Very few species of primates have been studied so as to make possible a good comparison of their social grouping in natural conditions . . . [and] the social life in the wild of a species as well known as the chimpanzee still remains almost a complete mystery." (1961:1) Since then we have learned a great deal about the natural behavior of nonhuman primates. In particular we now know that short-term studies provide information that is frequently not verified in longer, more detailed studies. The importance of these longer studies (over many years) is particularly relevant to modeling of early human behavior, as a number of contributors to this volume point out. After more than two decades, it is time again to relate primate field studies in some meaningful way to early human evolution. Why should anthropologists be concerned about nonhuman primates?

The previous question provided the rationale for organizing a symposium in Chicago at the eighty-second annual meeting of the American Anthropological Association, November 19, 1983. It was felt that anthropologists in all subdisciplines should be aware of recent studies in primate behavior and of the relevance of these studies for the understanding and interpretation of early hominid behavior patterns. Therefore, a symposium entitled "Primate Models for the Evolution of Human Behavior" was appropriate at this time and place. Since most anthropologists who study primate behavior are also physical anthropologists it was also appropriate that the American Association of Physical Anthropologists should sponsor such a symposium.

Can field studies of primate behavior tell us anything about early human behaviors, or even about the origin of such behaviors? One could make a case for looking at a variety of models, including living human hunter-gatherers (discussed by Potts). Taking a broader perspective one could also include some nonprimates as models: the social carnivores have been considered by some anthropologists (discussed by Susman) as appropriate for understanding the social behavior of our presumed "carnivorous" early ancestors. But, as Strum and Mitchell state, "In the end, anthropologists favored primates, arguing for phylogeny over ecology and emphasizing homology rather than convergent analogy."

The purpose of this symposium was to focus on the primate models alone, thus manifesting the value and importance of field studies of nonhuman primates within an anthropological framework. The contributors were asked to present their papers in such a way as to reflect this concept. Discussion at the symposium was taped, transcribed, and the papers were revised in light of the discussion. The paper by Marks, presented at the same meeting but in a different symposium, was considered particularly appropriate and has been included here as well. After the papers were finalized, Irven DeVore and John Tooby kindly consented to review them and write a final chapter relating the papers to a broader general framework of the process of anthropological modeling. The papers are presented in three sections.

The first section of the book deals with what Tooby and DeVore (this volume) refer to as hominid scenarios. These are models based on the proposition that some "key" behavioral innovation was involved in the evolutionary divergence of the human line from the ape line. Morphologically the earliest hominids differed from their ape-like forebears in possessing features reflecting bipedality and/or reduction in the anterior dentition (canine and incisors). The fossil evidence cannot yet clearly distinguish which of these features preceded the other; they may have begun to develop simultaneously. Most theories of hominid divergence assume that bipedalism was the earliest major hominid morphological innovation and seek its behavioral precursors. Other scenarios (e.g., Jolly's hypothesis) assume that dental changes came first and seek a dietary rationale. Irrespective of which morphological innovation initiated the hominid lineage, most would agree today that some key *behavioral* feature, or features, preceded the morphological changes. Over the years several such innovative behavioral features have been suggested.

The earliest scenario suggested was that of Man the Hunter. This idea was developed by Darwin and received its most noted recognition in Robert Ardrey's *African Genesis* (1961) and *The Hunting Hypothesis* (1976). Hunting was probably not the key behavioral feature in redirecting hominid evolution (see article by Tanner, for example), and is not included as a major focus of this volume. The role of hunting in previous reconstructions is elaborated by Susman, however, who points out that when it became clear australopithecines were the hunted and not the hunters, evidence for hunting by the earliest hominids evaporated. In the final chapter Tooby and DeVore emphasize that hunting *is* a part of the hominid foraging pattern and its role *later* in the human evolutionary process remains to be properly assessed. After all, humans *do* eat more meat than does any other primate even though the diet of most hunter-gatherer groups consists largely of plant foods.

Another popular scenario is Clifford Jolly's "seed-eaters" hypothesis (1970, 1973) that the basic hominid adaptation was feeding on small objects such as seeds. Potts refers to this adaptation in his discussion of primate models. Many introductory textbooks have also adopted this scenario. For example, Hoebel and Weaver state: "the first adaptation which differentiated the hominid line from that of the hominoids (dryopithecines) was a ground-dwelling, seed-and-small-object-eating adaptation that led to frontal dental reduction and bipedalism." (1979:106) This hypothesis is based on at least two untenable assumptions, however; that (1) certain dental characters signify both small-object feeding and terrestriality—which is not always the case since pandas (Sicher, 1944), *Cebus* monkeys (Kinzey, 1974), and mountain gorillas (Groves, 1970) all have the requisite dental complex; and, (2) *Ramapithecus* is the earliest hominid fossil—an assumption that is no longer valid (Andrews and Cronin, 1982; Pilbeam, 1983; Wolpoff, 1982; see also Kay, 1985).

In 1972 a Welsh writer, Elaine Morgan, proposed the Aquatic Ape scenario in which she suggested that the initial human adaptation was to life in the sea. The heat of the Pliocene, she claimed, drove ancestral females to the water to avoid predators and to cool off. The men followed. There, hairlessness (as on aquatic mammals), erect posture (to keep the head above water), and stone tools (to open shellfish as do sea otters) were all adaptations to the aquatic environment. Her vivid imagination has produced exciting reading, although there is no fossil evidence to support this just-so story. One attraction of her scenario, however, is that it shifted the emphasis away from Man the Hunter.

Another scenario is Owen Lovejoy's hypothesis (1981) that the key human innovation was an enhancement of reproductive fitness through monogamous pair bonding, reduced feeding competition, and increased male parental investment through provisioning. There are several problems with this hypothesis. For example, data from chimpanzees indicate that it is adult females (rather than adult males) who most frequently share food with their young. Crockett disagrees with several aspects of Lovejoy's hypothesis; the monogamous mating aspect is discussed by Kinzey in chapter six; and Tooby and DeVore discuss the scenario at length in the final chapter. Lovejoy's hypothesis attempted to keep the hominid males "in charge" in the face of a growing awareness of the importance of gathering rather than hunting in the hominid transition.

This brings us to the scenario of Gathering by Females. The gathering hypothesis proposes that since all apes (and most humans) eat predominantly plants, a key innovation that led to a separate hominid evolutionary line was the regular use of tools to gather plants. The importance of gathering among contemporary peoples was initially described by Richard Lee (1968) in a book ironically entitled *Man the Hunter*. Lee pointed out that in tropical hunter-gatherer societies some 60–80% of the diet is usually gathered plant food; they are, in fact, *gatherer*-hunters. In 1970, at the 69th Annual Meeting of the American Anthropological Association, Sally Linton provided the counterpoint to "Man the Hunter" in a paper she later published as "Woman the Gatherer" (Linton 1971). Linton pointed out problems in dealing with only half the species when theorizing about behavior and she suggested that gathering plants predated hunting. She also suggested that the earliest tools were almost certainly used for gathering plants. This idea became "The Gathering Hypothesis", and was developed more fully in the mid 1970's and early 1980's by Nancy Tanner, Adrienne Zihlman and Frances Dahlberg (Tanner and Zihlman 1976; Zihlman and Tanner 1978; Dahlberg 1981; Tanner 1981; Zihlman 1981, 1983; Tanner 1983).

Tanner was thus one of the first to suggest the early importance of gathering (as contrasted to early hunting) in human evolution. In chapter one of this book Tanner further reviews and develops The Gathering Hypothesis. She reconstructs an African stem-hominoid, and hypothesizes that natural selection and sexual selection were both significantly involved in the subsequent divergence of the human lineage from what she calls the ape stem. Gathering, she suggested, grew out of a generalized ancestral hominoid behavior pattern which already had developed "considerable potential for behavioral diversity." This capacity for behavioral diversity, common to both humans and chimpanzees, combined with molecular, morphological and fossil data indicating their phylogenetic closeness, makes studying the chimpanzee valuable in creating a model of an ancestral African hominoid. Recent field data indicate that among chimpanzees it is the female who uses tools most often and most persistently to obtain food, whether plant *or* animal. Among human gatherer-hunters most plant food (as well as some animal food) is also collected by females. Tanner states that the initial use of tools was specifically for the gathering of plants, and there was a subsequent sequence in the elaboration of the use of tools for food-getting; the invention of tools for container-making, pirating of carnivore kills, skinning, butchering and eventually hunting, fishing, then agriculture, all came much later. In chapter one, Tanner focuses on reconstructing characteristics of what she calls an ape stem population, and how the innovation of gathering was involved in the hominid transition.

Most of the time nonhuman primates consume food where they find it. A significant early hominid behavioral innovation was the transportation of resources. Hewes (1961) was the first to suggest that hominid bipedalism arose in connection with the carrying of food. Carrying made bipedalism advantageous. In view of the current controversy whether early hominids were scavengers or hunters (Shipman, 1983, 1986) it is significant that Hewes suggested scavenged meat was one of the earliest food items carried.* Subsequently he offered supporting evidence from several examples of nonhuman primates as bipedal food-carrying models (Hewes, 1964). Isaac (1976) elaborated on this idea and suggested that the significant innovation was transporting resources to a common gathering spot which he called a home base at which food sharing took place. In chapter 2, Potts suggests a variation of the home base scenario in which the earliest hominid tool sites, roughly 2 million years ago, functioned as "caches" for stone tools to which animal carcasses were transported for processing. Potts believes that this kind of reconstruction of the behavior of Lower Pleistocene hominids requires archeological data and cannot be modeled by any *one* living nonhuman primate (a view also espoused by Wrangham, Susman, and Strum and Mitchell). Potts suggests instead that primate models can help form hypotheses about various hominids, but cannot test them. (A similar point is made by Strum and Mitchell.) A full understanding of early hominid behavior patterns requires looking at living gatherer-hunters as well. Potts points out, however, that a simple analogy between extinct hominids and either living gatherer-hunters or living primates is unreliable largely because of human uniqueness. In the final chapter, Tooby and DeVore expand at length on the way in which human uniqueness compounds the difficulty of the modeling process.

---

* He suggested that food transport to a lair was followed by use of tools to cut up the scavenged carcass and then the meat was shared (Hewes, 1961).

The second section of the book looks at a series of individual primate-derived models. Two models have been used most frequently for interpreting the origin of human behavior: the baboon (a more analogous model) because, like humans, it is primarily terrestrial with an arboreal ancestry; and, the chimpanzee (a more homologous model) because, of the living nonhuman primates it is the most closely related to humans. This closeness of relationship disregards the recent suggestion of a particularly close relationship between humans and orangutans (Schwartz, 1984a, 1984b), and reflects much early work in anatomy, physiology, and embryology as well as recent studies on DNA hybridization (Sibley and Ahlquist, 1984). In addition to the baboon and the chimpanzee several other models are discussed.

In the first model of this section, Wrangham attempts to reconstruct early hominid social relations by looking at variability in patterns of social behavior in African apes and humans, and developing a list of shared features—phylogenetically conservative traits—which he believes were present in the common ancestor. This is an innovative approach for deriving an "ancestral suite" of hominid behaviors (although it resembles the suggestion long ago of Bartholomew and Birdsell [1953] of the possibility of extrapolating from behavioral data on other mammals. But, that was before field data were available for most primates, and before the development of the cladistic method.) Wrangham states, "The aim is to find out whether it is a useful approach, rather than to provide a full description of ancestral social organization." But, Wrangham does reconstruct several characteristics of a common ancestor: closed social networks, female exogamy without alliance bonds between females, males having sexual relationships with more than one female, and male-dominated hostile intergroup encounters. He believes that variability among living hominoids can best be understood in terms of two evolutionary pressures: optimal foraging theory to explain some of the differences in social organization, and reproductive competition to account for the formation and structure of groups. Though ape patterns can thus be understood, they also show that even small ecological differences have large consequences for social behavior. This means that our models of early hominid behavior will remain speculative until we know more about their ecology. Wrangham argues (as do both Potts and Susman) that no one living ape provides a "best fit" model for human behavior, but by doing a comparative socioecology of the living apes and humans, it may be possible to arrive at archetypal hominoid behaviors as a base line for the origin of hominid behavioral patterns.

In the next chapter, Susman shows how the baboon model was based on justifiable but incorrect interpretations of the fossil record. He suggests the same pattern of false assumptions—in this case an exclusively savanna-grassland environment for the earliest hominids—may influence the concept of the open-woodland chimpanzee as a hominid model. Susman describes both bipedal and arboreal aspects of australopithecine morphology and suggests that if the chimpanzee is to be used as a model, both savannah and forest forms must be compared. The fossil record now indicates that "the common ancestor of African apes and hominids was forest-adapted to a greater extent than we once thought," and thus strictly forest-adapted pygmy chimpanzees assume special importance. They have more cohesive social groups and reduced intragroup aggression compared with common chimpanzees—behaviors that may well have been important in the earliest hominids.

In chapter 5, Strum and Mitchell take an historical perspective in their review of studies of baboon behavior. They discuss three features that previous baboon models have emphasized: predation, aggression, and dominance. In each case they discuss the way in which these behaviors are or are not common in this ground-dwelling primate and might, or might not, reflect trends in early hominid behaviors. The baboon received an early surge of interest as a model, but more from the general public than from the scientists doing the field work. According to Strum and Mitchell, early concepts about primate society were primarily generalizations about baboon society, which then became the basis for reconstructions of early hominid social life. Now, in contrast, long-term studies of baboons by Strum and others provide provocative insights not anticipated by the earlier studies. To make interpretive generalizations about human behavior, Strum and Mitchell plead for detailed, long-term field studies with a comparative approach. They insist on a model using more than one species in more than one place and time, and suggest that a simple analogy between any one primate, such as the baboon, and early hominids "should be abandoned."

It has been suggested that early hominids were monogamous (Lovejoy, 1981), yet no living monogamous primate provides a useful model for early hominids. Kinzey discusses the behavior of monogamous primates, and compares those species which have a monogamous mating system (e.g., gibbons and titi monkeys) with a group which has recently been shown to have a form of extended family structure (e.g., marmosets and tamarins). The former tend to be behaviorally conservative and stereotyped; whereas, the latter are behaviorally and ecologically more plastic. The implication is that among human families forms of extended family have greater potential flexibility and adaptability than isolated nuclear families. The latter appear to occur only among industrial societies or in gatherer-hunter groups where, for ecological reasons usually related to a need for mobility, foraging in large groups would be counterproductive. Increased adaptability in monogamous human groups is obtained through increased social networks by means of kin ties, as well as through the development of non-kin relationships.

In chapter 7, Crockett reviews studies of howler monkeys, emphasizing data on sexual dimorphism, diet and foraging strategy, infanticide, and seasonal versus habitat differences in activity patterns. Even though *Alouatta* has not been used as a hominid model *per se*, conclusions from studying howlers—the longest and most extensively studied nonhuman primate—have significance for studies of human ancestry. Several lessons may be learned from the howlers: (1) A single species—such as the earliest hominid—may occupy a wide range of habitats, even though it has a single "feeding niche". (2) Howlers teach us that natural selection may operate on the two sexes differently and therefore the behavior of females may have constrained evolution of the behavior of males, or vice versa. (3) Skeletal material can lead to erroneous predictions with respect to adult sex ratio. (4) Seasonal differences in behavior may be greater than habitat differences. In this context it is significant that Grine (1984) recently suggested that dental differences between gracile and robust australopithecines may have been due largely to *seasonal* differences in diet encountered by the latter. Many have argued that primates, and especially chimpanzees, make the best models for human behavior because of their close phylogenetic relationship, but Crockett demonstrates quite convincingly that "we should seek the application of larger principles of evolutionary theory to particular categories of behavior." In their summary chapter, Tooby and DeVore emphasize the application of principles of behavioral ecology and evolutionary theory as appropriate analytic sources for (strategic) modeling.

The third section of the book deals with paleoecological models. These are reconstructions that depend on particular methods that use features of living animals, especially primates, for the development of evolutionary principles. Marks' methodology is cytogenetics and Sussman's is morphophysiology of digestion.

Marks proposes a new approach to the determination of ancestral social structure. He looks at chromosomal patterns and relates them to behavioral features of living animals. He proposes that reduction of barriers to gene flow results in inhibition of genetic drift, thereby favoring chromosomal homogeneity; patchy, discontinuous environments result in the accumulation of chromosomal changes. Marks presents evidence from macaques and baboons and from gibbons, respectively, to support his prediction. The former have large mobile troops with frequent transfer of individuals which inhibits genetic drift, together with karyotypic uniformity; the latter have small territorial groups which favor genetic drift, together with karyotypic diversity. From a comparison of ape and human chromosomal karyotypes Marks infers that the social structure of the earliest hominids should in general be chimpanzee-like and/or gorilla-like. While this is not a surprising prediction, it is surprising that such a prediction can be made from the study of chromosomes! We are a long way from predicting precise behavioral patterns from the chromosomes, but Marks provides considerable insight in this direction.

In chapter nine, Sussman proposes that ancestral diet can be inferred from conservative features of the digestive tract of related living animals. Among populations of the same species of primate living in different habitats, certain aspects of diet and foraging behavior seem to remain constant, even when plant species in these habitats differ radically. Further, certain conservative features of alimentary tract morphology can be related to these dietary propensities. This implies that dietary adaptations are conservative among primates. Drawing largely from morphophysiological research, Sussman introduces and defines the concept of "species-specific dietary pattern" and discusses how this concept might be useful in the study of the evolution of human dietary adaptations. Finally, based on these studies, he suggests that early hominids were mainly frugivorous omnivores that consumed a relatively minor proportion of animal matter—a conclusion not inconsistent with the models of Tanner, Potts, Susman, and Crockett.

Chapter 10 summarizes the theoretical issues developed in this book. Tooby and DeVore discuss the concept of modeling and they explore the distinction between referential and conceptual models. Most of the models discussed in the book are referential—and Tooby and DeVore believe they all are deficient because, among other things, they explore similarities between the human and the nonhuman model and ignore human uniqueness—a point also made by Potts in chapter 2. If there is any model that is to be truly useful in the interpretation of early human behavioral patterns, it will be an eclectic model—that is, no *one* model is appropriate for all parameters. Humans *are* unique! Tooby and DeVore bring the story full circle. DeVore was one of the earliest anthropologists to look at primate behavior in the wild and, together with Washburn, to develop a referential model for human behavior based on baboon behavior. Now, Tooby and DeVore suggest that the earlier model, and in fact every referential model, is inadequate and that what is needed is a conceptual model. According to them, "A powerful conceptual model for reconstructing hominid evolution does not yet exist . . ." but Tooby and DeVore suggest ways in which it may be constructed, based on behavioral ecology and evolutionary theory.

Primate patterns are patterns of social interaction and "there are as many sets of primate patterns as there are different kinds of primates." (Dolhinow, 1972:vi). But the study of nonhuman primates is not a useless endeavor devoid of any relationship to humans; rather, the variety and scope of behavioral differences are the result of two interacting factors—habitus and heritage, as William K. Gregory long ago suggested. We have made great strides in the past 30 years, but we are still trying to sort out the precise influence of each. "To progress," as Tooby and DeVore conclude at the end of this volume, we "must discard prime mover and single species primate models of human evolution, and instead recognize that evolutionary biology provides the conceptual model that will organize our understanding of hominids." We hope that this book will provide a stimulus for such a synthesis.

I

Behavioral Innovations

CHAPTER ONE

The Chimpanzee Model Revisited and the Gathering Hypothesis

NANCY MAKEPEACE TANNER

A CHIMPANZEE MODEL OF WHAT?

Chimpanzees prove particularly useful for reconstructing a model of behavioral and morphological characteristics of the population from which hominids diverged. Phylogenetically, the chimpanzee also may be the living ape most closely related to humans. Chimpanzees do not provide a model of the earliest hominids themselves. For that we need a hypothesis—and I recommend the Gathering Hypothesis—to take us from ape stem[1] to early hominid.

This chapter presents a fresh characterization of natural and sexual selection, outlines relevant phylogenetic information from molecular primate studies, delineates the ape stem adaptation behaviorally and morphologically, and presents important new data regarding how and why the gathering innovation very likely was involved in the transition from ancestral ape to early hominid. The chapter does not deal with the entire expanse of human evolution, from ancestral ape to *Homo sapiens*. A careful step by step approach to this complex analysis, utilizing research results relevant to each period, is required to avoid such common problems as ignoring one to two *million* years of highly probable tool use by bipedal hominids *before* stone tools are recognizable in the archeological record.[2] For my analysis of other periods, I refer the reader to prior work on environmental factors related to human food-getting styles over time and space (Tanner, 1983) and on australopithecine speciation (Tanner, 1981, 1985a); and I hope you will wait patiently for a presentation of how australopithecine evolution, plus further critical innovations, provided the foundation for *Homo erectus* to emerge (Tanner, in preparation).

3

Just as Darwin's original theory of gradual human evolution from animal ancestors received and still receives opposition from those who believe in "man's" creation by God, so too new theoretical implications of contemporary research may not be entirely grasped when gender concepts are still partially guided by traditional western cultural values and beliefs.

Here the significance of the chimpanzee for understanding human evolution, specifically for the process of becoming human, is outlined in a context of theory and data, and gaps in information are pointed out to encourage future research.

EVOLUTIONARY THEORY

Until the 1970s concepts of human evolution encouraged exploration of the "Evolution of Man" whereas little research relevant to women or children occurred. While creationists formed Eve from Adam's rib, evolutionary studies tended to omit females. The "generic masculine" of the English language influenced Darwin's title, *The Descent of Man and Selection in Relation to Sex* (1871), and unbeknownst to researchers, crept right into the formulation of research questions and the interpretation of data for over a century. Actually, all parts of a population are significant and must be examined. This chapter outlines refinements of theory and interpretation of data which become feasible when women and children are included in the study of human evolution.

First, we must return to Darwin's concepts of natural selection and sexual selection. Natural selection largely concerns birth and the food, health, and learning of the young. It has acted primarily upon the processes of food-getting and learning during most of the long course of human evolution, rather than upon competition, power or death among adult males. It is only because such concepts and beliefs relate to certain traditional themes of western culture *and* because such features have also become genuinely important in certain striking instances that they are often given so much weight. For example, large national political structures were invented and widely adopted during just the last several thousand years of history, in contrast to the many million years of human evolution. Nations began only after the invention of agriculture made large concentrations of people feasible. Thus, international political skills have not had nearly as long to develop as small-group social skills and therefore interactions within and between large groups, especially when cultures and languages differ, are still far more awkward than within small communities. Should international conflict by nuclear warfare occur, there could be a question of species survival. However, in this kind of crisis situation, style of competition and form of conflict become significant for both the nations involved and our species as a whole, regardless of whether the politicians engaged are male *or* female. Far more often, it is whether babies stay alive and healthy, and reach adulthood able to obtain food themselves, that are fundamental to natural selection during the course of evolution.

Sexual selection, as well as natural selection, is centrally involved in the evolutionary process as Darwin long ago proposed (Darwin, 1871). Sexual selection during human evolution has followed what Darwin identified as the common pattern. It did not undergo a reversal for humans as Darwin thought, presumably in response to 19th century European sexual concepts and values. This means that female sexual selection is highly significant, and that sexual selection more than natural selection accounts for certain types of features: for example, bright male bird feathers or attractive and practical aspects of the human penis.

I define foraging and predation as the largely opportunistic ob taining of plant and animal food, respectively, usually without tools; in contrast, gathering and hunting involve both tools and forethought. In the archeological record, stone tools begin to appear in relative abundance only some one to two million years *after* the earliest bipedal hominid fossils. The period I describe in this chapter is immediately prior to the earliest hominids and considerably before recognizable stone tools. Potts (Chapter 2) speaks of a later period, *after* stone tools appear. The ancestral apes, as all apes today, were primarily foragers with a little predation. Here we examine the process of how our ancestors began to obtain their food differently.

The five major assumptions I find useful in constructing an evolutionary sequence from ancestral ape, through a transitional population, to the earliest hominids, are: (1) all parts of the population are significant and must be examined, including women and young; (2) natural selection primarily concerns the continued food, life, health and learning of the young; (3) sexual selection, as well as natural selection, has been significant in the evolutionary process, and correlates with extent of parental investment in offspring (Darwin, 1871; Trivers, 1972; Tanner, 1981); (4) gathering food plants with tools far preceded hunting large mammals with tools, although "insect hunting" with tools may have occurred among ancestral apes, as occurs among chimpanzees today; and (5) culture is the human adaptation, the mode of storage and transmission of our many patterns for the different types of food-getting and social life; it is the primary means by which human physiological omnivory proves extremely effective. With culture, curiosity, and choice, humans have been able to spread into most environments on this globe and are beginning to develop means for planetary and interstellar exploration (Finney and Jones, 1985; Tanner, 1985a).

The synthesis and analysis of already available field, fossil and laboratory data led me to suggest the chimpanzee as a model for an ancestral ape (Tanner 1981, 1985b). Today, further molecular studies are available which are relevant in determining primate phylogeny, and new field data on chimpanzees not only provide significant additional information on social interaction and food-getting but also show why the invention of gathering with tools almost certainly was an early innovation, an innovation in which females were deeply involved and which was passed on to subsequent generations by observation and teaching. These new data test and support both the Chimpanzee Model and the Gathering Hypothesis.

TRACING APE RELATIONS TO HUMANS: MOLECULAR EVIDENCE ON PHYLOGENY

Two decades of laboratory comparisons of monkeys, apes and humans have much to offer. From the extensive molecular comparisons of living humans and apes a clear cut phylogenetic framework is apparent, placing humans closer to African apes *(Pan* and *Gorilla)* than to Asian apes, and among the Asian apes placing the orangutan *(Pongo)* closer to us than is *Hylobates.* Within the African apes, some molecular studies find that chimpanzees and humans are closest; for example, see Table 1.1 and Figure 1.1.

Relative degrees of closeness can be readily ascertained at the molecular level, forming the basis for construction of a phylogenetic tree as was done by Sibley and Ahlquist (1984) on the basis of DNA-DNA hybridization/disassociation tests (Figure 1.1). There are also other types of molecular studies that are relevant to determining ape-human phylogenetic relationships (Table 1.1). Body proteins have been compared by several methods; for example, by studying direct amino acid sequencing and by indirect comparison through immunization and electrophoresis techniques. Similarities in blood group systems have been tested, and similarities in spermatozoa and endocrines have been examined. Chromosomes themselves are being studied, with banding patterns compared in detail; and relative degrees of similarity between humans and other primates have been tested through ribosomal and mitochondrial DNA hybridization/ restriction sequencing; as well as through nuclear DNA-DNA strand hybridization/disassociation. The hybridization/disassociation process is one by which excellent indices of degrees of closeness can be obtained, providing a means for building an accurate phylogeny.

Prior to Sibley and Ahlquist's study of primate DNA-DNA hybridization, samples from all ape genera frequently were not included in each molecular comparison, as can be seen in Table 1.1; their detailed study is therefore especially useful for updating and completing the ape-human phylogenetic tree.

Sibley and Ahlquist[3] (1984) were the first to demonstrate convincingly a particular closeness between humans and chimpanzees in their phylogeny. But similar findings had actually been made in prior molecular studies (see Table 1.1)—for example in comparisons of human and chimpanzee blood proteins (Goodman, 1976; Goodman et al., 1983; Goodman et al., 1984; Mintz et al., 1984; Robinson et al., 1985) as well as chromosome banding patterns (Dutrillaux, 1980; Yunis and Prakash, 1982) and mtDNA (Hasegawa and Yano, 1984; Hasegawa et al., 1985).[4]

The many molecular indications that the divergence of human from ape was relatively recent is compatible with the recent appearance of early members of the human line in the fossil record. The earliest fossil remains of hominids known to be at least partially bipedal *(Australopithecus afarensis)* date from about 3–4 Mya (Johanson and White, 1979; Jungers, 1982); and molecular dating estimates of the ape-human divergence presently range from roughly 2.6 Mya to about 8 Mya.[5] The most significant conclusion from molecular studies is that whatever the molecular comparisons, humans and living great apes (especially African apes, and in particular the chimpanzees) are extremely similar and evidently closely related.

WHAT CAN WE TELL WITHOUT FOSSILS OF THE APE STEM?

The phylogenetic framework obtained from primate molecular results has been combined with hominid fossil information available elsewhere (Tanner, 1981, 1985b; Skelton et al., 1986) to produce Figure 1.2.

The place to look for fossils of an ape stem is Africa; they should occur between 4 and 8 Mya (Sibley and Ahlquist, 1984; see also Figure 1.2). Save for a few fossil fragments from eastern Africa, 4–6.5 Mya, African hominoid fossils from this period are not yet known, although *Sivapithecus/Ramapithecus* (a pre-pongid, pre-hominid form) lived in Africa several million years prior to this (Laporte and Zihlman 1983).

Partly because fossils of an ancestral ape have not yet been found, I have suggested constructing a model of that ancestor. This model is a *conceptual* framework. Do not let the fact that I include discussion of the possible morphology of the ancestral ape mislead you into assuming that a theoretical model—such as a chimpanzee model for an ape ancestor—is analogous to or as limited as the meaning of

Table 1.1. Molecular Studies of Similarities Between Humans and Apes. The evidence from a variety of researchers, molecular materials and methods over more than two decades usually has

Year	Researcher(s)	Apes Sampled	Electrophoresis	Immuno-Reaction	Amino Acid Sequencing
1986	Koop et al.	Orang utan, compared to Common chimpanzee and Gorilla from study by Chang and Slightom			
1985	Hasegawa et al.	Common chimpanzee. Gorilla. Orangutan. Gibbon			
1985	Udea et al.	Common chimpanzee. Gorilla. Orangutan. 2 species of Gibbon			
1985	Robinson et al.	Gorilla. Orangutan. Gibbon		Chimpanzee	
1984	Chang and Slightom	Common chimpanzee. Gorilla			
1984	Mintz et al.	Common and Pygmy chimpanzee. Gorilla. Orangutan. Gibbon		Chimpanzee	
1984	Harris et al.	Common chimpanzee. Gorilla			
1984	Sibley and Ahlquist	Common and Pygmy chimpanzee. Gorilla. Orangutan. Gibbon. Siamang			
1984	Goodman et al.	Common chimpanzee. Gorilla			
1984	G. Wilson et al.	Common and Pygmy chimpanzee. Gorilla. Orangutan. Gibbon			
1983	V. Wilson et al.	Common chimpanzee. Gorilla. Orangutan		Gorilla	
1983	Goodman et al.	Common and Pygmy chimpanzee. Gorilla			
1983	Dunnette and Weinshiltoum	Common chimpanzee. Gorilla. Orangutan. Gibbon			
1982	Goodman et al.	Common chimpanzee. Gorilla. Orangutan. Gibbon			Chimpanzee
1982	Yunis and Prakash	Common chimpanzee. Gorilla. Orangutan			
1982	Brown et al.	Common and Pygmy chimpanzee. Gorilla. Orangutan. Gibbon.			
1981	Ferris et al.	Common and Pygmy chimpanzee. Gorilla. Orangutan. Gibbon			
1980	Dutrillaux	Common and Pygmy chimpanzee. Gorilla. Orangutan			
1980	Seuánez	Common and Pygmy chimpanzee. Gorilla			
1978	Azen et al.	Common chimpanzee. Gorilla. Orangutan. Gibbon	African apes		
1978	Bruce and Ayala	Common and Pygmy chimpanzee. Gorilla. Orangutan (Bornean). Orangutan (Sumatran). 2 species of Gibbon. Siamang	Great apes		
1977	Gillespie	Common chimpanzee. 2 species of Gibbon			
1977	Seuánez et al.	Common and Pygmy chimpanzee. Gorilla. Orangutan			
1976	Seuánez et al.	Common chimpanzee. Gorilla. Orangutan			
1976	Benveniste and Todaro	Common chimpanzee. Gorilla. Orangutan. 2 species of Gibbon. Siamang			
1975	Martin et al.	Common and Pygmy chimpanzee. Gorilla. Orangutan			
1975	Cronin	Common chimpanzee. Gorilla. Orangutan. Gibbon		African apes	
1973	Romero-Herrara et al.	Common chimpanzee. Gibbon			Chimpanzee
1972	Kohne et al.	Common chimpanzee. Gibbon			
1972	Hoyer et al.	Common chimpanzee. Gorilla. Orangutan. Gibbon			
1971	Doolittle et al.	Common chimpanzee. Gorilla. Orangutan. Siamang			African apes
1967	Sarich and Wilson	Common and Pygmy chimpanzee. Gorilla. Orangutan. Gibbon. Siamang		Chimpanzee	
1966	Sarich and Wilson	Common chimpanzee. Gorilla. Orangutan. Gibbon. Siamang		Chimpanzee	
1963	Goodman	Common and Pygmy chimpanzee. Gorilla. Orangutan. Gibbon	African apes		
1963	Klinger et al.	Common and Pygmy chimpanzee. Gorilla. Orangutan. Gibbon			
1962	Goodman	Common chimpanzee. Gibbon			Chimpanzee
1960	Zuckerkandl et al.	Common chimpanzee. Gorilla. Orangutan	African apes		

Study Methods with Proteins

demonstrated African apes to be closer to humans than Asian apes, and among the African apes, more often shows chimpanzees closer than gorillas.

Gene Sequencing	Study Methods with Genetic Materials				Study Summary Ape(s) closest to *Homo sapiens*
	Chromosome Band Comparison	DNA-DNA Hybridization/ Disassociation	rDNA or Mitochondrial DNA Hybridization/ Restriction and Sequencing	Other	
African apes					African apes (η -globin gene)
			Chimpanzee		Chimpanzee
				Gorilla	Gorilla (C_ε gene) Chimpanzee (cortico-steroid binding globulin)
African apes					African apes (η -globin gene) Chimpanzee (blood serum)
African apes		Chimpanzee			African apes (η -globin gene) Chimpanzee
African apes			Chimpanzee		African apes (η -globin gene) Chimpanzee
			Chimpanzee		Gorilla (electrophoresis) Chimpanzee (mtDNA)
				Chimpanzee	Chimpanzee (haemoglobin)
				Gorilla	Gorilla (serum DBH) Chimpanzee
	Chimpanzee				Chimpanzee
			African apes		African apes
			African apes		African apes
	Chimpanzee				Chimpanzee
				Gorilla	Gorilla (spermatozoa morphology) African apes (Pb and PPb protein in saliva) Great apes
		Chimpanzee			Chimpanzee
				Gorilla	Gorilla
		African apes		African apes Asian apes	African apes African apes (DNA-DNA hybridization/disassociation) Asian apes (Type C baboon viral genes)
				Gorilla	Gorilla (spermatozoa morphology) African apes
					Chimpanzee
		Chimpanzee Chimpanzee			Chimpanzee Chimpanzee
					African apes
					Chimpanzee
					Chimpanzee
					African apes
	Chimpanzee				Chimpanzee
					Chimpanzee African apes

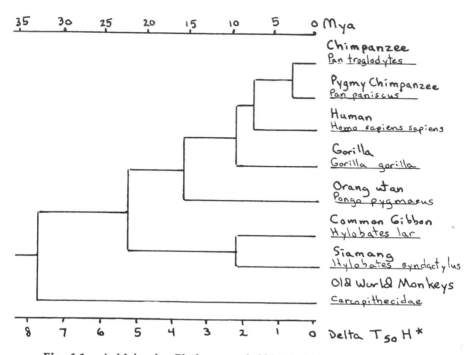

Fig. 1.1: A Molecular Phylogeny of Old World Primates. A phylogenetic tree built from detailed DNA-DNA hybridization/disassociation laboratory tests (Sibley and Ahlquist, 1984). These molecular tests provide indices of relatedness among primates. Chimpanzees are shown to be closer to humans than gorillas; and both African apes are considerably closer to humans than are any of the Asian apes. This phylogeny was calibrated by assuming a 16 Mya divergence for the Asian orang utan. Discovery of a different separation date for *Pongo* would change absolute time (dates of divergence) but not relative time (degrees of relatedness). Although "molecular clock" efforts are of interest, the primary significance of molecular experiments is in obtaining indices of relatedness which provides a phylogenetic framework.

* Relative *T*emperature at which *50%* of *H*ybridized DNA separates.

"model" in physical constructions such as "model airplane". Here I use the term "model" to refer to a framework of ideas, ideas regarding behavior as well as morphology. This is why, even should fossil information eventually become available, field studies of living apes will still prove extremely relevant to reconstructing the behavior of extinct pongids. I find the chimpanzee by far the most thought-provoking; however, comparisons of chimpanzees with other great apes and African pre-pongid, pre-hominid fossils also can be useful in pinpointing common features of the ape stem.

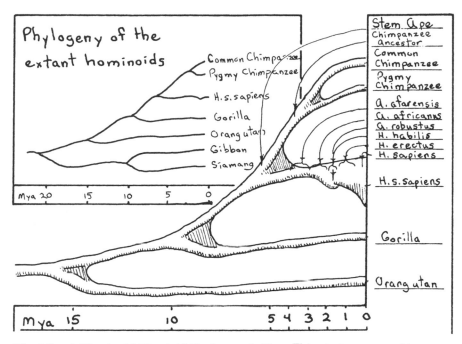

Phylogeny of the extant hominoids

Common Chimpanzee
Pygmy Chimpanzee
H. s. sapiens
Gorilla
Orang utan
Gibbon
Siamang

Mya 20   15   10   5   0

Stem Ape ancestor
Chimpanzee ancestor
Common Chimpanzee
Pygmy Chimpanzee
a. afarensis
a. africanus
a. robustus
H. habilis
H. erectus
H. sapiens
H.s. sapiens
Gorilla
Orangutan

Mya 15   10   5 4 3 2 1 0

Fig. 1.2: A Hominoid-Hominid Phylogenetic Tree. This phylogeny combines molecular and fossil data to show the relationships of humans today, fossil hominids, African apes and the Asian orang utan.

(I) ADAPTION, MORPHOLOGY AND SELECTION

Chimpanzee, gorilla and orangutan all rely heavily upon trees, each species with tree-swinging and tree-climbing locomotor abilities. Therefore, the stem-ape doubtless also relied heavily on trees. The African apes are both more terrestrial than the orangutan; so too was the earliest hominid. However, on the ground African apes knuckle-walk whereas the earliest known African hominids are already bipedal, without anatomical indication of prior knuckle-walking. The African ape stem probably had not yet evolved either physical specialization (knuckle-walking *or* bipedalism), but it probably had already begun to make use of the ground more than had *its* ancestor.

In extrapolating from the present to the past we are on solid ground with respect to the ancestral ape's diet: all apes eat high proportions of plants (Teleki, 1981; Jones and Sabater Pi, 1971; Schaller, 1976; Chevalier-Skolnikoff et al., 1982; Galdikas and Teleki, 1981; Susman, this volume; Sussman, this volume). Chimpanzees eat primarily woodland fruits, although they occasionally eat other kinds of plants and small or young animals. The gorilla is quite specialized, eating mostly leaves, stems and grasses, and has a digestive tract which can handle great quantities of cellulose (Chivers and Hladik, 1980). Asian apes also eat primarily plants, including large amounts of fruit. One can even state: all primates, including monkeys and prosimians as well as apes, eat large quantities of plants. The stem-ape almost certainly also relied heavily on plants.

In terms of the Gathering Hypothesis *per se,* the Chimpanzee Model is not essential: Whatever the ancestral ape was like it probably ate mostly plants, and early human tool innovations probably were to obtain plants. The Chimpanzee Model goes beyond this to elucidate features of the ape stem, *and* recent data on chimpanzees provide important new clues as to *how* the ape-human transition may have begun.

Early australopithecines *(A. afarensis)* are known already to be bipedal. A young female found at Afar, Ethiopia, has a human-shaped pelvis (AL 288), and footprints of two others indicating they were walking bipedally have been found at Laetoli (Leakey and Hay, 1979; Johanson et al., 1978).[6] The skeleton and footprints date roughly from 3–3.5 Mya. Combined with the strong evidence of terrestrial bipedal walking, some *A. afarensis* show fingers, wrists, and toes similar to those of chimpanzees who engage in aboreal climbing and suspension (Stern and Susman, 1983). For this reason, Stern and Susman report that "in our opinion *A. afarensis* is very close to what can be called a 'missing link'" between a prior African population and subsequent gracile and robust australopithecines (1983:314). Although *A. afarensis* was already bipedal, some could still use trees as effectively as an ape. Some also show more ape-like facial prognathism than do subsequent australopithecines (Ferguson, 1983).

There are two species of chimpanzees. Size and degree of sexual dimorphism are the anatomical features in which pygmy and common chimpanzees differ most. Great apes and fossil hominoids also differ considerably, especially in size. Here *Australopithecus afarensis,* the earliest known and most ape-like of the hominids, can help decide how to characterize an ancestral ape *A. afarensis* provides clues as to which chimpanzee's anatomy—*Pan troglodytes* or *P. paniscus*—is more likely to be similar to that of the ancestor of human and chimpanzee lines. Size will be examined first, then sexual dimorphism.

There has been a certain amount of controversy concerning the suggestion that *P. paniscus,* the smaller and less sexually dimorphic chimpanzee, might provide an especially effective prototype for a prehominid ancestor (Zihlman et al., 1978; Zihlman, 1979; Johnson, 1981; Latimer et al., 1981; Cronin, 1983; Sarich, 1983; Zihlman, 1984). This controversy began over how to interpret the averages of

measurements taken on 21 adult pygmy chimpanzee skeletons, hous-
ed at the Musée Royale de l'Afrique Centrale, Tervuren, Belgium
and at the Museum of Comparative Zoology, Harvard. The *P. paniscus*
pelvis and limb measurements were compared with measurements
from a combined sample of several australopithecine fossils. This
sample included *A. afarensis* (AL288-1 and AL1291b from Afar) and
africanus (Sts 34, Sts 1513, Sts 7 and Sts 14 from Sterkfontein),
which—although they came from sites that are quite distant geo-
graphically, in northeastern and southern Africa—provide the earliest
hominid fossil specimens indicating bipedalism. They date from about
2.5–3 Mya. Also measured were parts of more recent *A. africanus*
(Tm 1517 and OH8 from Kromdraai and Olduvai, eastern Africa),
which date from 2 Mya or less (Zihlman, 1979). The *P. paniscus*
averages proved startlingly similar to those of *Australopithecus* representing several regions and over a million years in time. The limb
measurements were the most similar;: the pelves were the most
different. This in itself is important possibly indicating that pelvic
change was particularly significant in the physical establishment of
the human line.

The limb and pelvic measurements showed that australopithecines
were rather small, as are pygmy chimpanzees. Both the earlier *A.
afarensis* (about 3–4 Mya) and the subsequent *A. africanus* (about
2–3 Mya) fossils also were small. The australopithecines' weight
estimates ranged from 32–35 kg.; pygmy chimpanzees' weight ranges
are similar, about 31–35 kg. (Zihlman, 1979). The small size of early
Australopithecus, as well as the existence of a comparatively small
chimpanzee make it quite probable that the ape that was ancestral
to both chimpanzee and human lines also was relatively small (Jungers and Susman, 1984; Sibley and Ahlquist, 1984).

Although the ape stem may have resembled the pygmy chimpanzee
with respect to size, it probably was more sexually dimorphic than
either humans *or* pygmy chimpanzees are today, resembling the
common chimpanzee in this feature. Long before either great apes
or humans evolved, primate sexual dimorphism, was quite large in
the African hominoid *Proconsul africanus* that lived about 17–22
Mya (Pilbeam, 1984). Similarly, the subsequent hominoid *Sivapithe-
cus/Ramapithecus*—whose fossils are found in Africa from about
14–12.5 to about 17 Mya and in Europe and Asia from about 5.5
to 13 or 14 Mya—exhibits considerable sexual dimorphism; so too
does the southeast Asian great ape, the orangutan, which is probably
its descendant. In Africa today, considerable sexual dimorphism continues among gorillas. The common chimpanzee maintains less size
and dental sexual dimorphism than other great apes, but still much
more than pygmy chimpanzees (Rodman and Wrangham, 1979;

Kinzey, 1984). The earliest hominids retained substantial sexual dimorphism as indicated by *A. afarensis* (Latimer et al., 1981). Fossils found in the Hadar formation, Afar, Ethiopia, dating from about 3–4 Mya, exhibit a range of dental and body sizes which Latimer et al. (1981) report to be similar to those in the sexually dimorphic gorilla. If the degree of sexual dimorphism of the African ape stem resembled that of *A. afarensis,* earlier hominoid fossils, gorilla and orangutan, then sexual dimorphism has decreased somewhat for common chimpanzees, and decreased considerably more for humans and pygmy chimpanzees.

This reduction of sexual dimorphism during evolution of the chimpanzee and human lines is intriguing. In recalling the importance of sexual selection as well as of natural selection in the Darwinian theory of evolution, I suggest that sexual selection was involved in the reduction of sexual dimorphism. Female sexual selection may have been particularly pertinent. Female sexual choice has been observed among common chimpanzees in the wild (Tutin, 1975), demonstrated by a female presenting to a male of her choice, avoidance of sex, and occasionally by walking out of sexual intercourse already underway. Extensive non-verbal, largely gestural, sexual communication concerning desired sexual position has been observed among pygmy chimpanzees at Yerkes (Savage-Rumbaugh et al., 1977; Savage-Rumbaugh et al., 1978). An interesting possibility is that the greater reduction of sexual dimorphism in contemporary humans and pygmy chimpanzees may have involved nonverbal transmission of information about matters such as desired sexual position, in a context of frequently exercised female sexual preference.

Another example of how sexual selection could have been relevant for both hominids and pygmy chimpanzees, is demonstrated by reduction of large male canine teeth. Females may have come to prefer to mate more often with males who kissed effectively than with those who growled at them and displayed large canines. Occasional kissing between common chimpanzees in the wild has been observed (Goodall, 1967). Similarily, sexual selection may have been a factor in the evolution of hominid male bipedalism. As Freud long ago noted, an erect, unclothed male with an erect and quite visible penis might have proven noticeable and attractive.

To summarize, quite a bit can be suggested concerning adaptation, morphology and selection in the ape stem by comparing pygmy chimpanzee, common chimpanzee and early fossil hominid. Further information is added when data from the other great apes and earlier primate fossils are included. Adaptively, the African ape stem probably resembled all great apes in its considerable use of trees. Behaviorally it probably spent more time on the ground than the Asian orangutan, but had not yet evolved physical adaptations for terrestrialism found in either African pongids (knuckle-walking) or hominids (bipedalism). Increased terrestriality may have preceded both subsequent terrestrial specializations that evolved in Africa. The ape stem probably ate mostly fruits but also many other plants and some animals. Morphologically the ape stem probably was relatively small but was more sexually dimorphic than humans today. In the first feature it was more like the pygmy chimpanzee; in the second, more like the common chimpanzee. Reduction of sexual dimorphism among later humans and pygmy chimpanzees probably was related to sexual selection.

(II) BEHAVIOR AND LEARNING

Chimpanzee behavior remains the most instructive for building a model of stem-ape behavior from which the human line could diverge. Because much field research concerns the common chimpanzee, more accessible and more known, comments here will concern *Pan troglodytes* (the common chimpanzee), unless specifically noted to describe *Pan paniscus* (the pygmy chimpanzee).

All apes have a relatively limited habitat compared to humans, but common chimpanzees utilize a wider range of environments than do pygmy chimpanzees or gorillas. Common chimpanzees make considerable use of sparse forest woodlands and are even known from one quite arid region. Common and pygmy chimpanzees eat a majority of fruits but both also eat other plant parts and many different kinds of plants, plus occasional small animals, giving them a greater tendency towards omnivory than other apes—a capacity important to the human line.

Common chimpanzees have the capacity not only to use more than one ecological niche, but the sizes of their ranges vary correlated with environmental setting. Ranges are smaller in more lushly forested regions than in drier less wooded areas. For example, in tropical forest regions the range may be only about 7–20 km² for a community of 40–80 animals; whereas in savanna woodlands a community of about 30–50 covering a range of about 190 km² is common, and at the more arid extreme a group of only 15–40 chimpanzees may range over as much as 700–750 km² (Tanner, 1981:85–86; Reynolds and Reynolds, 1965; Sugiyama, 1968, 1973; Itani, 1979). This is a difference of about 7 to 750 km² from smallest to largest range. However, the range in community sizes is far narrower, from only about 15 to 80 animals. The vastly greater range of sizes in human social groups is a major difference between humans and any of the apes.

Both common and pygmy chimpanzees associate in flexible, changing, diverse social groups (Kitamura, 1983; Sugiyama and Koman, 1979). Mothers and offspring, or siblings, have the most frequent and long-term contact within communities but other associations form as well. Social networks among females have been described in some detail among members of an open-air free-ranging zoo community in The Netherlands by de Waal (1982).

In the wild, interactions between communities differ, and this variability relates both to situation and communication. Females, especially when in estrus, may visit a neighboring community to check out the males, sometimes engaging in sexual interaction while there (Nishida and Kawanaka, 1972; Sugiyama, 1973; Goodall, 1973a, 1975). Adult female interactions between communities, other than sexual activities, have not been widely reported. Adult males exhibit several types of intergroup behaviors such as greeting by touching another male's genitals (Sugiyama, 1969), ignoring another male, and displaying or fighting (Goodall, 1979).

Because of the common emphasis on survival by fighting in many approaches to natural selection, and due to the greater ease in observation, aggressive interaction tends to be more widely reported than other forms of social interaction, and therefore important information on chimpanzee aggression already exists. Aggressive incidents are highly influenced by actual situation. For example, in the summer the chimpanzees at the Arnhem Burgers' Zoo in The Netherlands are allowed to range in the open air during the day (de Waal, 1982). In the cold Dutch winters they are kept in a large heated building; there, aggressive incidents become almost twice as frequent as during the summer open-air ranging. Fighting has also been observed considerably more frequently at Gombe—the region in Africa where Jane Goodall and associates have been studying chimpanzees for about a generation—than is usually seen at other areas. There, fights are most often observed in group concentrations near banana provisionings and appear to be much less frequent when groups are foraging in the wild. Also at Gombe heavy fights, some accompanied by killings, have been noted between two different communities in recent years. These intercommunity fights and killings occurred in a situation of population pressure after a new community entered the region in response to humans usurping their area for agricultural purposes, and after an extended period of increased intracommunity fighting associated with the concentrations of food in banana provisioning (Goodall, 1968c, 1977; Riss and Busse, 1977; Tanner, 1981).

In sexual interactions, a range of behavior is also evident among common chimpanzees in the wild: females most often accept sex from several males during short periods of time, usually when in estrus, but sometimes may travel with just one male for several days or even up to a few weeks while foraging for food (Tutin, 1975).

Only common chimpanzees have been observed using tools for food-getting in the wild, although in captivity some tool use by both species of chimpanzees and by orangutans has been seen (Chevalier-Skolnikoff et al., 1982; McGrew, 1981). Common chimpanzees have been observed in "cognitive mapping" of a test area, an ability which may be used in foraging for food in the wild. A chimpanzee may even "lead" other chimpanzees to find what it was shown, thus communicating referential information by nonverbal means in experiments (Menzel, 1973, 1974; Menzel and Halperin, 1975; Tanner, 1981). Several chimpanzees also have been trained in use of human language symbols; a few have even learned to use symbols with each other as well (Tanner and Zihlman, 1976b; Savage-Rumbaugh et al., 1978; Gardner and Gardner, 1978). In captivity, common and pygmy chimpanzees both can recognize themselves in mirrors, perhaps thereby indicating some "sense of self" (Gallup, 1970). These are all capacities once thought to be unique to humans, indicating our distinction from apes. Today, after the biochemists have shown us how closely relted humans and apes are, it is reassuring to find out how intelligent they are and of real interest to see how much human psychologists can assist them to learn!

To summarize, chimpanzees have considerable capacity to learn; they sometimes use tools in food getting and eat many kinds of plant foods plus a few animals; community sizes vary slightly and traveling ranges vary considerably; and various social and sexual interactions are exhibited within and between communities. Of the "great apes", the chimpanzee is the least physically specialized to a specific environment and is behaviorally the most flexible. The ape stem behaviorally was probably quite similar in these behavioral features.

Ancestral Apes and Human Gathering: What was the Transition to Human Like?

When hominids split from apes it is highly likely that the initial innovations in tool use for food-getting were for obtaining plants: plant gathering with tools was early and important. Recent observations of chimpanzee tool use in food-getting serve to explain how this may have begun to occur. New field data on chimpanzee tool use and transmission of skills will be presented in the next section. Before that, however, I shall describe the Gathering Hypothesis in more detail.

The Gathering Hypothesis proposes that an early transitional hominid innovation—one that would make obtaining sufficient food more feasible during a move from forest into savanna woodlands and grasslands—was the beginning of regular use of tools to collect plant food. The significance of gathering has now been widely discussed, with regard to how much gathering is utilized among contemporary peoples and with regard to its probable role in the hominid divergence from an ape-like ancestor (Lee, 1968, 1979; Linton, 1971; Gale, 1974; Tanner and Zihlman, 1976a; Zihlman and Tanner, 1978; Dahlberg, 1981; Tanner, 1981, 1985; Zihlman, 1981).

Because of the greater nutritional stress on females in pregnancy, lactation, and due to food sharing with young, gathering was most significant for females and probably a female change in "way of life" that occurred during the transition from an ancestral ape to the early ape-like hominid, A. afarensis. In this transition forested areas around lakes and along rivers probably were often used to obtain sufficient plant food. Females may not only have begun to walk bipedally but may have initially continued to move skillfully through the trees. This is indicated by the finger, wrist and toe measurements of A. afarensis (A.L. 288–1) the bipedal female known as "Lucy" (Stern and Susman, 1983).

Among gathering mothers natural selection was strong for bipedalism: for walking from one forested area across grasslands to another, for freeing the hands for tool-use in obtaining food, for carrying babies and food (Hewes, 1961) (especially prior to the invention of effective slings and containers), and for tool making. Whereas natural selection was more pertinent for bipedalism among gathering mothers, sexual selection was more significant for male bipedalism since their penises (expecially when "upright") could be noted more readily when they walked bipedally.

Walking bipedally assisted movements from forests, and across savanna grasslands to woodlands along river beds or near lakes. Gathering assisted in making use of both savanna grasslands and savanna woodlands, as well as in the utilization of a wider variety of plant foods than was common among ancestral apes. Gathering, together with ever-increasing innovations, learning, and information transmission, encouraged specialization in foods and food-getting to become more and more a cultural matter in a growing range of environments in the evolution of Australopithecus into Homo erectus, then Homo sapiens.

For transitional hominids who may have been moving out from jungle regions to make use of the savanna, the use of tools in gathering could make plant food—including new types of plants in the new environment—much more readily accessible. Regular tool use for food-getting could assist in the addition to the diet of plants more difficult to obtain than forest fruits, thereby making possible an early beginning of the development of that special human talent for exploiting more of the environment. In this way, gathering was probably significant to the actual process of becoming human itself. The learned technique of gathering (tool use to obtain plant food over a wider ecological range than utilized by the ancestral ape) bent the early hominid "way of life"—the australopithecine adoptation— towards a reliance on figuring out how to use tools in new ecological settings and on the social transmission of information (where to find foods, and how to make and use tools). This "figuring out" and "passing on" how to obtain new foods in new regions proved beneficial to hominids—in a feedback, interrelated manner—with physical changes involved in bipedalism and brain evolution (Geertz, 1973).

Humans today are a highly omnivorous species eating many forms of plants plus numerous animals as well (Teleki, 1981; Sussman, this volume). Within this general diversity, gathering and hunting peoples still rely heavily on plants in much of the world. Among most agricultural peoples, especially but not only in tropical areas, plant food is also very widely used. In temperate regions, meat is more prominent as a food among westerners than among Asian peoples. Only in the far North, among fishing and hunting groups such as the Eskimo where plant foods are not readily available, has the diet come to comprise largely animal food. In dietary terms, there has been a pattern of change over time and space—from that of an ape-like ancestor (who probably ate some 90% or more plant food and 10% or less animal food), to modern gathering and hunting humans in tropical areas of the world today (who still eat some 60–70% plants but have increased the animal portion of their diet to 30–40%, over time), to hunting-fishing peoples of the far North who eat largely animals (Hiatt, 1974; Dahlberg, 1981; Tanner, 1983).

The initial use of tools was specifically to gather plants; there has been a subsequent sequence of tool elaboration for food-getting since becoming human, combined with additional innovations in technology and techniques. Tools, for gathering came first; periodic subsequent inventions of tools for use in container-making, carnivore-kill pirating, skinning, butchering, and eventually hunting small and large animals, fishing, and planting gathered seeds in hoe, then plow, agriculture came much later over the several million years of human evolution (Tanner, in preparation).

THE GATHERING HYPOTHESIS: NEW DATA ON CHIMPANZEE TOOL USE

Recent reports of chimpanzees using wood sticks and rough, un-shaped rocks to hammer open nuts lend support to the Gathering

Hypothesis (Boesch and Boesch, 1981, 1983, 1984). Wild common chimpanzees in the Tai National Park, Ivory Coast, place nuts on tree roots or flat stones on the ground, or even sometimes on branches in trees, and break them open by hitting the nuts with sticks or rocks. This type of hammer-anvil arrangement is used to crack nuts open to get at food. Knowledge of chimpanzees' use of tools to obtain food, such as by this hammer-anvil arrangement, helps us realize that a fairly intelligent ancestral ape could have taken the step from such opportunistic tool use during foraging, to tool-making and more regular use of tools in plant gathering.

I have been asked why I stress female involvement in early gathering. Why wasn't plant food primarily obtained by the males, to bring to females and young back at camp? Or at least, even if regular camps were not yet utilized by the earliest hominids, why didn't males gather as much as females? After all, some 3 or 4 million years later, after planting became more widespread than gathering, both sexes appear to be quite thoroughly involved in agriculture in many parts of the world. These are all relevant questions. However, the evidence supports early tool use primarily by females to obtain plant food—probably as early as in the actual transition from ancestral ape to human. In this regard, the data on chimpanzee nut-cracking with tools is especially relevant: it is female chimpanzees that use tools the *most* to crack open the nuts. See Table 1.2.

Female chimpanzees use tools more than do males to obtain food, whether it is in more frequent nut-cracking with tools as reported by Boesch and Boesch (1981, 1983, 1984) or over longer periods of time in insect-collecting with tools as reported by McGrew (1979, 1981). Chimpanzee females use tools more often to obtain food, they

Table 1.2. Chimpanzee Nut-Cracking in Tai National Park, Ivory Coast. Females do more of all nut-cracking with tools. In particular they do much more of the more difficult cracking of coula nuts in trees and cracking panda nuts on the ground. Data from Boesch and Boesch (1984).

	Cracking of Coula Nuts			Cracking of Panda Nuts
	Ground	Tree	Total	Total
Female	336	68	404 Observations	92 Observations [*]
Male	225	6	231 Observations	37 Observations [*]

* Boesch and Boesch (1984) believe that for cracking panda nuts 89 and 19, for females and males respectively, is a more accurate representation. These are the numbers of nut-cracking sessions begun before arrival of human observers (nut-cracking sessions were often heard before they were seen). Males were more habituated to the researchers and more likely to crack nuts during presence of observers. The Boesches therefore believe that there is comparatively more male panda nut-cracking listed in Table 4 than ordinarily occurs in the wild.

continue using tools to obtain food over longer periods, and sometimes they even obtain food with tools in less social settings than males (Boesch and Boesch, 1984; McGrew, 1979).

Chimpanzee females also use tools in more complex ways for food-getting than do males. Boesch and Boesch (1981, 1984) report that it is less difficult to crack coula nuts on the ground than to crack them in trees or to crack panda nuts. For the easier coula nut-cracking on the ground, the chimpanzee needs only to think of a tool after perceiving nuts; and it can see what it wants to use as hammer and anvil simultaneously. When deciding to crack coula nuts in a tree, the chimpanzee generally sees none of these requisites simultaneously; some sort of conceptualization or "thinking ahead" appears necessary. Skill is also of a higher order in nut-cracking in trees, for when working in the trees "faultless transfers of hammer and nuts between the mouth, hands and feet between phases of work" are required (Boesch and Boesch, 1981: 591). Similarly, panda nut-cracking "also appears more difficult than coula-cracking on the ground, as it requires exact positioning of the nut at least three times during the opening process and a precise dosage of strength. Furthermore, some of the stone transports for the panda nut-cracking imply high cognitive capacities" (Boesch and Boesch, 1981: 591). In their earlier report (1981) the Boesches noted 66 females and 36 males in simple coula nut-cracking in trees and the difficult panda nut-cracking they observed 55 females and 5 males, and 40 females but just 2 males, respectively. Later (1984), with more observations, their figures were: coula nut-cracking on the ground 336 females and 225 males; for the more difficult coula nut-cracking in trees and for panda nut-cracking they observed 68 females and 6 males, plus 92 females and 37 males, respectively (Table 1.2).

Chimpanzee mothers take an active part in the tool-using apprenticeship of their female offspring by rewarding the daughters' attention with nuts or affection or even by supplying them with tools. To quote the Boesches: "the skill of female chimpanzees at Tai suggests the possibility that the first human tool-makers were women" (1981:592).

Human women continue to gather far more than men in regions where gathering remains a significant form of human subsistence, as in the tropics. The data on chimpanzees indicate also that females first *began* to gather frequently.

In the wild, chimpanzee young are carried by or hold on to their mothers much of the time from birth to about three or four years of age. During these early years the young obtain food from their mothers, largely by nursing, but mothers also share food they obtain by foraging and predation. This means that there's enough time for some body and brain growth after birth, before a youngster must become entirely self sufficient; and also there is extensive learning opportunity through extended close contact with the mother and constant observation of her.

In the transition from ancestral ape to human the children of gathering mothers had a better chance of adequate nutrition; in the new savanna environment this gave them a far better chance of survival. Once developed, the gathering innovation spread rapidly and widely within the small diverging population. Their close kin— the ape stem and evolving chimpanzees—in the nearby forests did not need to become gatherers. The efficient foraging of the ape stem remained effective in a suitable environment, as foraging also remained effective among the evolving chimpanzees.

The transitional hominid youngsters saw their mothers using tools for gathering; transitional mothers, like chimpanzees, probably taught daughters to some extent; and children's play might have included both finding the sorts of plants their mothers found, and playing with and learning to make the tools their mothers made and used. The very beginning of the shift from ancestral ape to human therefore was probably one that relied on innovation and learning. Is it any surprise that Holloway recently claimed that the brain was becoming more complex much earlier in human evolution than previously supposed? Holloway (1983) reports that the AL 162–28 (Australopithecus afarensis) endocranial cast does not show the crescent shaped "ape-fissure," or lunate sulcus, on the surface of the brain. This could imply some hominid brain reorganization as early as 3–4 Mya, although Falk (1985) does not reach this conclusion. Among these early hominids, the human learning-culture direction almost certainly was underway in behavior, and possibly a human-like direction already may have begun to appear in early hominid endocranial anatomy as well. Even very small brain reorganization or increase in brain size and/or complexity would fit well with the new pattern of learning for food-getting; the diverging hominid line may have already begun an adaptive pattern in which learning and tradition would come to play a major role.

Female chimpanzees regularly share food with their offspring (Silk, 1978). This is the case for nuts opened with tools at Tai, as well (Boesch and Boesch, 1984). Combined with pregnancy and nursing, food sharing with young puts far greater nutritional stress upon females than on males. There was a practical reason for transitional hominid females, who were feeding not only themselves but also their young during pregnancy and by nursing and sharing food with offspring, to initiate and continue a more efficient method of collecting plant food (gathering plants with tools) as they were moving out onto the savanna. Males could still meet their own needs much of the time by continuing to forage without tools. Male chimpanzees have been observed sharing food with females occasionally—but it has been small quantities of meat obtained without tools (through predation) and large fruits, obtained without tools (by foraging) that they have been observed to share (Boesch and Boesch, 1984). Therefore male sharing with females, among chimpanzees at least, does not particularly predispose them towards tool use to obtain food.

The Gathering Hypothesis therefore simply makes sense. Transitional hominid females, in communities that were moving into a new environment and becoming separated from an ancestral forest ape population, probably began using tools even more often for getting at hard-to-open food like nuts, then invented slightly more complex tools and techniques to gather plants in the new environment where fruits weren't as available. Recall that for chimpanzees to obtain enough forest fruits in a dry region their range expanded as much as thirty to one hundredfold in order to maintain a "chimpanzee-type" diet. For transitional hominids input from more regular tool use could be of real assistance in expanding the types of plants that became available in the new environment. The transitional and early hominids utilized their new gathering tools more frequently and on a more regular basis than chimpanzees use tools. Over time hominids gradually came to use tools for obtaining, collecting, carrying and processing a variety of plants in addition to simply cracking open nuts as do chimpanzees at Tai National Park. Gathering became more and more important to transitional and early hominids for a new food quest in a new locale.

CONCLUSION

With refinement of the concepts of natural and sexual selection, study of the total population (females and children as well as males), and exploration of the process of evolution step by step, human evolution is not a major biological mystery just as it does not require a special moment (as in creationism) to separate us from our close relatives, the apes.

Human evolution is a straightforward happening, one that has occurred step by step, with each step viable for its time, not taken with an end in sight or with the idea of somehow becoming American. It can be said to be "luck" that our earliest ancestors took up the development of gathering, which ended up working so well in so many environments, while our near relatives kept to foraging and predation without tools, for at that time the two lifestyles, if each undertaken in the appropriate environment, were both quite effective.

Yet gathering allowed the ever increasing use of many different environments, while foraging and predation restricted the other descendants of the ape stem to smaller and unfortunately dwindling areas. As Geertz has said, "One of the most significant facts about us may finally be that we all begin with the natural equipment to live a thousand kinds of life but end in the end having lived only one." (1973:45).

The emphasis on field studies of divergent species of primates and among highly different human cultures gives anthropology a very special resource. Primate field studies *and* cross-cultural fieldwork both are extremely important in fossil and archeological interpretation; laboratory comparisons of primates are also very significant to human evolution. These are all subdisciplines of anthropology. This is what makes anthropology, as a total field, so full of riches for the study of human evolution.

Given the persistent and increasing molecular data demonstrating close ties between humans and African apes, especially the chimpanzee, the comparison of common and pygmy chimpanzees with early hominid fossils provides a useful, straightforward procedure for deducing possible features of the stem population that was ancestral to all three: *P. troglodytes, P. paniscus* and *A. afarensis*. Anatomically, the ancestral ape probably was rather small but somewhat sexually dimorphic. From this African ape stem, size has increased for humans whereas sexual dimorphism has decreased.

In reconstructing the behavior of such an ape stem population, the many excellent field studies of chimpanzees do indicate that the ancestral ape may have possessed quite wide-ranging mental and social capacities. Range and population sizes of chimpanzee communities differ, correlated with ecological factors. Chimpanzee styles of sexual interaction and numbers of sexual partners differ situationally, partly correlated with hormones, but at least partially related to the interests and preferences of the parties involved. Interactions between various communities can also differ: from sexual interaction, pleasant excitement and a variety of greetings, ignoring each other, nervousness and defecation, or small scale fighting, to the killing that was seen at Gombe during population pressure and after their years of lesser fights during banana provisioning.

From the fact that all apes rely more heavily on plants than on animals for food, it is highly likely that the ape stem did so as well. Innovations in plant-getting tools and techniques plus the utilization of teaching and learning with communication in gathering, assisted the move out into a less well-known environment for those ancestral apes that were becoming human.

New information on chimpanzees continues to support a chimpanzee-like model for the stem-ape and to fit well with the hypothesis that early innovations by women, especially innovations of tools, techniques and sharing knowledge about plant gathering, were very much involved in the transition of the ancestral ape to the earliest hominid. For example, (1) Sibley and Ahlquist's data on human-ape-monkey DNA-DNA hybridization/disassociation verify the phylogenetic closeness of humans and African apes, and show the particular closeness of humans and chimpanzees; (2) chimpanzees are the only apes in the wild among whom certain populations are reported to use tools regularly in food-getting for nut-cracking and insect collecting; (3) Boesch and Boesch's recent observations of chimpanzees cracking nuts with tools show the most skillful tool use to be by female chimpanzees; they further report much more frequent tool use by females than by males in nut-cracking, just as noted by McGrew for insect-fishing; (4) chimpanzee mothers regularly share food with offspring, and siblings and others sometimes do so also, until the young have learned how to forage for sufficient food for themselves; and (5) Boesch and Boesch also report that chimpanzee mothers reward their daughters for learning to use tools. The process of mother-daughter teaching and learning in chimpanzee tool use appears to be a practical innovation by chimpanzee mothers given the nutritional needs of females in pregnancy, lactation, and food-sharing with offspring. An increased degree of tool use with teaching and learning for gathering in the transition from ancestral ape to human is hypothesized.

Cross-cultural studies continue to indicate that a high proportion of the food obtained and eaten by peoples of gathering-hunting societies in tropical regions is plant food provided by women from their gathering techniques, often amounting to 60 or 70% of the food, although meat brought in by men who may have spent long hours looking for animals does not go unappreciated. In Australia women collect small animals along with their gathering (Gale, 1974), and among the Agta of northeastern Luzon women and men hunt jointly, (Estioko-Griffen and Griffen, 1981). The fossil record evinces that the earliest hominids appeared in the tropics, where plant gathering continues to provide the highest proportion of food in contemporary societies living by gathering and hunting. The earliest known human fossils appear in Africa, in a somewhat different environment than that of apes but nonetheless near the regions where our closest kin, the African apes, still live. The nearest of those ape kin, the chimpanzees, eat large proportions of plants, sometimes even using tools skillfully to open nuts—plant food which otherwise would not be readily available. Transitional and early hominids were intelligent enough not only to do likewise, but to take the further steps of making and relying on tools for regular gathering which then operated in a feedback manner with the evolution of the brain.

Both the daily and generational courses of natural selection have more to do with healthy babies being born and continuing to stay alive and well until they too reproduce, than they do with aggression, or power, even though such features can be involved in creating crises of survival from time to time. Sexual selection is considerably more significant in the evolutionary process, including human origins, than has been acknowledged since Darwin wrote *The Descent of Man and Selection in Relation to Sex* (1871). Unfortunately, it was the first half of his title—his unknowing use of the "generic masculine"—that partially misguided many studies for over a century. Women actually have been very much involved from the very beginning, both in sexual selection and in gathering.

NOTES

1. When fossils of the immediate ancestor to hominids are found, they will not be identical with any living ape. However, there may be sufficient similarity to living apes for the term "ape" to be appropriate. I will therefore speak of the ancestor from which the human line branched as an "ancestral ape" or an "ape stem".

2. Earlier tools were probably wood or other organic materials that we have not yet identified in the archeological record.

3. Sibley and Ahlquist have done more than 900 experimental sets involving at least 18,000 DNA-DNA homolog hybrids over the past decade. They have studied birds as well as primates (Sibley and Ahlquist, 1986).

4. At the time of the earlier findings it was still common to pictorialize an equidistant phylogenetic trichotomy of humans and African apes—*Homo, Pan,* and *Gorilla*—according to an earlier phylogenetic tree suggested by Sarich and Cronin (1976). This is a phylogeny many researchers have utilized; and it is the one I used (Tanner 1981, 1985b).

5. At present Sibley and Ahlquist (1984), and Hasegawa et al. (1985), calibrate their molecular phylogenies differently, resulting in African ape-human divergence times ranging from 8 to 2.6 million years ago, respectively. Using 16 Mya as a calibration point for the divergence of the Asian orangutan, as do Sibley and Ahlquist, results in divergence times of about 10 Mya for gorilla and 8 Mya for chimpanzee, with the chimpanzee line splitting again about 3 Mya into common and pygmy chimpanzees. These are the estimtes I currently utilize.

However, Hasegawa et al. (1984, 1985) in working with mitochondrial DNA sequence data from which they constructed a similar hominoid phylogeny, have experimented with calculations based on other calibration points—estimates of both 90 Mya and of 65 Mya favor the more recent 65

Mya estimate because "no convincing fossils of the living orders of placental mammals have been found from the Cretaceous period . . .," and "the presumed holocaust that occurred at the end of the Cretaceous some 65 Myr ago, may have been responsible for starting a new radiation of placental mammals . ." (1985:161). According to their results indicating "the chimpanzee as the unique closest relative of humans among extant apes" (Hasegawa et al., 1985:162), they calculate the final divergence of chimpanzees from humans to be only about 2.68+0.61 Mya and suggest the possibility that the earliest known human ancestor, *A. afarensis,* and the chimpanzee ancestor still mated occasiionally, thereby accounting for many of the remaining molecular similarities between humans and chimpanzees. Intriguing as this suggestion of mating between chimpanzee ancestor and diverging hominid may be, it is not required in order for field studies of chimpanzee behavior and anatomical comparisons of *A. afarensis* with *P. troglodytes* and *P. paniscus* to be relevant in construction of an ape stem model.

6. The footprints have been variously interpreted as mother and child (Konner, 1986) and as large male and small female (Lovejoy, 1981).

CHAPTER TWO

Reconstructions of Early Hominid Socioecology: A Critique of Primate Models

RICHARD POTTS

INTRODUCTION

Information about the behavior of living primates has increased enormously over the past twenty years. During this time the data base about early hominids and their habitats has also grown rapidly. Paleoanthropologists attempt to use data from actual traces of hominids and their environmental settings to reconstruct hominid behavior and ecology. New methods of analysis have enabled inferences about early hominid locomotion, diet, tool use, and other aspects of behavior and ecology. Recent findings and changing assumptions in paleoanthropology suggest that there are important limitations in using living primates to reconstruct the behavior and socioecology of early hominids. This chapter will discuss (1) the kinds of fossil evidence for early hominid behavior; (2) whether there is a method for choosing accurate primate models for hominid behaviors that cannot be inferred directly from the fossil record; (3) the problem of possibly unique behaviors among early hominids, as suggested by archeological evidence and (4) the importance of primate behavior research for the study of early hominid adaptations.

PALEOANTHROPOLOGICAL INFERENCES

This section provides a brief overview of the kinds of prehistoric data which help to reconstruct early hominid behavior and ecology. This overview will serve to indicate gaps in our knowledge about early hominid behavior and, thus, where living primate models might be most welcome.

Certain aspects of hominid behavior and ecology can be more readily inferred, or directly tested, with evidence from the geological record. The evidence falls into three major categories: hominid fossils, paleoenvironmental data, and archeological data. Use of this evidence to reconstruct hominid adaptations requires inferential principles or analogies established from modern animals and environments. Often living primates contribute importantly to uniformitarian and analogical bases for reconstruction. Each of the three categories of evidence will be considered below.

Hominid Fossils

Hominid fossils provide data on skeletal morphology and its modification during an individual's lifetime (growth, biomechanical alterations, and changes due to diet and pathology). When arranged chronologically, fossils provide information which helps to test ideas about phylogeny. Paleoanthropologists have also used fossils to assess important behavioral and ecological characteristics of early hominids. Some examples are body size (Steudel, 1980), sexual dimorphism (Wolpoff, 1976; Trinkaus, 1980), locomotion (Preuschoft, 1971; Lovejoy et al., 1973; Stern and Susman, 1983), hand function (Napier, 1962; Susman and Creel, 1979), and diet (Kay, 1981; Grine, 1981, 1984; Walker, 1981). Inferences about behavior and body size depend on how well observable anatomical traits correlate with inferred characteristics. For instance, accurate body weight estimates require high correlations (with low standard errors) between body weight and measurable traits—e.g., femur length (Steudel, 1981) or skull length (Wood, 1979). That is, any given value measured from a fossil should correspond to a narrow range of body sizes.

Modern primates are important for testing correlations between morphological variables, on the one hand, and body size or anatomical functions, on the other. However, inferences about early hominids are extrapolations beyond known primate species. This often leads to disagreements among paleoanthropologists about those inferences. Body size estimates of hominids again provide an example of the problems involved. Many researchers consider it inappropriate to use regression formulas across different populations of *Homo sapiens*. If so, then the application of a body weight regression across species (from living to extinct species) is difficult to justify. Furthermore, interspecific regressions and correlations between body size and metric variables are affected by differences in locomotor and other behavioral characteristics. This may partially explain why interspecific and intraspecific body size regressions sometimes differ (Steudel, 1981, 1982a, 1982b). Thus, an estimate of hominid body size must take into accout postural/locomotor equivalence between early hominids and the reference sample on which the estimate (regression) is based (Wolpoff, 1983). It is probably unjustified to base body weight estimates for bipedal hominids on regressions for quadrupedal primates. A similar problem occurs in functional interpretations of fossils. Modern *Homo sapiens* is the only biped on which to base behavioral inferences from early hominid fossils. Bipedalism in modern humans is usually treated as a functionally uniform pattern of locomotion, though considerable anatomical variation is involved. Yet the overall postcranial anatomy of Plio-Pleistocene hominids appears to lie outside the range of modern human variation (Lovejoy et al., 1973; Oxnard, 1975; Stern and Susman, 1983; Walker, 1973; Zihlman, 1978). Some researchers contend that a functionally modern pattern of bipedalism also occurred in these hominids (Robinson, 1972; Lovejoy et al., 1973; Lovejoy, 1978). Others disagree; unique morphological patterns and morphological similarities to arboreal primates are thought to be functionally significant, indicating a behaviorally different pattern of bipedalism from that in modern humans (Preuschoft, 1971; Robinson, 1972; Susman and Stern, 1982; Jungers, 1982; Stern and Susman, 1983). Judgments about early hominid locomotion, of course, are limited in that no living primate shows the same combination of postcranial features observed in the fossils. Nonetheless, further biomechanical studies of living primates potentially offer a way to assess alternative behavioral interpretations of fossils. (See Wood, 1978, for a detailed treatment of methods of functional analysis of fossils.)

This brief discussion of behavioral and body size interpretations from hominid fossils brings up the issue of unique adaptations among extinct hominids and the difficulty of recognizing them. This is a problem which will be explored later with regard to archeological reconstructions of hominid activities.

Paleoenvironmental Evidence

Inferences about paleoenvironment and ancient geomorphology are possible from fossil and geological evidence. An ecological context for early hominid behavior is provided by reconstructions of paleoenvironments. Accordingly, paleoenvironmental data help in building and testing adaptive scenarios for hominid evolution (e.g., Laporte and Zihlman, 1983). Some techniques of paleoenvironmental analysis (e.g., oxygen isotopes) concern broad, even worldwide, climatic events. Others apply to sediments within small areas, such as single paleontological sites or sedimentary basins. These latter methods (e.g., lithofacies and pollen analyses) yield more detailed information about local habitats where hominids lived. Yet even localized paleoenvironmental reconstructions often may not provide the kind of resolution (e.g., seasonality) necessary to make some important ecological inferences about early hominids.

Paleoenvironmental interpretations are obtained from four major areas of research. First, sedimentological studies aim to identify different sediment types (lithofacies) based on particle size, mineralogy, and sedimentary structures. This information permits reconstruction of depositional environments and ancient geomorphological settings, such as the distribution of lake, lake margin, deltaic, and riverine zones (e.g., Hay, 1976). Second, geochemical studies, such as those on oxygen isotope ratios, provide evidence for climatic fluctuations, including glacial cycles and changes in rainfall (Shackleton, 1967; Cerling et al., 1977).

A third source of paleoenvironmental data is fossil plants. Pollen, in particular, has been used in reconstructions of early hominid environments (Bonnefille, 1979). Since many plants do not leave a pollen record, fossil pollen samples give a biased picture of local and regional vegetation. Detailed reconstructions of vegetation from pollen analysis are problematic, especially when mosaics of vegetation are involved which may lack modern analogues, such as suggested for the Asian Miocene (Pilbeam et al., 1979). Thus, fossil pollens, especially the frequency of montane forest species, have been used mainly to infer ancient rainfall patterns rather than detailed, local vegetation.

Faunal remains are a fourth source of information about ancient environments. Inferences from faunal assemblages about ecological communities depend on taphonomic studies of bone preservation and time averaging (Behrensmeyer and Hill, 1980; Behrensmeyer, 1982; Shipman, 1981). Some species are more sensitive to ecological conditions than others. Microfauna (e.g., rodents, insectivores, small birds) tend to be better indicators than large animals of climatic/ecological changes. But at present taphonomic biases seem to be less clearly understood for small animals than for large mammals. Due to small size, microfauna are affected greatly by taphonomic processes which destroy bones or remove them from their original habitat (Dodson, 1973). Large animals are also subject to important, and better studied, taphonomic biases. Large mammals, in particular, have been used to reconstruct broad climatic and vegetation patterns where hominids lived (Vrba, 1980; Potts, 1982).

Archeological Evidence

Compared with the kind of information available from living species, inferences made from archeological evidence about early hominid behavior and ecology are very limited. Behavioral inferences include the use of stone tools, techniques of their manufacture, and functions of some artifacts (Isaac, 1976; Keeley and Toth, 1981; Toth, 1982). The outcrop sources of stone tool materials can sometimes be identified (e.g., Hay, 1976). Accordingly, direct inferences can be made about the minimum distances over which hominids ranged to get and transport those materials. The existence of archeological sites relatively undisturbed by water action implies that early hominids carried stone to certain, delimited areas and discarded artifacts over the landscape. The transport of parts of animal carcasses to archeological sites also can be shown from study of faunal remains (e.g., Potts, 1982, 1984a). The means of acquiring animal tissues (i.e., various modes of hunting and scavenging) can be assessed from data on skeletal age of animals and skeletal part (Vrba, 1980; Binford, 1981; Klein, 1982; Potts, 1983). Identification of stone tool cutmarks on faunal remains (Potts and Shipman, 1981; Bunn, 1981) shows that early hominids used animal tissues. The fact that hominids were involved with the animal bones on early archeological sites implies that Plio-Pleistocene hominids ate more meat than do nonhuman primates (Isaac, 1978a; Bunn, 1981). Yet it is unclear how often meat was consumed or what percentage contribution meat made to early hominid diets (Isaac and Crader, 1981; Potts, 1984a). Further levels of interpretation attempt to explain in adaptive terms why hominids produced clusters of stone artifacts and animal bones and to reconstruct the ranging patterns and socioecology of early hominids (Isaac, 1976, 1978a, 1980). Some of these interpretations (e.g., the existence of home bases) will be discussed later.

This brief overview of paleobehavioral/ecological information from the fossil record indicates crucial gaps in our knowledge about early hominids. Although the living primates offer an important context in which to view reconstructions of hominid diet or locomotion, the fossil record potentially provides the only adequate tests of what particular hominids ate and how they moved. On the other hand, early hominid social behavior, social organization, and most demographic and life history characteristics are difficult, at best, to infer directly from the fossil evidence. The issue here is how living primates can help in this regard.

I will focus on two problems concerning the use of living primates to reconstruct hominid social and demographic characteristics. The first is whether there are adequate criteria for choosing specific primate models for particular periods of hominid evolution. The second problem is whether reconstructions based on living primates take into account possibly unique behaviors in early hominids. Since particular species of living primates may exhibit behaviors and socioecological features not seen in other species, it is possible that the behavior and socioecology of early hominids also were not like those observed in any modern primate. Although extant species provide a wealth of models of early hominid socioecology, even these may be too limited to reconstruct the unique trajectory of hominid behavioral evolution.

PRIMATE MODELS

One goal of field primatology has been to explain variations in primate social organization. Relationships between ecological and social variables have been especially important in developing a theory on this (Crook and Gartlan, 1966; Eisenberg et al., 1972; Jolly, 1972; Clutton-Brock and Harvey, 1977; Richard, 1985). Yet few researchers seem to recognize that "the problem of the emergence of hominid social organization would be one test of the explanatory power of such a theory" (Reynolds, 1976: 74). Rather, interpretive leaps about early hominid social life, guided by the characteristics of living species, are often considered necessary in the study of hominid evolution (Lancaster, 1968; Isaac, 1976). Since the fossil evidence provides few clues about behavior, modern species are used as analogues for early hominids. Living animals facilitate reconstructions of early hominid adaptations (e.g., Brace, 1979).

The problem is that living species offer a variety of plausible models for early hominid adaptations. The earliest hominids inhabited areas characterized by a mosaic of habitats, including open plains, woodland, and gallery forest (Van Couvering, 1980). Thus, behavioral and ecological analogues for early hominids can be chosen from species which inhabit a wide range of ecological zones. Those who believe that hominids originated under very specific selection pressures may choose from many specific adaptive models to characterize early hominids (e.g., hunting models, gathering models, baboon models). Others point out that because behavioral flexibility and variability typify all higher primates, hominids also have always been able to adapt to a wide variety of conditions. An emphasis on omnivorous diets rather than on a narrow range of foods, such as meat or nuts, is an example of this line of reasoning (Harding and Teleki, 1981).

Is there a method for selecting one plausible model over another? Is there a sound rationale to infer that early hominid social systems, group size and composition, or life history characteristics were like those of one living species but not another? Further, do living species necessarily provide good models for early hominid socioecology?

Interpretations of early hominid behavior are typically based on (1) analogies with living animals, and (2) adaptive reasoning to account for behavioral differences between modern humans and other primates. The major goal is to bridge the behavioral gap between humans and other primates. Direct analogies emphasize the behavioral continuities. The best behavioral reconstructions also account for major adaptive differences (e.g., regular tool use in humans). To incorporate distinctive human traits into an evolutionary scenario, judgments must be made about the ecological conditions under which such traits were beneficial to hominids. Adaptive reasoning plays this judgmental role.

An example of this latter aspect of behavioral reconstruction comes from Brace (1979). Early hominids were adapted to savannas as are modern baboons; yet humans are tool users whereas baboons are not. It is reasoned that use of a simple digging stick by early hominids would have greatly increased their available food supply. Thus, digging sticks were probably used by the earliest hominids.

As is typical of adaptationist reasoning, the reconstruction is plausible, but there is no clear reason provided by Brace to choose it over other plausible adaptive models which do not mention digging sticks. Further, it is unclear whether the use of a digging stick might have occurred first at 2.5 million years rather than 4 or 5 million years ago. That is, the timing of this behavioral novelty cannot be specified.

Analogies, or species-specific models, are derived from animals which are either phylogenetically close to humans (e.g., chimpanzees; see Tanner, and Susman, this volume) or species believed to be adapted to ecological conditions which also prevailed where early hominids lived (e.g., terrestrial baboons; a historical summary of the baboon as a model for early hominids is provided by Strum and Mitchell, this volume). Many researchers contend that living chimpanzees are the best model for the last common ancestor of hominids and the African apes (e.g., Tanner and Zihlman, 1976a; Zihlman et al., 1978; Tanner, 1981; Tanner, this volume). Accordingly, the earliest hominid is considerred chimp-like. As a result, an ape-human dichotomy is created. Early hominid adaptations are on a continuum between ape-like and human-like. For example: "Living chimpanzees represent the kind of population from which we evolved. Contemporary gathering-hunting peoples provide data on evolved patterns. We can then look at the two ends of the continuum and try to fill in the missing parts." (Tanner and Zihlman, 1976a: 587–588).

The problem with placing early hominids along a chimp-human ccontinuum is that it precludes considering unique adaptations off that continuum. Information from the hominid fossil record suggests that such unique adaptations did occur. For example, the cheek teeth of *Australopithecus* were larger and capped with thicker enamel than in either living chimpanzees or humans. Thus, in this aspect of dental anatomy *Australopithecus* did not fall on the proposed continuum. Other features of early hominid crania (e.g., supraorbital torus) and postcranial anatomy (e.g., skeletal robusticity) indicate that early *Homo* also did not fall on a chimp-human continuum in certain features. While it is easy to see whether early hominid morphology fits on the continuum, it is less easy to judge whether a simple ape-human dichotomy portrays adequately the behavioral and ecological characteristics of *Australopithecus* and early *Homo*.

Many researchers, in fact, do not ascribe strictly to this continuum. For instance, analogues for early hominids are often based on tropical, open country monkeys *(Papio, Erythrocebus, Theropithecus)*. These analogues suggest adaptive changes which occurred when hominid ancestors shifted from a closed vegetation habitat to savannas sometime between 14 and 2 million years ago. Large mammalian carnivores are also a popular source for analogies. A standard interpretation of the earliest archeological evidence 1.8 to 2.5 million years ago is that a shift to meat-eating and hunting characterized early *Homo*. Although this interpretation has been questioned (Binford, 1981; Zihlman, 1981; Shipman, 1983; Potts, 1984a), some researchers replace a chimp or baboon model with a carnivore model, emphasizing social cooperation and food sharing, to describe the adaptation of early Pleistocene hominids (Schaller and Lowther, 1969; King, 1975; Thompson, 1975, 1976). As an alternative, human hunter-gatherers also join the pool of possible living analogues for tool-making hominids that lived during the Plio-Pleistocene.

Each modern analogue has its proponents. The reasons for choosing a particular analogue often conflict, as do the resulting models of early hominid behavior. A brief comparison between two models illustrates this point. A recent reconstruction by Brace (1979) suggests that large game hunting is the basis of human adaptation. Many others have also proposed this idea (e.g., Dart, 1953; Washburn and Lancaster, 1968; Ardrey, 1976). In contrast, Tanner (1981; Zihlman, 1983, Tanner and Zihlman, Tanner, this volume 1976a) maintains that the initial and most important innovation in human evolution was the gathering of plant foods and specifically not the hunting of animals. Both scenarios are plausible and consistent with the fossil evidence. Brace and Tanner provide the rationales underlying their reconstructions. In Tanner's model, comparisons between apes and humans help to determine ancestral behavior patterns. The predominance of plant foods in the diets of modern chimpanzees and hunter-gatherers is emphasized. Thus, Tanner focuses on an important change within the herbivorous pattern of chimps and humans, i.e., the gathering of plant foods. In contrast, Brace's model is more concerned with adaptive analogues off the chimp-human continuum. He considers how the adaptations of animals to open savannas would have modified an initial ape-like ancestral condition. Hunting behavior is considered by Brace to be one of those adaptations.

The problem in choosing the right analogue might appear to be circumvented if it is acknowledged that many animals provide useful models for reconstructing early hominid adaptations. In fact, some paleoanthropologists have adopted this viewpoint. For example, Campbell (1979) points out that there are close similarities in social organization between monkeys, apes, human hunter-gatherers, and social carnivores. Given these similarities, Campbell maintains that "we do not need to postulate any major development in social organization during hominid evolution" (Campbell, 1979: 301–302). This compromise viewpoint shows the problem of accepting or rejecting plausible analogies, whether based on animals phylogenetically close to early hominids or ostensibly similar in behavior. Monkeys, apes, modern humans, and large carnivores may show general similarities in sociality, but different species vary widely in socioecological characteristics. We are still left with the problem of trying to choose the most accurate analogy or combination of analogies for early hominids. As is made clear by Campbell's comment, all models seem appropriate when superficial similarities are emphasized; this eliminates the important question—the unique trajectory of hominid behavioral evolution.

Problem of Behavioral Uniqueness

The accuracy of behavioral or socioecological models depends in part on how well they allow for behavioral uniqueness among extinct hominids. Field primatologists document and try to account for variations in social systems in living species. Ecological variables are thought to be especially important in determining the social, demographic, and life history characteristics of species (Jolly, 1972; Krebs and Davies, 1978; Hinde, 1983; Richard, 1985). By adopting this orientation toward socioecology, paleoanthropologists should also consider (1) possible ecological differences between early hominids and living primates, including modern humans, and (2) the difficulties of explaining or predicting social characteristics from ecological features. Early hominid soocioecology can be evaluated if ecological factors known to influence social characteristics can be studied in the fossil record. This section will illustrate how socioecological factors can be inferred for tool-making hominids from the Plio-Pleistocene. Problems for socioecological models based on living primate species will be considered.

Attempts to reconstruct the behavior of Plio-Pleistocene hominids, 2.5 to 1.5 million years ago, are faced with the possibility of unique adaptations, i.e., unlike those of modern humans or other primates. Plio-Pleistocene hominids lived 2 to 6 million years after the divergence of hominids from African apes, according to most recent estimates; and they preceded modern *Homo sapiens* by about 1.5 to 2.0 million years. As noted previously, these hominids show some features found in no modern hominoids (e.g., cheek tooth morphology). Further, the presence of more than one contemporaneous hominid species provided an adaptive context which differed from that during both earlier and later periods of hominid evolution. Therefore, Plio-Pleistocene hominids do not have a particularly close temporal connection with either modern humans or the last common ancestor, and there is reason to believe that adaptive differences occurred.

The earliest archeological sites, nonetheless, seem to provide evidence of a Plio-Pleistocene behavior pattern for which there is a good modern analogue, i.e., human hunter-gatherers. However, socioecological reconstructions of the hominids that made these early sites illustrate the problems with analogies based on modern species. A modern analogue (tropical hunter-gatherers) is the traditional source of interpretation of the earliest archeological sites. Yet paleoecological inferences from archeological data conflict with important aspects of this analogy. These inferences provide an alternative to a traditional analogical viewpoint for discussing the socioecology of early hominids.

The earliest archeological sites come from the period 2.5 to 1.5 million years ago. Sites over 2.0 million years old are rare and have not yet been studied fully (Harris and Johanson, 1983). In contrast, sites in the 2.0 to 1.5 million year period have been studied in detail from taphonomical, paleoecological, and behavioral viewpoints. The archeological sites from Bed I at Olduvai Gorge are perhaps the best known sites from this period (Leakey, 1971). They are discussed in this section. Description of the sites and detailed data analyses are contained in other sources (Potts, 1982, 1984a, 1984b). A brief description and summary of analyses pertinent to hominid ecology will serve here.

Most of the archeological sites from Bed I Olduvai have several features in common, as originally described by Leakey (1971). A concentration of stone artifacts and animal bones, 10 to 20 meters in diameter, defines each site. These are called "type C" sites by Isaac (1978; Isaac and Crader, 1981). The animal bones are broken and represent a variety of species, particularly mammals ranging in size from small gazelle to elephant. Stone artifacts consist of a variety of tools, cores, waste flakes, and unmodified raw material. A variety of raw materials were used. Some of the sources were approximately 2 to 3 kilometers from the excavated sites (Hay, 1976; Potts, 1982). Taphonomic studies indicate that hominids transported both animal bones and stone artifacts to well-delimited spots on the ancient landscape, though other agents besides hominids were also important in the formation of these archeological sites (Potts, 1982, Potts and Shipman, 1981; Bunn, 1982).

The dominant interpretation of the Olduvai sites is that they were home bases—i.e., spatial nodes of social activity and food sharing among early hominids (Isaac, 1976, 1978a; Campbell, 1982; Fagan, 1983). It has been assumed that early archeological clusters of bones and stone artifacts are indistinguishable from hunter-gatherer camp-sites; thus, "they seem to indicate that the movements of Plio-Pleistocene hominids were organized around a home base" (Isaac, 1976: 500). One implication of the home base hypothesis is that modern, tropical hunter-gatherers constitute a reasonable model of the foraging behavior and social group characteristics of Plio-Pleis-tocene hominids. As a result, a wide range of distinctively human characteristics are also implied in the home base interpretation. These include daily use of tools, regular eating of meat, divison of labor, language, and delayed reciprocity in social feeding (Isaac, 1976, 1978a; Potts, 1984b).

Behaviorial comparisons between humans and nonhuman primates have helped to identify two salient features of human home bases (Table 2.1). These features are safety and food sharing. First, Wash-burn and DeVore (1961b) characterized hominid home bases as safe places where injured, sick, elderly, or young members of the social group could stay while others foraged. They point out, in contrast, that in Old World monkeys and apes, all group members move from their sleeping locations during the day. Second, Isaac (1978a, 1980, 1983a) has pointed out that in nonhuman primates, individuals feed themselves as they forage, whereas humans often exhibit an addi-tional feeding pattern—the transport of food to a home base for sharing with other foragers.

The early archeological sites from Olduvai are often believed to be the best evidence for early hominid home bases, characterized by both safety and food sharing. However, the home base interpre-tation has been questioned recently by Isaac (1983a) and others (Binford, 1981; Potts, 1982, 1984b). Detailed study of the earliest Olduvai sites shows some contradictions to a model based on tropical hunter-gatherer socioecology (Potts, 1982, 1984b). First, taphonomic analysis indicates that animal bones were brought to these sites by hominids probably over periods of at least several years. This period

Table 2.1.

Characteristics of the home base concept	Nonhuman Primates	Humans	Ref.
Safety	All group members move during daily round.	Some members (injured, sick, elderly, young) stay at home base.	Washburn and DeVore, 1961b
Food sharing	Individuals feed-as-you-go.	Delayed food consumption; food taken to home base.	Isaac 1978a, 1983a

of bone accumulation is much longer than the period over which modern, tropical hunter-gatherers reoccupy their campsites. Second, patterns of bone modification indicate that carnivores, such as hyaenids and felids, had visited these sites during the entire period of bone accumulation. They damaged the bones, possibly as extensively as hominids did, and had access to complete bones rich in meat and marrow. Damage inflicted by carnivore teeth and by hominid stone tools to the bones within each site assemblage, and sometimes to the same bone, suggests that hominids and carnivores had competed at least in an indirect way over animal tissues carried to these sites. Finally, the animal bones from Olduvai are not modified as intensively as are bones processed for meat and marrow at modern campsites. For example, 9% of the total number of major limb bone specimens from Olduvai sites are complete. This contrasts with only 1.2% complete limb bones from a sample of 16 !Kung San campsites (Yellen, 1977). Relative inefficiency in bone/meat processing by Olduvai hominids may explain why carnivores were attracted repeatedly to these sites of bone accumulation (Potts, 1982, 1984b; Potts and Shipman, 1981).

It is difficult to reconcile a home base interpretation to these findings about the processing of animal tissues and site utilization by Olduvai hominids. The hunter-gatherer analogy is based primarily on the fact that Olduvai hominids accumulated artifacts and animal bones, as do modern hunter-gatherers. This general similarity begins to fade in the light of taphonomic findings and paleoecological inferences from the archeological sites. In particular, the presumed safety of the home base seems violated by evidence for high potential, and actual, competition between early hominids and carnivores over animal tissues at these sites. The removal of bones from carcasses by hominids probably reduced the chances of direct interaction with predators. However, repeated transport of animal tissues to sites probably resulted in costs from carnivore competition that differed from those incurred by modern hunter-gatherers. The latter have a variety of means to deal with potential predators and carnivore competitors. These include fire, more complete or efficient bone/ meat processing activities, and possibly more effective weapons than possessed by Olduvai hominids. Moreover, evidence for repeated attraction of carnivores to these sites suggests that hominids had to adapt their movements and their use of sites and animal tissues to the activites of large carnivores in a way unknown among recent hunter-gatherers. Hominid use of these sites as refuges of safety and, therefore, as central areas for social activity appears doubtful. This implies that social activities were not focused at the primary locations where stone and animal food resources were transported.

These behavioral and ecological inferences from archeological data have implications for socioecological reconstruction. Resource acquisition and predator pressure are considered to be major determinants of primate social adaptations (Jolly, 1972; Bernstein and Smith, 1979; Richard, 1981; Wrangham, 1983a, 1983b). If, as suggested here, Olduvai hominids differed from modern hunter-gatherers in these traits, it is possible that they also differed in their social organization and demographic characteristics. A generalized interpretation of the earliest sites at Olduvai is needed which relies less on socioecological analogies to modern hunter-gatherers. It is clear that early hominids transported at least two kinds of resources to these sites—stone tool material and animal bones. Although resource transport by tropical hunter-gatherers involves a socioecology focused around transient home bases, the carrying of resources to sites by early hominids need not imply similar social or demographic characteristics to those found in their modern counterparts.

To show alternatives to the hunter-gatherer home base model exist, I have suggested previously a "stone cache" interpretation for the early Olduvai sites (Potts, 1984b). This idea takes into account faunal assemblage features noted previously to conflict with the home base analogy. These include long periods of bone accumulation by hominids at sites, modification of the bones by carnivores over the period of bone accumulation, and relatively inefficient processing of bones at these sites. Further, the stone cache idea is based on the general notion tht hominids transported stone artifacts and food resources requiring stone tool use to the same places.

According to the stone cache interpretation, sites were established throughout the hominid foraging range. Figure 2.1 shows one scenario where 6 sites were produced around a central source of stone raw material. The sites are situated in the various vegetation and sedimentary zones known to have existed 1.8 million years ago at Olduvai

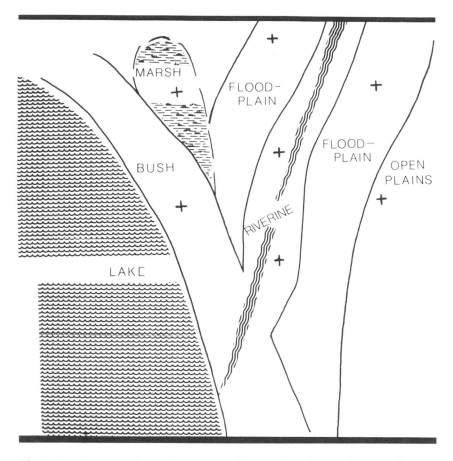

Fig. 2-1.   Reconstruction of six stone caches produced around a central stone raw material source (+). The caches occur in a variety of sedimentary and vegetation zones known to have existed at ancient Olduvai.

(Hay, 1976; Potts, 1982). Sites were produced by carrying stone raw material from outcrops to delimited locations in the foraging area. The stone material was useful for making cores and tools which were re-used over the long term. Hominids located animal tissues already detached from the skeleton, or they cut portions from carcasses with tools carried from caches of stone. Bones were transported to a nearby cache, and the tissues were processed quickly and incompletely. The site was then abandoned. Carnivores were attracted repeatedly to the bone assemblages at each cache and to some of the same bones modified by hominids. This scenario does not specify how frequently hominids visited caches or where they went after leaving a cache, since no archeological evidence at present seems to bear on these questions. The existence of social bases away from the caches (and bone accumulations) or sleeping areas similar to those of nonhuman primates seems likely.

This brief scenario illustrates an alternative interpretation to the home base model. Whether or not the stone cache idea is correct in detail, a general resource transport interpretation of the Olduvai sites does not imply a socioecology centered around home bases, as in human hunter-gatherers.

Furthermore, important differences from nonhuman primates can be noted. Hominid foraging at Olduvai must have incurred competition with predators unlike that faced by other higher primates, especially since the latter do not exploit large mammals. Stone and food resources were transported in a manner unknown among nonhuman primates. The archeological sites do bear some resemblance to chimpanzee nut-cracking sites, which also contain tools and food refuse (Sugiyama and Koman, 1979b). But the similarity is superficial. Foraging by Olduvai hominids differed in that it involved transport of foods (at least animal tissues) to their sites, whereas chimpanzee nut-cracking sites occur at the source of the food itself. As for hunter-gatherers, modern nonhuman primates appear to differ from Olduvai hominids in aspects of foraging ecology and predator avoidance.

It is important to note that living primates still offer numerous plausible models of Olduvai hominid socioecology. For example, did early hominids at Olduvai move in social groups resembling those of hunter-gatherers—i.e., changeable in composition but composed of several family units which consistently reunited at a social base to which artifacts and bones were not taken? Were they like common chimpanzees, living in communities of males and females which ranged independently throughout an area and formed short-lived parties (Goodall, 1975; Harcourt and Stewart, 1983)? Were they like pygmy chimps, which form more stable parties of males and females than do common chimps (Kuroda, 1979)? Or do multiple male-female groups (as in common baboons) or "family units" (hamadryas baboon) which shift as a cohesive unit while foraging best portray the social groups of Olduvai hominids?

There is no specific paleoecological inference for ancient Olduvai which suggests at present that one of these analogues is more appropriate than the others. In fact, each of the analogues seems consistent with a general resource transport interpretation of the Olduvai sites. On the other hand, differences in foraging and predator avoidance suggest that Olduvai hominids may have had social strategies found in none of these modern species. Archeologists assume that concentrations of stone artifacts and animal bones specify important aspects of hominid social and economic organization. This assumption is correct only if a hunter-gatherer model is applicable. In contrast, other mammals which accumulate resources or leave debris (e.g., porcupines, hyenas, chimps at nut-cracking sites) seem to provide no general model of sociality, group size, composition, or organization.

Olduvai provides excellent data about ancient ecological settings and hominid activities. Yet this information does not direct us to a particular living primate model to reconstruct hominid socioecology. Wrangham (this volume) suggests that it is not possible to reconstruct a model of this from living forms because of behavioral variability in the African apes. In response, some might remark that the fòssil record has left us with yet another mystery (cf., Reynolds 1976: 73). However, the study of human behavioral evolution is possibly furthered by knowing that long-persisting species of extinct hominids thrived with adaptations for which there is no modern parallel.

VALUE OF PRIMATE STUDIES

This chapter has focused on problems of applying socioecological analogies from living primates to early hominids. Analogies are often based on assumed or superficial resemblances. In contrast, analysis of the prehistoric record suggests that early hominids may have differed from living primates in ecological features which influence species' social and demographic characteristics. The differences implied in socioecology would be masked by analogies adopted from living species. This analysis exemplifies the shortcomings of static models of adaptation based on particular modern primates. Despite this critique, primate studies continue to be a valuable source of ideas and information pertinent to hominid evolution. Primate behavior research is valuable to the study of early hominid adaptation for several reasons.

First, testable hypotheses about hominid evolution can result from comparisons between living nonhuman primates and particular species of early hominids. An example is Jolly's seed-eating hypothesis, developed in part from anatomical comparisons between terrestrial monkeys and extinct hominoids (Jolly, 1970, 1973). In response to this hypothesis, dietary analyses of early hominid teeth have shown that while a grass-eating adaptation can be dismissed, small, hard objects were probably a part of the diet of early hominids (Walker, 1981; Kay, 1981). In order to test hypotheses based on comparisons with living primates, such hypotheses must identify the species or period of hominid evolution to which they pertain. Furthermore, they should specify aspects of hominid anatomy, diet, behavior, or ecological setting which can be evaluated ultimately with data from the geological record.

Second, the idea of human behavioral evolution is founded on comparisons between humans and nonhuman primates (Jay, 1968b; Lancaster, 1968; Isaac, 1976). These comparisons help to define the endpoints of the trajectory of hominid behavioral evolution. However, knowing the differences and similarities between humans and other primates does not make the evolutionary trajectory straightforward. In particular, neither behavioral comparisons nor living primate models inform us about the rate of behavioral evolution or help to identify unique hominid behaviors for which there is no appropriate primate analogue.

Finally, studies of modern primates can explore processes of behavioral variation and change. Research oriented toward adaptive processes can show the conditions (e.g., ecological, social) under which certain behavioral variations resembling human behaviors occur (e.g., Reynolds, 1976; Strum, 1981). A distinction between *results* and *processes* is an important one (Richard 1981). Field studies of primates not only describe the static results of adaptation but also show *how* primates adapt and *how* behavioral variations arise. It is the application of static primate models to early hominids that yields the methodological difficulties and conflicting reconstructions discussed earlier.

For example, the fact that chimpanzees hunt does not necessarily mean that hunting was practiced by protohominids or by *Australopithecus*. However, it is useful to know the ecological and social conditions under which higher primate hunting is practiced and becomes more frequent (Strum, 1981; Strum and Mitchell, this volume). If evidence for these conditions can be recognized in the hominid fossil record, then the process of hominid behavioral evolution, in this case the development of hunting, can be studied. As another example, the fact that chimpanzees make tools does not mean that all species of early hominids made tools, even though this is plausible. Yet behavioral traditions, including patterns of tool use and food preparation, have been documented in chimpanzees (McGrew et al., 1979; Boesch and Boesch, 1984; Tanner, this volume) and macaques (Frisch, 1968; Kummer, 1971). Transmission of behavior patterns across generations in these species indicates that modern human cultural processes (e.g., language) are not the only means to explain traditions. This has implications for how traditions of early hominid stone tool manufacture are interpreted.

If the goal of studying hominid behavioral evolution is to understand the unique events which led to modern humans, then primate studies may contribute greatly to this end by showing how unique aspects of socioecology and behavior arise in primates. The emphasis here is on process, not static analogies. Problems in understanding modern primate adaptations (Richard, 1981) can inform us about some of the difficulties in reconstructing early hominid socioecology. The problem of unique hominid adaptations can be illustrated by living species. Assuming that only the anatomy and geographic distribution of a living species is known, misleading models of its behavior and social organization result from analogies with other modern primates.

As an example, would we be able to reconstruct the socioecology of *Papio hamadryas* from its anatomy, inferences about diet, and knowing that it occupied cliffs in dry habitats? Table 2.2 presents some of the salient features of hamadryas social groups and compares them with the social systems of related monkeys. The baboon morphology of *P. hamadryas* might suggest that a general baboon model would provide the best socioecological reconstruction. However, the social and demographic characteristics of hamadryas contrast greatly with what occurs in other *Papio* baboons (Dunbar, 1983). A savanna baboon model would miss unique aspects of hamadryas socioecology and would preclude an evolutionary study of what made *P. hamadryas* a distinct species. The social systems of geladas and hamadryas baboons are superficially similar. But important differences do exist (Table 2.2). The similarities appear to have evolved for rather different ecological reasons, and the contrasts reflect important differences in social behavior (Dunbar, 1983). Social grouping in hamadryas appears to be an adaptive response to foraging under conditions of scarce food resources. However, some aspects of hamadryas social organization have perhaps their closest parallels in gorillas, which live in a very different kind of habitat. Strong social bonds occur between hamadryas females and the leading male, whereas relatively weak relationships occur among females. This situation is similar to social group relationships in gorillas, where females tolerate one another but have strong bonds to the leading male (Harcourt, 1979a, b). Yet due to phylogenetic distance and differences in ecological setting, it is doubtful that gorillas would be considered as a model for hamadryas social relationships. Even so, the behavioral/ecological reasons for this pattern of social relationships are different in the two cases (Harcourt and Stewart, 1983).

The point of this exercise is that unique and evolutionarily important aspects of primate socioecology—whether in the past or present—may be masked by supposedly plausible reconstructions based on other primates. Furthermore, accurate analogies might be overlooked because of taxonomic and broad ecological dissimilarities. The usual rationales for selecting modern primate analogues for the behavior of other primates, including early hominids, are not reliable.

Table 2.2. Some distinctive socioecological characteristics of *Papio hamadryas* and comparisons with other *Papio* species, gelada *(Theropithecus)*, and patas *(Erythrocebus)*. Information from Dunbar and Dunbar (1975), Dunbar (1983), Kummer (1971), and Richard (in press).

Socioecological Feature	Appearance of Feature in Hamadryas Baboons	Comparisons with Other Primate Species
Social grouping	1-male reproductive units aggregate into bands.	Unlike all other *Papio*, but similar kind of social grouping to geladas. Patas have 1-male units but lack large band aggregates.
Band foraging movements	Highly coordinated; strongly controlled by males, who keep individual 1-male units from dispersing.	Unlike geladas: males do not maintain tight control over group movements.
Social relationships	Weak social bonds among females.	Unlike geladas: reproductive unit is maintained by strong female bonds.
	Strong female relationship to harem male.	A different kind of alliance occurs in geladas. Unlike patas: no herding/defense of females by male.
	Strong social bonds among males.	Unlike geladas: 1-male units unite with and disperse from the band easily. Unlike patas: hostile male interactions.

Returning to early hominids, paleoanthropology aims to document and explain how humans evolved. Yet attention should also be paid to anatomical and behavioral variations within the hominid clade, including differences from modern humans. Rather than using modern primate analogies to make interpretive leaps about early hominid behavior, this latter aspect of paleoanthropology adopts the theoretical goals and interpretive issues of modern primatology. Inferences about early hominid socioecology are subject to at least the same difficulties faced by primatologists in accounting for socioecological variations in modern primates. Accordingly, unique behaviors and adaptive variations among the hominids are important to discover; and they imply variations in socioecology, as they do among modern primates. Consequently, one of the significant tasks of paleoanthropology is to ascertain how modern human adaptations emerged from a more variable set of behavioral possibilities which existed among early hominids.

Unifying paleoanthropology and behavioral primatology in this way makes the reconstruction of early hominid socioecology extremely difficult. To make this possible, primatologists must work toward a better understanding of socioecological determinants in primates. From this, paleoanthropologists can try to develop methods to infer those ecological features which best predict social characteristics. This dialectic between paleoanthropologists and primatologists is based on an optimistic view, namely, that primate socioecology, in fact, can be understood and the development of inferential methods in paleoanthropology and paleoecology has only begun.

SUMMARY

Does an adequate method exist for choosing primate models to reconstruct early hominid socioecology? Conflicting models, based especially on chimpanzees and baboons, have been advocated previously without much concern for testing those models with evidence from the geological record or without considering possibly unique adaptations among early hominids. The issue of uniqueness is discussed for Plio-Pleistocene hominids from Olduvai. Re-evaluation of the earliest archeological sites at Olduvai suggests that (1) Olduvai hominids interacted with the carnivore community and had to deal with predators in ways not usually faced by nonhuman primates or hunter-gatherers; and (2) hominids foraged in a manner unlike nonhuman primates or human hunter-gatherers (namely, they transported resources but not to home bases having the same social functions as modern campsites).

Variations in foraging and in predator avoidance strategies are deemed important determinants of socioecological variation in living primates. Evidence for different hominid adaptations from those known among living primates suggest that there is no single primate species which serves as an appropriate socioecological analogue. Thus, the use of *particular* species either as models or to create a simple evolutionary continuum (chimp to human) is questionable. If paleoanthropology concerns behavioral variation and uniqueness in hominids, its goals become much more closely allied with those of behavioral primatology. Documentation and explanation of species' differences in behavior and socioecology are important in the study of living primates. A similar approach can be adopted in the study of hominid adaptations. In this approach superficial similarities between early hominids and living primates are de-emphasized. Instead, behavioral differences and the emergence of modern human adaptations from a more varied set of early hominid behaviors and socioecological adaptations are emphasized.

II

Primate-derived Models

CHAPTER THREE

The Significance of African Apes for Reconstructing Human Social Evolution

RICHARD W. WRANGHAM

INTRODUCTION

There are three ways to use African apes to reconstruct hominid social organization. They can provide models for the behavior of an ancestral species; they can be used to test theories of social behavior; or they can be compared with humans to identify phylogenetically conservative traits. This essay does the latter. The aim is to find out whether it is a useful approach, rather than to provide a full description of ancestral social organization. To explain and justify the search for conservative traits, which has not been made before, I begin by placing it in the context of prior analyses.

First, particular species have been argued to provide good behavioral models of human ancestors. Several authors, for example, have suggested that our ancestors once behaved like baboons *Papio* sp. (see review by Strum and Mitchell, this volume) or chimpanzees *Pan troglodytes* (Reynolds, 1966; Goodall and Hamburg, 1975; Tanner, 1981; McGrew, 1981). The ideas these models generate are often plausible and thought-provoking, but their value is limited by their initial assumption: they assume that the social organization of human ancestors was similar to that of a living species. Possibly it was. But it is much more likely that for several million years our ancestors have had forms of social organization not seen in species living today. This means that even "the best available model" (Tanner, 1981) may not be good enough. Reconstructions based on a model therefore need a system for deciding which kinds of behavior seen in a living species are most likely to have occurred in human ancestors.

The second and more circuitous way of using animal studies promises just such a system, by explaining animal behavior. Field data provide the testing ground for theories designed to explain the distribution of social behavior in different species (Emlen and Oring, 1977; Krebs and Davies, 1984). These theories are then used to "predict" how hominid ancestors behaved, based on their probable ecology (e.g., Bartholomew and Birdsell, 1953; Schaller and Lowther, 1969; Lovejoy, 1981; Baer and McEachron, 1982). The value of this method naturally depends on the quality of the theories, which come from behavioral ecology and have solved a variety of behavioral puzzles (e.g., Krebs and Davies, 1984). Despite the successes and growing importance of behavioral ecology, however, it is undoubtedly premature to rely on it to "predict" the behavior of fossil species. The problem is that although it is a promising field, the rules which it has found for explaining species differences in social organization are still tentative. This is particularly true for primates, where even the broad outlines of the relationship between ecology and social organization are the subject of disagreement. It is an open question, for example, why many primates live in groups at all, or why in some species males move between groups while in others females do, or why some species are monogamous and others are not (e.g., Clutton-Brock and Harvey, 1977; Wrangham, 1980; van Schaik and van Hooff, 1983). Again, though theories have been proposed to explain differences in ape and human societies, they are no more than sketches focussing on a few key variables, and there is no consensus on their validity (e.g., apes: Wrangham, 1979a, 1985; Harcourt and Stewart, 1983; Ghiglieri, 1984; Rodman, 1984; humans: Harris, 1979; Orlove, 1980; Irons, 1983). It may be only a few years before reliable explanations of species differences in social organization are found, but it is misleading to suggest that they have been found yet. The present state of the art means that attempts to use behavioral ecology to reconstruct hominid behavior are no stronger than those which use chimpanzees or other apes as models: even Lovejoy's scheme, which is the most elaborate to date, is riddled with speculation (Allen et al., 1982; Isaac, 1982). This problem would exist even if we had a clear picture of the ecology of human ancestors. The fact that we don't (Pilbeam, 1984) only makes the problem worse.

In view of these problems this chapter explores the third approach, phylogenetic comparison, which offers a quicker, though ultimately weaker, system for recognizing probable aspects of ancestral social organization. The principle of the analysis is that because humans and the three living species of African apes are derived from a common ancestor (CA), the probability of a given behavior occurring in the ancestor can be judged from its distribution in the four descendants. If it occurs in all four species, it is likely (though not certain) to have occurred in the CA because otherwise it must have evolved independently at least twice. If the four species differ with respect to a particular behavior, nothing certain can be said about the CA. The aim, accordingly, is to distinguish between aspects of hominoid social organization which are shared, and therefore phylogenetically conservative, and those which are variable.

If shared behaviors occur, the distinction is useful for two reasons. First, it shows which kinds of behavior are most likely to have occurred not only in the CA but also in intermediate species between the CA and its living descendants. These behaviors can be viewed as part of an "ancestral suite" which, though admittedly hypothetical, offers a logical starting point for behavioral reconstruction at any time during human evolution. It will not always be correct, but it is unlikely to be far wrong.

Second, it contributes to an understanding of hominoid behavioral ecology because it helps to clarify the relationship between social behavior and ecology. Humans, gorillas and the two species of chimpanzee apparently have little in common ecologically: they have different diets, habitats, and technologies. This means that if they share common features of social organization, there are few ecological factors which can easily be held responsible. It is still unknown, of course, whether ecological explanations will account for the social radiation of the hominoids. However, the analysis of inter-specific correlations of behavior and ecology will undoubtedly help to resolve the question, by subjecting the few tight correlations to hard scrutiny. Previous correlations across primates have always excluded humans, and have mostly been concerned with easily quantifiable variables, such as group size, rather than with social relations. Thus there is every possibility that important relationships lie undiscovered. Even though ultimately we must rely on principles which have been tested in a wide range of species, our closest relatives are still a good source of hypotheses.

METHOD

Ape-Hominid Phylogeny

Biochemical, paleontological and morphological studies provide a reasonably clear picture of ape and human evolutionary relationships (Fig. 1). Common chimpanzees and bonobos (*Pan paniscus*) are more closely related to each other than to any other hominoid (Zihlman and Lowenstein 1983; see also list of molecular comparisons, Tanner, this volume). In the ancestry of humans, gorillas (*Gorilla gorilla*), and the two chimpanzees, it is still uncertain which pair diverged last. The most likely scenario links gorillas and chimpanzee ancestors most closely (Ferris et al., 1981; de Bonis, 1983; Cronin, 1983; Gantt, 1983; Kluge, 1983). In Figure 3.1, however, the relationship is shown as a murky three-way split because the evidence is still contradictory. Hemoglobin analysis, for instance, shows two amino acid substitutions which suggests that chimpanzees and people form the most recently diverged pair (Goodman et al., 1983), a view supported by recent studies of DNA hybridization (Sibley and Ahlquist 1984). Chromosomal evidence makes it unlikely that a three-way split actually occurred (Mai 1983), but for the purposes of this chapter the phylogeny in Figure 1 is adequate: it is conservative and does not argue for any particular one of the contradictory viewpoints.

Orangutans (*Pongo pygmaeus*) are not considered here because it is normally considered that their ancestors diverged from the African ape-human stem well before the emergence of hominids (Ciochon 1983). An alternative case has been made, however, in which orangutans and hominids form a single clade, more closely related to each other than to the African apes (Schwartz 1984a, 1984b). If orangutans were indeed the closest living relative of humans, the conclusions here would have to be revised. The method would still be applicable, however.

Behavioral Comparisons

The value of the analysis depends both on the quality of the data and the relevance of the behavioral variables. First, the social behavior of apes has been well described at a few sites, but little is still known about the range of variation among populations of the same species (Table 3.1). (Susman, this volume, summarizes the behavior of the pygmy chimpanzee, and compares the behavior of the common chimpanzee - ed.) Many aspects of social organization are known to be variable, however, including both grouping patterns and social relationships (below). This means that current views of the social behavior of African apes may be biased by the available studies, which are far from representative. Thus social relationships among lowland gorillas *G. g. gorilla,* for example, have never been studied. Even for chimpanzees, which are the best-known species, there are no long-term data on an open-country or forest-living population, or on the western or central subspecies (*P. t. verus and P. t. troglodytes*), or from areas where they are sympathetic with gorillas. Furthermore, at the two long-term chimpanzee sites in Tanzania, a proportion of the population has had intermittent access to foods provided by observers, which raises the possibility that their behavior has been seriously modified as a result (Reynolds, 1975; Ghiglieri,

1984). It seems unlikely, however, that such provisioning would have seriously influenced the variables considered here (see Goodall, 1983). Fortunately, behavioral differences between species are usually more extreme than the degree of variation within them, but the shortcomings of the data should be borne in mind.

Intraspecific variation is a major problem, of course, for simple characterizations of human behavior, and it can only be treated superficially here. The main focus is on "egalitarian" societies in the sense of Service, (1967), i.e. tribes or bands without state organization. This by no means eliminates variation, but at least reduces it. The quality of cross-cultural data is often questionable because of sample bias or poor reporting (Barnard, 1983), and caution is therefore necessary.

Second, the behavioral variables selected for analysis are those which theory suggests are primary determinants of other aspects of social organization (Wrangham, 1982). They are adult grouping patterns, relationships among mothers, relationships among breeding males, sexual relationships and intergroup relationships. These are considered to be fundamental aspects of social organization because they reflect rather directly the reproductive strategies of breeding adults, which are themselves influenced strongly by ecological var-

Table 3.1. Major Field Studies of the African Apes

	>10 Yrs.	2–10 Yrs.	Site	Reference
GORILLA				
G.g. gorilla	–	–		
G.g. graueri	–	1	* Kahuzi, Zaire	Yamagiwa 1983
G.g. beringei	1	–	Virunga, Rwanda	Fossey 1983
BONOBO				
P. paniscus	–	2	Wamba, Zaire	Kano 1982
			Lomako, Zaire	Badrian and Badrian 1984
CHIMPANZEE				
P.t. verus	–	2	Bossou, Guinea	Sugiyama 1981
			Mt. Assirik, Senegal	Baldwin et al. 1982
P.t. troglodytes	–	–		
P.t. schweinfurthii	2		Gombe, Tanzania	Goodall 1983
			Kasoge, Tanzania	Nishida and Uehara 1983
		2	Budongo, Uganda	Suzuki 1979
			Kibale, Uganda	Ghiglieri 1984

The tables include all studies which have contributed data on the social relationships of African apes. Purely ecological studies are not included.
* Kahuzi gorillas show traits of both G. g. graueri and G. g. beringei. They are sometimes classified as G. g. beringei (Goodall and Groves 1977).

iables. The social relationships of nonbreeding adults and juveniles, by contrast, are expected to be adapted to those of breeding adults.

SOCIAL ORGANIZATION OF AFRICAN APES AND HUMANS

Grouping Patterns

Grouping patterns are summarized in Table 2. First the stability of parties (i.e., feeding or traveling groups) varies. From long-term observations of the two eastern subspecies (*G. g. beringei* and *G. g. graueri*) mixed-sex parties of gorillas are known to be stable over several months or more (Virunga: Harcourt et al., 1981; Kahuzi: Yamagiwa, 1983). They are presumed to be similarly stable in West Africa (Harcourt et al., 1981). Parties of chimpanzees and bonobos, by contrast, break up and reform on a daily or hourly basis in all habitats (Kuroda, 1979). The same is true, of course, for all human populations. The difference between gorillas and other species means that phylogenetic comparison provides no direct evidence about the stability of the CA's parties.

The comparison of grouping patterns does suggest, however, that the social networks of the CA, as opposed to its parties, were semiclosed and stable. Closed social networks are particularly obvious among gorillas because almost all affiliative interactions occur within the stable groups (Fossey, 1983). Among chimpanzees, by contrast, occurrence of closed networks was not suspected during the first few

no clear evidence about parties

closed social networks

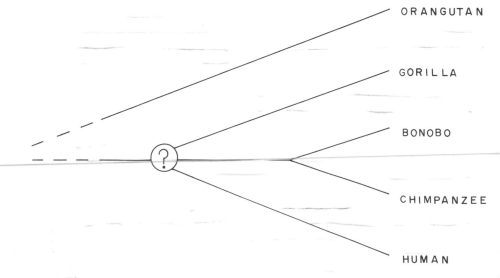

Fig. 3-1. Phylogeny of the Hominoids.

years of field study. Long-term data at Kasoge and Gombe have now shown, however, that affiliative relationships between adult males occur strictly within fixed sets of up to 16 or more males, and that relaxed interactions between males from different networks are rare or nonexistent (Nishida, 1979; Goodall, 1983). Female networks are less rigidly closed than those of the males, as shown by mothers who occasionally associate with males from more than one network (Wrangham, 1979b). Uehara (1981) and Goodall (1983) have argued that such females are normally in the process of transferring their affiliations, and that both sexes should be regarded as living in a closed social group (cf. Kawanaka, 1982, who concurs on the basis of female behavior in an intergroup interaction). Closed networks, known as communities or unit-groups, are now assumed to occur at all chimpanzee study sites (Table I), though they have only been conclusively demonstrated in Tanzania (i.e. for *P. t. schweinfurthii*). They include from 19 (Gombe: Kahama) to 106 (Kasoge: M-group) individuals of all ages. So far as is known, all chimpanzees are members of such a community.

Bonobo grouping patterns resemble those of chimpanzees. The occurrence of closed communities at Wamba, for example, is strongly implied by 217 temporary subgroups, or parties, observed at an artificial feeding site. Each party was composed wholly of individuals from one of two groups visiting the feeding ground (P-group or E-group). The only exception was a single "mixed" party consisting of two anestrous females (Kano, 1982). Bonobo communities at Wamba differ from those of chimpanzees by being larger (up to 120 individuals) and by being subdivided into three or more relatively permanent subgroups (Kitamura, 1983). The bonobo communities observed at Lomako also show evidence of subdivision, though they are similar in size to chimpanzee communities (Badrian and Badrian, 1984).

The social networks of many contemporary peoples are more open than among most nonhuman primates, because even in populations at low density individuals routinely have friends or trading partners in a variety of camps or villages (e.g. Wiessner, 1982). Furthermore, camp membership can change in a number of different ways, including by the aggregation and dispersal of camps, and by households or individuals moving independently between camps (e.g. Turnbull, 1965). Nevertheless, the very existence of discrete camps or villages, which appears to be universal in pre-State societies, indicates that networks of daily social interaction are semiclosed. Among most peoples these boundaries of daily interaction conform (or conformed) to other boundaries, such as clanship, land rights and symbol use, and their importance is thereby intensified. Even where camp membership is comparatively flexible, individuals are members of discrete political groups such as a band, and they carry their group membership with them when they join a new group.

I conclude that African apes and people share a strong tendency towards closure of their social networks. This is in contrast to orangutans, which have completely open networks (Rijksen, 1978; Galdikas, 1979; Rodman, 1979). Most primates, however, have closed social networks, and from the present data it would be surprising if the CA did not also have them.

The final aspect of grouping patterns considered here is whether some individuals spend their time alone. Table 3.2 shows that adult males commonly travel alone in all the CA's known descendants. Lone travel by mothers, by contrast, is variable. It is unknown in gorillas, whereas in chimpanzees it can average as much as 65% of the mother's day-time (e.g. at Gombe, Wrangham and Smuts, 1980). Bonobos are intermediate. In Wamba, for example, mothers are occasionally found alone but normally travel in relatively stable subgroups with particular males (Kano, 1982). Accordingly, no inference can be made about the tendency for female CAs to have traveled alone, whereas males can reasonably be expected to have done so. This contrasts with savanna baboons, *Papio anubis*, for instance, where males normally travel alone only in the temporary circumstances of transferring between groups (Packer, 1979; but see Slatkin and Hausfater, 1976).

Relationships Among Females

Relationships among female African apes and among women are striking because they contrast sharply with the better studied African monkeys. Table 3.3 shows that female exogamy is a universal trend in African apes and people, resulting in mothers spending their time with females who are normally only distantly related to themselves. It is only a trend, however: female residence patterns are clearly variable between different groups of people, and possibly in other species also.

For gorillas, female migration from the natal group is based solely on data from the Virunga, where eight out of ten adolescent or nulliparous females are known to have left the group where they were born (Harcourt et al., 1981, Yamagiwa, 1983). Fossey (1982), for example, reported that 17 females had transferred a total of 30 times. Though the trend for female exogamy is clear, it is not invariable: at least two Virunga females have given birth in their natal groups.

Among Tanzanian chimpanzees at least 12 nulliparous females have been observed emigrating from their natal communities, and

Table 3.2. Grouping Patterns.

	Party Membership	Social Network	Lone Mothers	Lone Males
Gorilla	Stable	Closed	No	Yes
Bonobo	Variable	Closed	Yes	Yes
Chimpanzee	Variable	Closed	Yes	Yes
Human	Variable	Semi-closed	Yes	Yes
Common Ancestor	?	Closed	?	Yes

Tables 3.2 to 3.6 show only the dominant trends. There are numerous exceptions discussed in the text.

Table 3.3. Relationships Among Females.

	Breed in Natal Group	Frequency of Forming Alliances With Females
Gorilla	Rarely	Rare
Bonobo	Rarely?	Unknown
Chimpanzee	Rarely	Rare
Human	Rarely	Rare
Common Ancestor	Rarely	Rare

Table 3.4. Relationships Among Males

	Breed in Natal Group	Frequency of Forming Alliances With Males
Gorilla	Rare	Rare
Bonobo	?	Rare
Chimpanzee	Common	Common
Human	Common	Common
Common Ancestor	?	?

Table 3.5. Sexual Relationships

	Mating System	Length of Sexual Relationships
Gorilla	Polygyny	Long-term
Bonobo	Promiscuity	Short-term (?)
Chimpanzee	Promiscuity	Short-term
Human	Polygyny	Long-term
Common Ancestor	?	?

Table 3.6. Intergroup Relationships

	Quality	Active Participants	Stalk/ Attack	Territorial Defence
Gorilla	Hostile	Males	Yes	No
Bonobo	Tense	?	?	?
Chimpanzee	Hostile	Males	Yes	Variable
Human	Mainly Hostile	Males	Yes	Variable
Common Ancestor	Hostile	Males	Yes	?

Table 3.7. Reconstructions of the Social Organization of Human Ancestors[1]

Reference	This Chapter	Tanner 1981	McGrew 1981	Baer & McEachron 1982	Lovejoy 1981
Method	Phylogenetic Comparison	Chimpanzee Model	Chimpanzee Model	Behavioral Ecology	Behavioral Ecology
Species	Common Ancestor	A Late Prehominid	The Earliest Hominid	The Earliest Hominid	An Early Hominid
(1) Closed social network	Yes	—	Yes	Yes	—
(2) Party composition	?	Unstable	Unstable	Stable	Unstable
(3) Females sometimes alone	?	Yes	Yes	No	Yes
(4) Males sometimes alone	Yes	Yes	Yes	No	Yes
(5) Female exogamy	Yes	—	Yes	No	—
(6) Female alliances	No	—	No	Yes	—
(7) Male endogamy	?	Often	Yes	No	Yes
(8) Male alliances	?	—	Yes	—	—
(9) Males have single mates	No	No	No	No	Yes
(10) Length of sexual relationships	?	Short	Short	Short	Long
(11) Hostile relations between groups	Yes	No	Yes	—	—
(12) Males active in intergroup encounters	Yes	—	Yes	—	—
(13) Stalking and attacking	Yes	—	—	—	—
(14) Territorial defence	?	—	?	—	—

[1] The Table shows only traits discussed in this chapter.
Key: "—" variable not considered; "?" no decision possible.

13 females have joined new communities (Uehara, 1981; Goodall, 1983). As in gorillas, mothers also transfer occasionally (Nishida, 1979); and a few females (at least two) have given birth in their natal communities (loc. cit.). No tendency has been found in either species for related females to follow each other to the same group or community, but it remains possible that it will be found.

There are fewer data available for bonobos. Kano (1982) observed two nulliparous females each associating with two different communities; they appeared to be migrating in a way similar to that observed in female chimpanzees. Two additional nulliparous females and one mature mother visited one of the study communities temporarily. From these observations Kano (1982) concluded that females typically emigrate from one community to another.

Among people, sex biases in exogamy vary radically among different societies, but a strong tendency has been reported for small-scale societies to practice female exogamy. Among hunter-gatherers, for example, Ember (1978) showed that only 16% of 179 societies recorded in the Ethnographic Atlas are matrilocal, i.e., having female endogamy. A further 19% of societies are classified as bilocal or avunculocal, i.e. having variable patterns of female residence, while in the remainder female exogamy was reported as the norm. Similar results were obtained in van den Berghe's analysis (1979) of 857 societies including all economic types: 13% are matrilocal, and 13% bilocal or avunculocal. These data suggest that the tendency for female kin to live together as mothers is expressed rarely compared to the tendency to leave their natal groups. Caution is necessary in interpreting the numerical data because it is possible that there is a consistent discrepancy between reports of residence practices and the behavior as it actually occurs, or that the reports are simply wrong (Barnard, 1983). Nevertheless there is no doubt that most human societies are substantially more similar to the African apes in their tendency for female exogamy than they are to Old World Monkeys, which show clear patterns of female endogamy in many species (Wrangham, 1980). This means that the CA can also be expected to have shown a strong trend towards female exogamy.

A similar conclusion can be drawn concerning female alliances. Alliances are relationships in which individuals predictably support each other in contests against conspecifics, such as in competition over resources. They are a striking aspect of the social organization of females in many primates, such as macaques and savannah baboons, because they influence numerous aspects of social behavior (Hinde, 1983).

In Tanzanian chimpanzees associations between females are typically the consequence of attraction to a common stimulus rather than to each other (Nishida, 1979; Wrangham and Smuts, 1980), and alliances are infrequent (Goodall, 1968b). As among gorillas (Harcourt, 1979a; Yamagiwa, 1983), mothers are reported to associate preferentially with those who have infants of similar age (loc. cit.). (This has been reported also in Bossou, [Sugiyama and Koman, 1979a], and Kibale, [Ghiglieri, 1984]. It is a curious result because the only evidence of alloparenting behavior is by nulliparous females, [Nishida,

1983b].) Long-term supportive relationships between females are unknown except between mothers and daughters who have occasionally raised infants in the same community (Goodall, 1983). It is possible that examples will be found elsewhere, however. Thus in some field studies adult females spend more time with each other than at Gombe or Kasoge (e.g. Bossou, Sugiyama and Koman, 1979a), suggesting that the quality of social relationships may also differ. Chimpanzee females are certainly capable of developing supportive and powerful relationships with each other, as shown by de Waal's (1982) observations in Arnhem Zoo, Holland.

minimal femal alliances

Individual relationships have barely been described in bonobos, but as with gorillas and chimpanzees it is clear that females rarely have dominance interactions with each other. Alliance relationships must be correspondingly unimportant, because no coalitionary interactions have yet been described. There are two important ways, nevertheless, in which bonobo females differ from chimpanzees. First, during intense interactions, such as when begging for food, they commonly rub each other's genitals (Kuroda, 1980; Badrian and Badrian, 1984). This appears to be an affiliative behavior, and its occurrence suggests that female bonobos have more complex relationships than female chimpanzees do. Second, subgroups within bonobo communities are reported to have a more stable set of females than of males (Kitamura, 1983).

less mutual support among females

Nevertheless, like all the apes, female bonobos are clearly less supportive of each other than are female macaques and baboons, who regularly intervene on each other's behalf in dominance interactions (Hinde, 1983). In the same way, human females have relationships which may include strikingly friendly aspects, but they rarely involve physical aggression or systematic alliance relationships in which women form predictable alliances against other women (Irons, 1983). This is not to say they are unknown. In some societies such relationships can be very important. Competition between matrilineal clans over women's rights to land, for example, provides a parallel to the behavior seen in Old World monkeys (e.g. among the Hopi, who are also matrilocal, Forde, 1934; see also Irons, 1983). In most societies, however, long-term female relationships involve friendships rather than competitive alliances. The similarity of female relationships among African apes and people and their difference from those of terrestrial Old World monkeys suggest that the CA probably also had females with tolerant, potentially friendly but rarely coalitionary relationships.

female relations in CA

Relationships Among Males

Like relationships among females, male relationships in African apes and humans have unusual qualities compared to the best-known monkeys. In group-living monkeys the dominant trend is for males to breed away from their kin, and to have primarily competitive, unsupportive relationships with other males (Packer, 1979; Wrangham, 1980; but see Cheney and Seyfarth, 1983, who show that emigrating male vervet monkeys *Cercopithecus aethiops* may associate with male kin in their new group, and Strum and Mitchell (this volume), for references to alliances in male baboons.). The "matrilocal" monkey trend is clearly reversed in chimpanzees and people, nor is it shown by gorillas or bonobos. This raises the possibility that the CA could also have had the unusual tendency for patrilocality.

Among chimpanzees the only clear cases of male migration between communities have been of two juveniles, 4 to 5 years old, who joined a community in the company of immigrating females (probably their sisters) (Goodall, 1983). The disappearance of males from an isolated community at Bossou also implied the possibility of male migration (Sugiyama, 1981). Apart from these observations, all chimpanzee migrations between communities have been by females (above); and at least seven males have been observed to mate as adults in their natal communities (Goodall, 1983). The consequence is that brothers and other close male relatives typically live together as adults. As expected from this pattern, male chimpanzees are reported to show strong associations and alliances, sometimes (but not always) with close kin. Sugiyama (1968; Sugiyama and Koman, 1979a), Bygott (1979) and Nishida (1979, 1983b) describe such relationships for four study sites, but at one site where close observation is possible (Kibale) they have not been observed (Ghiglieri, 1984).

Among people the majority of societies are patrilocal (e.g., in hunter-gatherers, 56 to 62 percent [Ember, 1978]; in all economic types, 69 percent [van den Berghe, 1979], 82 percent [Harcourt, 1978]). Again, therefore, related males tend to live together as adults, and they are highly supportive of each other, often in fraternal interest groups (e.g. Tiger, 1969; Otterbein, 1974; Chagnon, 1980).

No strong conclusion can be drawn about male kin associations in the CA, however, for two reasons. First, for bonobos the evidence is inadequate to judge whether related males normally live together. Based on facial resemblances between young adult males and older mothers, Kano (1982) argued that male bonobos do stay in their natal communities, but direct observations are lacking. Caution is appropriate in judging male bonobo residence patterns because both at Wamba and at Lomako male social relationships appear much less supportive and important than in chimpanzees (Kuroda, 1979, 1980; Badrian and Badrian, 1984). Male bonobos groom each other less than females do, for instance, and coalitionary aggression among males has not been seen, in striking contrast to chimpanzees (loc. cit.). Evan if CA males lived in multi-male networks, therefore, it should not necessarily be assumed that they formed such strong social bonds with their male kin as chimpanzees and many humans do.

Second, in most gorilla groups (64 to 77 percent, Harcourt et al., 1981) there is only one silverback, and hence probably only one breeding male. Related males therefore tend to live apart as adults, which could also have been true of the CA. This prohibits conclusions about the associations of CA males, but the gorilla evidence nevertheless follows the chimpanzee pattern by suggesting that male kin may breed together. Thus Fossey (1983) reported only two pairs of breeding males: one was considered to be father and son, and the other to be paternally related brothers. (Relationships were judged from patterns of association from the juvenile period to adulthood.) Future data may show that bonobos and gorillas share with chimpanzees and humans a consistent trend for breeding males to associate with their kin. Present data show merely that this is the likeliest finding. See Table 3.4.

Sexual Relationships

Sexual relationships can be polygynous, polyandrous, promiscuous or monogamous. In polygynous species, several females mate exclusively with one male, whereas in polyandrous species several males mate exclusively with one female. In promiscuous species neither sex mates exclusively, and in monogamous species both sexes do. Table 3.5 summarises sexual relationships both in these terms and according to the stability of sexual partnerships.

Gorillas and the two chimpanzee species differ in both ways. Gorillas are polygynous even in groups having more than one mating male: different females mate different males, and the choice of partner follows long-term affiliative bonds (Harcourt et al., 1980). Chimpanzees and bonobos are promiscuous because within communities adults mate any potential partners: receptive females often mate with several different males in a day, and almost always do so within an estrous period (Tutin, 1979; Kuroda, 1980). Temporary monogamous relationships (consortships lasting up to a few weeks) also occur in chimpanzees. They are commoner at Gombe (where they were considered responsible for 50% of 14 conceptions [Tutin, 1979] than in Kasoge (where only one consortship was seen in 28 months [Hasegawa and Hiraiwa-Hasegawa, 1983]. Although consortships provide evidence of short-term mate choice by females (Tutin, 1979), long-term relationships (i.e. consistent consort relations over several months) do not occur. The rather stable associations of male and female bonobos (Kano, 1982) suggest that long-term partnerships might be found within their promiscuous system, but no data are available yet.

The fact that gorillas and the chimpanzees differ so clearly means that it matters little how human sexual relationships are classified. This is convenient because patterns vary so much, both between and within societies, that general trends are elusive. This is particularly true of female sexual relationships. Though women in most societies are enjoined to mate exclusively with one male (either in polygynous or monogamous relationships), some people practice promiscuity as a cultural norm (Flinn, 1981), and in others it occurs at high rates despite institutional disapproval. Whatever mating system humans are considered to have, there is no indication whether CA females had short-term or long-term relationships, or whether they mated several males or only one.

Sexual relationships of males also vary in many ways, but in one respect gorillas, bonobos and chimpanzees are similar: breeding males normally have sexual relationships with more than one female. (An exception occurs when there is only one female in a gorilla group, which happens in some 10% of groups.) In a majority of human societies polygyny is practiced widely (e.g. 93% of 130 African societies [van den Berghe, 1979], particularly by the more powerful males (Chagnon 1980). Even in societies with a monogamous marriage system, mating practice is routinely promiscuous because many individuals have covert sexual relationships. This is in contrast to many monogamous primates, where males have not been seen to be polygynous (i.e. the "obligate", monogamists, such as gibbons *Hylobates* spp. [Wittenberger and Tilson, 1980]. Too little is known about sexual relationships to be sure that hunter-gatherer societies are commonly polygynous or promiscuous, but they certainly are sometimes (Tindale, 1974). Thus the comparison suggests that successful CA males also had sexual relationships with more than one female, but whether they were short-term or long-term is not indicated.

The wide range of sexual behavior of apes and humans prevents further conclusions. Thus humans have private and often nocturnal copulations, compared to the public and largely diurnal copulations of chimpanzees; sexual interactions are initiated primarily by females in gorillas, but by males in chimpanzees (Harcourt et al., 1980); female chimpanzees and bonobos have obvious sexual swellings, unlike gorillas and humans; aggressive competition for matings (as opposed to competition for a mating relationship) is rare among gorillas or humans, but it is common among chimpanzees (particularly in the days just before detumescence of the sexual swelling, when ovulation is likely to occur [Tutin, 1979; Hasegawa and Hiraiwa-

Hasegawa, 1983]; matings are restricted to a short oestrous period
(1 to 3 days) in gorillas, a long oestrous period (9 to 12 days of
maximal tumescence) in chimpanzees, and not at all in humans; and
copulations are brief and numerous in chimpanzees, long and few
in gorillas, and long and numerous in humans (Harcourt et al., 1980).
Thus phylogenetic comparisons offer little direct insight on the sexual
behavior of the CA.

Intergroup Relationships

Four aspects of intergroup relationships are summarized in Table
3.6. As in most animals intergroup interactions are infrequent in
apes, and are therefore poorly known. They appear to have the
profoundest significance, however.

For gorillas intergroup interactions have been seen in the Virunga
and in Kahuzi. In the Virunga about 80 percent of encounters involved
violent displays, and 50 percent involved physical aggression by adult
males (Harcourt, 1978). Severe wounding (Harcourt, 1978) and probably death (Baumgartel, 1976) of adult males can result. Furthermore
five out of a total of 38 observed infants have apparently been killed
by attacks from adult males during intergroup encounters (Fossey,
1979, 1981). In Kahuzi three interactions were reported by Yamagiwa
(1983). There was no physical violence, but there were fierce displays
in two of them. Furthermore an infected wound which led to the
death of a breeding male was apparently caused by attacks from a
lone male.

Intercommunity interactions observed to date in bonobos have
involved vocal contests and avoidance of confrontation at distances
where attacks were not possible, both at Wamba and Lomako (Kano,
1982; Badrian and Badrian, 1984). Smaller parties retreated from
larger parties. Since the total number of observations is still less than
10, few generalizations about bonobo intercommunity encounters can
be made, but it is evident that they are at least tense.

In chimpanzees, intercommunity relationships are well known only
in Kasoge and Gombe. At both sites encounters of the type described
for bonobos have been seen regularly. In addition, however, parties
composed mainly of males have been observed patrolling at the edge
of the community ranges, making charging displays at members of
other groups, and (at Gombe only) violently attacking them (Nishida,
1979; Goodall et al., 1979). At both sites intercommunity interactions
are almost invariably hostile. At Gombe the deaths of five adult
males and one adult female appeared to be the direct result of severe
attacks seen to be made by males from a neighboring community
(Goodall, 1983). These attacks have been described in detail (Goodall

et al., 1979). As many as seven further deaths of adults are suspected to have been the result of intercommunity aggression, in interactions involving three communities at Gombe and two at Kasoge (Goodall, pers. comm., Kawanaka, 1981). Five infanticides have been reported in intercommunity interactions (Kawanaka, 1981).

The widespread tendency for intergroup hostility between human groups is well recognized for agricultural and industrial societies (e.g. Wright, 1965; Otterbein, 1974; Beer, 1981). Among hunter-gatherers it is sometimes considered that neighboring groups were typically peaceful (e.g. Lee and DeVore, 1968). Ember's (1978) analysis of 50 representative hunter-gatherer societies shows, however, that 64% are considered to have had warfare at least once every two years. This is a very high rate of intergroup violence compared to other animals. Together with the ape evidence it implies that many populations of the CA are likely to have had hostile intergroup relationships as a normal part of their social organization.

Table 3.6 shows the nature of the encounters. Among gorillas, chimpanzees and humans, the main participants are males, and this is probably true also for bonobos (Badrian and Badrian 1984). In many Old World monkeys, by contrast, escalated intergroup aggression is carried out by females as well as by males (Cheney, 1983). Unlike many primates, therefore, the CA can be expected to have had males as the principal active participants in intergroup encounters.

Furthermore the encounters may have involved other patterns unusual in monkeys, namely stalk or pursuit followed by violent physical attact. In gorillas and chimpanzees encounters occur not only when groups meet by chance, but also when members of one group seek those of another by sound, sight or tracks (Fossey, 1981; Goodall et al., 1979). Stalking and killing are well known in human intergroup encounters, of course (e.g. see references in Durham, 1976), but they have not been seen among bonobos.

Finally, the ape data give no indication whether the CA is likely to have been territorial. Gorilla groups have extensively overlapping home ranges which vary in location between years. They show no evidence of territorial defense (Casimir and Butenandt, 1973; Fossey and Harcourt, 1977). Male chimpanzees, by contrast, sometimes make efforts to repel intruders from their own community ranges, and can thus be considered at least partly territorial (Goodall et al., 1979). It is certain, however, that the enormous community ranges occupied by open-country chimpanzees (200 sq km or more [Baldwin et al., 1982] are too large to be defended as territories. Human groups show a similarly wide range of degrees of territoriality (Dyson-Hudson and Smith, 1978).

DISCUSSION

The Significance of the Ancestral Suite

The results of the comparisons are summed in Table 3.7. Eight characteristics are considered to be similar in living species, while six vary. Further data on variation are needed to make this conclusion more precise, but it shows that there is marked similarity in the social organization of African apes and humans. It is difficult to judge whether the shared characteristics are primitive or derived with respect to the ape stock, becaue there is only one comparison (with the orangutan) on which to base a conclusion. This means that no conclusion can be reached about how long these traits were present before the common ancestor evolved. We are confined to thinking about the common ancestor itself.

Thus the CA is implied to have commonly had closed social networks, hostile and male-dominated intergroup relationships with stalk-and-attack interactions, female exogamy and no alliance bonds between females, and males having sexual relationships with more than one female. Six other traits, by contrast, vary in their occurrence among the CA's descendants, and therefore do not provide direct clues to the ancestral social organization. Though any feature in the ancestral suite might in fact have been absent in the CA, the results are useful for two reasons.

Reconstructing Ancestral Social Organization. First, the existence of an ancestral suite means that it should be taken into account when reconstructing hominid behavior. This is not only because it provides clues to whether particular traits occurred, but also because several of the traits in Table 3.7 are likely to influence other features of social organization. Intergroup relationships and the stability of parties are two such features which have previously been treated arbitrarily despite their considerable importance.

Thus Lovejoy (1981) and Tanner (1981, and this volume) proposed models of early hominid social organization without considering the possibility that intergroup relationships occurred and were hostile. Intergroup interactions in the living species clearly create strong selection pressures for cooperative and protective relationships within groups. The present analysis shows that the simplest hypothesis is that hostile intergroup relationships occurred in ancestral species also, so reconstructions which ignore them are unlikely to be accurate.

On the other hand the stability of parties varies between living species, so this feature should be "predicted" only with the aid of a strong argument. Previous analyses have been less cautious. Tanner (1981), McGrew (1981) and Lovejoy (1981) considered parties unstable, whereas Baer and McEachron (1982) considered them stable. Neither view has adequate support. In living primates party stability appears related to the intensity of feeding competition, and hence to food distribution, but precisely how is not yet understood (Clutton-Brock and Harvey, 1977; Wrangham, 1986). A confident reconstruction of party stability is unlikely to be made until this principle has been worked out and applied to the food distribution of ancestral species.

This is a critical issue because the stability of parties can be expected to affect many other aspects of social organization. For instance, among diurnal primates long-term and exclusive sexual relationships occur only in species with stable parties, such as the polygynous units of gorillas or hamadryas baboons *Papio hamadryas* (Kummer, 1968), or the many monogamous groups (Wittenberger and Tilson, 1980). This is presumably because males must be present to be effective mate-guarders. It implies that unstable parties and exclusive relationships (Lovejoy, 1981) are an improbable combination, unless a system such as language provides help in absentee mate-guarding. By limiting the effectiveness of mateguarding, unstable parties could affect not only the stability of sexual relationships, but also (as a result) the extent of paternal investment, the pattern of sexual behavior, and the form of male-male competition (Alexander and Noonan, 1979). A key ecological problem for behavioral reconstruction, therefore, is whether stable parties were possible.

Explaining Hominoid Social Organization. The second benefit of these results is their demonstration that there are several types of behavior which are unusual in other primates, yet occur in four closely related species which have major differences in their ecology. Explaining the common features is therefore a difficult problem, with only two obvious kinds of solution other than coincidence. The superficial answer is "phylogenetic inertia". The most useful meaning of phylogenetic inertia in this instance is that shared aspects of social organization are brought about by some other shared characteristic. For example, highly developed cognitive abilities might be responsible for the common behavioral features. There is a problem, however, in envisioning how such a process would work. A further difficulty is that although some of the common features (such as intergroup raiding) occur in very few other mammals, others (such as the lack of female alliances) are comparatively widespread. Explanations based on phylogenetic inertia are therefore unlikely to be useful on their own.

Alternatively, subtle ecological similarities may still prove to account for the common behavioral features. Food distribution, for instance, may not appear to be similar across the different African apes, yet it has been argued to differ consistently from the food distribution of Cercopithecine monkeys, with the result that among apes, unlike monkeys, there is no advantage to female alliances (Wrangham, 1980). Again, compared to monkeys African apes may be so much less vulnerable to predators that they can afford to travel in much smaller groups (van Schaik and van Hooff, 1983). Development of such hypotheses will eventually show whether phylogenetic inertia is needed as an explanatory device at all.

Comparison With Single-Species Approaches

The phylogenetic approach differs in two ways from reconstructions based on single species. It uses several species; and it uses them not as models, but as indicators of conservative features of social organization. It thereby avoids two common problems with single-species reconstructions (Landau et al., 1982). First, the method allows ancestral species to be unique. Instead of assuming that early hominids behaved like a particular species, it frees them to have novel types (or combinations) of features which vary in their occurrence in living species. Second, it avoids relying on criteria of unknown importance, such as a carnivorous lifestyle or a treeless habitat. Nevertheless, in the present analysis it suffers several concomitant disadvantages, the effects of which should be reducible in the future.

First, it reconstructs only a limited repertoire. Of course, this chapter has been confined to a narrow set of variables concerned with social relationships. A wider net could add more variables to the ancestral suite, including an average group size less than 10, a population density of less than 5 per sq km, a home range of at least 7 sq km, and occasional infanticide (Wrangham, 1986). But variable features will continue to be excluded unless methods are found for judging the probability of their occurrence in an ancestor. An improved behavioral ecology is one such method, as discussed. A resolution of the three-way phylogenetic split (Fig. 1) into two two-way splits is a second. And a third method will be possible when it is clear whether the bonobo or the chimpanzee is closer to their common ancestor, because the social organization of the derived form (which is probably the bonobo) [Johnson, 1981] can then itself be taken as derived. At present phylogenetic comparison has fewer "predictions" than a model built faithfully on chimpanzees (McGrew, 1981, Table 7), but its power will grow as cladistic analysis of the hominoids improves.

Second, it takes no advantage of potentially useful information from paleontology, archaeology or paleoecology (Potts, this volume).

It ignores the influence of bipedalism, for instance, or central place foraging, or habitat type. This is because phylogenetic comparison applies to the CA and all its descendants, rather than to particular species. Features like this must certainly be used in the reconstruction of particular species, however.

The Importance of Intraspecific Variation

The present analysis has focused on central tendencies. This is a useful device for making comparisons. Substantial variation is thereby ignored, however, and must be considered again in reconstructions. This includes variation with seasons, demographic structure, population density, and habitat, all of which are known to influence primate social behavior (e.g. Altmann and Altmann, 1979; Baldwin et al., 1982). The characteristics in Tables 3.2 through 3.7 are species-specific, but they are a typology only of central tendencies, not of inevitable outcomes.

For instance, the comparisons in this chapter go against a recent trend which has downplayed the significance of aggression in human history (Table 3.7, Leakey and Lewin 1977). However, it is important to note that the view taken here is different from the classic naturalistic suggestion that humans have an evolutionary history of inevitable territorial aggression (Ardrey, 1970; Lorenz, 1967). First, there is no implication that territoriality occurred at all. Second, intergroup aggression was not necessarily universal (though it might have been). Instead, its distribution may have depended on ecological conditions, as is probably true of chimpanzees and certainly is of humans (Durham, 1976), baboons (e.g. Hamilton et al., 1976) and many other animals.

Reconstructing such features will therefore depend on understanding their adaptive significance, and hence why they occur in some environments and not others. We are thrown back again on behavioral ecology and other explanatory principles. Phylogenetic comparison gives no ultimate answers, but it points to the productive questions. And it reminds us that whatever else animals teach us, we should avoid typological thinking.

ACKNOWLEDGMENTS

D. Cheney, R. Hames, W. Kinzey, R. Seyfarth and B. Smuts made valuable comments. This chapter was prepared while the author was a Fellow at the Center for Advanced Study in the Behavioral Sciences. I am grateful for financial support provided by the National Science Foundation (BNS 76–22943).

CHAPTER FOUR

Pygmy Chimpanzees and Common Chimpanzees: Models for the Behavioral Ecology of the Earliest Hominids

RANDALL L. SUSMAN

INTRODUCTION

The notion of an African ape-human clade and an ape-like hominid ancestor was first clearly enunciated by Huxley (1863) on the basis of anatomical similarities between humans, chimpanzees and gorillas. Darwin (1871) later incorporated these notions in his own thinking on hominid evolution. From comparisons between humans and living apes, Darwin and Huxley, as well as others, such as Haeckel (1896), were able to develop vivid images of the earliest hominid in the virtual absence of a fossil record. Haeckel (1896), while conceding that the earliest true humans appeared only with the advent of speech and enlarged brains, hypothesized that *bipedalism* marked the very beginning of hominid evolution. Without a fossil record, Haeckel's hypothesis remained untested, but Darwin (1871) maintained that one day the fossil evidence would "fill in the gaps" between humans and great apes.

The fossils Darwin anticipated appeared with the announcement of *Australopithecus africanus* (Dart, 1925). Since geologists at the time thought that the geography of South Africa in the Pleistocene was similar to that of the present, Dart (1926) turned to the South African savanna and its most successful primate inhabitants, chacma baboons, for interpretation of the habitat and behavior of these early hominids. Baboon fossils were prominent elements in the South

African cave assemblages that yielded *Australopithecus,* and Dart felt that the open country and rigors of savanna life rapidly selected for similar traits (such as intelligence and meat-eating) in both baboons and early hominids. Dart observed first-hand the carnivorous proclivities of baboons and hypothesized that the early hominids must also have been hunters subsisting in large part on meat (Dart, 1957, 1959). This hypothesis was supported by supposed bone tools and weapons found with *Australopithecus* at the South African sites. For Dart, baboons provided clues as to how small-brained, predatory man-apes such as *Australopithecus* might have existed on the South African veldt. He viewed carnivory, tool behavior and intelligence as three elements of an adaptive pattern. The savanna was a place where selection would favor "quick wittedness" for both the capture and killing of prey and for escape from predators. (See review of the baboon model by Strum and Mitchell, this volume.)

The themes of terrestriality, meat-eating, and a regimented social organization necessary for the exigencies of life on the savanna recur in all of the theories of human origins that have been proposed in the 30 years following Dart's announcement of *Australopithecus* (Dart, 1926 *et seq.;* Washburn, 1957; Oakley, 1961a). Oakley (1961a) believed that apes were "forest creatures," subsisting mainly on plants and insects while all humans ate animal flesh. He felt, as did Dart (e.g., 1957, 1963) and others, that baboons, that were observed to eat wild and domestic animals, were perhaps more like early hominids than were any of the apes. Because the advent of bipedality had long been held as a fundamental hominid trait (Darwin, 1871; Haeckel, 1896; Weidenreich, 1947) models, such as Oakley's, also attempted to integrate bipedalism with the earlier themes of terrestriality, meat-eating, and tight-knit social organization. Washburn, the leading figure in the promotion of anthropologically oriented primate field studies, also believed in the predatory nature of the australopithecines. In 1957 he wrote that meat-eating engendered hunting and attendant traits such as cooperation, division of labor, sharing of food, territoriality, and tool use. Washburn became a leading proponent of the view that hunting (and meat-eating) was the major force in the social and psychological evolution of early humans. Reflecting the influence of Dart, (and others such as Robert Broom), Washburn and Lancaster wrote, "In a very real sense our intellect, interests, emotions and basic social life all are evolutionary products of the success of the hunting adaptation (Washburn and Lancaster, 1968).

Washburn and DeVore (1961a) conducted one of the first anthropologically focused field studies and further popularized the baboon model, although they refrained from over-representing the similarities between baboon and tribal human society. Washburn and DeVore felt that baboons (in this case olive baboons) provided a test case for how a primate might solve the problem of coming to the ground. Their studies revealed a number of fascinating facts about baboon life. These included the relative extensiveness of troop ranges (compared to those of earlier studied arboreal primates), the existence of well-defined dominance hierarchies, and a varied but overwhelmingly vegetarian diet. Washburn and DeVore (1961a), however, confirmed the carnivorous proclivity of baboons documenting one instance of olive baboons killing and eating a young vervet monkey, and two instances of predation on newborn Thompson's gazelle during their two-month study in 1959. They also observed dominance interactions and concluded that the dominance heirarchy strictly defined and controlled intragroup aggression and aided in troop defense. Adult male baboons acting cooperatively could successfully defend the troop against formidable predators such as leopards and cheetah. In the presence of these and other dangers such as lions, and snakes, Washburn and DeVore noted that the occurrence of trees (as sources of escape and sleeping refuges) limited the distribution of baboon troops as much as did the availability of food and water.

While drawing many inferences on early hominid ecology from a baboon-like model, Washburn and DeVore concluded that early man was distinctively different from baboons in the possession of food sharing, cooperation, bipedal locomotion, intelligence and language. Like Dart, they hypothesized that selection for hunting (including the killing of large animals) might account for the aforementioned complex of early hominid behaviors and morphological traits.

Since the early 1960s, this savanna-based model has strongly influenced field studies by behavioral ecologists and anthropologists. Attention has been directed not only to nonhuman primates, but also to social, open country carnivores. Mech (1970), Kruuk (1972) and Schaller (1972), considered the implications for social organization of cooperative hunting by wolves, hyenas and lions, respectively. Later Schaller and Lowther (1969), Cachel (1975) and King (1975) applied these carnivore models in reconstructing the sociology of early hominids. Like the baboon models, all of the carnivore models assumed that early hominids were adapted or in the process of adapting to open country. In addition, the carnivore models relied on the assumption that hunting per se (not simply meat-eating) was a key element in the early hominid adaptive shift and later speciation and hominids (Cachel, 1975). Schaller and Lowther (1969), in stating a case for the social carnivore model, noted that while many nonhuman primate species exhibit fairly closed social groups similar to human hunters and carnivores, the latter two share the additional trait of cooperative hunting behavior—a behavioral mode that would be especially significant for hunting large prey in open terrain (Schaller and Lowther, 1969). Like Washburn and DeVore (1961a) the proponents of carnivore models assumed that early hominids not only hunted, but they hunted large prey (Schaller and Lowther, 1969).

When Jane Goodall undertook her pioneering study of chimpanzees, she was strongly influenced by the predation hypothesis (Goodall, 1963). At the time when Goodall began her fieldwork, the view of chimpanzees held by Oakley and others was that man's closest relatives were forest-dwelling vegetarians distinguished from hominids, who were savanna-dwelling, killer apes. Goodall's early field work revealed that chimpanzees were not the strict vegetarians that Oakley supposed. In a preliminary report on the initial 15 months of her long-term study she observed (over a period of 800 hours) the consumption of ants, termites, gall fly larvae, and most significantly on three occasions, the capture and consumption of a young bush pig, a bushbuck, and one monkey (Goodall, 1968b). As Goodall's study unfolded over the decade of the 1960s, the chimpanzee moved to the center of anthropological interest. (At the same time dramatic new hominid fossils were being uncovered in East Africa, not far from the site of Goodall's work). The long-term studies at Gombe documented the conditions surrounding chimpanzee predation including the social behavior associated with it (Teleki, 1973; 1981). Despite the attention given to predation, few species of primates are significantly predatory. Strum and Mitchell (this volume) discuss factors that appear to explain the restricted distribution of predation among nonhuman primates.

Goodall also reported on what has been called tool-using: the ability of chimpanzees to use twigs to remove termites from their nests and to use leafy wadges as "sponges" for drinking. Goodall outlined the basically frugivorous diet of chimpanzees and noted that their overall behavioral "adaptability," including rudimentary hunting and tool-using, indicated that chimpanzees were comparative "generalists" among higher primates. Goodall's work did much to alter the "definition" of hominid. As a result of the studies of the Gombe chimpanzees, it became apparent that the behavioral differences which separated humans from chimpanzees were of a subtle, continuous, quantitative nature.

Brain (1972) was the first to reconsider the "killer-ape" hypothesis seriously (as well as the evidence for interpersonal violence in *Australopithecus,* [Dart, 1957]). The notion of *Australopithecus* as killer apes, first developed by Dart (1926, 1957) and later popularized by Ardrey, was based in large part on the claim that holes in specimen SK 54 were blows inflicted by a fellow australopithecine. Brain showed that the supposed flint projectile embedded in the type skill of *Paranthropus* (the robust australopithecine, TM 1517) was less probably from a fellow hominid and more likely the result of debris falling from the cave roof onto the skull. Claims of fractures and traumatically induced pathologies in the Taungs child, STS 60, and other specimens were also cast in doubt by Brain (1972). From studies of leopard lairs in Kenya, Brain showed that australopithecines were commonly victims of leopard predation. Brain's work weakened the notion of *Australopithecus* as predator. Instead a view of early hominids as prey emerged.

Brain convincingly demonstrated that the supposed bone tools and "weapons" of Dart's "osteodontokeratic" culture could not be attributed to the activities of *Australopithecus*. Rather, he showed that the South African hominid sites of Swartkrans, Kromdraai, Sterkfontein, Makapansgat, and Taung (all caves during the Plio-Pleistocene) acted as catchments that accumulated feeding remains of various carnivores and scavengers such as leopards, hyenas, and porcupines (Brain 1970). In a compelling discussion of the Swartkrans site, Brain demonstrated the fit of the canine teeth of a Swartkrans leopard into holes in the skull of a young robust australopithecine (SK 54). Brain suggested, based on observations of the feeding behavior of wild leopards, how the hominid prey was likely consumed in a tree at the mouth of a limestone cave. During or after feeding by the leopard, the bones of the young hominid fell or were washed into the catchment and included in the cave deposit. Other studies by Brain on the fossils themselves and on the feeding behavior of extant owls, porcupines, hyenas, leopards, and cheetahs, provided convincing evidence that *Australopithecus* was the hunted (or scavenged) rather than the hunter.

The work of Brain and others, suggests that the killer-ape models of hominid behavior and social organization were based on understandable but incorrect interpretations of the fossil record. With the data we now have from field studies in a variety of habitats and with a greatly expanded fossil record, it is well past the time to rethink not only the killer-ape but also the savanna model. One general question we might ask is *when* and *how* did the earliest humans abandon their hominoid heritage, leave the trees, and become full-time bipeds. This is a question that Darwin posed as he, and most subsequent human evolutionists, recognized the significance of coming to the ground and achieving a two-legged, striding manner of locomotion. One can now pose this question more directly given our expanded knowledge of the naturalistic behavior of primates and the great number of fossils of foot, leg, thigh and hip (as well as the upper limbs) we now have of early hominids. We can ask, "Do these fossils look (and, therefore, did they act) like tree dwellers, ground dwellers, apes, or monkeys, or did they represent some unique combination of the above? Do they lie on a morphological and behavioral continuum from the ape to the human grade? Or do they fall off of this continuum? The fossils give us the clues; they point to the direction that our comparative field studies and our anatomical research should take.

As discussed below, our detailed examination of the fossils (Jungers, 1982; Stern and Susman, 1983; Susman *et al.*, 1984, 1985) and those of others (Senut, 1980; Tuttle, 1981; Tardieu, 1983; Senut and Tardieu, 1985) show that *Australopithecus afarensis* was at least a part-time climber and that morphologically they were bona fide members of the Hominoidea, ape-like in some features; human-like in others. While different parts of the anatomy of *A. afarensis* can be likened to apes or humans, the "total morphological pattern" in *afarensis* is unique. The pattern is not so unique, however, that it prohibits our drawing functional inferences with regard to each anatomical region and inferences as to the behavior and habitus of *A. afarensis* (Jungers, 1982; Stern and Susman, 1983; Susman *et al.*, 1984, 1985).

Initially new evidence of the Hadar hominids seemed to do little to alter interpretations of the earliest hominid (Johanson and Edey, 1981; Laporte and Zihlman, 1983). Even though the new species, *Australopithecus afarensis* was half a million to a million years older than previously known *A. africanus* and as much as 2 million years prior to *Homo habilis*, most workers simply widened their interpretations (Lovejoy, 1979; Johanson and Edey, 1981; Oxnard, 1984). Others, however, viewed the Hadar hominid fossils as representing a very different hominid grade (Stern and Susman, 1983; Susman et al., 1984, 1985). Stern and Susman (1981) provided a model for the evolution of human bipedalism wherein vertical climbing is seen as the mode of locomotion that preadapted the pongid hip for hominid bipedality. The Hadar hominids were viewed as largely forest (rather than strictly savanna) adapted and it was speculated that their dependence on the forest continued beyond the point at which hominids began to evolve longer lower limbs, develop a low, broad, ilium with outwardly oriented lesser gluteal muscles, a short hamstring moment arm, shorter foot with straight lateral toes, adducted great toe, and a wide heel.

Other aspects of the paleobiology of the Hadar hominids also suggest a forest adaptation (Susman et al., 1984). These include small body size (30 kg for adult females) and the evidence of forested conditions, in addition to more open environments, in the African Plio-Pleistocene (as indicated by faunal and paleobotanical remains). In light of these facts we might learn most about the habitus of

Australopithecus by comparing and contrasting data from the studies of deciduous (open) woodland chimpanzees with those on forest species. *Pan paniscus* is the most forest adapted of the African apes and as such it becomes important as one potential source for understanding the behavior and ecology of the earliest hominids.

SOCIOECOLOGY OF FREE-RANGING PYGMY CHIMPANZEES

Pygmy chimpanzee social groups consist of cohesive units of males, females and immatures (Kuroda, 1979, 1980; Kano, 1982; Badrian and Badrian, 1984). The majority (68%) of groups encountered in the Lomako Forest are mixed groups of 5–10 individuals, including immatures (Badrian and Badrian, 1984). At Wamba mixed groups of 11–15 individuals account for 74% of the sightings (Kuroda, 1979). Kano (1983) similarly reports that mixed groups averaging 8 animals account for 70% of the total at Yalosidi. At Lake Tumba, pygmy chimpanzees form small groups of less than 10 individuals (Horn, 1980). Pygmy chimpanzee groups, however, frequently aggregate into larger "communities". The largest community aggregations observed in the Lomako Forest and at Wamba are around 55 individuals, although larger groups may sometimes form (Kuroda, 1979; Badrian and Badrian 1984). Large groups (>20 individuals) are more common at Wamba than in the Lomako. Large associations of pygmy chimpanzees at both sites are related to temporary concentrations of preferred fruits and abundances of localized food sources. Three such foods, *Dialium pachyphyllum* (Leguminosae), *Uapaca guinensis* (Euphorbiaceae), and *Antiaris toxicaria* (Moraceae) occur in tall (>40m) trees with large crowns. These trees may accommodate as many as 17 animals (Badrian and Malenky, 1984). Male groups and isolated groups of females with young are rare in pygmy chimpanzees (Kuroda, 1979; Kano, 1983; Badrian and Badrian, 1984).

Pygmy chimpanzee females appear to be sexually receptive even when they are carrying very young infants, and females may cycle within one year of giving birth. Thompson-Handler et al. (1984) suggest that the increased receptivity of pygmy chimpanzee females may play a social cohesive role, reinforcing male-female bonds. Other evidence supports this hypothesis.

The general levels of agonistic behavior are low in pygmy chimpanzees. Kano and Mulavwa (1984) report that the greatest frequency of agonistic behavior is observed at their "artificial feeding place"; agonistic encounters between males increase from less than one per social group/hour (0.70) under natural conditions to 3.26 per social group/hour. But even at the artificial feeding place, encounters between males and females were infrequent. In the naturalistic setting, agonistic encounters were most frequent during feeding, directed from a high ranking male to lower ranking male (Kano, 1983). At Yalosidi, Kano observed only one agonistic interaction in 68 hours (Kano, 1983). Females, especially multiparious ones, express little or no fear of males and often supplant and take food from males (Kano and Mulavwa, 1984). Taking of food from males by females often involves or leads to copulation (Kano, 1984; Thompson-Handler et al., 1984).

The high level of male tolerance and permanent associations of male and female pygmy chimpanzees are reinforced by grooming and sexual behavior. One such behavior, peculiar in its relative frequency to pygmy chimpanzees, is the high frequency of male-female grooming associations (Fig. 4.1). In pygmy chimpanzees, male-female pairs represent 25% of all grooming observed in the Lomako and 48% of the grooming at Wamba, while in common chimpanzees male-male grooming and female-infant grooming pairs exceed those of males and females. Other manifestations of the bonding between male and female pygmy chimpanzees are seen in the tolerance of males for females as well as in young begging and taking animal and plant food. (Badrian and Malenky, 1984; Kano and Mulavwa, 1984). Another manifestation of affiliative behavior in pygmy chimpanzees is seen in what has been termed genito-genital rubbing (Kuroda, 1980; Kano, 1980; Thompson-Handler et al., 1984). Genito-genital rubbing is thought to reduce tension between females. Interactions between female pygmy chimpanzees such as genito-genital rubbing are frequently observed during episodes of food sharing (Kano, 1984). As noted during food sharing, male-female sexual behavior also serves to reduce tension (Kuroda, 1980; Thompson-Handler et al., 1984). Pygmy chimpanzees may have a prolonged swelling phase of the menstrual cycle (Savage Rumbaugh and Wilkerson, 1978; Thompson-Handler et al., 1984) and female pygmy chimpanzees copulate throughout their menstrual cycle (Thompson-Handler et al., 1984). Thompson-Handler found that, in the Lomako, once females began to cycle, they retained a swollen perineum and did not return to a 0-stage of swelling (Thompson-Handler et al., 1984).

Food sharing is another manifestation of the cohesiveness of pygmy chimpanzee society. Kuroda reports that the high tolerance among individuals results in males and females sharing food as well as females sharing food with their young (Kuroda, 1984). At Wamba the sharing of plant food has been reported Kuroda (1984) and in the Lomako Forest pygmy chimpanzees kill and share animal food as well (Badrian and Malenky, 1984). At Wamba both naturally occurring fruits such as *Dialium* and artificially provisioned sugar

Fig. 4.1 Male-female grooming.

cane is shared among the group. Tolerance on the part of adult males is seen by the fact that they may be supplanted from feeding positions by younger individuals and females. In the Lomako males share the meat of small ungulates with females and young. During the meat eating episodes females were allowed to take parts of the carcass after copulating with the male possessors (Badrian and Badrian, 1984; Badrian and Malenky, 1984).

COMPARISONS OF PYGMY AND COMMON CHIMPANZEES

Overall, as Kano (1982) noted, chimpanzees and pygmy chimpanzees share common elements of their social organization; large communities are made up of smaller subunits. The units, however, differ between the two species. The basic social unit or subgroup in pygmy chimpanzees consists of roughly equal numbers of adult males and females together with immatures (socionomic sex ratio of .55). Pygmy chimpanzees have higher male-female, and female-female affinities. Group cohesion is maintained by numerous behaviors seen in pygmy chimpanzees and observed only rarely in common chimpanzees. As mentioned before, these include genito-genital rubbing in females, lengthened phases of sexual receptivity on the part of females, high tolerance of group members by the dominant males and widespread food sharing.

All of the above signal a cohesive social group and Shea (1983) has suggested that this, coupled with the reduced sexual dimorphism (including reduced dental dimorphism [Kinzey, 1984]) of *Pan paniscus* (compared to *Pan troglodytes*), may be a reflection of the reduced level of intragroup aggression in *Pan paniscus*. It may also reflect the more arboreal habitus of pygmy chimpanzees and a more closed breeding system whereby pygmy chimpanzee females emigrate from their natal group but may remain within their community. Kano (1982) recorded few episodes of copulation when groups numbered less than 10 individuals while in larger community aggregations there was more excitement, including aggressive encounters, genito-genital rubbing, display (branch dragging) and copulation. This led Kano to the conclusion that the community aggregations were more significant social units than the smaller foraging units.

While pygmy chimpanzee social groups consist of males, females and immatures (68% of groups in the Lomako, 74% at Wamba), social groups of common chimpanzees are less commonly mixed (30% at Gombe [Goodall, 1968b]; 47% at Mahale [Nishida, 1979]). The frequency of mixed groups of forest chimpanzees (37% at Budongo) is comparable to that for other common chimpanzees (Reynolds, 1965; Reynolds and Reynolds, 1965). Pygmy chimpanzees clearly do not subscribe to the pattern in common chimpanzees in which all male parties patrol large home ranges and females are frequently found alone with their offspring or with other females. Common chimpanzee males forage over a wider area which covers the ranges of several females. Males associate principally with estrous females (Wrangham, 1975; Suzuki, 1977; Pusey, 1979). Wrangham (1980) has suggested that females with offspring operate to maximize their foraging efficiency while male groups range over a wide area determined by reproductive opportunity and access to females.

The mixed groups of pygmy chimpanzees devote roughly 30% of their daily activity to feeding (Kano and Mulavwa, 1984) while common chimpanzees at Gombe devote 43% of their activity to feeding (Teleki, 1981). The day ranges of Gombe chimpanzees, which average 4 to 6 km (Wrangham, 1975), also exceed those of pygmy chimpanzees (2.4 km [range 0.4–6 km, n=91]) (Kano and Mulavwa, 1984). Pygmy chimpanzees devote up to 80% of their feeding to arboreal foods (Kano and Mulavwa, 1984) (Fig. 4.2); common chimpanzees devote roughly 62% of their feeding activity to exploitation of arboreal foods. Kano and Mulavwa (1984) note that the stratum most frequently utilized for feeding by pygmy chimpanzees at Wamba are the crowns of emergent trees.

Pygmy chimpanzee groups tend to be larger than those of common chimpanzees. The greatest frequency of groups is 11–15 animals (Kuroda, 1979) with roughly equal male-female ratio (socionomic sex ratio = .55 [Kano, 1982]). At Gombe the modal group size of common chimpanzees is 2–4 (Goodall, 1968b) while in the Budongo Forest it is 2–6 individuals (Reynolds, 1965). In both pygmy and common chimpanzees these groups are units of larger communities which may aggregate into larger, temporary associations when food is abundant (in the case of pygmy chimpanzees) or when estrous females are consorting with males (in common chimpanzees).

The topic of food sharing has been given a great deal of attention recently (McGrew, 1979; Galdikas and Teleki, 1981; Strum, 1981; Teleki, 1981) because of the persistent notion that a fundamental human adaptation was cooperation between the sexes and a division of labor (Washburn, 1957). Pygmy chimpanzees commonly share all manner of foods including small (*Dialium* spp.) and large (*Anonidium mannii*) fruits, provisioned foods such as sugar cane, and, in the Lomako Forest, the meat of small ungulates such as duikers (*Cephalophus* spp.). All the meat-eating episodes in the Lomako probably involved males as the captors and primary possessors. Common chimpanzees also share plant and animal food (Teleki, 1973; McGrew, 1979). In the common chimpanzee males are the principal captors of small mammals while females are the predominant termite gath-

Fig. 4.2 Pygmy chimpanzees feeding.

erers. The length of time expended by females to gather termites and ants is greater than that expended by males (Goodall, 1968b). Forty-seven percent of female fecal samples contained insect remains compared to 27% for males. As a whole Gombe chimpanzees spent only 3% of the total time under observation engaged in termite fishing. Pygmy chimpanzees consume insects (Badrian et al., 1981; Badrian and Malenky, 1984; Kano and Mulavwa, 1984) but termite fishing has not been observed at either Wamba or in the Lomako Forest. It may be that termite fishing, which is an independent activity engaged in by females, is less prominent in socially coherent pygmy chimpanzee society where females do not forage by themselves.

HUMID RAINFORESTS VERSUS DECIDUOUS WOODLANDS AS ECOLOGICAL SETTINGS AND DETERMINANTS OF SOCIAL BEHAVIOR

When compared with that of common chimpanzees, pygmy chimpanzee society displays many elements that are generally seen in forest versus open-country primates. Decreased day range, increased incidence of arboreal feeding, and less time budgeted for feeding. The relaxed levels of intraspecific agonistic behavior, the increased sexual receptivity, the reduced period of lactational amenorrhea, and the reduced sexual dimorphism in pygmy chimpanzees versus common chimpanzees may also reflect the reduced stress on pygmy chimpanzee social organization. This may in turn relate to the pygmy chimpanzee's comparatively stable forested habitat with reduced seasonality, relaxed feeding competition, and reduced predator pressure by comparison with the more open country, ground-dwelling common chimpanzee. In the Congo Basin of central Africa the seasonality is mild while in drier areas of western (McGrew et al., 1981) and eastern Africa (Itani, 1979) seasonal fluctuations in food availability are more marked. In addition to behavioral differences, numerous anatomical features of pygmy chimpanzees, such as smaller size, long curved fingers and toes, longer scapula and others, may also be viewed as features related to an arboreal habitus (for detailed discussion of this subject see Senut, 1978, 1980; Senut and LeFloch, 1981; Tardieu, 1981; Tuttle, 1981; Jungers, 1982; Stern and Susman, 1983; Susman, et al., 1984, 1985; Senut and Tardieu, 1985).

CONCLUSIONS

Whereas Washburn and others in 1961, at the time *The Social Life of Early Man* was written, built their reconstructions of early hominid behavior largely on comparative primatology of open country species and on a meagre fossil record of South African hominids, we now have an enhanced perspective based on many field studies of ecologically diverse primates (and other mammals) and a great wealth of fossil evidence. We also have at our disposal a number of elegant analyses of the fossil material (e.g. Brain, 1970; Lovejoy, 1975). The hominid discoveries in eastern Africa at Hadar and new interpretations of the paleontological and archeological record (Isaac, 1981; Potts, 1984a, this volume) offer the possibility that the common ancestor of African apes and hominids was forest adapted, or at the very least, more dependent on an arboreal habitus than was once thought. If so, the savanna model (Lancaster, 1978; Zihlman and Brunker, 1979; Lovejoy, 1981; Johanson and Edey, 1981; LaPorte and Zihlman, 1983) requires modification (Susman et al., 1984).

Pygmy chimpanzees provide one important source of data for reconstructing models of hominid behavior. Not only do social structures and behavior differ in the two chimpanzees, but morphological differences are also seen in the distinctive black skin, small ears, whiskers and dark pelage (Coolidge, 1933), less robust skeletal anatomy and skull (Fenart and Deblock, 1973; Cramer, 1977; Zihlman et al., 1978) reduced dentition (Johanson, 1974; Susman and Jungers, 1981; Kinzey, 1984) and reduced sexual dimorphism in *Pan paniscus* (McHenry and Corruccini, 1981; Shea, 1983; Jungers and Susman, 1984). In addition, differences in pygmy and common chimpanzees are seen in locomotor behavior, dietary preferences (including differences in animal prey species), and vocal repertoire.

The "model" I accept as the most likely representative of the earliest hominids by definition is a composite one. The fossil record itself suggests that the African apes hold the most important clues to our own evolution. Lovejoy (1982) has noted

> Modern human social behavior is completely irrelevant to that of emergent hominids. Humans are products of at least 2 million years of intense social evolution. Their mating and reproductive behavior are saturated with religious, symbolic, and relational structures. Almost no vertebrate species is less suited to the reconstruction of early hominid behavior.

As Haeckel stated almost one hundred years ago, ". . . no single one of the existing man-like apes is among the direct ancestors of the human race; they are all the last scattered remnants of an old catarrhine branch, once numerous, from which the human race has developed as a special branch and in a special direction (Haeckel, 1896:181)." Just as the morphology of the earliest hominids is a mosaic of primitive (hominoid) and derived (hominid) traits (see McHenry, 1975) the behavior and ecology of these hominids is almost certainly unique. The nature of the elements in the pattern can only be resolved by the paleontological record. (For a contrasting opinion see Wrangham, this volume.) How the elements of the pattern articulate in an adaptive complex will be determined by behavioral-ecological data garnered from the many different social systems and ecological settings in which extant primates are found.

The combination of morphological adaptations for climbing and bipedal walking found in the earliest hominids, *Australopithecus afarensis*, imply a broad range of behaviors and a wide ecological niche. The conception of the earliest hominids as savanna-dwelling, terrestrial bipeds does not account for the small size, relatively short lower limb, mobile ankle, long forefoot, curved toes, and ape-like toe joints of *A. afarensis*. While these early hominids did walk bipedally on the ground at least some of the time (as attested to by their hip and thigh morphology and fossil footprint tracks) they may, at the same time, have remained equally (or better adapted) for climbing and life in the trees. If so, then models of early hominid ecology and social behavior must incorporate data from extant forest apes to a far greater extent than they have in the past.

ACKNOWLEDGEMENTS

I thank the government of the Republic of Zaire and the Institute for Scientific Research, Kinshasa, for their support of our field work. The Lomako Forest Pygmy Chimpanzee Project has continued with help from many individuals. I thank Dr. Nkanza Dolumingu, Kabongo Ka Mbulamata, Noel Badrian, Nancy Thompson-Handler, Richard Malenky, Frances White, Franz Christaans, Lofinda Bongenge, Ikwa Nyamaolo, Bofaso Bosenja, and Lokuli Isekofaso. All work has been carried out with funding from NSF (grants BNS 8218236 and BNS 831120601).

I am grateful to John Fleagle, Bill Jungers and Susan Larson for many useful comments on this manuscript. Thanks to Richard Malenky who took the photographs in figures 4.1 and 4.2.

Finally, thanks to Warren Kinzey, who many years ago sparked my interest in physical anthropology, for inviting me to contribute to this volume.

CHAPTER FIVE

Baboon Models and Muddles

SHIRLEY C. STRUM
and WILLIAM MITCHELL

INTRODUCTION

Baboons have captured the imagination of humans since ancient times and where the two species of primates lived next to each other, baboons figured prominently in both mythology and culture. Since baboons were watched only casually, ideas about them were often projections of human fears, desires and concerns. However, baboons have also held an historically important place in scientific efforts to understand human behavior. This paper considers the place of baboon studies in recent and future evolutionary reconstructions as an illustration of new directions in the development of nonhuman primate models for human evolution. But first let us trace the history of baboons in evolutionary studies.

THE HISTORY OF BABOON MODELS

Our history should really begin with the pioneering work of Eugene Marais (1940; 1969) who studied baboons in South Africa in the late 1800's. Marais watched several troops over extended periods and had a modern evolutionary perspective, asking interesting questions about the evolution of human behavior. Marais' insights were half a century ahead of their time. Yet due to a peculiar set of circumstances (see Ardrey's introduction in Marais, 1969, for details) this research had no impact on scientific thinking then or later. By contrast, Zuckerman's study of hamadryas baboons (Zuckerman, 1932) at the London Zoo in the 1930's created a model of primate society that influenced interpretations of nonhuman and human behavior for decades. In the three years preceding his observations, 130 hamadryas baboons had been caged in a 100 by 60 foot enclosure. Ninety-four baboons died, either directly or indirectly as a result of males fighting with each other over access to females. Aggression between males continued during Zuckerman's observations. Though it is now easy to see the inaccuracies in his conclusion that primate society was based on sex and organized by dominance, itself derived from aggression, these biases were less apparent at that time given the lack of field data on primate behavior. Generalizing from particular baboons to primate society was made easy by the theoretical perspective of that era.

Carpenter's field studies of several species of monkeys and apes (Carpenter, 1934; 1940; 1942) provided much needed naturalistic and comparative data. Sadly, little of the new primate data found its way into interpretations of human evolution and further field investigations were made impossible by World War II. Interest was rekindled in the 1950's when a variety of nonhuman primate species were studied worldwide. Among these (see, for example, Jay, 1965; Southwick et al., 1965), it was the baboon studies of Washburn, DeVore, and Hall (e.g. Washburn and DeVore, 1961b; DeVore and Hall, 1965) that gave the field its working definitions of important concepts such as the "primate group", the "primate male" and the "primate female" and identified the role played by aggression and dominance in primate society. Washburn and DeVore made evolutionary interpretations of the adaptive nature of what they saw among baboons (Washburn and DeVore, 1961b; DeVore and Washburn, 1963) and used both their data and their interpretations to speculate directly about the evolution of human behavior. Because baboons and early hominids shared the same ecology with a similar primate biology, they reasoned that the baboon data could help identify the problems facing ancient humans and offer suggestions about the solutions available to hominids. Baboons were also used to define what was uniquely human by contrasting living humans and baboons. The themes that emerged directly from the baboon model included: the adaptive nature of aggression, its use and control through a male dominance hierarchy, the differences in roles between males and females, and the relationship between aggression, dominance and reproductive success. The important themes that emerged from the comparison with living humans were: the uniqueness of hunting as a human adaptation (with implications for culture, communication and social interactions) and the interaction between ecology and social organization and between environment and behavior.

> . . . we have tried to stress those aspects of baboon ecology
> which are of the greatest help in understanding human
> evolution. Obviously, man is not descended from a baboon,
> and the behavior of our ancestors may have been very

different from that of living baboons. But we think that in a general way the problems faced by the baboon troop may be very similar to those which confronted our ancestors. . . . Finally, we would stress that survival is a complex process, and that all the factors which lead to reproductive success must ultimately be considered . . . with the coming of man, every category is fundamentally altered and evolution begins to be dominated by new selection pressures. Some measure of how different the new directions are may be gained from the study of the ecology of baboons . . . (DeVore and Washburn, 1963:366).

Although the baboon studies represented some of the best field data of the time, in retrospect we can see that the "baboon model" had a disproportionate impact on our ideas about primates. Equally good data from studies on other species that were at variance with the baboon model had a limited audience (e.g. Hall, 1965b; Jay, 1965; Simonds, 1965). Even Carpenter, whose earlier description of howler monkey society (Carpenter, 1934) stood in direct opposition to the baboon model, made a very baboon-like reinterpretation in the 1960's emphasizing competition, dominance and aggression; in the earlier interpretation, howler society was the ideal "communism" (Carpenter, 1965). (See Crockett, this volume, for a review of howler monkey studies.) Haraway (1978) has recently traced the special appeal of the baboon model, or rather the issues that the baboon model raises, within the modern human political and social context. While this and similar interpretations (Martin and Voorhies, 1975; Reynolds, 1976) may remain controversial, what is most important for the present discussion is that our concepts about *primate* society were, for many years, actually generalizations about *baboon* society. This then became the basis for our reconstructions of the social life of early hominids.

The initial demise of the baboon model resulted from accumulating data on other species (see Jay, 1968a) and information on baboons in other areas (Rowell, 1966a, 1966b, 1969a, 1969b; Ransom, 1971). Primate variability, recognized by Marais at the turn of the century, was now a confirmed fact with critical implications for the use of primate behavior in evolutionary reconstructions. The new position was this: if it was as risky to generalize from baboons in one area to baboons in another area, how could broader generalizations be made about nonhuman primates and how could these be extended, by way of simple analogy, to early hominids?

The existence of primate variability also created a controversy over the importance of phylogeny and ecology (e.g., Gartlan, 1968; Struhsaker, 1969). The argument was whether we should be searching for traits of biological ancestry—homology—or traits that converged in response to environmental requirements—analogy—in our evolutionary models of early hominids. The new data on chimpanzees in the wild (Goodall, 1968a, 1968b, 1968c, 1973) propelled chimps into the key role as "the model". The phylogenetic closeness of chimpanzees to humans was clearly reflected in their many human-like behaviors (Lancaster, 1975), yet social carnivores also made a brief bid for the role of prototypes for early hominids (Schaller and Lowther, 1969; Thompson, 1975; Cachel, 1975; King, 1975). In the end, anthropologists favored primates, arguing for phylogeny over ecology and emphasizing homology rather than convergent analogy.

Ironically, just as specialists were abandoning the baboon model, the popular press and nonspecialists interested in interpreting human evolution adopted and championed that view of primate society (e.g., Ardrey, 1961; Campbell, 1966; Tiger, 1969; Tiger and Fox, 1971; Birdsell, 1972; Ricklefs, 1973). [A different view, that the baboon model reflected incorrect interpretations of the hominid fossil record, is put forward by Susman, this volume.-ed.] The demise of the early scientific models was not followed by a new synthesis because primate variability was little understood. Two factors appeared important (some variation was closely linked to differences in ecology and other variation was obviously tied to differences in phylogeny), but which took precedence and how the interaction occurred was still unclear. Recently, behavioral ecology has stimulated a renewed interest in interpretations based on animal behavior. The focus has shifted, however, from evolutionary interpretations which were unconsciously "good of the group" or "good of the species" to ones based on individual selection linked to the extended genome of the kin group and through reciprocity to unrelated individuals (Wilson, 1975; Trivers, 1971). This theoretical perspective suggests that all primates, in fact all animals, can be understood in the same terms, the evolutionary factors that motivate behavior making baboons as useful as chimpanzees and social carnivores in efforts to understand human evolution. Though still lacking an all encompassing framework, both recent data and current theory suggest a direction to take. If all primates, in fact, all animals, can be understood in the same evolutionary terms, the concept of a "best" model must be faulty. The real advantage of the data on nonhuman animals, then, is to define principles and processes that work in an evolutionary context; the nonhuman primate data can show these in operation in complex societies. The primate baseline can be created in two ways, either from comparisons of populations of the same (or different) species or from comparisons of longitudinal data of a single population. In this manner, the human origins story is set at its starting place.

DEFINING PRINCIPLES AND PROCESSES

To illustrate how the primate data can be used, we will draw on the second type of data, the longitudinal study of one group in one population of olive baboons *(Papio anubis)*. These have been variously known as the Pumphouse Gang, the Gilgil baboons, and the baboons of Kekopey. The details of their behavior are published elsewhere (Strum, 1975, 1976a,b, 1981, 1982, 1983a,b, 1984, in press). Here we will summarize a few points that are relevant to evolutionary interpretations of human behavior.

Hunting

Primates are an omnivorous order, yet only a few species are truly predatory. Most early interpretation of human evolution (Washburn and Avis, 1958; Spuhler, 1959; Campbell, 1966; Krantz, 1968; Washburn and Lancaster, 1968) assumed that hominids were the only primate species that hunted (but see Dart, 1953 and Oakley, 1961b). Observations of the hunting behavior of Gombe chimpanzees (Goodall, 1968b) caused a significant shift in this position. Critical to both viewpoints are the conditions that select for primate predation; without discerning these we cannot model the evolution of human hunting.

Pumphouse baboons appear more predatory than the Gombe chimpanzees, having the highest predatory rate of any nonhuman primate (1 kill per 12 hours of observation recorded in 1973).

Predation in the Pumphouse troop can be opportunistic, the common pattern in other baboon populations, but these baboons also have developed more complicated tactics such as extended searches and stalks and coordinated relay chases. Searches for prey can last up to 2 hours and take the baboon over 2 miles from the troop. Meat is sometimes shared between hunters and their relatives and friends, a divergence from the baboon's usual reluctance to share food. Finally, predatory behavior in Pumphouse developed as a "tradition" with important differences between the sexes and between individuals of each sex (see Strum, 1975, 1976a,b, 1981, 1983b for details).

We gain new insights about why so few species of primates are significantly predatory from these data. Three sets of factors, ecological, social, and individual played a role in the development and elaboration of the Pumphouse predatory pattern and could, in prin-

Table 5.1. Prey Species

| | 1970–1971 | | 1973 | | 1975 | | 1976–1977 | |
	No.	%	No.	%	No.	%	No.	%
Thomson's gazelle								
(Gazella thomsoni)	16	34	33	33	—	—	9	20
Dikdik								
(Rhynoctragus kirki)	8	17	7	7	2	13	5	11
Steenbok								
(Raphicerus campestris)	1	2	6	6	1	6	1	2
Impala								
(Aepyceros melampus)	1	2	1	1	—	—	—	—
Klipspringer								
(Oreotragus oreotragus)	—	—	1	1	—	—	—	—
Antelope, sp. indet.	5	11	—	—	—	—	—	—
Hare								
(Lepus capensis)	12	25	41	41	9	56	24	53
Bird	1	2	11	11	4	25	5	11
Small mammal, sp. indt.	3	6	—	—	—	—	1	2
Total	47	100	100	100	16	100	45	100

Note: These figures should be compared with caution, since different observation methods were used in 1970–1971 and the other three periods, and different numbers of observation hours were involved in each period.

ciple, help explain the restricted distribution of predation among nonhuman primates.

At the broadest ecological level, there must, of course, be suitable prey. The baboon data highlight what suitabillity means for an unspecialized primate. Baboons only take prey smaller than themselves since they are unable to solve the problems of capture and consumption of larger individuals. They cannot match the speed of older antelopes, for example, but they can catch young ones. (See Fig. 5.1.) They can only eat prey which is small enough to restrain since they do not deliver a death blow. Lacking the teeth and jaws of a true carnivore, they have great difficulty getting at the meat and bone through the thick hide of larger or older prey.

The next ecological level is that of foraging strategies. The chances of finding prey must offset the energy expended in search and capture. Opportunistic predation, the common baboon pattern, is distinct from systematic pursuit in the investment of time and energy. The possibility and advisability of systematic predation is related to several factors. Habitat type plays an important role. Some habitats have more prey than others and within habitats, visibility makes the prey more or less detectable. The baboons' primary foraging determines home range, thus baboon herbivory restricts baboon predatory opportunities to the species living in these essential habitats. Purely opportunistic predation, within any habitat, limits the frequency and extent of a predatory habit. Systematic pursuit is warranted only

Fig. 5-1. Adult male baboon finishing consumption of an infant Thomson's gazelle.

with group-living prey species because their easy visibility, their aggregation, and group size insure that more prey will be available to offset the costs of systematic pursuit.

The presence of other predators who might be dangerous competition is the final ecological factor that plays an influential role in baboon predation. The dangers of attack by large predators is irrelevant to opportunistic baboon predation which occurs within or near the troop, allowing the baboon predator some margin of safety. However, predation upon baboons does become an important consideration when predatory activities take an individual away from the protection of the troop.

Using the Pumphouse information we can list the ecological conditions for the development of a predatory pattern that extends beyond opportunism. There must be visible, suitably sized, group-living prey in the primary foraging habitats and a reduction in indigenous predators for these prey. This implies both an open niche and relative safety from interference competition for the primate predator. Stated this way, we soon realize that such conditions are rare for most baboon populations and for most populations of non-human primates.

Furthermore, the baboon data suggest that the necessary conditions for the development of primate predation/hunting may not, in themselves, be sufficient. Not all opportunities are exploited, even when they are obviously advantageous. What is ecologically possible must also mesh with what is socially and individually possible. Developing a serious predatory interest requires more than an open niche (see Strum, 1976a,b, 1981). At a minimum, elements of predatory behavior should exist within the species repertoire or there should be a range of social and foraging behaviors that can be used in the new pattern. The impetus for the change must also come from somewhere, either at an individual or social level. Once initiated, social facilitation and observational learning play a crucial role, as do psychological and social factors that can inhibit or constrain predatory behavior (see Strum, 1976a,b, 1981 for a detailed discussion).

The role of social and psychological factors is derived directly from the Pumphouse baboon story, as it has unfolded over the past 13 years. For example, Pumphouse males have differing tendencies to be away from the troop. In order for sophisticated hunting techniques to develop, a hunter had to leave the troop to follow herds of Thomsons gazelles. The "psychological" and social differences between males played a critical role; at times they inhibited such developments, when the males who were the primary predators were also uncomfortable leaving the troop, and at times they facilitated a more sophisticted pattern, when a change in relations among males allowed a particular male to take the lead in predatory pursuits. One key male who liked to wander, began the long-distance hunts and served as a model for other males. They copied him and thus began a new "tradition". Without this male the new hunting techniques might never have developed.

Another example of the importance of social and psychological factors is found in the difference between male and female baboon predatory behavior. Both sexes relish meat and some females try harder and are more successful in obtaining it than some males, but only males developed the more sophisticated hunting techniques. Females never joined the consumption of a carcass until it was brought back to the troop or the troop could clearly be seen. (See Figs. 5.2 and 5.3.) They were among the first to leave if the troop moved off, even when there was still meat left to eat. Female conservatism, for that is what it was, makes good evolutionary sense. Lone females are at greater risk than lone males. In addition, the migratory life that males lead certainly has an emotional corollary that would make it easier for them, than for females, to be away from the troop. The limitations may be more than psychological. Males, in fact, have more free time than females as a result of their different sizes, their different nutritional requirements and their different reproductive investments. In such ways social and individual factors can constrain or facilitate the elaboration of predatory behavior. Even for a group or individual that finds itself in the appropriate ecological situation, opportunities can not always be taken.

We can begin to consider the relevance of baboon behavior for interpretations of human evolution using these data. First and foremost, they help establish a baseline for the predatory component of nonhuman primate subsistence behavior. Intelligent questions can then be formulated about the changes that necessarily occurred during the journey from the nonhuman pattern to the human one. Hominids, with their own unspecialized primate anatomy, had to overcome obstacles that seem to limit baboons. How did they solve the problem of prey size, the problem of prey availability, the problem of competition with other predators? Though these are not new questions, they take on added meaning when we consider how changes might have actually happened. We can assume that early hominids were at least as complex as baboons and we can use baboons to identify processes that may have facilitated or inhibited the developments documents in the fossil record. Perhaps it is the multiplicity of factors

Fig. 5-2. Adult female baboon in consort bringing her consort male to consumption episode. She is the female with the highest interest in meat-eating in the troop.

Fig. 5-3. Primary predatory male, and initiator of sophisticated hunting, attended by female and infant friend as he uses fingers to scoop out brain from skull of immature Thomson's gazelle.

contributing to changes in predatory behavior which is the most important new emphasis of the baboon data. In particular, the sophisticated hunting that developed in 1973 can be seen as a response to the rare convergence of a number of factors. We are forced by this comparison to eliminate single factor explanations for even small shifts in primate behavior.

Selective forces operating on hominids were not acting on a *tabula rasa*. It is therefore important to consider the susceptibility of the existing primate patterns to modification, the advantages and disadvantages of any shift for a hominid predator, and the compromises in behavior and social organization necessary and possible once an extensive predatory existence became important to a group-living primate.

We gain a new sense of how changes occur within complex primate groups, including early hominids, from the baboon example. The role of the individual assumes a new preeminence. Since we are considering behavioral changes, adaptive shifts can be rapid, taking only a few months or years and can just as rapidly vanish when the conditions, both necessary and sufficient, disappear (Strum, 1981). Changes in predatory behavior can even occur without any major change in ecological conditions, altering as a result of social or reproductive factors not normally linked with subsistence.

Armed with this approach we have educated hypotheses, telling us what we should accept as evidence and, perhaps, even redefining what is considered as uniquely human. The divergence of the hominids from nonhuman primates in areas such as cooperation, division of labor, strategy, and cognition is widely linked to the development of the human gathering and hunting pattern. Yet the baboon data illustrate that all of these traits have precursors among the nonhuman primates. Differences could be heightened by increasing selection on already existing tendencies. To illustrate this point let us consider some current ideas about the origin of human sex differences. Both the proponents and opponents of the hunting hypothesis (see Ardrey, 1961; Washburn and Lancaster, 1968; Birdsell, 1972; Tanner and Zihlman, 1976a; Lovejoy, 1981; Tanner, 1981) suggest that the basic divergence between the sexes was a hominid adaptation to the savannah. Yet baboons, with evolutionary origins preceding the hominids by millions of years, without tools or language and without the human division of labor, have "humanlike" emotional differences between males and females that limit what they do and seem comfortable doing. What, then, is uniquely human? Where did it originate? Does it represent a continuity with past sex differences or an innovation?

Seeing human evolution through baboon "spectacles" appears a useful first step; we can identify processes and principles that may explain the limited predatory behavior among nonhuman primates and the problems that early hominids had to overcome to create the human adaptation.

Dominance and Aggression

Baboon predatory behavior has obvious importance for interpretations of human evolution but ideas about male dominance and aggression that emanated from the baboon model have had an equal impact on evolutionary reconstructions of the life of early hominids. Here too the data on Pumphouse baboons are relevant.

The traditional baboon dominance hierarchy of males organized according to status gained by aggression is not found among Pumphouse males (Strum, 1982). The important dimension for these males is their length of residency in the troop, not agonistic dominance. Residency predicts both who wins fights and who gets the resources but these two factors are inversely related. Males who are new to the troop are aggressively dominant toward the long-term residents yet it is these residents who have greater access to and success in getting the limited resources, including estrous females.

We can make sense of this sytem only by understanding that baboons have nonaggressive or social alternatives they can use in both competition and defense. Since these "social strategies" (Strum, 1982, 1983a, 1984, in press; Western and Strum, 1983) depend on a knowledge of the troop and on an established set of relationships, the newcomer male is at a distinct disadvantge, lacking both vital information and the allies critical for social maneuvering.

Only 25 percent of the consort turnovers, in which one male takes over a female from another male, are actually the result of aggression in Pumphouse (Strum, 1982 and in prep.). The majority of takeovers result from social strategies that depend on social skills, social knowledge, and the cooperation of the consort female. Fighting over an estrous female is only part of the battle; unless a female allows him to copulate, a male will not sire any offspring. Females cooperate significantly more with males who are friends than with nonfriends. Friends are individuals who have invested both time and energy cultivating a social relationship, one that forms the basis for social reciprocity between them and that precedes and supercedes the brief period of sexual receptivity (Strum, 1982, 1983a).

This "system" is partly a consequence of male migration. Evolutionarily, males leave their natal group to avoid inbreeding. However, at the proximate level, no matter what male motives might be, migration creates a group in which some males are strangers, feared and avoided, while others are friends and relatives, seen as sources of support and protection. Aggression is still important but it loses its centrality when caught up in the complex network of kinship, friendship and social strategies (Strum, in press). Therefore, when

Table 5.2. Dominance and Consort Rank Correlations (Consorts, N = 381)

Dominance rank	Consort rank	N	Correlation r_s	P
(1) Yearly total agonism	Yearly total	7	−0.57	>0.05
(2) Quarterly total	Quarterly total			
(a) 1st quarter		5	−0.1	>0.05
(b) 2nd quarter		7	0.18	>0.05
(c) 3rd quarter		7	−0.5	>0.05
(d) 4th quarter		7	−0.57	>0.05
(3) Yearly total	Cycle of fertilization and two previous cycles			
(a) Total	Total consorts	7	−0.67	>0.05
(b) Total	Consorts, D–3 to D	7	−0.79*	<0.05
(4) Yearly total	Cycle of fertilization			
(a) Total	Total consorts	7	−0.47	>0.05
(b) Total	Consorts, D–3 to D	7	0.04	>0.05

* Significant

Pumphouse baboons use aggression for competition and defense, it is only one among several options, more often than not, the most difficult to employ, the riskiest, and the least successful given the complexities of the social group (Strum 1982, 1983a, 1984 in press).

We can use these few baboon facts, as we did with the evidence on predation, to discuss the evolution of human behavior. The first suggestion offered by the baboon evidence is the most startling: that the functional view of aggression, which marked a major advance in the study of animal behavior (Strum, in press), may have over-emphasized the role of aggression in daily life. Evolutionary success for any member of a baboon group depends on the ability to manipulate the social context as much, or more, than it depends on aggression. This is certainly also true of other primates, although the actual evidence is limited (e.g., Yerkes, 1940; Goodall, 1968a, b; Kummer, Goetz and Angst, 1970; Goss-Custard et al., 1978; Shapiro, 1978; Bygott, 1979; Markowitz, 1979; Packer, 1979) and must be true, to some extent for other mammals (but see Strum, in press, for restrictions). Manipulation and social intelligence clearly predate the human experiment.

More surprising, agonistic dominance is not an organizing principle for male baboons. This jeopardizes the foundation of many popular and scientific interpretations of human behavior originally grounded in baboon society (Ardrey, 1961; DeVore and Washburn, 1963; Morris, 1967; Tiger, 1969; Tiger and Fox, 1971; Pfeiffer, 1972). What then is the role of male dominance in human society? Should we view it as unique or does it have precursors in the nonhuman primate repertoire?

Finally, knowing that "lowly" baboons are capable social strategists has important implications for how we characterize aggression among other primates, including humans. If aggression is just one strategy among several, and if it is often the least effective and riskiest option, the selection should have been for a flexible response preparing an individual for the possibility of aggression but not locking him into an aggressive reaction. Finding such flexibility among baboons changes the evolutionary timescale in a significant way. Baboon social st rategies imply that no matter how ancient aggression might be, the social alternatives we observe today are certainly older than previous interpretations have suggested (Strum, in press). Once created, these social alternatives must have quickly displaced aggression from its pivotal place as *the* strategy to that of a tactic in a larger array of options (Strum, in press b). With more evolutionary time and greater selective pressure for the devlopment of flexibility, it becomes increasingly difficult to posit the inevitability and centrality of aggression among higher primates, including humans.

Such a view does not mean that aggression is unimportant for mammals, for primates, or for baboons. Many of the differences between male and female baboons are clearly the consequence of the anatomy of aggression in males. Nor does it mean that we should expect humans to be unaggressive. Aggression still has a place as a tactic. Yet once alternatives exist, aggression can seldom be the ultimate solution. The alternatives allow individuals to circumvent aggression, reverse its outcome, redress grievances, and the like. The original winner, faced with the ineffectiveness of his aggression as the loser switches tactics, is forced to respond with his own social options.

Previous evolutionary scenarios (Washburn and Hamburg, 1968; Lancaster, 1975) suggested that the shift in the role of aggression in society came with the advent of language. Before language, all communication had to be by action, and aggression was an important method of communication about competition and dispersal. This argument still has validity yet an earlier shift is suggested by the baboon data, one which also placed a premium on intelligence, learning and the development of social skills.

Politics

Let us summarize our current view of Pumphouse baboon society (Strum, 1982, 1983a, 1984, in press), then see how this may modify our ideas about the evolution of human behavior. Because Pumphouse baboons use and need social strategies, social relationships appear to be as critical to their survival as food and water. Social relationships represent investments by one individual in another (Kummer, 1978a,b), creating a system of social reciprocity where complementary benefits are carefully tuned, "tit for tat" (Strum, 1982, 1983, 1984 in press). If we take friendships between males and females as our example, the process is best illustrated when a new male transfers to the troop. Females are fearful of this "stranger" but he chooses a female to follow, signaling friendly intentions while trying to approach. Finally his persistence, patience and friendly overtures win him acceptance. He stays close to the female, grooms her and intervenes on her behalf when she gets into trouble with other troop members. Once established, the female shares responsibility for the friendship; she follows the male and grooms him and the pair spend time together, feeding, resting, and socializing. In addition to his assistance during aggressive interactions, the female can rely on the male's support of her family, and his presence gives her access to some resources and reduces the interference from other troop members. On his side, a male can count on a female friend's cooperation in several critical situations. Friends have significantly more consorts than nonfriends and friendly females cooperate more with their consort partner. A male is less likely to lose a female to the aggressive challenge of other males, more likely to copulate successfully, and have more time to feed and rest during a consort when he is with a female friend (Strum, 1982). In addition, male baboons use females as agonistic buffers against the aggression of other males in much the same way they use infants (Strum, 1983a, 1984). The success of this tactic depends upon the female's cooperation which is tied to the previous friendly relations between the male and the female.

Social relationships, such as friendships between males and females, are crucial to both partner's survival and success in the group. Baboons invest in these relationships far in advance of gaining any benefit from them and also seem to understand the relative effectiveness and usefulness of different sets of social ties (Strum, 1983a, 1984). Within this setting, size or physical prowess do not yield the "political" power over others that we might expect. A big male, although built as a fighting machine, needs the cooperation of the small infant or the female that he uses as an agonistic buffer if he is to defend himself successfully against the aggression of another male. This same big male needs a female's cooperation to be reproductively successful even if he aggressively claimed her from another male. Females and infants have powerful leverage through the system of social reciprocity created by social relationships. Pumphouse baboons certainly appear to develop and manage social resources in order to gain an advantage, both in the short and longer term.

Just as in the previous examples on predation and on aggression and dominance, we can identify principles about baboons that aid us in interpretations about the evolution of human behavior. First, the origins of politics appear to predate the human adaptation. Baboons lack the human political institutions but the interpersonal machinations in a babon troop and in a small-scale human society seem politically very similar. If human politics are part of a primate continuum, what, then, is the origin of human differences? When and how did they devleop and what kind of evolutionary shift do they represent?

Second, aggression is not the only means baboons and other nonhuman primates have at their disposal when they compete with or defend themselves against conspecifics. Given the complexity of baboon social strategies, we must argue for a continuum rather than a dichotomy in the primate order. What were the human evolutionary developments? What role did language and culture play in further elaborations? What was the influence of modes of subsistence on human politics? What effect does group size, population density, patterns of migration have on the evolution of politics?

Third, one sex does not hold the political power. To focus upon the inherent advantages of male size ignores the complexity of the social system and the intricacies of real power within at least one nonhuman primate group. The Pumphouse baboon data directly contradict the baboon model that has been the basis of may generalizations about human society (e.g., Ardrey, 1961; DeVore and Washburn, 1963; Morris, 1967; Tiger, 1969).

Fourth, the biological necessity of outbreeding forces one sex to migrate leaving behind the benefits of familiarity and kinship of the natal troop. An inevitable social scenario is set in motion, creating basic sex differences in behavior, in tactics, and in strategies which may have relevance to human differences (see Western and Strum, 1983).

Finally, the discovery of social complexity among Pumphouse baboons is a surprise. Baboons have neither the large brains nor the phylogenetic closeness to humans of chimpanzees, a species where complexity is both expected and documented. A comparison between baboons and chimpanzees suggests that there are at least two origins of primate complexity. The first, as illustrated by Pumphouse baboons, results from the constant presence of many conspecifics, including both relatives and strangers, creating a strong selective pressure for social manipulation. Other factors which might play a role in this type of social complexity are the impossibility of escape (either emotionally or strategically), the high density of individuals, and the costs of aggression, both physical and social (see Strum, in press). What results is a system of social reciprocity involving kin and nonkin in an array of different tactics and strategies.

A second type of complexity is illustrated by the Gombe chimpanzees. Large communities of chimps are constantly forced to fragment and reunite in response to the distribution of resources (Wrangham, 1979a, b). In order to function as a social group they must cope with individuals who have become "temporary" strangers. The chimpanzee solution is an elaborate repertoire of reassurance and appeasement gestures, greater intelligence and the ability to manipulate conspecifics within each of these temporarily stable groups (Goodall, 1968a, b; Teleki, 1973; Bygott, 1979; de Waal, 1982). We can now ask an interesting new question: what is the origin of human social complexity? Is it the same as for baboons, or the same as for chimpanzees, some combination of both, or neither?

DISCUSSION

Simple descriptions of primate behavior were extremely helpful in early attempts to understand the evolution of human behavior. yet, description alone cannot provide the answers to either the important questions about the basis of behavior or those about which evolutionary processes are at work. The comparative approach is not new. Earlier primate models of human evolution used a form of comparison. What we would like to suggest is that the comparative approach must be applied in a more sophisticated and rigorous fashion; simple analogies and direct comparisons between any one primate species and early hominids should be abandoned. For example, if Pumphouse baboons did X, or some variant of X at one point in time, we have no way of knowing whether the earliest hominids did X, the opposite of X or some variant of the variant of X. The comparative primate data, whatever the form of the comparison, takes us a great deal further than any simple analogy, illustrating what is possible for a primate and providing principles that can be used in a variety of applications. Placing what is possible within the context of hominid biology, anatomy, and ecology, suggests what was probable for these ancient human primates. Future *models* should concern themselves with processes and principles since, we would argue, these represent the only valid starting place for evolutionary reconstructions.

The *muddles* continue where we use old data and old ways of thinking, and where we use theory without a sense of what animals actually can do, or use data too narrowly. There are other muddling influences of equal importance. We know that the human brain has difficulty comprehending multidimensional phenomena. A first step in any description or analysis is necessarily the making of simplifying assumptions. But too often the original simplification is forgotten and the conclusion that is reached is that the phenomenon is actually simple (Strum, 1978). Single factor explanations, so prevalent in past evolutionary reconstructions, are a good case in point. While they may be a reasonable starting place, they are an inadequate end to the intellectual journey when no other routes have been explored.

The evolution of human behavior is the focus of more than one scientific discipline. As rigorous as our scientific models try to be, many muddles come from outside the scientific arena. Consciously, or unconsciously, we define the limits and expectations of our current society when we trace the origin and evolution of human behavior (see Latour and Strum, in press). As a result, many interpretations reflect strong but unconscious commitments. An obvious example is the controversy over the evolution and evolutionary significance of differences in human sex roles. Some scientists have used current primate data and evolutionary theory to bolster previous interpretations (Popp, 1978; Symons, 1979; Hrdy, 1981) while other have used the same data and theory to counter them (Tanner and Zilhman, 1976a; Tanner 1981; Lovejoy, 1981). The radical swing of the pendulum reflects not so much the implicit truth of the new data but rather the range of emotional, social and political commitments that confront each other simultaneously. Science is not *simply* politics, but neither is it "value free" (Latour and Woolgar, 1979) and outside factors inevitably intrude when we attempt to interpret something as important as the evolution of human behavior (see Haraway, 1978a, b).

CONCLUSION

The study of nonhuman primates, for those interested in reconstructing human evolution, offers several significant contributions. The primate data provide a baseline to begin the journey and provide the principles that can be applied to primates, human and otherwise, generally and specifically. The recent nonhuman primate data also reveal a greater continuity between nonhuman and human primates. This is a constructive shift that makes our evolutionary scenarios more believable since evolutionary processes have difficulty creating things *de novo*.

More and more we have insights about how evolutionary changes occur in complex primate groups. With this knowledge, understanding what is possible for primates, we are only left to discover what was probable for the early hominids.

Research on baboons has played an important role in scientific efforts to understand the evolution of human behavior. As significant, in our opinion, is the perspective gained from the history of baboons models about the pitfalls of evolutionary reconstruction and the places where muddles still remain. These muddles, created by our human brain, our human emotions, our old data, and our earlier methods must be addressed if the study of nonhuman primates is to have a significant place in our future evolutionary reconstructions.

ACKNOWLEDGEMENTS

The research on which this paper is based was funded during the past thirteen years by the following organizations: Fyssen Foundation (Paris), L.S.B. Leakey Foundation, National Science Foundation, New York Zoological Society, University of California, San Diego, Wenner-Gren Foundation and World Wildlife Fund-US. The government of Kenya has generously granted permission for the research and the Institute of Primate Research, Nairobi has provided local sponsorship. many individuals provided useful discussions of ideas incorporated in this paper and they deserve acknowledgement: Donna Haraway, Bruno Latour, Johan Western and the students in several classes concerned with primate models.

CHAPTER SIX

A Primate Model for Human Mating Systems

WARREN G. KINZEY

In this chapter I will argue that monogamy is correlated with relative behavioral and ecological inflexibility, at least in the non-human primates. More complex social systems—including polygamy and promiscuity—provide greater flexibility both behaviorally and ecologically. Monogamous primates, on the other hand, are behaviorally more conservative, and ecologically more restricted. This interpretation has implications for social organization in humans—for understanding and possibly for improving human conditions, in terms of parental care, child rearing, and education.

First, a few definitions are needed. Animal populations have mating systems called *monogamy* (in which an individual "reproduces sexually with only one partner of the opposite sex" [Wickler and Seibt, 1983]) and *polygamy* (in which an individual reproduces with more than one such partner). Many have suggested that polygamy includes *polyandry* (in which a female reproduces with more than one male) and *polygyny* (in which a male reproduces with more than one female).[1] When both sexes have more than one partner, mating is promiscuous. Thus, we may view mating systems as monogamous, polygynous, polyandrous, or promiscuous. (See also Wrangham, this volume.)

Human mating systems and family structure have long been of interest to anthropologists and sociologists who have interpreted them in a variety of ways. One of the most pervading ideas has been that of virtual universality of the monogamous mating pattern, coupled with the old idea that human monogamy was somehow superior to, or at least more evolved than, the harem system of baboons (Zuckerman, 1932) or communal mating in howler monkeys (Carpenter, 1934). Thus, it came as no surprise when the first field study of an ape, the gibbon, (Carpenter, 1940) supported the notion that monogamy was the highest form of social system. For example, Coon wrote, "the gibbon ... is nearest to man in its behavior, including sexual habits, [and] in its family composition. The gibbon is organized into mongamous family groups, and there is no reason to believe that human families have ever been formed characteristically in any other way." (1948: 3,43–44). Even though gibbons are now known to be the *only* consistently monogamous hominoids, (see Wrangham, this volume), monogamy is still thought by many, especially in the Western world, to be the *most* common human mating system. Further, the assumption that monogamous mating is the basic and most widespread human system underlies Lovejoy's (1981) hypothesis that it was one of the earliest hominid innovations. Monogamy is definitely *not* the most common human mating system, as will be seen below.

I look at the consequences of human mating systems from the vantage point of having studied nonhuman primates in their natural habitats, and conclude that mating systems not only have different evolutionary histories (see, for example, Eisenberg et al., 1972), but also different adaptive values (see Ripley, 1984, for further discussion). Among nonhuman primates a monogamous mating system appears to have the least long-term adaptive value. Although the reason for this is not clear, irrespective of its cause the same may be true among humans; there may be good reason why monogamy is the *least* common human mating system.[2] Seen from the point of view of the nonhuman primates monogamy has the least *long-term* adaptability. Why, then, does monogamy occur at all? As among nonhuman primates, human monogamy occurs in a small number of cases in which specific ecological factors make it advantageous. Further, when monogamy does occur in humans, it is generally accompanied by a variety of relationships that increase the potential for social networks. The lack of social networks is the major disadvantage of monogamy per se. Promiscuity does not normally occur in *any* human society, but polygyny and polyandry taken together are much more frequent than monogamy. They encompass a greater extension of social networks than monogamy; they have greater long term adaptability, and consequently they are more common. Probably the majority of cultures in the world practice some form of extended family in which the living group contains more than a single pair and their children.

Monogamy is common in birds but is relatively rare, though widely distributed, in mammals. The term *pair-bonded* has often been equated with *monogamous* but the two are not precisely synonymous. A pair-bond is a permanent *social* relationship between an adult male and adult female whose family structure includes their dependent offspring (Eisenberg et al., 1972); whereas, monogamy is a sexual or reproductive relationship. In this paper I use the term monogamy to refer only to obligate monogamy (in the sense of Kleiman, 1977).[3]

Monogamy occurs in less than 3 percent of mammalian species (Kleiman, 1977) and according to Hrdy (1981) occurs in 18 percent of primate species. The latter figure is too high, however, since many callitrichid species which she includes are now known not to be monogamous (Sussman and Kinzey, 1984; Abrahamson, 1985; Terborgh and Goldizen, 1985; Goldizen, 1986). Monogamy occurs in only 12 percent of anthropoid primates.

The monogamous species of higher primates are listed in Table 6.1 Among the ceboid primates of Central and South America all the monogamous species occur in a single subfamily, the Pitheciinae *(sensu* Rosenberger, 1981), and they all appear to feed upon a uniformly dispersed patchy food supply found primarily in small-crowned fruit trees (Robinson et al., 1986). The inclusion in the subfamily Pitheciinae of all the ceboid species that are consistently monogamous, and the possibility that one of the non-monogamous members of the subfamily, *Chiropotes,* includes aggregations of monogamous subunits (Robinson et al., 1986) suggest that monogamy was the primitive condition for this group.

Based on the presence of monogamy in these forms, Eisenberg (1977, 1981) has suggested that monogamous pairing was an ancient trait within the New World primates as a whole, and that from it the other forms of social structure in the Central and South American primates may have evolved (Eisenberg et al., 1972).

Among the Old World monkeys (Family Cercopithecidae), monogamy is rare and is found only in three species whose closest relatives in each case are not monogamous. In contrast, all the members of the Old World lesser ape family, Hylobatidae, are monogamous.

Table 6.1. Monogamous Anthropoid Primates

Family Cebidae
    Aotus—owl monkey (1 species, nocturnal)
    Callicebus—titi monkeys (3 species)
    Pithecia—saki monkeys (2–4 species)

Family Cercopithecidae
    Cercopithecus neglectus—de Brazza's monkey
    Presbytis potenziani—Mentawi Island langur
    Nasalis (Simias) concolor—simakobu monkey

Family Hylobatidae
    Hylobates—gibbons and siamang (9 species)

Family Hominidae
    Homo sapiens (facultative)

As Wittenberger and Tilson have astutely noted, "no single hypothesis is sufficient to explain all known instances of monogamy." (1980:198). Wilson (1975) suggested three possible causal conditions for monogamy, and Wittenberger and Tilson (1980) increased this list to five. In primates, monogamy has certainly evolved for more than one reason, under a variety of ecological conditions: (1) as an advantage of group living (in diurnal species) over solitary living (in nocturnal species), mostly among the lower primates, but including *Aotus*; (2) as a means of defending scarce and valuable resources; and (3) as a response to human predation. In humans it is facultative; that is, it occurs under some conditions, but not others, and perhaps not for the same reason in all cases.

The owl monkey, *Aotus*, is nocturnal and is one of several primates that are both nocturnal and monogamous. Others include: tarsiers, *Avahi*, and *Lemur mongoz* (the only nocturnal lemur). All nocturnal primates are either solitary or monogamous. *Aotus* evolved from an ancestor which was diurnal and either it became monogamous subsequent to its shift to nocturnality, or the diurnal ancestor of *Aotus* was monogamous. The latter is the more likely explanation and accords with the special adaptive significance of nocturnality in *Aotus* (Wright, 1982, 1985b).

"At least three species [of monkey] . . . appear to have adopted monogamous mating systems as a facultative response to predation by humans during historical times. In each case [de Brazza's monkey (Gautier-Hion and Gautier, 1978), the Mentawi Island langur (Tilson and Tenaza, 1976) and the simakobu (Tilson, 1977)] . . . the monogamous species is the only nonpolygynous member of its genus." (Hrdy, 1981:45) (*Cercopithecus hamlyni* is a possible exception, as it may also be monogamous [Gautier-Hion and Gautier, 1978; Jon Hart, pers. comm.].)

Very little is known of the behavior of saki monkeys in the wild, except that they are monogamous and live "in small family groups that rarely exceed four animals." (Buchanan et al., 1981:402)

The remaining monogamous primates are the gibbons (including the siamang), and the titi monkeys. The social behavior of both these groups is relatively well known: for all three species of titi monkeys through the work of Mason, Robinson, Wright, and Kinzey (Kinzey, 1981), and for 8 of the 9 species of gibbons (summarized by Chivers, 1984). Throughout their range, in addition to the features noted above, they have a unimodal activity period, being most active in the morning and declining in the afternoon; they feed primarily on small scattered fruit sources with leaves contributing a variable component of the diet. "Gibbon food preferences limit them to certain kinds of forest with distinctive features of food supply." (Chivers, in press) Their behavior is stereotyped with little regional variation. As Marks points out, however, (this volume) the genetic picture of gibbons favors genetic drift—cytogenetic diversity despite the lack of behavioral diversity.

The titi monkeys in the Neotropics, similarly, are behaviorally and ecologically relatively homogeneous, (although one species does appear to be restricted to a specialized habitat in vegetation growing on white sand soils [Kinzey and Gentry, 1979]). Throughout their range in the Neotropics they have limited relationships with other species of primates, infants are carried by the adult male, grooming is an important social activity, they have relatively small home ranges, and they are quite uniform osteologically, differing among themselves only slightly in body size.

The monogamous family, though it is widely distributed within the order Primates (at least 25 percent of all genera have at least one species that is monogamous), is quite uncommon (only 12 percent of anthropoid species are monogamous) and appears to be rather stereotyped behaviorally, and lack plasticity ecologically. "Lifestyles are remarkably similar among monogamous primates." (Hrdy, 1981:39) Monogamous primates also share similarity in the size and distribution of resources in space and time (Wright, 1985a). "Resources that provide the bulk of the diet are small and occur in uniformly dispersed small patches which cannot accommodate large groups. . . . Exclusion of other small groups from these limited resources leads to selection for pronounced territoriality." (Wright, 1985a:244) When a group is larger than that of a monogamous family more interindividual relationships are possible, if only by virtue of group size alone. This contributes to potential variability in behavior.

What are some of the possible mechanisms that might account for the lower levels of behavioral and ecological variability in monogamous primates? Evidence indicates that compared with other primates, monogamous primates eat lower quality diets (Fragaszy and Mason, 1983; Gaulin and Kurland, ms.), have an inferior ability to perceive spatial relationships (Gaulin and FitzGerald, 1986), and have minimal levels of role differentiation (McKenna, 1982).

In contrast to monogamous primates, one example that is adapted to a wide variety of habitats is the family Callitrichidae—perhaps in part because of the nature of their family pattern. The early laboratory data led most reviewers to believe that the callitrichids were monogamous (e.g., Redican, 1976; Kleiman, 1977; Leutenegger, 1980; Redican and Taub, 1981).

Based on field data, however, all the marmosets and tamarins clearly do not have a monogamous mating system. Tamarins have been observed to live in groups with changing group composition

(Dawson, 1977; Neyman, 1977), often with more than a single pair of adults. In four cases in which copulations were observed in two-male groups, both males mated with a single female—polyandrous mating (Terborgh and Goldizen, 1985; Goldizen, 1986). The additional non-related animals in the group, both young and adult, assist in the care of the young, and we believe (Sussman and Kinzey, 1984) that "the adaptive strategy of this system is to increase the care, and thus the survival, of offspring." Changing composition of groups and a ratio of males:females greater than 1:1 have also been observed in marmosets (Hubrecht, 1984).

If Eisenberg (1977) is correct in suggesting that monogamous pairing is an ancient trait among the New World primates, then the family Callitrichidae may have evolved their complex social system from monogamy to what Sussman and Kinzey (1984) have called "a small multimale group with a communal rearing system, that tends toward polyandrous mating."

How could this system have evolved in callitrichids? According to Wittenberger and Tilson (1980:200), monogamy should occur "in territorial species if pairing with an available unmated male is always better than pairing with an already mated male." This condition, in which monogamy may be advantageous *only* for females and their progeny, is an adequate explanation for all species of primates, according to Wittenberger and Tilson. Apparently marmoset and tamarin females have found a way to make polyandry *more* advantageous than monogamy through tolerating and encouraging communal rearing.

The marmosets and tamarins are remarkable in the breadth of their habitat tolerance: they "are found in a variety of habitat types and the home ranges of most species are characterized by a mix of habitats usually including an abundance of edge. . . . Groups of some species of tamarins merge temporarily . . . some populations are territorial while others share large portions of their home ranges. Differences in ranging behavior and in mechanisms of group spacing seem to be dependent more upon environmental factors than upon phylogeny" (Sussman and Kinzey, 1984). There is evidence of a variety of habitats, a wide range of group sizes, and of home range sizes. For example, marmosets and tamarins occur in both dense tropical rain forest as well as in Brazilian cerrado (open savannah with patches of stunted vegetation).

What may be important in groups like the callitrichids is what Campbell (1979) has called the "organizational plasticity" of behavior. He describes this in chimpanzees, among which he says, that "the environment constrains and permits certain behaviors so that in the open savanna woodland we see a different organization from that seen in forest. This organizational plasticity is part of chimpanzee behavioral potential, no doubt shared by hominids." (1979:302) Similar organizational plasticity is seen in baboons, as well as in marmosets and tamarins, and perhaps, to a greater or lesser extent, in virtually all the primates except in those that are monogamous.

Ripley (1984) has presented a similar point of view in a different framework. She argues that "increased social flexibility and geographical distribution . . . may foster persistence of the lineage" (Ripley, 1984:39), that is, may promote long-term evolutionary success. Ripley points out that some animals (including beavers and termites among non-primates) and humans achieve long-term success "by controlling the productivity of the ecosystem rather than by adapting to it." Adapting to it is, of course, what the nonhuman primates have done.

Even though humans control their environment as well as adapting to it, does the relationship between behavioral plasticity and complex social organization in the nonhuman primates suggest anything about facultative monogamy in humans?. Examination of Murdock's (1957) world ethnographic sample of 565 cultures indicates that only 20% of human societies are monogamous. Of these, 21% live in bands living a marginal existence, such as !Kung, Andaman Islanders, Polar Eskimo, and pygmies, and another 20% are Western industrialized societies. Since I argue that it is the extension, or augmentation, of relationships outside the monogamous family unit that makes such monogamous relationships successful, it is relevant that Wrangham and Ross (1983) recently presented data to show that in the Efe pygmies success, as measured by wealth rank in males, depends on the number of helpers which in turn is determined by kinship ties— exactly what I would have predicted. Nimkoff and Middleton (1960) demonstrated from HRAF data long ago that there is a highly significant correlation between type of family system and subsistence pattern; the independent, or monogamous, family is the most common in hunting and gathering cultures. Monogamy is also common in agriculturally based societies. Looking again at the world ethnographic sample, 88% of all monogamous societies are either hunting/gathering or have agriculture as the dominant subsistence activity. Put another way, 83% of societies in which agriculture is the dominant means of subsistence favor some kind of nuclear family arrangement (Coult and Habenstein, 1965). The ecological similarity to gibbons and titi monkeys is significant: primitive agriculturalists have dispersed, uneven resources, which must be defended and harvested by a single male and female pair in a limited territory.

Thus, monogamy in humans occurs in large part in ecologically marginal areas or in Western society. As Hrdy has suggested, "Monogamy in humans may be a matter of ecological necessity, or it may be imposed by legal sanctions" (Hrdy, 1981:36). But, monogamy in Western society probably did not originate through legal or moral sanction—that came later. Leibowitz (1982) has suggested that the common denominator of nuclear families, whether among collector-hunters or in industrialized societies, is that they occur "in conjunction with a need for mobility." (1978:183) Another possibility is that monogamy in industrial societies is simply a holdover from the agricultural past.

Murdock (1949) claimed the nuclear family to be universal and polygyny to be merely an aggregation of nuclear families. However, Murdock was using the term "monogamy" to describe a *social* system; whereas, I use the term in its biological sense to describe a *mating* system. These two uses of the term monogamy must not be confused, as Wickler and Seibt (1983) made clear in their review of monogamy. In fact, it is the very aggregation of families in a social sense that Murdock described that is important in humans. These are institutionalized forms of kinship ties, and they assist relationships among individuals at a variety of levels.

Is there a difficulty with the legally imposed sanction of monogamy in human families? In Western society this may be so. In *"Coming of Age in Samoa"* Mead spoke strongly of the fragility of the nuclear family. Contrast the availability of relationships in a nuclear family with those available in extended families. Mead, in contrasting Western society with that of Samoa suggested that a family community larger than that of a nuclear family "seems to ensure the child against the development of . . . crippling attitudes [as an adult]." (1928:118) She went on to say that "it is not pleasant to realize that we have developed a form of family organization [in the United States] which often cripples the emotional life, and warps and confuses the growth of many individuals' power to consciously live their own lives." (1928:119) Mead was speaking of the isolated nuclear family whose isolation she resented. The problems appear to be minimized when strong personal relationships are extended to a sphere outside that of a single nuclear family, whether the extension be institutionalized or informal.

Leibowitz (1978) points out that monogamous groups vary in the degree to which they use kinship networks—in Western society they are used "only in emergencies or under extreme conditions" (1982:183), whereas, most other nuclear family groups have extensive network relationships. In summarizing research on hunter-gathering groups she says that "for the Andamanese . . . as in other collecting-hunting societies, marriage contracts effectively tie individuals and groups of people into extensive and extended relationships. For us, marriage ties two people together while relatives, friends, and neighborhood cohorts may never exhange so much as a smile." (Leibowitz, 1978:183) In the majority of human societies these relationships are institutionalized through extended kinship groups, frequently—but not necessarily—developed through polygamous mating. Nuclear families are isolated and independent *only* under special circumstances—whether in hunting-collecting or industrial societies (Leibowitz, 1978).

Western society also has institutionalized relationships which are not the result of extended kinship groups, an important adjunct to the paucity of relationships within the nuclear family. Fraternal and sororal organizations, rotary clubs, and the like, serve the purpose of providing relationships that in most non-Western societies are provided by large kinship groups. An increase in the number of "kin" relationships may also be obtained inadvertently through divorce and remarriage: in that sense there is a certain adaptiveness to divorce. The support of two or more families by divorced men could even be viewed as an economic form of polygyny.

Thus, in Western society there is the opportunity for extending the family social unit through non-kinship groups. This is analogous in some ways to the communal breeding system in marmosets and tamarins. "The adaptive strategy of this system [in marmosets and tamarins] is to increase the care, and thus the survival, of offspring." (Sussman & Kinzey, 1984) In humans, the adaptive strategy of non-kin social extensions (rotary clubs, fraternal organizations, godparents, close personal friends. etc.) is similarly to further one's well-being, including the well-being of offspring, and/or to provide outlets for social relationships that are not available within the framework of the limited size of a nuclear family.

The nonhuman primate model, therefore, suggests that there is adaptive value, or long-term evolutionary success, in having social extensions beyond the independent mating unit, whether they be through kinship ties, as in the majority of human societies, or through the formation of non-related relationships and organizations typical of Western society.

Although it may be difficult to establish a causal mechanism for lower levels of behavioral and ecological variability in monogamous primates, the cause of morphological variability is well established. Rates of evolutionary change are positively correlated with amounts of genetic variation, which in turn are "directly proportional to changes in allelic frequencies." (Dobzhansky et. al, 1977) In monogamous mating the potential for allelic change is reduced compared with that of polygamous matings. If the same mechanisms apply to behavior and ecology, we should expect less behavioral and ecological variability in monogamous species. This, indeed, is what is observed.

ACKNOWLEDGMENTS

I am grateful to the following people for comments on various drafts of this chapter: Mel Ember, Helen Fisher, Eleanor Leacock, and Suzanne Ripley. I thank Kim Kramer and Suzanne Walker for editorial assistance. The research was supported, in part, by grants from the Research Foundation of the City University of New York.

FOOTNOTES

1. In parallel with the division of polygamy, monogamy might be divided into monandry (when a female mates exclusively with one male) and monogyny (when a male mates exclusively with one female). However, when more than one monogynous male mates with a single female the reproductive unit becomes polyandrous and, similarly, when more than one monandrous female mates with a single male the unit becomes polygynous. The distinction, therefore, is not useful in this paper.

2. Monogamy is the least common mating system so long as serial monogamy is excluded and systems are classified on the basis of what is permissible not what is actually practiced. (See also footnote three.) These distinctions will be elaborated at another time.

3. Most authors do not distinguish between serial monogamy and polygyny. The major exception is Fisher (1984, ms.). In this paper I use the term monogamy *only* to refer to life-long monogamy. According to Kleiman (1977) Type I monogamy does not involve pair-bonding. To the extent that her Type II monogamy refers to a permanent relationship and involves only a single pair and their offspring, Type II monogamy (obligate monogamy) is the social equivalent to pair-bonding.

CHAPTER SEVEN

Diet, Dimorphism and Demography: Perspectives from Howlers to Hominids

CAROLYN M. CROCKETT

Carpenter's (1934) pioneering field study of mantled howler monkeys stood alone for decades as the only relatively complete picture of a primate population. In methodology and description of behavior, his field study remained unequaled by any primate studies until the 1960s, and is still worth reading today. However, even with fifty years of research on howler monkeys and their society, we have just touched the surface. Studies of other howler species have revealed some fascinating and challenging differences, as well as similarities, that remain to be fully explained. Long-term studies of many species in a variety of habitats seem to be the only way to understand the complex evolution of primate societies. This perspective should alert us to be cautious in drawing conclusions about our own ancestry.

When this volume's editor asked me to contribute a chapter addressing the relevance of howler monkey studies to the evolution of hominids, I balked. My research orientation has been behavioral ecology rather than anthropology, and my background in hominid evolution is spare indeed. However, inspired by a recent seminar program at the University of Washington titled "Early Hominids: Evolution and Environmental Settings," I agreed to attempt this assignment. My focus is rather narrow, the genus *Alouatta,* but perhaps my conclusions have broader significance for studies of human ancestry.

My particular scientific interest is the evolution of social organization and how to account for the diversity of societies that animals display. This interest has led me to focus upon primates. The order Primates comprises approximately 200 species which collectively live in nearly every type of "society" described for mammals. Given their various adaptive radiations, primates allow convenient and illuminating comparisons of related species in the same environment, related species in different environments, and unrelated species in similar environments. Thus, we can begin to untangle the complicated interactions between phylogeny and ecology.

Howler monkeys are a good primate group for analysis for several reasons. First, there are six howler species (genus *Alouatta*), most living in a diversity of habitats. Thus, we can investigate a group of related species in both similar and different environments. In fact, *Alouatta* is one of the best-known primate genera, having been studied in a wide variety of habitats and seasonal conditions, in some sites over a period of years (Crockett and Eisenberg, 1986). Second, the six species are largely allopatric, with geographic distributions reported to overlap in only three small locations (Figure 7.1). To the extent that the populations are different, we can rule out competition with close relatives (i.e., members of the same genus) as a factor producing these differences. Third, the New World howlers can be compared with the very distantly related Old World primates which have adapted to a similar ecology: predominantly arboreal exploitation of a vegetarian diet. Thus, we can assess the extent of convergent evolution leading to similarities in social organization. However, howler monkeys also pose some interesting problems of their own (Crockett and Eisenberg, 1986).

The major part of this chapter reviews some howler monkey data pertaining to the topics of sexual dimorphism, diet and foraging strategy, seasonal versus habitat differences in major activity patterns, and infanticide. In the last section, I present some conclusions inspired by studies of howler monkeys which may have relevance to hypotheses about hominids.

SEXUAL DIMORPHISM

One general problem area has to do with sexual dimorphism. Of the six species, *Alouatta caraya* and the subspecies *A. fusca clamitans* show sexual dichromatism (Crockett and Eisenberg, 1986). In both cases, males change color around puberty while immatures are approximately the same coloration as adult females. In *A. caraya* the males become black and are thus substantially darker than their olive-buff female counterparts (Shoemaker, 1978). In *A. f. clamitans* the males become reddish while most females in this subspecies remain brown (a few adult females are also reddish, and apparent hybrids between the two subspecies of *A. fusca* have been collected [Kinzey, 1982]).

Fig. 7-1. Approximate distributions of *Alouatta* species adapted from Wolfheim (1983). Distribution of *A. fusca* and *A. caraya* in southeastern Brazil derived from collection locations reported by Kinzey (1982); dashed line is approximate boundary between *A. fusca fusca* (north) and *A. fusca clamitans* (south). Black dots indicate areas of sympatry reported by Smith (1970), Hernández-Camacho and Cooper (1976), and Crespo (1982). Uncertain areas of distribution indicated by "?" (adapted from Wolfheim (1983)). Asterisk (*) is location of Rylands' (1981) study area whose primate fauna includes *A. seniculus;* dotted line connects this location to rest of *A. seniculus* distribution, since this area is outside the distribution reported by Wolfheim (1983).

No overwhelmingly convincing hypothesis to account for sexual dichromatism in this genus has been proposed. Thorington et al. (1979) relate pelage color to solar isolation which varies across habitats, and to some extent, across howler species distributions. These authors suggest that howlers in areas of greatest exposure to the sun have the lightest fur. However, *A. caraya* poses an obvious problem for this hypothesis in that the adults of this species represent the lightest and darkest extremes of pelage in all *Alouatta*. (It should also be noted that some other Neotropical primates show clinal variation in pelage which is not consistently related to habitat nor latitude [Hershkovitz, 1977]. Furthermore, studies by Walsberg et al. [1978] indicate that under windy conditions dark coats may actually acquire less heat load than light coats, because dark coats are more affected by convective cooling.) Thorington et al. (1979) suggest that because *A. caraya* is exposed to the greatest seasonal extremes in temperature due to its southern latitude and upland distribution, the advantages of dark versus light pelage also vary seasonally. This, of course, does not really address why sexual dichromatism evolved in the first place.

A good guess is that sexual dichromatism has something to do with signalling sexual identity and, thus, is a result of sexual selection. Of the two sorts of sexual selection (Robinson, 1982), female choice of distinctive males (epigamic selection) seems a more likely selective pressure than intrasexual competition for mates (but see Hershkovitz, 1979). Table 7.1 lists the seven primate species with dramatic sexual dichromatism in body pelage. In six of the seven species (all but *A. fusca clamitans),* males are black. In all four genera where it occurs, one or more but not all species are dichromatic. In *Alouatta* and *Hylobates,* males change color at puberty (Shoemaker, 1978; Hershkovitz, 1977) while in *Lemur macaco,* males and females are dichromatic at birth (Harrington, 1978). In *Pithecia pithecia,* the male's pale face ring is evident at birth (Hanif, 1967), but infants of both sexes are dark and the female gradually lightens (Shoemaker, personal communication).

Sexual dichromatism in primates is not consistently related to intrasexual competition as estimated by mating system: one would expect male-male competition to be greatest in polygynous species, but sexual dichromatism also occurs in monogamous primates (Table 7.1). One could argue that distinctive males might be more intimidating in male-male encounters, but such encounters are not normally as intense or frequent in monogamous species compared with polygynous ones. Correspondingly, we might expect sexual dichromatism to be more common in polygynous species if distinctive coloration were favored by intrasexual selection. However, more than half of the dichromatic species are monogamous.

The common feature that can be detected among the seven dichromatic species is the possibility of natal female emigration. Female emigration has been well documented in *Alouatta seniculus* and *A. palliata* (Crockett, 1984; Clarke and Glander, 1984), and an adult female and juvenile *A. pigra* not associated with a troop (Schlichte, 1978) also may have been emigrants. In the former two species, the emigrant females form new troops with extratroop males (male how-

Table 7.1.   Primates with Dramatic Sexual Dichromatism in Adult Body Pelage[1]

Family *Species*	Social System	References
Cebidae		
Alouatta caraya	Polygyny	Shoemaker 1978; Thorington *et al.* 1984
A. fusca clamitans	Polygyny[2]	Kinzey 1982
Pithecia pithecia	Monogamy[3]	Hershkovitz 1977, 1979
Hylobatidae		
Hylobates concolor	Monogamy	Macdonald 1984
H. hoolock	"	"
H. pileatus	"	"
Lemuridae		
Lemur macaco	Polygyny	Harrington 1978; Pollock 1979

[1] In the genera *Pithecia, Hylobates,* and *Lemur,* two or more other species have sexual dichromatism to a lesser extent, for example in coloration of fur on parts of the head or more subtle shade differences in dorsal pelage (Hershkovitz, 1979; Macdonald, 1984). It is not clear from available descriptions whether *A. f. clamitans* is actually more dichromatic than, e.g., *Lemur fulvus rufus.*

[2] Social system by analogy to other *Alouatta* (Crockett and Eisenberg, 1986).

[3] Monogamy suspected on basis of small size of groups (Macdonald, 1984; Robinson et al., 1986). The *P. pithecia* in Mittermeier and van Roosmalen's (1981) study site were found in "family" groups. The census of Vessey et al. (1978) found a mean group size of 3.3 individuals (range 1–5; n = 10), but they reported that groups usually had one adult male and one to two adult females. Such a census, however, might not be able to differentiate nearly mature natal animals from reproductive adults.

lers also emigrate) or else join existing troops. No long term studies of either *A. caraya* or *A. fusca* have been published, but I fully expect that they too will show some female emigration. *Hylobates* and apparently most *Pithecia* live in monogamous family groupings (Robinson et al. 1986) (Table 7.1). Thus, unless a parent dies, offspring of both sexes must emigrate and find their own mates. In *Lemur macaco,* Pollock (1979), summarizing data from Petter (1962), reported one instance of an adult female joining a group (four adult males disappeared and three males joined groups during the same period). Therefore, in all of these cases of pronounced sexual dichromatism, the trait could have evolved and became fixated through some process of epigamic selection, since females who emigrate from natal troops are in a position to "choose" the males with whom they join and eventually mate. This is not the case in social systems where females stay put and males compete with each other to join troops and mate with females. Female choice of one of several males does occur in such societies (reviewed by Robinson, 1982), but which males are available to choose from is usually predetermined by conflicts among males.

My incompletely developed hypothesis of female choice of distinctively colored males does have some limitations (other than the obvious one of sparse data). For example, it could be argued that not all species with female emigration have sexual dichromatism. What I am proposing, though, is that females "choose" distinctive males simply because they are different. Thus, evolution of sexual dichromatism depends on chance mutations upon which selection (in this case by females) can operate. Once distinctive males begin to be "chosen," it becomes highly disadvantageous for males to be non-distinctive, and the trait should spread rapidly.

Another puzzling facet of sexual dimorphism in *Alouatta* is that the testes of *A. palliata* do not descend visibly until puberty while the testes of *A. seniculus, A. pigra* and *A. caraya* descend in infancy (reviewed in Crockett and Eisenberg, 1986). Thus, to field researchers the sexes of immature *A. palliata* are indistinguishable unless the monkeys are captured. *Alouatta palliata* also shows much less sexual dimorphism in body weight and in hyoid volume than *A. seniculus* and *A. caraya* (Thorington et al., 1979; Sekulic, 1981). (The hyoid is involved in the production of the characteristic roaring vocalizations for which the howlers are named [Sekulic, 1981]). Compared to the other species for which data are available, *A. palliata* troops have the highest adult female to adult male sex ratio (Crockett and Eisenberg, 1986). This is opposite from the general pattern for primates in which the adult sex ratio, reflecting male-male competition for females, is positively correlated with sexual dimorphism (Clutton-Brock and Harvey, 1977a). Nevertheless, it would seem that male body size, hyoid volume, and age at testes descent are all products of sexual selection, probably intrasexual selection.

So we have a situation in which some of the most interesting and relevant characteristics of *Alouatta* would never appear in the fossil record. Only skeletal material would be preserved (probably *excluding* the delicate hyoid). Based on such material, we would have some idea of the variation in weight dimorphism, but it would lead us to the wrong prediction with respect to adult sex ratio. We would be unlikely to guess correctly about the ways in which sexual selection might be shaping the evolution of this genus. Yet on the basis of some of the traits that I have described, it is clear that *A. palliata, A. seniculus,* and *A. caraya* have gone in somewhat different directions.

HOWLER DIETS

In contrast to the divergent results of sexual selection in *Alouatta*, the diet and foraging strategy of all species studied appear to be very similar. Wherever they live, howlers eat leaves, fruits and flowers. *Alouatta palliata* and *A. seniculus* are by far the best studied. These two species occur in the widest range of habitat types, from mountainous and lowland evergreen rainforests to lowland swamp forests and highly-seasonal semideciduous habitats (Crockett and Eisenberg, 1986). A comparison of the percent of feeding time spent on leaves, fruits, and flowers shows that *A. seniculus* falls within the intraspecific differences among *A. palliata* studied in different habitats (Figure 7.2). Similarly, the number of different food plant species varies more intraspecifically than interspecifically, and the variation seems to be due primarily to differences in plant diversity among the habitats studied (Table 7.2).

Many of the same plant families are eaten from site to site, with variation related to availability. Overall, the most important family is Moraceae especially the figs, *Ficus*. The second most important family is Fabaceae (=Leguminosae). These two families monopolize the top ten food species of *A. palliata* (Milton, 1980; Glander, 1981; Estrada, 1984) and also figure importantly in the diets of *A. seniculus* (Mittermeier and van Roosmalen, 1981; Gaulin and Gaulin, 1982;

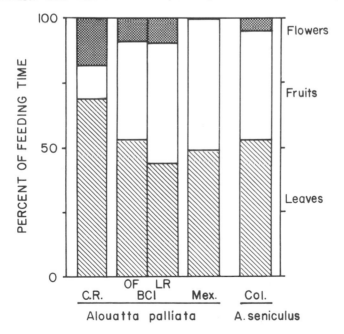

Fig. 7-2. Percent of feeding time spent eating leaves, fruits and flowers comparing *Alouatta palliata* in Costa Rica, Panama (two habitats), and Mexico with *A. seniculus* in Colombia. See Table 2 for description of habitat types and references.

Table 7.2. Number of Plant Species Eaten by Howlers in Different Habitats

Species Location[1]	Habitat	Plant Species # Eat (Avail)		Families # Eat (Avail)[2]	
A. palliata					
Costa Rica	Semideciduous Forest	62+	(96+)	26+	(37+)
BCI	Moist Semideciduous				
	OF: Mature forest	73			
	LR: Secondary forest	73	(112+)[3]		
	Total different	109[4]		41	
	In common	37			
Mexico	Evergreen Rainforest	27+	(44+)	15+	(22+)
A. seniculus					
Colombia	Montane Evergreen				
	Forest	ca. 34			
Venezuela	Semideciduous				
	Gallery forest	62	(78+)[5]	27	(30+)
	Open woodland	39		23	
	Total different	73[4]		32	
	In common	28		18	

[1] Study areas and references: Costa Rica: Finca La Pacífica (Glander 1978, 1981). BCI: Barro Colorado Island, Panama (Milton, 1980; OF = Old Forest; LR = Lutz Ravine). Mexico: Las Tuxtlas, Veracruz (Estrada, 1984). Colombia: Finca Merenberg (Gaulin and Gaulin, 1982). Venezuela: Hato Masaguaral (Crockett, in prep.).
[2] # Eat (Avail): Number of different plant species and families eaten by a single study troop (number available in habitat); number followed by "+" indicates that only tree species are included (lianas and epiphytes excluded).
[3] Lutz Ravine tree species identified by Thorington et al., (1982).
[4] Total different consumed by two study troops, one in each habitat.
[5] Gallery forest species diversity from Troth (1979).

Crockett, in prep.) and *A. fusca* (Chitolina and Sander, 1981). During a short study, *A. pigra* spent over 90% of feeding time eating Moraceae, more than 87% on one species alone (Schlichte, 1978). In the only study where Moraceae did not figure prominently in the howlers' diet, trees of this family were very rare (Glander, 1978). One species of *Ficus* was only the tenth-ranked species eaten, but based on its low density had the highest selection ratio (i.e., percent of feeding time divided by percent of trees available of this species [Glander, 1981]). The scarcity of Moraceae in Glander's (1978, 1981) study area may partly account for the low percentage of fruit in the howlers' diet at this Costa Rican site (Figure 7.2). *Ficus,* unlike most other Neotropical trees, is not seasonal in its fruit production, and where relatively common provides howlers a source of fruit for much of the year (e.g., Milton, 1980).

Howlers of three different species spend a similar 11 to 19% of daytime in feeding (Milton, 1980). Howler foraging strategies, food selection and harvesting techniques appear to be remarkably similar across sites and species (e.g., compare Milton, 1980; Glander, 1981;

Gaulin and Gaulin, 1982; and Estrada, 1984). Howlers are quite selective, feeding on seasonally available items. The general pattern is to concentrate on one or two primary food sources in a day, supplemented by other items eaten in smaller amounts. The primary food sources vary from month to month, depending on availability. During some months the main food source may be a species flushing new leaves while during others it may be a species bearing ripe fruits. Howlers' average daily travel (day range) varies from under 200 to about 700 meters across sites and species (Crockett and Eisenberg, 1986). The length and direction of travel is largely a function of the distribution of the principle food resources being used at the time (Milton, 1980; Estrada, 1984; Crockett, in prep.).

Wherever howlers are, irrespective of species membership, they seem to be making their living in about the same way. The variation in dietary composition and its effects on foraging patterns can be attributed to habitat differences which cut across howler species boundaries. The conclusion that all howler species occupy the same dietary niche helps explain the essentially allopatric distribution of *Alouatta* (Milton, 1980).

SEASONS VERSUS HABITATS

For the past six years I have been studying red howler monkeys *(Alouatta seniculus)* at Hato Masaguaral, a ranch in the *llanos* or plains of central Venezuela. The climate is highly seasonal with a discrete wet and dry season, each of about six months duration (Figure 7.3). The ranch is a protected reserve for hundreds of red howler monkeys living in two rather distinct habitats located only a few kilometers apart (Crockett, 1985, in prep.). This site therefore allows a rare opportunity to compare simultaneously the relative contributions of major habitat differences and pronounced seasonal differences to howler behavioral ecology.

The two habitat types are a gallery forest (GF) and an open shrub woodland (OW) described in some detail by Troth (1979; OW=discrete mata bajío and shrub woodland bajío). These two semideciduous habitats differ rather dramatically although they both fall within the lowland tropical dry forest zone (Holdridge, 1967; Ewel et al., 1976). The GF trees form a continuous canopy in most areas, reaching about 20 m in the area censused. The OW is characterized by grassland dotted with scattered shrubs and palms, clumps of small trees and shrubs (called "matas"), and small groves of trees (maximum ca. 14 m in height).

Of the animals in the 40–50 troops regularly censused over time, virtually all adults and many immatures are individually identifiable,

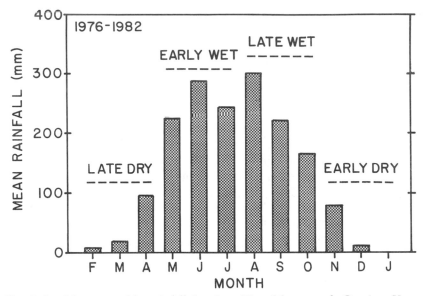

Fig. 7-3. Mean monthly rainfall (mm) at Hato Masaguaral, Guarico, Venezuela, averaged over seven years (1976–1982). Mean annual rainfall (1976–1982) = 1653 ± 329 mm. May through October is the wet season and November through April is the dry season.

some marked with permanent ear tags (e.g., Thorington et al. 1979). During 20 consecutive months, I collected detailed behavioral data on two troops, one dwelling in each habitat type. These data were gathered during 115 dawn-to-dusk observation periods recording feeding behavior, social behavior, activity patterns, and so on, for each troop member. In addition, detailed ecological data were collected from the home ranges of the two troops. These data included phenological assessment of the vegetation (i.e., the fruiting, flowering, and leafing patterns of the plant species eaten) and plant abundance transect sampling to estimate the density of all food plant species. The data on food availability allow assessment of foraging strategy, e.g., to determine whether the howlers are selectively feeding on particular items at different times of the year as has been reported for *Alouatta* at other sites (Milton, 1980; Glander, 1981; Gaulin and Gaulin, 1982; Estrada, 1984).

The botanical diversity is considerably greater in the GF than the OW, and the diversity of plant species eaten by GF red howlers is also greater (Table 7.2). The plant abundance transects revealed that the density of red howler food species differed greatly between habitats for some plants but was very similar for others (Crockett, in prep.). The home range size of the two troops was markedly different, being about 26 ha for the GF troop and only about 6 ha for the OW troop (and 25% of that was open grassland).

The availability of food plant parts varies seasonally (Milton, 1980; Glander, 1981; Crockett, in prep.). Furthermore, the maximum daily temperatures at Hato Masaguaral are noticeably hotter in dry season, averaging ca. 36.3 degrees Celsius compared to 34 degrees in the wet season (Troth, 1979). The difference is magnified because most trees are leafless during the sunny dry season, while both leaves and cloud cover attenuate solar radiation in the wet season. Thus, it would not be surprising to find that the red howlers' behavior differed somewhat in the two seasons.

To ascertain the relative effects of season versus habitat on some aspects of red howler behavior, I did some preliminary analyses comparing activity patterns of the two study troops in wet versus dry season. Data are derived from 70 days over 10 months, five in the wet season and five in the dry season. At that time, the OW troop had 9–10 members and the GF troop had 7–8 members, each with one adult male, two adult females, and natal immatures. During the dawn-to-dusk observations I recorded scan sample data (J. Altmann, 1974) on each troop member every 15 minutes. However, the preliminary data presented here are "activity scores" indicating the predominant activity of the troop during 3420 15-minute intervals. Thus, the percentages in Figs. 7.4 to 7.7 *should not be* considered as estimates of the time that individual red howlers spent in these activites, but rather as estimates of the percent of the daytime (or hour of day) that the troop as a whole spent engaging in the major activity categories.

Figure 7.4 compares the percent of 15-minute intervals that the GF and OW troops spent in five major activity categories, wet and dry seasons combined. The activity categories are as follows:

1. "Resting": All individuals inactive for the entire 15-minute period with the exception that a young infant could climb around (as they often do during resting periods), and one other animal could engage in an activity like feeding or defecation.

2. "Mixed Activity": Intervals in which social interactions, defecation, and other activities by two or more individuals occurred, and that did not fit the criteria of the other four categories.

3. "Feeding": Intervals in which the majority of the troop spent more than 10 minutes feeding, and the troop traveled less than 50 meters.

4. "Travel-Feeding": Intervals in which the troops traveled more than 50 meters; traveling often was accompanied by feeding along the way.

5. "Howling": Intervals in which the troop howled. When howling bouts were less than 15 minutes in duration (which is usually
the case [Sekulic, 1982b; Crockett, in prep.], only the interval with
the most minutes of howling was scored as "howling."

Figure 7.4 shows that the troops spent the same percentage of
intervals engaged in howling but that they differed somewhat in the
other categories. The OW troop spent more intervals in mixed activity
and feeding than the GF troop which spent correspondingly more
time in rest and travel-feeding categories. The difference in travel-
feeding is consistent with the GF troop's larger home range and
longer average day range (Crockett, in prep.). The difference in resting
versus mixed activity cannot be fully explained until the scan sample
data are completely analyzed. However, the higher percentage of
intervals spent in mixed activity by the OW troop is likely related
to the greater number of juveniles, who often played while adults
rested.

In Figure 7.5, resting and mixed activity are combined as are
feeding and travel-feeding, and the data for dry and wet seasons
are separated. The dry season percentages for the three behavior
categories are virtually identical for both the GF and the OW troops.
In the wet season, the GF troop has a slightly higher percentage in

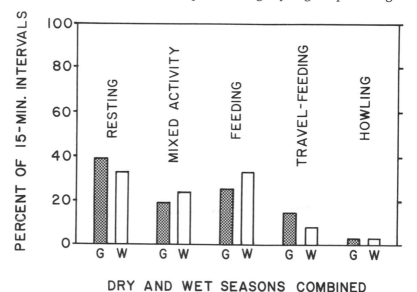

Fig. 7-4. Percent of 15-minute intervals that the gallery forest (G) and open
woodland (W) study troops spent in five major activity categories, seasons
combined (see text for definitions and sample size).

resting plus mixed and the OW slightly higher in feeding plus travel. However, the most obvious pattern is that the within-season similarity is greater than the within-habitat similarity. More simply stated, at Hato Masaguaral seasonal differences appear to have a greater effect on these major activity categories than do habitat differences.

This conclusion is even more strongly supported when diurnal variation in activity patterns are examined. Figures 7.6 and 7.7 show, respectively, percent of intervals resting and percent of intervals feeding and travel-feeding combined. The diurnal resting pattern within seasons is very similar for troops from different habitats, yet the patterns differ notably between seasons. In the dry season there is a peak of resting at midday coinciding with high temperatures then, while in the wet season, resting declines throughout the day until a sharp rise in the late afternoon (Fig. 7.6). Somewhat of a mirror image of resting, feeding is depressed at midday in the dry season and increases throughout the day in the wet season for both habitat types (Fig. 7.7). Spearman rank order correlations (Siegel, 1956), pairing percentages by hour of day, revealed significant positive correlations between GF and OW percentages for resting in both dry and wet season ($r_s = .66$, $<.02$, 1-tailed, n = 13, for both seasons), and for feeding in wet season ($r_s = .72$, $p <.01$, n = 13). Hourly percentages for feeding in dry season were not significantly correlated

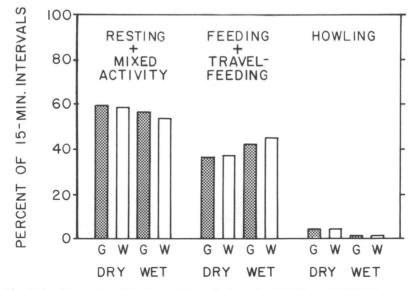

Fig. 7-5.   Percent of 15-minute intervals that the GF (G) and OW (W) troops spent in three major activity categories, comparing dry and wet seasons (see text).

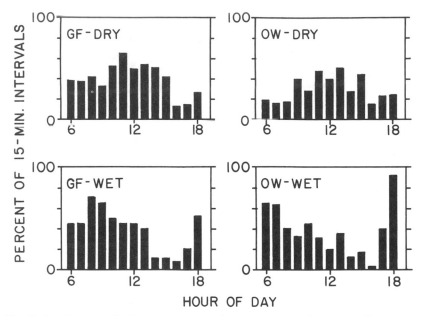

Fig. 7-6. Percent of 15-minute intervals spent resting by hour of the day, comparing habitats (GF and OW) and seasons (dry and wet).

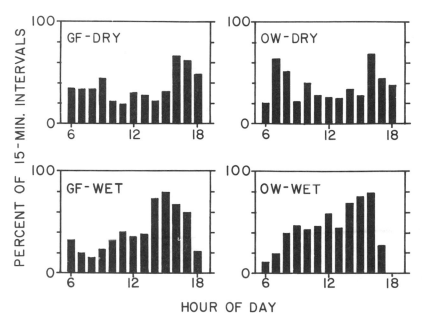

Fig. 7-7. Percent of 15-minute intervals spent feeding and travel-feeding, combined, by hour of the day, comparing habitats (GF and OW) and seasons (dry and wet).

between GF and OW habitats (r_s = .27, p> .05, n = 13), probably because the OW showed a more pronounced morning peak in feeding and travel (Fig. 7.7). None of the correlations comparing dry versus wet season percentages within habitats were significant (r_s = .10 [rest, GF], −.34 [rest, OW], −.15 [feed, GF], and .02 [feed, OW], n = 13 each correlation).

Similar seasonal differences in diurnal patterns of resting and feeding were found by Sekulic (1982a) in four other OW troops located several hundred meters from the OW troop that I studied. The wet season diurnal pattern of declining rest and increasing feeding throughout the day is also similar to that reported for *A. seniculus* in a wet montane forest, although in that study the howlers displayed a marked feeding peak at dawn (Gaulin and Gaulin, 1982).

Richard's (1978) study of another vegetarian primate, the prosimian *Propithecus verreauxi*, also demonstrated the importance of seasonal factors on behavior patterns. Her two study areas were 1500 km apart and differed considerably in annual rainfall. Both were seasonal, semideciduous habitats, although seasonality was more pronounced in the southern area which had less than half the annual rainfall and greater temperature extremes compared to the northern site. The habitats themselves differed in numerous ways including height, plant diversity, and botanical composition. Despite the rather dramatic difference in both rainfall and habitat features, in the wet season the amount and diurnal pattern of feeding were very similar between the habitats, with reduced feeding at midday. Unlike my red howler study, however, in the dry season the *Propithecus* in the two habitats differed significantly in time spent feeding and diurnal pattern of feeding. The *Propithecus* in the drier habitat fed less and showed a midday peak in feeding during the dry season, rather than a suppression. Part of the contrasting relationship between season and activity pattern in Richard's (1978) study may be related to the fact that the hottest daytime temperatures occurred in the drier habitat during the wet rather than dry season.

Thus, with respect to general patterns of behavior and "time budgets," it appears that in regions with strongly seasonal climates, seasonal factors have an effect which can equal or exceed habitat differences. The importance of seasonal factors is often overlooked, or habitat differences tend to be emphasized at the expense of seasonal factors. At the very least, these data suggest the dangers of comparing short term studies of different habitats when they did not occur during equivalent seasons. Some behavioral contrasts attributed to habitat variation may in fact reflect adjustments to seasonal variation in rainfall, temperature, and availability of different foods.

Primate Versus Carnivore Models of Early Hominid Behavior

King (1980) reviews evidence comparing the appropriateness of primate versus carnivore models for the reconstruction of early hominid behavior. He concludes that both animal groups can provide heuristic analogies, and which is more appropriate depends on the particular behavior in question. In contrast, Susman (this volume) concludes that carnivore models make additional assumptions, including hunting (not just meat-eating) specifically for large prey. I conclude this brief overview of howler society with a discussion of a behavior whose explanation clearly transcends taxonomic lines: infanticide.

In 1982, 32 scientists from around the world gathered to present evidence for the occurrence of infanticide in animals from invertebrates to humans (Hausfater and Hrdy, 1984). The data and discussion at the conference made it clear that there is no unitary explanation to account for infanticidal behavior. In fact, there are five major hypotheses (Hrdy and Hausfater, 1984). Four hypotheses are "adaptive" in that the reproductive success of the individual committing infanticide potentially can be increased through infanticide. These hypotheses are "Exploitation," "Resource Competition," "Sexual Selection," and "Parental Manipulation." The fifth explanation for infanticide, "Social Pathology," is nonadaptive in that no one directly or consistently benefits from infanticide. In nonadaptive cases, infanticide results from increased aggression levels (perhaps induced by overcrowding) or other lethal behaviors in which the infants are not intended victims but may accidentally get in the way.

Infanticide in humans occurs in a variety of circumstances that fits all five hypotheses, although infanticides attributable to parental manipulation (e.g., to promote birth spacing or eliminate offspring of the less desirable sex) and social pathology (no examples necessary!) are particularly common (Hrdy and Hausfater, 1984; Dickemann, 1984). Infanticide in nonhuman primates, however, usually can be explained by the sexual selection hypothesis, and appears to be quite widespread especially among primates with harem-type social systems. (There is, however, a great deal of controversy about the interpretation of nonhuman primate infanticide [Hausfater, 1984].

The sexual selection hypothesis is based on the concept that intrasexual competition for mates favors the evolution of traits which directly or indirectly enhance an individual's reproductive edge over others. In mammals, it is usually males that compete for females. In many species, a female conceives her next offspring sooner after the loss of her current infant than if it survives. In these cases, males may increase their reproductive success by killing a female's current offspring (sired by another male) and thereby have the opportunity to sire her next infant(s) sooner. Simply stated, to have offspring sooner means that an infanticidal male will on average have more offspring than non-infanticidal males. And in terms of reproductive success and fitness, more is better. Infanticide under these circumstances can be viewed as a male reproductive strategy.

The sexual selection hypothesis seems to account well for infanticide in many harem-type primate species, in which generally a single male mates with females in a group. The tenure of a male in the breeding position is relatively short, and since he may be ousted by another male at any time, quite unpredictable. Thus, any means to increase his reproductive output would be favored. Evidence supporting infanticide as a male productive strategy based on the sexual selection hypothesis comes from numerous primate species including mantled howler monkeys and red howlers (*A. palliata and A. seniculus* [Clarke, 1983; Crockett and Sekulic, 1984]).

The sexual selection hypothesis also best accounts for infanticide in various nonprimate species in which females give birth again sooner if they lose their current infants. Infanticide is especially well documented in lions (*Panthera leo*), and sexually selected infanticide may occur in some other carnivores as well (Packer and Pusey, 1984). A comparison of lions and red howler monkeys with respect to infanticide illustrates both the potency of sexual selection and its effects across taxonomic groups, since the similarities between these unrelated species are quite remarkable (Crockett and Sekulic, 1984; Packer and Pusey, 1984):

1. The actual observations of infanticides are few, despite the relatively good visibility in the field and the thousands of hours that these two species have been studied. In both species, males have been observed to kill infants.

2. Much circumstantial evidence is available to suggest that many infant disappearances are infanticides, and the number of suspected infanticides is quite large. These suspected infanticides coincide with invasions by new males (as do most observed ones). In both species, coalitions of more than one male are more successful at taking over troops or prides than are single males. In both species, suspected infanticides have been associated with attempted takeovers in addition to successful ones.

3. Pregnant lions rarely mate with new males (two cases [Packer and Pusey, 1983]), and pregnant red howler females have not been observed mating. Females of both species which are pregnant at the

time of a male change are likely to lose those infants shortly after birth (infanticide suspected). Thus, neither species appears to have an effective "pseudoestrus," whereby females might deceive new males about the paternity of their unborn offspring. Such an adaptation has been proposed for Hanuman langurs (*Presbytis entellus* [Hrdy, 1977]).

4. Females of both species resume mating shortly after losing infants, and the interbirth intervals to the subsequent offspring are shortened. This means that by killing infants of previous breeding males, new males can shorten the interval to the births of their own offspring.

5. New males in both species often succeed in siring the next crop of infants. However, in both cases, more than one male are usually involved in takeovers, and it cannot always be determined that the male who killed a female's infant is the same individual who sired her subsequent offspring. Nevertheless, infanticide in both red howler monkeys and lions seems best explained as a sexually-selected male reproductive strategy (Crockett and Sekulic, 1984; Packer and Pusey, 1984).

HOWLERS and HOMINIDS: SOME CONCLUSIONS

As a model for early hominid behavior which could very well have included infanticide, it does not seem appropriate to conclude that a nonhuman primate is a better model than a carnivore or vice-versa. Rather, sexual selection is an important concept in our understanding of the evolution of behavior in both taxa and also should apply to hominids. Furthermore, the fact that sexual selection has resulted in convergence in the behaviors of male invasions and infanticide in vegetarian red howlers and carnivorous lions emphasizes that such selection pressures can operate independently of those shaping a species' foraging patterns. Howlers and other nonhuman primates should not be considered models for hominid behavior simply because they belong to the same order. We should seek the application of larger principles of evolutionary theory to particular categories of behavior and see how their predictions fit various animal species. Only then can we make reasonable predictions about the behavior of our ancestors.

Are howlers a usable model for hominid behavior and society? Since howlers are folivore-frugivores, rather than frugivore-omnivores as our ancestors probably were (Sussman, this volume), we might rule them out entirely. Also, the Neotropical primates are not direct ancestors, so they cannot provide many homologies. However, as already suggested in the preceding paragraph, models of some aspects of behavior, such as those related to mating systems, clearly transcend taxonomic lines. In addition, studies of howlers and other group-foraging primates suggest that environmental variation must have had enormous effects on hominid behavior, including foraging strategies and activity patterns. Habitat differences *and* seasonal differences are both important components of environmental variation, and the importance of seasonal effects perhaps has not been given enough recognition. The specifics of the effects of habitat and seasonal factors on hominid behavior would depend a great deal on what was being eaten and how it varied in space and time both seasonally and in different habitats.

Howlers of all species studied appear to occupy very similar feeding niches, even though they dwell (both inter- and intraspecifically) in a wide range of habitat types. This brings up the possibility that hominids too, while basically "making their living" in a similar way throughout their geographic distribution, might have lived in a broader range of habitat types than is ordinarily proposed.

It is also important to keep in mind that selection can operate on the two sexes differently (Wrangham, 1979a). For example, I suggested a preliminary hypothesis that female choice of distinctive mates might account for sexual dichromatism in primates. One particularly potent analogy, and possible homology, between hunter-gatherer humans and their closest relatives the apes is that females often (or for some ape species, always) leave their natal groups (Service, 1966; Wrangham, 1979a). Wrangham (1979a; 1980) has suggested that food resource competition and acquisition may have greater effects on females than on males, while the behavior of males depends to a great extent on what those females are doing. This sex difference is linked to a female mammal's nutrient needs for gestation and lactation which must be maintained above a certain level or reproductive failure is inevitable. Since howler monkeys also show female emigration, which in red howlers at least seems to reflect female reproductive competition (Crockett, 1984), howlers may in this regard help us predict hominid behavior. Thus, since natural selection often operates on the two sexes differently, theories of human evolution ought to consider what both sexes of hominids might have been doing, and how the behavior of one sex might have constrained or directed the evolution of the behavior of the other sex.

Lovejoy's (1981) reconstruction of hominid evolution does incorporate some of the points mentioned here. He suggests that hominid ancestors occupied a variety of habitats, from grasslands to canopy forests, and that this diversity was produced in part by climatic changes leading to increased seasonality. He proposes that increased seasonality favored evolution of characteristics which would reduce food competition between the sexes, and he suggests that females (the smaller sex) occupied smaller home ranges. Furthermore, he argues that the evolution of bipedality derived from males provisioning their mates, by carrying food in the hands, and thus increasing offspring survival. Males were larger than females because they could thereby travel farther and obtain and carry more food, and large size might aid in defense against predators. Although Lovejoy does not explicitly state this, larger male size could be viewed as an epigamic trait in that females might prefer ("choose") mates that were large because they would be better providers.

A key aspect of Lovejoy's (1981) theory is that hominids had a monogamous mating system, a characteristic that is inconsistent with the sexual dimorphism in hominid size (*Australopithecus afarensis* was quite dimorphic in body size; references in Lovejoy, 1981). In nonhuman primates, sexual dimorphism in body size is best explained by sexual selection due to sex differences in reproductive potential (Gaulin and Sailer, 1984). It is difficult to accept that larger male size in hominids was not accompanied by greater variance in male than female reproductive success and some degree of polygyny. Lovejoy's (1981) arguments about size differences to reduce food competition are not entirely convincing. The only two nonhuman primates that have a marked degree of sexual segregation in food exploitation are orangutans *(Pongo pygmaeus)* and chimpanzees *(Pan troglodytes)*; dietary composition differs somewhat and male ranges are larger than females' (Galdikas and Teleki, 1981). In both of these species, sexual dimorphism in body size is consistent with male reproductive competition and polygynous mating systems. It may be that reduced competition between the sexes for food is sometimes a consequence of sex differences in body size evolved for other reasons. However, the advantage to a particular male of minimizing food competition with a female can be realized only if she is raising *his* offspring (or is related to him) and female/offspring survival is increased. This advantage can be achieved if a single male (or possibly a "brotherhood") excludes other males from access to the females and their food, and such exclusivity can occur in either polygynous or monogamous societies.

Despite these criticisms, I believe that Lovejoy (1981) has suggested some thought-provoking ideas, many of which may turn out to be correct. The discrepancy between hominid sexual dimorphism and proposed monogamy could be reconciled if not all adult females were able to reproduce, for example through social subordination by other females as found in some monogamous canids (Kleiman and Eisenberg, 1973). Larger males then might be more successful at defeating smaller males in competition over mates, and/or females might choose larger males who might be better able to provision them. Recall that several species of howlers show variation in sexual dimorphism and demography that are unlikely to be preserved in the fossil record, and that sex differences in size of red versus mantled howlers might lead to erroneous predictions of socionomic sex ratio. These and other insights gained from a relatively well-known taxon like *Alouatta* suggest that there are undoubtably some important aspects of our hominid ancestry that will never be ascertained, even if we have the entire fossil record at our disposal. Some guesses based on the few fossils presently available are likely to be completely wrong. This leads me to recommend that those interested in reconstructing hominid behavior not become too attached to their hypotheses.

ACKNOWLEDGEMENTS

My research on red howler monkeys has been supported by the Smithsonian Institution, Friends of the National Zoo, National Geographic Society, and my husband Robert Brooks. I thank the Tomás Blohm family for making Hato Masaguaral available as a research site. Thanks also to Warren Kinzey for asking me to contribute to this volume, and for his infinite patience.

III

Paleoecological Models

CHAPTER EIGHT

Social and Ecological Aspects of Primate Cytogenetics

JON MARKS

INTRODUCTION

Inferences about primate behavior, I shall argue in this chapter, can be made from the apparently unrelated realm of primate cytogenetics, by virtue of significant regularities in the tempo of evolutionary change in the karyotypes of various primate lineages. These regularities involve an empirical, and plausibly causal, association between social and ecological variables on the one hand, and extent of karyotypic diversity on the other.

Cytogenetics, or the study of cellular components of heredity, the chromosomes, has traditionally been among the most arcane areas of biology. The most well-understood chromosomes from an evolutionary perspective are those of the fruitfly, *Drosophila*, but one cannot easily extrapolate from this genus to others. For example, the larval salivary chromosomes of the fruitfly present a level of resolution far more fine than any presently achievable in mammals. Additionally, the fruitfly possesses a group of adaptations for maintaining specific linkages of alleles, such as lack of crossing-over in meiosis of the male, and the prevalence of chromosomal inversions, which seem to have no counterpart in mammals.

Mammalian cytogenetics only came into its own in 1970–71, with the simultaneous development of several techniques permitting the identification of individual chromosomes on the basis of gross banding patterns. Previously, the chromosomes could only be seen as uniformly stained silhouettes; now, not only can they be identified, but aspects of their structure, such as internal rearrangements, have become fairly easy to detect. Yet with the novelty of these techniques, the level of evolutionary investigation is comparably primitive; it consists for the most part merely of documenting chromosomal differences between species.

Primate cytogenetics is presently, and curiously, less a subdiscipline of primatology than of clinical genetics. Thus, while fairly copious data exist on the karyotypes of various primates, students of primate cytogenetics generally have not attempted to implicate these data in the greater drama of primate biology and evolution. These data have most frequently been used to infer phylogeny, and often with heterodox results (Chiarelli, 1966, 1972, 1975; Jones, 1976; Miller, 1977; Bernstein et al., 1980; Yunis and Prakash, 1982).

Elsewhere I have argued that the most reliable chromosomal data are quite consistent with orthodox views of hominoid phylogeny (Marks, 1983a). There are, however, other questions to which the study of primate chromosomes may be addressed; in particular, questions of evolutionary process, which have remained largely unexplored in evolutionary cytogenetics.

ASPECTS OF CHROMOSOMAL EVOLUTION IN PRIMATES

The most commonly used method of preparing chromosomes, both in clinical and evolutionary studies, is known as G-banding. This involves the activity of a mild protease (such as dilute preparations of trypsin or pancreatin), followed by staining with a standard biological dye, Giemsa. The procedure gives every chromosome pair in the karyotype a distinctive pattern of longitudinal bands, which may be compared across individuals, or across taxa.

Unfortunately, it is not known precisely what these banded regions represent. The chromosome itself is a transient entity (that is, visible only at metaphase of cell division), formed by the coiling of the genetic material and its extensive complexing with proteins. The pattern of bands on a chromosome is in some way related to the DNA sequence of the region (Comings, 1978; Miller et al., 1983), though not determined by it. Any change in the nucleotide sequence is impossible to detect in the light microscope; and conversely, a difference in the staining of a chromosomal region may reflect only differential coiling of the genetic material, and not necessarily a difference in nucleotide sequence. Additionally, active informational genes are now known to represent only a tiny portion of the genome (Bodmer, 1981)—and indeed Ohno (1982) has likened the relationship between genes and genome to oases in a desert. Therefore, any chromosomal change is probably unlikely to affect either the structure or the expression of any gene.

The literature on human clinical chromosomal anomalies is also instructive. While quantitative changes in chromosomes usually result in phenotypic abnormalities, balanced changes (i.e., rearrangements) are generally phenotypically passive. The vast majority of heterozygotes, and the few homozygotes which have been detected, are phenotypically completely normal. Even when clinical abnormalities are detected, the phenotype is usually not attributable directly to the karyotypic change (Vine et al., 1976; Riccardi and Holmquist, 1979; Callow et al., 1979).

It thus appears that, as a first approximation, chromosomes may be regarded as essentially passive receptacles of the genetic information, and their alterations as adaptively neutral. The kinds of alterations by which primate karyotypes are seen to differ from each other are as follows:

1. *Inversions.* These involve the reversal of polarity of a chromosomal segment. If the inversion includes the centromere, it is pericentric; if not, it is paracentric.

2. *Translocations.* These refer to the transfer of a chromosomal segment to a different chromosome. If the translocation is a bilateral exchange between two chromosomes, it is a reciprocal translocation; if it is the unilateral transfer of material, it is non-reciprocal.

3. *Fusions.* These involve the union of two chromosomes to form one large chromosome, maintaining the genetic information content, but reducing the number of chromosomes.

4. *Fissions.* These are obviously the reverse of fusions.

5. *Insertions.* These involve the intercalation of a chromosomal segment, and may be unbalanced.

6. *Deletions.* These are obviously the reverse of insertions.

7. *Gain or Loss of Heterochromatin or Other Redundant DNAs.*

Certain classes of redundant DNA are able to be rapidly amplified or diminished in the genome (Dover, 1981). These include the repeated genes for ribosomal RNA, and the satellite DNAs, which are known to have species-specific localizations on chromosomes, although the modes by which they expand, contract, and move are not well understood. They are therefore generally not useful as phylogenetic markers.

A curiosity concerning these mutational modes is that certain clades seem to be characterized by "favoring" certain karyotype differences. Pongid karyotypes primarily differ from one another by inversions (Miller, 1977); hylobatid karyotypes are reported to differ primarily by translocations (van Tuinen and Ledbetter, 1983); *Cercopithecus* karyotypes differ primarily by fissions and heterochromatin; and lemurids by fusions and fissions. This phenomenon was given the name "karyotypic orthoselection" by White (1973), although it is far from clear that any selective mechanism is involved.

RATES OF CHROMOSOMAL EVOLUTION

Quantitative discussions of chromosomal evolutionary rates are almost always limited to changes in chromosome number or arm number (Wilson et al., 1975; Bush et al., 1977; Imai and Crozier, 1980; Imai et al., 1983), as these are already quantitative in character. Yet these numerical techniques can only treat fusions and fissions, as these change chromosome numbers; and a small subset of inversions and translocations, as these may change arm numbers. That is, the majority of chromosomal evolutionary phenomena cannot be included in these calculations. And consequently, although *Hylobates concolor* (2n=52) and *H. syndactylus* (2n=50) would seem by these quantitative methods to be as different from each other as *Pan troglodytes* (2n=48) is from *Homo sapiens* (2n=46), this is quite misleading. The *Pan* and *Homo* karyotypes can be easily aligned to show massive identity and similarity of chromosomal bands (Turleau and de Grouchy, 1972); while *H. concolor* and *H. syndactylus* cannot (van Tuinen and Ledbetter, 1983). (See Figure 8.1.)

There is as yet no accurate way to express quantitatively the extent of chromosomal divergence among species. If an inversion is qualitatively different in its formation and transmission from a translocation, then it is certainly unreasonable to give them equal weight in a numerical treatment. Further, there is a major problem with regard to the replicability of chromosomal comparisons. Chiarelli (1982) has shown that simply between the karyotypes of *Macaca mulatta* and *Cercopithecus aethiops,* several groups of researchers have differed widely as to the extent of similarity detectable, the kinds and quantities of changes detected, and matches of specific chromosomes across the genera.

Obviously, the study of rates of primate karyotype evolution is still embryonic. Yet there are at least qualitative and relative statements which can be made on the subject at present, which may have some implications for the study of primate social structure.

Arnason (1972) noted that cetaceans and pinnipeds were karyotypically conservative, whereas rodents were karyotypically diverse. Since the taxa are of comparable age, Arnason inferred that this diversity was a rate-phenomenon, that is, different amounts of change in similar amounts of time. He then sought to explain these differences in the microevolutionary dynamics presumably experienced by these organisms. Cetacea and Pinnipedia, he reasoned, live in predominantly aquatic environments. Their environments are generally continuously distributed, with few barriers to gene flow presented by the ocean.

Rodents, on the other hand, live in patchier environments, are distributed more discontinuously, and are generally less vagile. Thus,

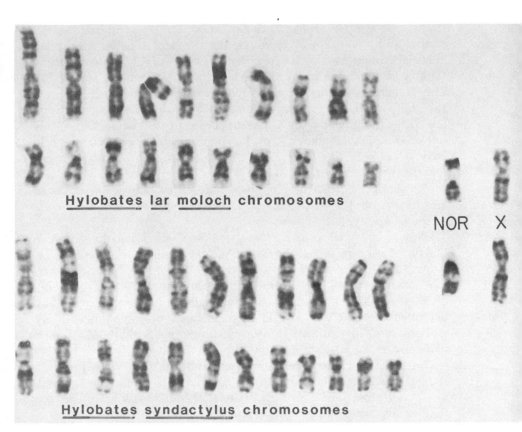

Fig. 8-1. Chromosomes of a hybrid gibbon *(Hylobates lar moloch* x *Hylobates syndactylus)*. This individual has 47 distinct chromosomes, of which only the X-chromosomes and nucleolar-organizer-bearing chromosomes can be reliably paired. The hapoid complement of *H. lar moloch* is above; *H. syndactylus* is below. The viability of such hybrids suggests that the genetic material may be drastically reorganized within the karyotype, without altering significantly its expression or regulation. In the closely related hylobatids, such chromosomal reorganization has taken place in a relatively short span of time. (Courtesy of Dr. Roscoe Stanyon.)

chromosome changes might be expected to accumulate in rodents, by virtue of the action of genetic drift, while chromosome changes may not be able to become established in aquatic mammalian populations, by virtue of the homogenizing effect of gene flow.

Although I believe Arnason's conclusions to have been insightful and fundamentally correct, the Cetacea and Rodentia are so grossly different in other ways, such as body size and reproductive rate (Bengtsson, 1980), or population size, or social dynamics—many of which are not well known—that they do not provide a neat paradigm case for an explanation of rate variation in karyotype evolution.

The gibbons (*Hylobates*) and papionine monkeys, (macaques, baboons, and mangabeys) however, do provide a better controlled "natural laboratory" for the problem. They are fairly close relatives, classified in the same Infraorder Catarrhini (Szalay and Delson, 1979). They reflect comparable taxonomic diversity, each being accorded subfamily status in presently non-standard classifications, Simpson (1945) for the gibbons and Chiarelli (1966) for the papionines. They reflect comparable amounts of biochemical diversity, according to Dene et al. (1976). They are also of comparable body size and reproductive biology.

The significant suite of biological differences between papionines and hylobatids lies in two areas: their socio-ecology and the extent of their karyotypic diversity.

Gibbons are well known from behavioral studies to live high in the forest canopy in pair-bonded, nuclear family social units (Carpenter, 1940; Ellefson, 1968; Chivers, 1972; Roonwal and Mohnot, 1977; Raemaekers, 1979; Gittins and Raemaekers, 1980; Gittins, 1980). They are territorial and not highly vagile, adult males defending delimited areas. Tilson (1981) has indicated that subadult Kloss's gibbons tend to establish territories contiguous with those of their parents.

The genetic picture which emerges from this sort of organization is one in which the operation of genetic drift should be favored. The social groups are small and if related individuals establish contiguous territories, presumably randomly inbred. If indeed chromosomal variations can be considered as nearly neutral mutations, then the microevolutionary forces which are favored by the gibbon's society and ecology should result in great amounts of cytogenetic diversity within the taxon.

At the other pole in behavior, the papionine monkeys are well known (despite the obvious variation among species) as living in large, mobile troops and traveling frequently on the ground They are generally polygynous and not pair-bonded (Hall and DeVore, 1965; Crook and Gartlan, 1966; Kummer, 1968; Itani, 1977). Further, several species of this taxon have been observed to peripheralize and transfer individuals among troops (Lindburg, 1969; Rowell, 1969a; Packer, 1975; Sugiyama, 1976). All of these factors should act at a microevolutionary level to inhibit genetic drift and to promote gene flow—and thereby favor *homogeneity* for chromosomal mutations.

If we consider the karyotypes of these two anthropoid groups, (see figs. 8.1 and 8.2) we find a striking concordance with the predictions derived from their social structure and ecology. That is, in the genus *Hylobates,* the gibbons, the *H. lar* superspecies has 2n=44, *H. hoolock* has 2n=38, *H. concolor* has 2n=52, and *H. syndactylus* has 2n=50.

Further, the similarity of their chromosome numbers overestimates the similarity of the karyotypes, as interspecific comparisons have proven to be exceedingly difficult (Dutrillaux et al., 1975; Tantravahi et al., 1975; Myers and Shafer, 1979; Couturier et al., 1982; Prouty et al., 1983; Stanyon and Chiarelli, 1983; van Tuinen and Ledbetter, 1983).

The macaques, baboons, and mangabeys, on the other hand, have an extraordinary uniformity of karyotypes. Not only the same chromosome number (2n=42) but also the identical banded karyotype, or a subtle variant of the identical karyotype, has been reported for all species of *Macaca, Papio, Mandrillus, Theropithecus,* and *Cercocebus* so far tested (de Vries et al., 1975; Rubio-Goday et al., 1976; Cambefort et al., 1976; Dutrillaux et al., 1979; Bernstein et al., 1980; Stanyon et al., 1980; Soulie and de Grouchy, 1981; Stanyon, 1982; Dutrillaux et al., 1982). (See fig. 8.2).

It appears, then, that the gibbons have experienced a considerably more extensive diversification in karyotype than the papionines have. Insofar as there is no evidence that the taxonomic radiation of either clade significantly preceded the other, this karyotypic diversity seems to be a rate phenomenon. The gibbons have changed more radically in karyotype than the papionines, over a comparable period of time. And this can be plausibly explained by their paradigmatic socioecological differences.

We may label the phenomenon of exceedingly rapid karyotype evolution "chromosomal tachytely" (Simpson, 1944; Marks, 1983b); and exceedingly slow karyotype evolution, as evidenced by the papionines, "chromosomal bradytely". The obvious questions are, what other primate groups exhibit differential rates of karyotype evolution, and are these similarly related to socio-ecological variables?

Among the prosimians, no group displays a conservatism of karyotype comparable to that of the semiterrestrial monkeys described above. With few exceptions, each prosimian species has a karyotype differing in some ways, but clearly approximating that of its closest relatives.

Nevertheless, Sussman (1972; 1974) has described several ecological and behavioral differences between *Lemur fulvus* and *Lemur catta* which support the idea of a connection between karyotype evolution and socio-ecology. *Lemur fulvus* lives higher in the trees than *L. catta*. The former inhabit "canopy forests", while the latter inhabit "brush and scrub forests", doing much of their traveling on the ground. Second, *L. fulvus* has a significantly smaller range, and is consequently less vagile, than *L. catta*. The *L. fulvus* home range was approximately 1 hectare, while the *L. catta* home range was about 9 hectares. A group of *L. fulvus* moved about 125 to 150

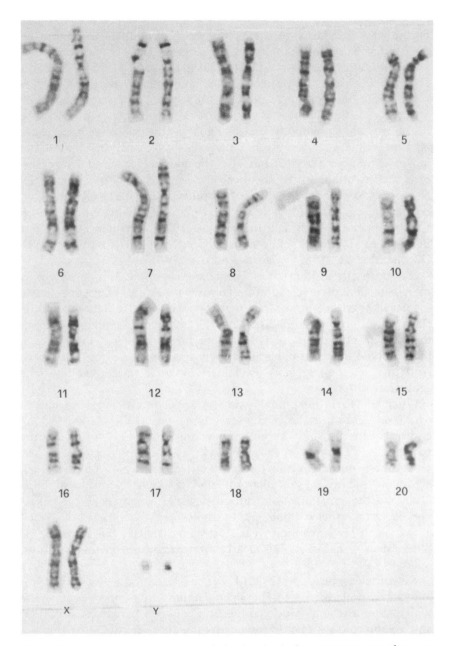

Fig. 8-2. Composite karyotype of the haploid chromosome complements of *Papio anubis* and *Macaca fascicularis*. *Papio anubis* chromosomes are the left of each pair; *Macaca fascicularis* chromosomes are the right of each pair. The striking similarity of each chromosome of *Papio* to each of *Macaca* indicates that little chromosomal change has accompanied the evolutionary diversification of this group. (Courtesy of Dr. Roscoe Stanyon.)

meters in a day, while *L. catta* moved over 900 meters. Third, the social group size, and thus presumably the effective population size, was considerably smaller in *L. fulvus* (averaging 9.5 individuals) than in *L. catta* (averaging 18 individuals). Fourth, Sussman noted a "tendency toward peripheralization of subordinate males in groups of *L. catta*", which did not apparently exist in *L. fulvus*. This observation had been previously reported by Jolly (1966), and more recently by Jones (1983). The latter additionally documents the transfer of these males between social groups.

These four contrasts between *L. fulvus* and *L. catta* mimic the social and ecological differences between the hylobatids and papionines, with *L. fulvus* being more "gibbon-like" and *L. catta* more "baboon-like". The smaller group size, greater tendency toward arboreality, and lesser degree of vagility of *L. fulvus* are all factors discussed previously in connection with the gibbons as theoretically tending to promote genetic drift and discourage gene flow. The opposite effects should occur in *L. catta*, strongly augmented by the transfer of males between groups, also paralleling the papionines, and a presumably rich source of gene flow.

Given these factors, we may make a prediction about the pattern of chromosomal variation in these lemurs. That is, *L. fulvus* should exhibit a tendency toward chromosomal diversification of populations to a greater degree than *L. catta*.

The chromosomes of lemurs have been quite extensively studied (Hamilton et al., 1977; Hamilton and Buettner-Janusch, 1977; Buettner-Janusch and Hamilton, 1979; Dresser and Hamilton, 1979; Rumpler and Dutrillaux, 1976; 1978; 1980; Dutrillaux and Rumpler, 1977; Martin, 1978). The available data indicate that *Lemur catta* has no subspecies and is apparently monotypic at 2n=56. *Lemur fulvus*, on the other hand, has several subspecies, some of which have karyotypic distinctions. Thus, *L. f. albocollaris* has 2n=48; *L. f. collaris* has a 2n=50/51/52 polymorphism; and *L. f. albifrons* has 2n=60, as do *L. f. fulvus* and *L. f. rufus*.

Lemur fulvus is clearly more likely to be differentiated into karyotypically distinct groups, below the species level, than *L. catta*, in considerable harmony with the idea that there is a significant relationship between socio-ecology and chromosomal diversity.

Considering the Neotropical monkeys we find the Callitrichidae considerably more conservative in karyotype than the Cebidae. The former family has chromosome numbers of 2n=44 and 46 and great similarity of karyotypes within the taxon (Chiarelli, 1975; Benirschke et al., 1982). The cebids, on the other hand, range from 2n=20 to 2n=62, with the most drastic intrageneric karyotypic divergence occurring between *Callicebus moloch* (2n=46) and *C. torquatus* (2n=20). *Callicebus personatus* has not yet been karyotyped.

Callitrichids are among the most vagile Neotropical primates. Animals frequently transfer between troops (Dawson, 1977; Neyman, 1977), and they have a communal breeding system (Sussman and Kinzey, 1984). These factors should favor chromosomal homogeneity. The genus *Callicebus*, on the other hand, is characterized by monogamy and territoriality, and lives in very small social groups (Kinzey, 1981; Kinzey and Becker, 1983). These observations suggest a strong concordance again between the behavioral and cytogenetic data.

Among the Cercopithecoidea, as discussed previously, the cercopithecine tribe Papionini (Szalay and Delson, 1979) is noteworthy for its conservatism in chromosome number and banding. Its sister group, the tribe Cercopithecini, (*Cercopithecus, Allenopithecus, Erythrocebus*) on the other hand, has chromosome numbers ranging from 2n=48 in *Cercopithecus nigroviridis* to 2n=72 in *C. mitis* (Chiarelli, 1975). These seem to be more easily matched across species than the gibbon chromosomes (Dugoujon et al., 1982a, b; Caballin et al., 1980; Dutrillaux et al., 1980). Nevertheless there is a striking contrast in degree of cytogenetic diversity between the two cercopithecine tribes. And although not as well studied either cytogenetically or behaviorally as the gibbons, the Cercopithecini (with the exceptiuon of *C. aethiops*, which is considered to be behaviorally convergent with the papionines) are generally more arboreal, less vagile, and live in smaller social groups than the Papionini (Clutton-Brock and Harvey, 1977a). Again, these are the sorts of behavioral differences which are expected to favor genetic drift and inhibit gene flow, and fuel the establishment of chromosomal variations among populations.

The Colobinae are not well known cytogenetically, but are reported to vary between 2n=44 and 2n=48 in chromosome number, and there are detectable differences among the karyotypes of related species (Soma et al., 1974; Zneimer et al., 1979; Dutrillaux et al., 1981).

Among the Hominoidea, the hylobatids are the only group possessing drastic variation in rate of evolution of the karyotype. The chromosomes of *Pongo, Gorilla, Pan,* and *Homo* can all be matched with little difficulty (Paris Conference, 1975; Turleau et al. 1972; Dutrillaux, 1979).

BEHAVIORAL INFERENCES ABOUT HOMO

Granting a significant relationship between behavioral and cytogenetic data, as I have atttempted to demonstrate, use of the chromosomal divergence of our species from its closest relatives should make inferences possible about the behavior of our ancestors. That is, if the extent of structural chromosomal diversity among taxa is influenced to some degree by social and ecological variables, are *humans* more or less divergent chromosomally from the Pongidae than any given great ape is from any other?

There are three possible outcomes: if humans have accumulated significantly more chromosomal differences, we might infer that our immediate ancestors, after the divergence from *Pan* and *Gorilla,* were more "gibbon-like" in social structure and ecology. If humans have accumulated considerably fewer differences, we might infer our immediate ancestors to have been more "baboon-like." And if humans have accumulated about the same amount of chromosomal diversity as *Pan* and *Gorilla,* we might infer that the common elements of chimpanzee and gorilla socio-ecology were common as well to the precultural ancestors of *Homo sapiens.*

Stanyon and Chiarelli (1982) studied the karyotypes of the Pongidae and *Homo* in an attempt to estimate the number of unique derived karyotypic changes for each lineage. If we try to avoid the problems of replicability of observation and evolutionary dynamics of repetitive DNA by considering only the most unambiguous changes of chromosome structure, we may combine the conclusions of Stanyon and Chiarelli (1982) with those of the Stockholm Conference (1978). The conclusions are that *Gorilla* has undergone unique structural changes of chromosomes V, VIII, X, XIV, and XVII; *Pan troglodytes* has undergone unique structural changes of IV, V, IX, and XVII; and *Homo* has undergone changes of II, IV, IX, and XVII.

Given the problems inherent in the analysis of comparative cytogenetic data already discussed, one would be advised to accept with some circumspection the specific nature and exact number of chromosomal changes just given. However, the conclusion that *Homo* has at least not gained many more or fewer unique derived chromosomal changes than its closest relatives seems to be well supported from the comparative data on their chromosomes.

From this analysis, we may draw the inference that the early hominids probably did not diverge radically from an ancestral chimp-like or gorilla-like social structure; that indeed, the social structures characteristic of our closest relatives are more likely to be better models for our ancestors than structures characteristic of more distantly related anthropoids.

The conclusion should not be surprising, and is certainly not radical. What is significant, at least to me, is that it can apparently be drawn from the study of chromosomes. That is, given a knowledge of chromosomes and phylogeny, it may be possible to deduce aspects of behavior.

The still-primitive state of primate cytogenetics effectively prohibits any stronger or more specific statements about primate biology at present. Indeed, this chapter is a highly theoretical account, although I have tried to season it liberally with appropriate data. As the study of primate chromosomes matures, a more vigorous interaction between primate ethology and primate cytogenetics is to be hoped for, perhaps with each generating hypotheses for the other to test.

ACKNOWLEDGEMENTS

I am grateful to Roscoe Stanyon for providing figures 8.1 and 8.2. I thank Warren Kinzey for soliciting this contribution and for his excellent editorial work. John Buettner-Janusch and the late Thomas J.M. Schopf encouraged me and gave constructive criticisms and discussion of some of the ideas in this paper. I would also like to thank the following people for support of various kinds: W. Rathje, J. Shen, and L. Howitt.

CHAPTER NINE

Species-Specific Dietary Patterns in Primates and Human Dietary Adaptations

ROBERT W. SUSSMAN

In recent years there has been a great deal of interest in research on the evolution of the human diet. This is reflected in a number of workshops, conferences and symposia held in the past few years. For example, in 1976 the Diet, Nutrition and Cancer Program, National Institutes of Health held a workshop on "Anthropology and Comparative Zoology: To Define Evolutionary Determinants of Dietary Adaptation and Natural Diet Patterns in Man"; the Plenary Session of the 1983 annual meetings of the American Association of Physical Anthropologists was entitled "Food for Thought: Diet and Human Evolution"; and in 1984 a Gordon Research Conference was held on "Diet and Human Evolution".

Throughout most of human evolution, subsistence was based on a gathering and hunting economy. It is only within the last 9 to 10,000 years that humans have cultivated their own food. We must assume that *Homo sapiens* developed certain dietary preferences that correlated with adaptations of the gastrointestinal tract during the long period of evolution of the genus. Do human gastrointestinal and dental adaptations reflect any of this past evolutionary history?

Research into this question revolves around a number of questions related to both recently adapted and phylogenetically conservative features. For example, is there something we might call a "natural" diet of man? As a result of their evolutionary history, are humans adapted for a specific type of diet? Are there correlations between digestive tract adaptations and dietary patterns in primates? If so, do any of these adaptations occur in humans? Can we find differences in digestive tract adaptations in human populations with different types of diets? Has the use of fire or cultivated crops greatly altered digestive tract adaptations? Finally, will studies of this sort lead to a better understanding of the evolution of human dietary patterns?

In this chapter, I, of course, will not be able to answer any of these questions. However, in light of the orientation of this volume, I will focus on how studies of diet and foraging behavior of non-human primates might lead to a better understanding of the evolution of human dietary patterns. First, I will describe the concept of "species-specific dietary pattern." I will then describe two field studies (Sussman, 1974, 1977, and Sussman and Tattersall, 1981), as well as a number of other studies of primates, to illustrate this concept. Third, I will review some of the dietary patterns found among primates generally and compare these to patterns found among human hunting and gathering groups. Finally, I will describe some of the possible relationships between these dietary patterns and morphophysiological adaptations.

SPECIES-SPECIFIC DIETARY PATTERNS

In recent years through numerous detailed studies of primate diets (see below), investigators have shown that two populations of the same species living in different areas will often feed on: (1) the same proportion of particular food items (e.g., fruits, flowers, leaves, insects, etc.); and (2) a similar number and proportion of plant species, even though the particular plant species may be entirely different. I have referred to these as *species-specific dietary patterns* (Sussman 1978). In other words, I hypothesize that each primate species is relatively fixed in certain features of its dietary preferences; although plant and or animal species eaten may differ in different localities, the types of items eaten and the degree of diversity of the diet remain quite constant. These dietary patterns are ultimately dependent upon the morphological and physiological adaptations of the species which, in turn, determine taste preferences, foraging patterns, and the ability to process and digest potential foods. Parameters used to measure dietary patterns are, for example: the percentage of different plant parts and animal prey in the diet; the total number of species eaten in a given time period; the percentage of the most-consumed species; the percentage of the five most frequently consumed species in the diet; and the percentage of the ten most frequently consumed species in the diet.

A quantitative measure of the diversity of the diet of a population can be determined by using the following index of dietary diversity (Rotenberry 1980):

$$I_D = \frac{1}{\Sigma P_i^2}$$

where P_i is the relative percentage contribution to the diet of the *ith* taxon or food category. This measure is similar to that of "niche breadth" of Levins (1968), Pianka (1969), and others, and gives an indication of the number of species or food items eaten as well as the relative proportion of time spent feeding on each food category. The potential values for this index range from 1.0 to infinity. A value of 1.0 would indicate that a study population ate only a single category of food over a particular period of time.

Thus, the index of dietary diversity gives an indication of the monotony or diversity of the diet of a particular study population over a certain, specified time period. Although this index is not comparative in itself, indices can be compared to determine whether different species have relatively specific or more generalized diets. However, only data collected over comparable time periods should be used in comparisons of dietary diversity among different study populations.

The similarity of the diets of different populations or species can be measured directly by using the "correlational index" (Stander 1970, Pianka 1973, Stacey, 1986):

$$I_C = \frac{\Sigma X_i Y_i}{\sqrt{\Sigma X_i^2 \Sigma Y_i^2}}$$

where X_i is the relative contribution of food category *i* to the diet of one population or species and Y_i the relative contribution of the same category to the diet of the second. This equation is similar to that of "niche overlap" of Levins (1968) and Pianka (1973), and has been used to estimate so-called competition coefficients. The index varies between 0 and 1. A value of 0 indicates that the two study populations have no foods in common, whereas a value of 1.0 signifies that they have identical diets (i.e. they eat the same food items in precisely the same proportions).

When comparing species-specific dietary patterns between different primate species, we often find that these patterns are not dependent upon taxonomic relationships. Closely related species often have very different diets, whereas many unrelated species have convergent dietary patterns. However, at some level, we would assume that there is a relationship between dietary patterns, foraging patterns, and anatomical and physiological adaptations. Unfortunately, in the examples that follow, comparable data have not always been collected and often the above indices cannot be computed. Therefore, I will necessarily be using different types of measures in an attempt to illustrate the usefulness of the concept of species-specific dietary patterns.

TWO LEMURS AND A MACAQUE: EXAMPLES OF SPECIES-SPECIFIC DIETARY PATTERNS

I first began to think of species-specific dietary patterns during a study of two closely related species of lemur in Madagascar: the ringtailed lemur *(Lemur catta)* and the brown lemur *(Lemur fulvus)* (Figure 9.1). This study was carried out in three separate forests (Figure 9.2): Antserananomby, where the two species coexisted; Tongobato, where the brown lemur was found alone; and Berenty, where the ringtailed lemur lived alone. Observations at Antserananomby were conducted during the dry season, whereas those at the other two forests took place during the wet season. This study has been described in detail elsewhere (Sussman 1974, 1977) and only certain aspects of feeding behavior will be discussed here.

Quantitative data were collected on the diet and feeding behavior of these two species and their diets were found to be radically different. The brown lemur had a very limited diet, feeding on a very narrow range of food items; the ringtailed lemur had a relatively

Fig. 9-1. (a) Ring tailed lemur *(Lemur catta)*. (b) Brown lemur *(Lemur fulvus)*.

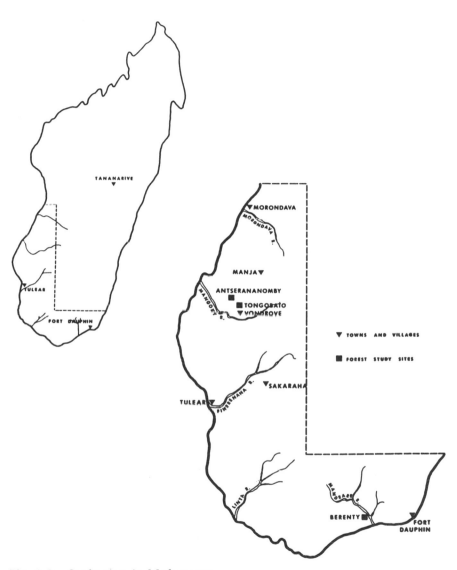

Fig. 9-2. Study sites in Madagascar.

diverse diet. The brown lemur ate only 8 plant species at Tongobato and 11 at Antserananomby, eating a total of 13 species in both forests combined. The ringtailed lemur fed on 24 plant species at each forest. Only three of these plant species were eaten by *L. catta* in both forests; they therefore fed on a total of 45 different plant species combined. Neither lemur was observed feeding on animal prey.

The diet of the brown lemur was further limited by the fact that a few species of plant made up a large portion of the diet and the leaves of *Tamarindus indica* (the dominant tree species in all three forests) were the main staple (Table 9.1). At Antserananomby, three species of plant constituted 85% of the diet: *Acacia rovumae*, *Ficus soroceoides* and *Tamarindus indica* (Table 9.1a). At Tongobato, *Flacourtia ramontchi*, *Tamarindus indica* and *Terminalia mantaly* accounted for over 80% of the diet (Table 9.1b). Tamarind leaves accounted for over 40% of the diet at Tongobato and over 75% during the dry season at Antserananomby.

The diet of the ringtailed lemur was more diverse than that of the brown lemur. Eight species of plant made up over 70% of the diet at Antserananomby (Table 9.1c). At Berenty, eight species of plant accounted for 80% of the diet (Table 9.1d). The tamarind tree provided 23–24% of the diet in the two forests, with tamarind pods and leaves providing approximately equal proportions regardless of season.

The parts of the plants eaten and the seasonal variation in diet were related to the foraging patterns of these two prosimians. Brown lemur groups had very small day ranges (125 to 150 meters) and home ranges (about one hectare). They stayed mainly in the canopy of the trees and rarely came to the ground. The ringtailed lemur moved 1,000 or more meters daily and had relatively large home ranges, averaging around 9 hectares. Ringtailed groups constantly surveyed their home range, covering the whole area every 7 to 10 days. Although this species fed in all forest strata, most group travel and almost one third of its feeding took place on the ground.

Both lemur species ate fruit, shoots, leaves, flowers, bark, and sap (Table 9.2). However, the restricted ranging pattern of the brown lemur corresponded to a dependence on the tamarind tree and a highly folivorous diet. In the dry season at Antserananomby, this lemur was able to subsist almost entirely on mature leaves, mainly from tamarind. In the wet season (Tongobato), it supplemented its mainly folivorous diet with readily available fruit (42%) and flowers (5%), though tamarind leaves still accounted for 42% of the diet. Because more fruits and flowers were available in the wet season, the index of dietary diversity at Tongobato was 3.19; during the dry season at Antserananomby it was only 1.70 (see Table 9.1). The pattern of plant part utilization by the ringtailed lemur did not change a great deal seasonally. Because the ringtails constantly surveyed their home range and fed in all forest levels, they were able to exploit a number of different resources over a wide area. Their constant movement was not related to any noticeable depletion of resources. Even during the dry season at Berenty, ringtailed lemurs were able to find and exploit many species of plant that were in

Table 9.1. The Number and Percentage of Individual Activity Records (IAR's) for Feeding on Identified Species of Plants and Indices of Dietary Diversity (I_D)

a. *Lemur fulvus rufus* at Antserananomby

Plant Species	Number of IAR's	Percentage of IAR's
Tamarindus indica	1802	75.68%
Leaves	1793	75.30
Fruit	9	0.38
Acacia sp.	156	6.55
Ficus soroceoides Bak.	141	5.92
Acacia rovumae Olia.	74	3.10
Terminalia mantaly	21	0.88
Quivisianthe papinae	18	0.75
Other	169	7.06
Total	2381	99.94%
I_D		1.70

b. *Lemur fulvus rufus* at Tongobato

Plant Species	Number of IAR's	Percentage of IAR's
Tamarindus indica	276	48.85
Leaves	237	41.95
Flowers	26	4.60
Fruit	10	1.77
Bark	3	0.53
Terminalia mantaly	127	22.47
Flacourtia ramontchi	69	12.21
Acacia rovumae Olia	38	6.72
Vitex beravensis	18	3.18
Other	37	6.54
Total	565	99.97%
I_D		3.19

c. *Lemur catta* at Antserananomby

Plant Species	Number of IAR's	Percentage of IAR's
Tamarindus indica	374	24.36%
Fruit	183	11.92
Leaves	174	11.33
Flowers	17	1.11

Small trees:
  Alchornea sp.
  Flacourtia ramontchi
  Grevia sp.
  Poupartia caffra H. Perr
	320	20.84

Ground plants (all species)	225	14.65

c. *Lemur catta* at Antserananomby—*Continued*		
Plant Species	Number of IAR's	Percentage of IAR's
Ficus soroceoides Bak	194	12.63
Vines (all species)	140	9.12
Quisivianthe papinae	94	6.12
Vitex beravensis	82	5.34
Ficus cocculifolia	40	2.60
Acacia rovumae Olia	18	1.17
Other	48	3.12
Total	1535	99.95%
I_D		6.37

d. *Lemur catta* at Berenty		
Plant Species	Number of IAR's	Percentage of IAR's
Tamarindus indica	519	22.97%
Leaves	274	12.13
Fruit	225	9.96
Bark	20	.88
Rinorea greveana H. Bn.	474	20.98
Pithecellobium dulce Benth.	433	19.16
Phyllanthus sp.	137	6.06
Melia azedarach L.	132	5.84
Ehretia sp.	130	5.74
Ground plants (all species)	124	5.48
Opuntia vulgaris Mill	84	3.71
Annona sp.	38	1.68
Vines (all species)	27	1.19
Other	161	7.10
Total	2259	99.91%
I_D		6.51

fruit and flower. The index of dietary diversity for *L. catta* was very similar at both forests, 6.37 at Antserananomby and 6.51 at Berenty (see Table 1).

The second study I wish to summarize was conducted on a group of long-tailed macaques *(Macaca fascicularis)* in Mauritius (Figure 9.3). These monkeys are not endemic to Mauritius but were brought to this small island from Java about 450 years ago (Sussman and Tattersall, 1981). Mauritian macaque males weigh about 7 kg. and females weigh about 4.5 kg. The monkeys found in the Mauritian savannah live in large groups of between 70–90 individuals. One of the long-term foci of this study was to compare dietary patterns and

Table 9.2 The Number and Percentage of Individual Activity Records for Feeding on Identified Parts of Plants.

a. *Lemur fulvus rufus* at Antserananomby

Part of Plant Eaten	Number of IAR's	Percentage of IAR's
Leaves	2123	89.16%
Fruit	161	6.76
Flowers	90	3.77
Bark	7	.29
Total	2381	99.98

b. *Lemur fulvus rufus* at Tongobato

Part of Plant Eaten	Number of IAR's	Percentage of IAR's
Leaves	275	52.08%
Fruit	224	42.43
Flowers	26	4.92
Bark	3	.56
Total	528	99.99

c. *Lemur catta* at Antserananomby

Part of Plant Eaten	Number of IAR's	Percentage of IAR's
Leaves	670	43.64%
Fruit	516	33.61
Herbs	225	14.65
Flowers	124	8.07
Total	1536	99.97%

d. *Lemur catta* at Berenty

Part of Plant Eaten	Number of IAR's	Percentage of IAR's
Fruit	1335	59.30%
Leaves	550	24.43
Flowers	137	6.08
Herbs	124	5.50
Bark, sap, cactus	105	4.66
Total	2251	99.97%

foraging behavior of populations living in degraded, savannah habitats with those inhabiting the undisturbed endemic, evergreen forest of Mauritius and, eventually, with the parent population in Indonesia. Given the extreme differences in plant species composition and distribution in these three areas, I hoped to determine whether a predictable, species-specific dietary pattern could be found among these long-tailed macaque populations.

Before going to Mauritius, I attempted to predict what the dietary pattern might be, given previous research on the morphology and behavior of *Macaca fascicularis*. From studies of molar morphology, Kay (1978) infers that the dietary adaptations of macaques range from highly folivorous to extremely frugivorous. *M. fascicularis* is intermediate in this range, having a molar morphology which suggests a diet consisting predominantly of fruit with some leaves and insects. From studies of gut morphology, Chivers and Hladik (1980) also indicate that these monkeys should be frugivores, tending towards folivory. Preliminary field studies in Malaysia support these predictions. MacKinnon and MacKinnon (1980) found *M. fascicularis* in Malaysia to have a diet made up of 72.5% fruit and flowers, 24% leaves and 4.7% animal prey. In a separate study, Aldrich-Blake (1980) found the diet to be composed of 70% fruit and flowers, 25% leaves, and 5% animal prey. These authors report that Malaysian long-tailed macaques are very eclectic feeders with a high level of short-term selectivity. They concentrate on a few food sources at any one time, but change this concentration as different resources become available.

Fig. 9–3. Mauritian long-tailed macaque *(Macaca fascicularis)*.

Although data have not been analyzed for the total 24 months of the Mauritian study, preliminary results from different seasons in 1977 and 1979 reveal a pattern very similar to that described for the Malaysian long-tailed macaques. In June to July 1977 a total of 21 plant species were eaten in 125 hours and from September to December 1979, 31 species were eaten in 200 hours: the indices of dietary diversity are 5.75 and 7.19, respectively. In both seasons, however, only 14 plant species were eaten over 1% of the time and only 6 of these species were fed upon in both years (Table 9.3). Furthermore, fruit from two species accounted for over 50% of the diet and five species accounted for between 65–75% of the diet (Table 9.4). In both years, the proportions of plant parts eaten were extremely similar to those reported for the Malaysian long-tailed monkeys (Table 9.5). Thus, as in Malaysia, the diet of the Mauritian macaque is mainly frugivorous but includes a relatively high proportion (almost 30%) of leaves and insects. As predicted, these monkeys feed on a large number of plant species but the major portion of their diet consists of a few species at any one time.

FURTHER EXAMPLES OF SPECIES-SPECIFIC DIETARY PATTERNS

Although data have often been collected using different methods and emphasizing different aspects of the diet, species-specific dietary patterns have been found in a number of species. I will only give a few examples here. Pollock (1977) observed two adjacent groups of indri *(Indri indri)* in Madagascar. He found that the percentages of plants making up the greatest part of the diet and the proportion of the different plant parts eaten by both groups was essentially the same (Table 9.6). From patterns of food choice each day, Pollock has the impression that the indris had an organized variability in their diet and "that a precise control of dietetic variety existed" (1977:54). This, further, was related to a highly organized strategy of feeding and ranging.

Milton (1980) studied two groups of howler monkeys *(Alouatta palliata)* in different areas of Barro Colorado. One of the forests (Lutz Ravine) was largely composed of secondary forest and the second (referred to as Old Forest) was undisturbed, mature forest. She found that the *number* of food species eaten in both forests was exactly the same, 73 plant species, but 75% of the particular *species* eaten were different (Table 9.7). The *number* of species of plants used for each of the three major dietary categories was also strikingly similar although the species used for these plant parts were mainly different. Milton states:

Table 9.3. Plant Species Eaten over 1% of the time by *Macaca fascicularis* during Two Seasons in Mauritius

(a.) June-July 1977 (125 hours) Species	%	(b.) Sept.-Dec. 1979 (200 hours) Species	%
1. Tamarindus indica	33	Tamarindus indica	27
2. Ficus sp.	22	Mangifera indica	23
3. Saccarum officinarum	8	Albizzia lebbek	7
4. Acacia eburnea	6	Eleocharis plantiginea	5
5. Leucaena leucocephela	5	Acacia concinna	3
6. Acacia concinna	3	Ficus sp.	3
7. Albizzia lebbek	3	Leucaena leucophela	3
8. Fucraea gigantea	3	Arctocarpus intergifolia	2
9. Cissus sp.	2	Samenea saman	2
10. Schinus terebinthifolia	2	Cassia occidentalis	2
11. Cassia sp.	1	Saccarum officianarum	2
12. Mariscus sp.	1	Cassia fistula	2
13. Hydrilla verticillata	1	Haematoxylon compehianum	2
14. Acalypha indica	1	Eichhormia crassipes	2
Total # of species eaten	21		31
Index of dietary diversity (I_D)	5.75		7.19

Table 9.4. Mean Percentage Item and Species Composition of Diet of Long-tailed Macaques in Two Separate Years in Mauritius

A. % of Species Eaten—1977				
Species	Part	%		
Tamarindus indica	pod	33	} 55%	
Ficus	fruit	22		} 74%
Saccarum officinarum	stem	8		
Acacia eburnea	pod	6		
Leucaena leucocephela	pod	5		

B. % of Species Eaten—1979				
Species	Part	%		
Tamarindus indica	pod	28	} 51%	
Mango	fruit	23		} 69%
Albizzia	flowers, stems, new leaves	7		
Eleocharis (grass)	stem	5		
Acacia concinna	leaves	3		
Ficus	fruit	3		

When examined separately, both study areas showed the same pattern in the number of food species used during the same period . . . Thus despite the differences in the forest between the two areas, both troops diversified the species used as food sources to the same extent (1980:59–60).

Table 9.5. Mean Percentage Item Composition of Diet of Long-tailed Macaques in Malaysia and Mauritius

	Malaysia			
	MacKinnon 1980	Aldrich-Blake 1980	Mauritius 1977	Mauritius 1979
Fruit & flowers	72.5	70	71	66
Leaves & stems	24	25	22	22
Invertebrates	4.4	5	5	4
?			2	7

The differences in plant species used by the two howler groups were mainly the result of differences in plant composition in the two study areas.

Struhsaker (1975, 1978) and Clutton-Brock (1972) studied different groups of red colobus *(Colobus badius)* in Uganda and Tanzania, respectively. Again the patterns of the diets of the two populations were strikingly similar, though the number of shared plant species was very small (Table 9.8). Struhsaker (1978) also found the diet of red colobus to be stable over a five year period (1970–1975), even though species composition changed somewhat over time.

The examples discussed so far are from highly folivorous primates, but more generalized, omnivorous primates show species-specific dietary patterns as well. Kavanaugh, (1978) for example, studied vervet monkeys *(Cercopithecus aethiops)* in two different forests for four months each. Although he found differences in the proportions of food items and of different food species in the diet of the two populations, certain aspects of the diversity of the diets were very similar. The range of species eaten during any monthly sample varied from 9 to 17 at one forest, and from 8 to 18 at the other. Furthermore, the top five species accounted for monthly minima of 52% in both forests and maxima of 83% and 81% at the two forests. Kavanaugh (1978) states:

> The diet varied seasonally within habitats and few species were common to more than one study site, but the total ranges of foodparts showed little variation between habitats . . . (p. 60) Interhabitat differences in the particular species eaten reflect differences in the availability of those species (p. 57).

Homewood (1978) studied mangabeys *(Cercocebus galeritus)* in two sites, Mchelelo and Mnazini, along the Tana River in Kenya.

Table 9.6. Percentage Composition of Diet of indri *(Indri indri)* in two study sites in Madagascar (from Pollock 1977).

	Group P	Group V
Top Ranked	14%	19%
Top Five	50%	50%
Young Leaves & Shoots	36.1%	32.2%
Fruit	26.4%	23.8%
Flowers	2.3%	0.0%
Mature Leaves	0.9%	0.2%
Unidentified	34.3%	43.8%

Table 9.7. Number of Different Species Eaten by Howlers *(Alouatta palliata)* in Two Studies in Barro Colorado Island. (From Milton, 1980)

	Old Forest	Lutz Ravine	In Common	Total Different
Total	73	73	37	109
Leaves	59	59	31	87
Fruit	25	23	12	36
Flowers	13	16	4	25

[data from samples over 9 month period in both study sites at B.C.I.]

Table 9.8. Number of Plant Species and Percentage Composition of Top Ranked Species Eaten by Red Colobus *(Colobus badius)* in two study sites in East Africa— Kibale (Struhsaker, 1975); Gombe (Clutton-Brock, 1972)

	Gombe (9 months)	Kibale (12 months)
Total # of Species	60	68 (5 in common)
% of top 5 ssp.	55%	55.9%
% of top 10 ssp.	78.4%	75%
Top Species	15.4% *(Newtonia)*	15.4% *(Celtis africana)*
Index of Dietary Diversity (H)	2.65	2.96

Despite major differences in vegetation and species composition, the percentage contribution of different food items was very similar for the monkeys in the two areas (Figure 9.4) The mangabeys at both forests concentrated on a few prolific species at any one time; the top five species for each month accounted for a median of 78% of the diet at Mnazini and 83% in Mchelelo. Comparing her study with a study by Quris (1975) in Gabon, Homewood found Mangabeys from West and East Africa to have very similar diets. As with the ringtailed lemur, *C. galeritus* did not greatly alter the food item portion of its diet seasonally or in different areas. Homewood emphasizes that the versatility and adaptability of the mangabey foraging, locomotor and social behavior "ensures relative dietary constancy (in terms of composition by item) despite environmental change" (1978:389).

In a study comparing three adjacent groups of savannah baboons *(Papio cynocephalus)* at Amboseli, Stacey (1986) found the amount of overlap in the individual plant species and plant parts eaten by the

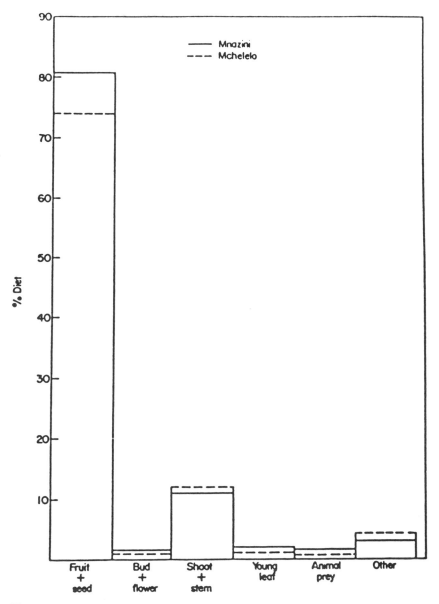

Fig. 9-4. Median percentage item composition of diet in Mangabeys *(Cercocebus galeritus)* at two study sites in Kenya. (From Homewood, 1978).

three groups (using the "correlational index", see p. 153) to be "surprisingly low". However, compared on the basis of general food types, the percentage of time spent feeding on each category was almost identical (Table 9.9). The index of dietary diversity was also similar among the three groups. Thus, the groups fed upon the same types of foods in very similar proportions, but the actual species utilized by each group were frequently different.

Finally, the diet of orangutans has been studied in two forests in Borneo (MacKinnon, 1974; Rodman, 1977) and in a Sumatran forest (Rijksen, 1978). In all three forests, the main food categories eaten were fruits, leaves, bark, and insects. The proportion of fruit and leaves eaten by the orangutan populations was similar (Figure 9.5). The amount of time eating insects by the Sumatran orangs was higher than that by the Bornean apes and the proportion of bark eating was lower. However, Rijken included the amount of time spent actually searching for and collecting insect food, rather than the actual feeding time. Given the different methods used in collecting feeding data, at this level, the dietary patterns in the three populations, representing two subspecies, are remarkably similar.

DIETARY PATTERNS AMONG PRIMATES

In the species discussed above there is an interrelationship among foraging pattern, diversity of diet, and seasonal variation in diet. Feeding patterns, as defined by types of food items eaten and relative diversity of the diet, appear to be species-specific and determined by the ecology, distribution, and evolutionary history of the primates concerned. The foraging and dietary patterns of these species are not unique among primates. As can be seen in Table 9.10, there are convergent patterns among unrelated species. As with the brown lemur, a high proportion of the diets of the purple-faced langur and of the black-and-white colobus are made up of leaves. During certain seasons, these species are able to exist almost exclusively on mature leaves and this correlates with very low dietetic diversity. Other species with similar dietary adaptations include the sportive lemur (Lepilemur) and gelada baboons (Theropithecus). The gray langur, red colobus, and ring-tailed lemur have more diverse diets and although they consume a fair proportion of leaf material, presumably they cannot subsist on diets composed exclusively of mature leaves.

Long-tailed macaques, vervet monkeys, mangabeys, baboons, and orangutans include some animal matter in their diets and, along with many other primate species, are omnivores. In fact, most species of primate are omnivorous (see Harding, 1981) and omnivory should be considered an evolutionarily conservative and generalized trait

Table 9.9. Percentage Item Composition and Dietary Indices of Three Groups of Baboons *(Papio cynocephalus)* in Amboseli National Park, Kenya. (From Stacey, 1986)

Food type	Percentage of Total Feeding Time			
	Limp's Group	Hook's Group	Alto's Group	All Groups
Grasses	38	40	43	41
Fruits	33	22	31	28
Seeds	12	27	12	18
Sap	10	7	7	8
Flowers	2	2	6	3
Leaves	2	1	1	1
Animal Matter	0	2	0	1
Miscellaneous	2	0	1	1
Index of Dietary Diversity (I_D)	13.37	13.93	14.14	
Index of Dietary Similarity (I_C)	*L&H*	*L&A*	*H&A*	
Plant Species	0.476	0.507	0.588 (very low)	
General Food Types	0.935	0.990	0.945 (almost identical)	

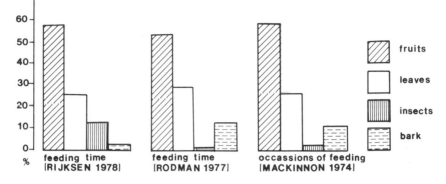

Fig. 9-5. Percentage item composition of diet of Orang-utans *(Pongo pyg-maeus)* at three study sites in Sumatra and Borneo.

among primates. Primates evolved from insectivores. However, it is very likely that the earliest primates became distinct from insectivores by taking advantage of the food resources offered by newly diversifying flowering plants (see Sussman and Raven, 1978). The earliest "primates of modern aspect" were small, nocturnal prosimians much like some of the extant lemurs and lorisids. The majority of these animals are primarily frugivorous but obtain most of their protein from insects. Presently, the only modern primates known to include a greater proportion of animal prey than plant material in their diets are the small-bodied *Galago demidovii, Arctocebus calabarensis,* and the three species of *Tarsier.* Among primates, the proportion of animal material included in the diet is related to body size. Small primates are able to obtain most of their protein needs from insects whereas larger forms must utilize leaves or other plant sources to fulfill some or all of their protein requirements. Because of the difficulty in obtaining a sufficient amount of insect prey, omnivorous mammals over 2 to 3 kg. in weight must rely heavily on social insects or on small vertebrates for protein (Charles-Dominique, 1975; Kay, 1975; Hladik, 1981; Terborgh, 1983). The ability to subsist without animal protein and to obtain all protein requirements from folivory is a more specialized, derived feeding adaptation among primates. Figure 9.6 is a hypothetical scheme of the evolution of general primate feeding adaptations.

Thus, omnivorous primates are mainly frugivorous and, depending upon body size, obtain most of their protein from insects or leaves. In all large, omnivorous, nonhuman primates, animal protein is a very small but presumably necessary component of the diet. Animals falling into this category usually have the largest home ranges and day ranges and the most diverse diets of all primates. Although there

Table 9.10. Dietary patterns among some diurnal, large-bodied primates

Species	Species of plants			Parts of plants and animal prey			References
	No. of plant species eaten	% of most utilized species	No. of plant species comprising majority of diet	% of mature leaves	% of other plant material (fruit)	% of animal prey	
1) Specialized folivores							
Brown lemur *(Lemur fulvus)*	8, 11	>60	3 (85%)	@70	30 (24)	0	Sussman (1977)
Purple-faced langur *(Presbytis senex)*	12 (>90%)	41	3 (70%)	60	40 (28)	0	Hladik (1977)
Black-and-white colobus *(Colobus guereza)*	6, 8	>70	3 (90%)	@60	40	0	Clutton-Brock (1975)
2) Folivore–frugivores							
Ring-tailed lemur *(Lemur catta)*	24	23	8 (70%)	34 (young & mature)	66 (46)	0	Sussman (1977)
Gray langur *(Presbytis entellus)*	25 (>90%)	@10	10 (70%)	21	79 (45)	0	Hladik (1977)
Red colobus *(Colobus badius)*	20 (>90%)	11	9 (70%)	20	80	0	Clutton-Brock (1975)
3) Omnivores							
Cebus monkey *(Cebus capucinus)*	54	Unspecified	36 (60%)	Small	80 (65)	20	Hladik and Hladik (1969), Oppenheimer (1968)
Toque macaque *(Macaca sinica)*	>40	Unspecified	22	Small	96 (77)	4	Hladik and Hladik (1972), Dittus (1974)
Vervet monkey *(Cercopithecus sabaeus)*	>65	7.2	12 (50%)	Small	87 (50)	13	Harrison (1984)
Chimpanzee *(Pan troglodytes)*	78	Unspecified	18 (80%)	Small	96 (68)	4	Suzuki (1969, 1975)
4) Human hunter/gatherers							
≠Kadi San Bushman	79	Unspecified	13	Small	96.4	3.6	Tanaka (1976)

Data represent yearly averages (Adapted from Sussman 1978)

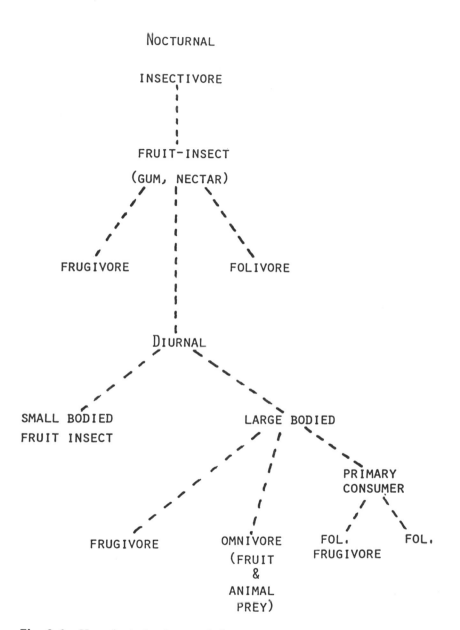

Fig. 9-6. Hypothetical scheme of the evolution of primate feeding adaptations.

has been a great deal of publicity given to the fact that some large primates, such as baboons and chimpanzees, include animal prey and especially small vertebrates in their diets, given the evolutionary history and dietary patterns of primates generally, this is not at all surprising. Table 9.10 lists the dietary patterns of some omnivorous primates.

For the purpose of comparison, Table 9.10 includes data on a human hunting and gathering group, the ≠Kadi San Bushman of the Kalahari. The study of this group (Tanaka, 1976, 1980) is one of the most detailed to date on the diet of modern hunters and gatherers. Because of the methods employed, the estimates shown in Table 9.10 are comparable to those obtained for nonhuman primates. At this level of comparison, the ≠Kadi San Bushman diet is very similar to that of nonhuman primate omnivores and most similar to that of the chimpanzee. It is probably not surprising to anyone that human and chimpanzee dietary patterns are generally similar, but it might be somewhat of a surprise that so little animal prey is eaten by these hunters and gatherers. However, this probably is not unusual. A number of estimates of the diets in these societies have also shown that most "hunters" subsist mainly by gathering, with 65% to over 80% of the diet being made up of plant material (Lee, 1968, 1969; Woodburn, 1968; Tanno, 1981). Given these behavioral data, the body size of early hominids, and their general dental and gut tract anatomy (see below), we may hypothesize that the earliest relatives of *Homo* were mainly frugivorous omnivores with a dietary pattern similar to that of modern chimpanzees, though the specific plant species and food items utilized are likely to have been quite different.

Table 9.11 presents a very preliminary and simplified classification of some of the major categories of feeding types found among primates. The classification is preliminary because of the paucity of comparative data on the diets of most nonhuman primates and simplified because it is likely that more classes and subclasses will be found as more data are gathered. Furthermore, even within the general categories, there is a great deal of variability possible at the species level. What is defined by these categories is not a specific set of diets, but groups of primates with relatively similar dietary patterns. Each species of primate is predicted to have a species-specific dietary pattern and those species filling similar ecological roles in different communities may have convergent dietary patterns. In this way, we may eventually be able to define specific feeding guilds among primates. These patterns probably exist in conjunction with certain limits in the range and proportion of food items that would constitute an acceptable diet for a given species. We assume that to some extent these dietary patterns and limitations are physiologically based.

Table 9.11. Primate feeding types

Size	Classification	Diet
	Nocturnal primates	
Small bodied (to @ 500 g)	Insectivores Insectivore–frugivores	@70% animal prey 50% animal prey
Large bodied (1–? kg)	Frugivores Folivores	Mainly fruit, little oɩ ɩ1o animal prey Mainly leaves, little or no animal prey
	Diurnal primates	
Small bodied (to @ 500 g)	Insectivore–frugivores	30–50% insects
Large bodied (over 1 kg)	Omnivores Specialized frugivores Folivore–frugivores Specialized folivores	Mainly fruit w/some animal prey Very high % fruit Little or no animal prey Mature leaves, no animal prey

RELATIONSHIPS BETWEEN MORPHOPHYSIOLOGY AND DIETARY PATTERNS IN PRIMATES

In figure 9.7, I present a model depicting how morphophysiology might mediate foraging and feeding behavior. In this model, I assume that the feeding niche of a species (and the morphological, physiological and, therefore, behavioral adaptations directly related to food exploitation) is evolutionarily conservative. Over long-term evolutionary history, behaviors, such as food preferences and the ability to find and exploit certain food items, are dependent upon morphophysiological adaptations that are phylogenetically conservative. Species-specific dietary patterns are the result of these conservative feeding adaptations, and the food selected from what is potentially available in any given habitat is determined to a large extent by phylogenetic adaptations. This would explain why sympatric species choose different resources, with potentially the same resources available, and why populations of the same species search for similar types of resources in different habitats. (It also gives us some insight into why models of optimal foraging strategy, which use resource distribution as an independent variable and do not take into account phylogenetic feeding adaptations, have proven to be relatively unfruitful.) Given this model, short term, population-specific foraging behaviors will depend upon specific patterns of food distribution and availability. At some level, perturbations and stresses caused by difficulty of access or the absence of certain foods will lead to changes in the normal patterns of food acquisition behavior and possibly to changes and selection at the morphophysiological level. However, behavior, and subsequently morphology, will only vary if the phylogenetically conservative species-specific patterns cannot be achieved.

Thus, we assume there is a relationship between certain morphophysiological characteristics and feeding and foraging behavior. Although variation occurs in the diet of a primate species, this variation is constrained by morphological and physiological adaptations. The diet is related, first, to specific morphological and physiological adaptations of the digestive tract of the species and, secondly, to environmental variables. Furthermore, the specific patterns of different species may be variable in different ways and a study of the types of *patterns* that exist among primates should be quite informative. The assumption that dietary patterns are conservative and may constrain changes in other variables underlies many arguments concerning the relationships between ecology and social structure (e.g., Lack, 1968; Crook, 1970; Denham, 1971; S. A. Altmann, 1974; Jarmon, 1974) although it is rarely made explicit (see, however, Clutton-Brock and Harvey, 1977b; Hladik, 1977, 1981).

The above discussion assumes that certain feeding adaptations are quite conservative and may allow us to predict dietary patterns. Recent research on primate dental and intestinal tract morphology indicates that this is so. For example, a number of investigators have been able to determine relationships between dental morphology and dietary propensity in a variety of primate taxa (Kay, 1975, 1978, 1981; Hylander, 1975; Rosenberger and Kinzey, 1976; Kay and Hylander, 1978; Kay et al., 1978; Kinzey, 1978). Kay (1975) showed that species which eat different proportions of fruit, leaves, and insects have different molar structure. Taking allometric adjustments into account, primates with folivorous or insectivorous diets tend to have proportionately larger molars with relatively longer shearing blades and higher crowns than do frugivorous species. Molars with thick enamel and poorly developed shearing crests correspond with

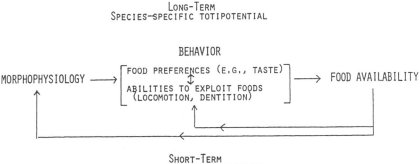

Fig. 9-7. Model representing relationships between morphophysiology, feeding behavior and food availability.

a diet made up mainly of fruit and especially hard nuts, seeds, and tough pods (Kay, 1981). Kay and Hylander (1978:174) state:

. . . any dietary interpretation based on morphology may be slightly out of phase with the present behavior. But if an animal's morphology were too far out of step with its environment, extinction would result. It is not surprising then that . . . minor dental variations correspond remarkably well with what is known of dietary preferences of species in the wild.

Dietetic differences among primates are also related to variation in digestive tract anatomy and physiology (Hladik, 1967; Amerasinghe et al., 1971; Hladik et al., 1971; Chivers and Hladik, 1980, 1984; Martin et al., 1985). In general mammals subsisting mainly on animal matter have a simple stomach and colon and a long small intestine. Those feeding on leaves have a complex stomach or an enlarged caecum and colon. Mammals that are mainly frugivorous have an intermediate morphology but tend towards one direction or the other depending upon the tendency to supplement their diet with animal matter or leaves.

The indication that certain adaptations of the intestinal tract were present in the ancestral mammalian condition (e.g., a dichotomy between fore-gut and mid-gut fermenting species, the possession of a caecum), suggests that *some* plant food was usually consumed, "and the common blanket reference to ancestral placental mammals as 'insectivorous' is therefore probably misleading" (Martin et al., 1985). In general, the alimentary tract of primates is relatively generalized with few extreme specializations (Hill, 1972; Chivers and Hladik, 1980, 1984; Martin et al., 1985). This is true of both the stomach, which generally remains a simple globular sac, and the small intestine, which varies somewhat in proportionate length but is fairly uniform in form and distribution throughout the primates. Only in the more specialized leaf-eating primates is some major gastric specialization encountered. This, again, indicates that the common ancestral primate was most likely an omnivore (i.e., fed on both plant and animal matter).

Given the fact that the proportions of different compartments of the intestinal tract are generally related to the proportion of foliage, animal matter, and fruit in the diet of mammals, Chivers and Hladik (1980, 1984) made interspecific comparisons of 78 mammals, including 48 primate species, in an attempt to describe and predict these relationships. By taking the ratio of surface area of the small intestine + ½ that of the stomach, caecum and colon ("potential area for absorption") in relation to body length, they could predict whether a species was mainly folivorous, frugivorous, or faunivorous at an 85% confidence level (except in the smallest sized animals) (Figure 9.8). Furthermore, among frugivores, the propensity to supplement the diet with leaves or animal protein could be predicted. Martin et al. (1985), using many of the same specimens as Chivers and Hladik, scaled gastrointestinal compartments in relation to metabolic requirements and body weight. Although mammals (primates as well as non-primates) with specializations for folivory separated out with multivariate clustering techniques, there was a "considerable lability among mammal species exhibiting less specialized guts." Both Chivers and Hladik (1980) and Martin et al. (1985) found that measurements of gastrointestinal compartments varied in captive and wild specimens of the same species.

Thus, at least at a general level, relationships exist between dietary patterns, dental morphology, and alimentary tract adaptations, and we may ask the question: Can relationships be found between morphology and diet in humans, and do these dental and gastrointestinal adaptations reflect past dietary patterns? As discussed above, Kay (1981, pers. comm.) found an inverse relationship between relative shearing capabilities of the molars and relative enamel thickness, with the latter adaptation being related to a greater proportion of fruit, seeds and hard objects in the diet versus foliage or animal matter. Human dentition, both modern and fossil, is characterized by having thick enamel.

In their comparative studies, Chivers and Hladik (1980, 1984) compared "coefficients of gut differentiation" (surface area of stomach + caecum + colon)/(surface area of small intestine) between faunivores, frugivores and folivores. The values for faunivores fell between 0.08 and about 0.55; for frugivores between approximately 0.33 and 2.0; the coefficient for folivores was between 1.0 and 6.0. In a preliminary study of modern human intestinal tracts from dissection specimens in an urban U.S. medical school, using the same methods as Chivers and Hladik, we found a coefficient of 0.62 (N=6, range 0.37–1.15). Thus, in this measurement of proportionate lengths of gastrointestinal compartments, the modern humans we measured fall within the middle of the frugivorous range, but slightly in the direction of faunivores. However, when we compare the relationship between potential area for absorption (surface area of small intestine and half the combined areas of stomach, caecum, and colon) and body length in a number of mammals (as per Chivers and Hladik, 1980), our measurements predict a faunivorous diet for this human population (Figure 9.8). Martin et al. (1985) also measured six human gut tracts and found that humans clustered with faunivorous mammals.

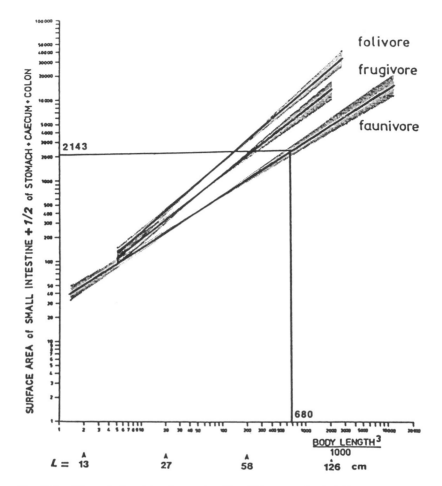

Fig. 9-8. The relationship, determined by Chivers and Hladik, 1980, between potential area for absorption (surface area of small intestine and half the combined areas of stomach, caecum, and colon) and body length in faunivores, frugivores and folivores in the form of regressions derived from individual data. The stippled areas demarcate the 95% confidence limits for the slopes; the three dietary groups are quite distinct at the 85% limit. Human data collected at Washington University (area for absorption = 2143; body length[3] = 680) fall within the faunivore range. (Adapted from Chivers and Hladik, 1980).

Do these results suggest that the "natural diet" of *Homo sapiens* is highly faunivorous? How can we reconcile interpretations from the general patterns of the gastrointestinal tract, the dentition, and modern hunters and gatherers' diets with allometrically corrected gut tract morphology? Are these measurements valid for interpretations of early human dietary adaptations and present dietary propensities? Unfortunately, I think that relative proportions of gastrointestinal compartments of modern humans will not help us understand the evolution of human dietary patterns—at least not until we know more about the physiology of digestion. There are too many unanswered questions. For example:

1. Gut tract compartmental dimensions appear to be quite malleable. Mammals, including primates, maintained in captivity exhibit different dimensions from wild-living conspecifics (Hladik, 1967; Chivers and Hladik, 1980; Martin et al., 1985), and presumably intraspecific variation might occur in wild populations with vastly different diets. How much of the morphology of humans in our samples is related to the high proportion of animal protein in the diet of modern Western industrialized populations? What would these dimensions look like in hunters and gatherers or highly vegetarian populations?

2. How have intestinal dimensions kept pace with the increase in body size over the past few generations? It is difficult to assess the effect of these rapid secular trends in height and weight on intestinal tract proportions.

3. Finally, and perhaps most importantly, how has cooking affected gastrointestinal adaptations over the past half million or so years? Just as the physical properties of foliage and insect chitin similarly affect the morphology of dentition (Kay and Hylander, 1978; Kay, 1984), cooked foods may require less extensive digestion than raw plant foods. Thus the use of cooked foods may have resulted in a morphology in humans similar to that in mammals with highly faunivorous diets.

Further comparative studies of the histology of the gut tract of primates in conjunction with detailed and quantitative studies of the food habits of natural populations are needed to determine if more precise dietary/digestive tract relationships exist. Studies of this type should lead to a better understanding of digestive physiology. However, whether we can ever determine the "natural diet" of man by such comparisons still remains an unanswered question.

SUMMARY

In this paper I have attempted to make the following points:

1) There are a variety of foraging and dietary patterns among primates; different species have generally obligate food habits in that the types of food items eaten and the degree of dietary diversity are relatively fixed.

2) There are a number of convergent dietary patterns among primates that are not taxonomically dependent; closely related species may have different food habits, while the diets of unrelated forms may be quite similar.

3) At least at a general level, in naturally occurring animals, relationships exist between dietary patterns and alimentary tract adaptations.

4) Studies of the dimensions of intestinal tract compartments in humans have not led to a greater understanding of the evolution of the human diet because the human diet has changed so rapidly and the intestinal tract is quite malleable.

5) The further study of species-specific dietary patterns among primates may lead to a better understanding of the role of primates in ecological communities and to the definition of primate feeding guilds.

6) Early hominids were relatively large animals, mainly terrestrial, and lived in edge or savannah habitats. There is no indication that they were dietary specialists. Most primates living in similar environments are mainly frugivorous and feed on a small proportion of animal protein, depending upon body size. Furthermore, these species have quite diverse diets (i.e. they eat a large number of food items and plant species), though some have seasonal specialties. Comparing dietary patterns of other primates living under these conditions, I suspect that early hominids were mainly frugivorous omnivores that consumed a relatively minor proportion of animal matter. Dental adaptations further indicate that they ate relatively small hard foods, or foods containing gritty material, at lease some proportion of the time. These latter foods could have been nuts, seeds (or fruit with hard seeds), hard pods, or possibly soiled roots.

ACKNOWLEDGEMENTS

I would like to thank Jerry Purvis, Betty Bacandreas and Jeff McKee for their assistance in preparation and analysis of the data from human intestinal tracts. I would also like to thank Steven Ward for making these specimens available. I appreciate the helpful comments made on various aspects of this paper by Richard Kay, Warren Kinzey, Tom Przybeck, Linda Sussman and participants of the symposium at the 1983 annual meetings of the American Anthropological Association. This research was supported in part by Research Fellowship

MH 46268–01 of the National Institute of Mental Health, United States Public Health Service, Research Grant BNS–7916561 of the National Science Foundation, and by a research grant from the National Geographic Society of Washington, D.C.

IV

Theoretical Issues

CHAPTER TEN

The Reconstruction of Hominid Behavioral Evolution Through Strategic Modeling

JOHN TOOBY
and IRVEN DEVORE

INTRODUCTION[1]

The reconstruction of hominid evolutionary history is a scientific problem of exceptional difficulty. Direct observation is impossible; fossil and archaeological evidence are scarce. It is also a pivotal problem, not only because of the scope and crucial character of the issues it addresses about modern human nature, but also because of the challenge it presents to evolutionary biologists. Humans are so singular a species, with such zoologically unprecedented capacities, that it is a major biological mystery how evolutionary processes could have produced us out of our primate ancestors. Yet unique cases are far from unsolvable in science, and many of them, such as Hamilton's (1964) and Williams & Williams' (1957) investigation of the enigma of sterile castes in eusocial insects, prove to be the stimulus for fundamental advances in the encompassing theories that seek to assimilate them. Hominid behavioral evolution can only be reconstructed through the use of powerful analytic models, and this article addresses the prospects for creating a model of hominid evolution that can, in fact, clarify how so unusual species was produced out of our primate ancestors.

Models are inherent to any scientific endeavor. Not only do they play a major role in the discovery and exploration of a subject, but a validated model is the final product of a successful scientific inquiry. The goal of research is to produce a validated model that both organizes and best interprets an expanding body of data. A model relates what was previously unrelated, allowing new inferences to be drawn: a model gives data meaning. Newton's theory of gravitation united Kepler's laws of planetary motion with the previously unconnected dynamics of terrestrial falling bodies. Einstein's theory of general relativity was validated by looking for a minor deviation in the apparent location of a star during a solar eclipse—a previously unlooked for and otherwise minor phenomenon. And Darwin's theory of natural selection elucidated the previously ungrasped connection between, for example, the breeding of pigeons and the descent of man. Models do not simply account for data already observed—on the contrary, as Einstein remarked, "it is the theory which decides what we can observe" (Heisenberg, 1971:63). Models (or theories) function as organs of perception: they allow new kinds of evidence and new relationships to be perceived (Popper, 1972).

Because unique zoological features are involved and direct evidence is difficult to obtain, models are essential for the reconstruction of hominid behavioral evolution. Innovative models provide the potential for supplementing the existing paleontological and archaeological record with new kinds of data and inferences. For example, the theory of neutralism allowed the use of biochemical data to create molecular clocks; these resulted in alternative datings and more informative phylogenies (Sarich, 1980). Marks (this volume) connected primate cytogenetics to primate social structure. In short, models offer the eventual prospect of alleviating the shortage of information about hominid evolution.

It is the hallmark of a good model that, as it allows more and more indirect evidence to be focussed on a problem, it also allows a continual expansion in the body of sound inference. While paleontologists have become understandably impatient with the flood of speculations about human origins, they need to temper their desire to ground their field in solid fact with the realization that empiricism and modeling are natural—in fact, inalienable—allies. Reconstruction using data alone, in the absence of models, is not a logical possibility (Popper, 1959, 1972). The question is not whether to use models, but rather *what kinds of models are useful? how should they be used? and what are the criteria for good models?*

REFERENTIAL AND CONCEPTUAL MODELS

There is continuing confusion over what kind of models will prove most useful in reconstructing the history of hominid evolution. Although many different types of models are used in science, we offer a simple distinction between *referential models* and *conceptual models.*

In a referential model, one real phenomenon is used as a model for its referent, another real phenomenon that is less amenable to direct study. An example is the use of animal models for humans in drug research, where ethics prevents the direct study of the effects of new drugs on humans.

For years, paleontologists have used referential models to reconstruct extinct species by comparing homologous features of the extinct form with a living one. Sometimes the fossil sample is disappointingly small; a single tooth, a piece of palate, the incomplete articular surface of a limb bone. Inferences from these fossil scraps to their analogous or homologous counterparts in living species are (or should be) rather modest.

The referential approach has been widely applied to behavioral evolution. As only bones, and not behavior, are preserved, attempts at behavioral reconstruction suffer from a one-stage-removed effect: the pieces of preserved skeletal material are first used to reconstruct a whole animal (technically, its skeleton), and this reconstructed specimen is then compared, by reference, to its nearest living counterpart. Such is the fascination with understanding behavioral evolution, however, that there has been no hesitation in proposing various living species as "models" for the behavior of our hominid ancestors. Typically, one or a cluster of prominent behavioral traits (such as "dominance" or "gathering") are advocated as the most illuminating approach to understanding hominid adaptation, and, at various times, different referential models have tended to dominate discussion: researchers have proposed common chimpanzees (e.g., Tanner, this vol.), baboons (see Strum and Mitchell, this vol., for review), living hunter-gatherers, various social carnivores (for review, see Teleki, 1981), and, recently, pygmy chimpanzees or bonobos (Zihlman et al., 1978).

Conceptual models, on the other hand, are not real phenomena. Instead, they are theories: sets of concepts or variables that are defined, and whose interrelationships are analytically specified. At its best, a conceptual model has elements that are well-defined and easily operationalized; the relationships between its variables are sharply constrained; and the assumptions on which it is based are validated (or at least realistic and clearly stated); the implications for specific applications of a conceptual model can be unambiguously deduced from these analytically interdefined variables (that is, it makes potentially falsifiable predictions); the same few elements economically explain a large range of phenomena, relating previously unconnected phenomena into new meaningful systems; these new systems of interpretation allow new kinds of inferences to be made from new data sets made relevant by the model; finally, new elements, when they are found necessary, can be defined and integrated into the model so that the model can be expanded to cover new domains and new phenomena. At its worst, a conceptual model is highly artificial and obscure; it rests on unstated, unrealistic, or shifting assumptions; it leaves unintegrated, or absent, factors known to be important; it yields conclusions that are trivial, obvious, or absurd. Paradigmatic examples of good conceptual models are Newton's mechanics, Euclid's geometry, Dalton's chemistry, and Darwin's theory of natural selection (especially when combined with genetics in the Modern Synthesis). In each case, an enormous array of phenomena can be deduced from a few tightly interdefined central concepts.

Although referential models can be very useful where appropriate, as in medical research, their use in "behavioral paleontology" presents serious difficulties and should be carefully circumscribed. We will argue that the reconstruction of hominid evolution requires conceptual models. Although we are still far from achieving conceptual models that are both powerful and validated, efforts to create such models will surely be more fruitful than attempts to view one or another living species as a reflection of our distant past.

THE LIMITATIONS OF REFERENTIAL MODELS

How does one choose a living species as a referential model for extinct hominids, and once chosen, how does one know along what dimensions the model species resembles the unobservable referent? All real phenomena—baboons, chimpanzees, modern hunter-gatherers—have an infinite number of arbitrarily defined characteristics, some of which they will no doubt have in common with the referent (extinct hominids), and some of which will differ. A conceptual model is needed to substantiate the claim that a living species is a good parallel to an extinct one, and it is just this conceptual model that is lacking.

Because there is no validated principle to govern the selection of an appropriate living species as a referential model, the use of such models is arbitrary. Moreover, the question of which parts of the model are relevant (that is, display patterns of covariance) is usually not well specified, but left implicit, vague or intuitive. Consequently, there is no standard by which one can evaluate the large literature that discusses various species, and, at the preference of the author, asserts that hominids "probably" were like baboons, bonobos, or whatever, because they share some trait or other. In the absence of a sound conceptual model, there seems to be no way of improving the standards of the argument, assessing the probability of any assertion, or for that matter of extracting any substantive contribution to the progressive reconstruction of hominid behavioral evolution.

Moreover, without a well-specified conceptual model, there are no grounds for inferring how observed differences between hominids and a model living species can be expected to modify hypothesized parallels. Baboons are quadrapedal and hominids are bipedal: Will this make any difference in whether dominance relations in baboons parallel dominance relations in hominids? Will it affect foraging patterns? If hominid males were more predatory than baboon males, how will that affect male-female relations? Without a conceptual model, there is no way to know.

The absence of any legitimate method for handling known differences between hominids and proposed referential model species has several unfortunate effects on those who rely heavily on referential research. First, referential models often lead to a disproportionate focus on the evolutionary period when differences between the model species and hominids is hypothesized to be at a minimum, that is, on the earlier more ape-like phases of our evolution. Unfortunately, this focus sheds little light on the forces that so significantly transformed the hominid lineage. Even if one were to learn everything about the hominid-pongid common ancestor, many of the most crucial questions about distinctively hominid evolution would remain unanswered: why we are humans and not chimpanzees, bonobos, or gorillas?

Second, and more important, because a referential perspective has no rigorous way to handle differences, similarities are emphasized at the expense of differences. The significance of the zoologically novel features of hominid evolution (such as high intelligence, language, sophisticated tool use, and an immense expansion in cultural traditions and learning) is de-emphasized or neglected. Discontinuities between hominids and catarrhines, such as bipedalism, (possibly) high degrees of carnivory, male parental investment, and male coalitional intergroup hostility, are similarly underemphasized. But organisms are systems of coevolved adaptations; a change in one feature resonates through the system, changing other features in the adaptive constellation. Hence, novel features will frequently alter the function and meaning even of identified similarities. Only uniquenesses can explain uniquenesses; one cannot invoke the features species have in common to explain their differences. By their nature, referential models tend to ignore or obscure the most important question in human evolution: where did our most crucial and novel adaptations come from?

Usually a referential model is conflated with, or presented as if it were the same as, a conceptual model about the referential species. So it was not simply savannah baboons that were proposed as a model for hominids, but a certain conception of male dominance relations in baboons (Washburn and DeVore, 1961b). When male dominance became less popular as a research perspective, the putatively more peaceful chimpanzee became a popular referential species (Tanner, 1981). As the aspects emphasized by the conceptual models implicit in these theories rotated in and out of fashion, the preferred referential model species changed—from baboons, to various social carnivores, to chimpanzees, to bonobos.

The perils and shortcomings of referential reasoning can be clearly seen if we take an example from another field entirely. Newton's theory of gravitation as applied to the orbital motion of the planets precisely tied together a number of different physical features into a single conceptual model (e.g., mass, the force of gravity, the year length of a planet, its orbital velocity, its distance from the sun). For the sake of analogy, assume that we know these physical features for all of the other planets in the solar system, but know only a few of them for the Earth. How, then, could we find out what Earth was like? We could use referential modeling, in which case we would propose that the Earth resembled Mars, or Jupiter, or Neptune, etc., and argue the relative merits of each case. This is clearly not a successful procedure, even if we found the "best" parallel planet by some criterion. At the very best, we are limited in the accuracy of our analysis by what parallels happen to exist.

The better strategy is to develop an appropriate conceptual model (in this case Newton's theory of universal gravitation), by finding the set of invariant relationships that exists between the variables known for the other planets. We could then take the few things that are known about the Earth, plug these parameters into our conceptual model, then precisely determine many (or all) of its unknown features. Newton used the other planets as data, not as models, and he used this set of data to derive and test the general principles that comprise the valid conceptual model of universal gravitation. By this method, the unique features of an unknown planet (in this analogy, the Earth), can be worked out. By the referential method, the Earth's uniquenesses would remain unknowable.

In short, the use of the referential approach should be discarded, and its literature assimilated into vertebrate behavioral ecology. Not only will this allow a better understanding of various primate species themselves, but it will allow the resulting conceptual models to address central questions of hominid evolution directly, including questions about the emergence of the many novel features of humans for which there are no tight parallels elsewhere in the primate world.

Strategic Modeling and Human Behavioral Evolution

Can a conceptual model be created that is powerful enough to allow the reconstruction of hominid behavioral evolution from available data? In other areas of science, the most successful conceptual models have been based on a strong deductive framework (e.g., the physical models of Maxwell, Newton, or Einstein). Fortunately, there exists in biology a set of principles with the requisite deductive power: evolutionary theory. By combining evolutionary theory (and its subdisciplines, such as behavioral ecology) with what is already known about primates and hominids, one can begin to construct and validate a specifically elaborated set of principles that together will comprise the desired conceptual model.

A central achievement of modern evolutionary biology has been the recognition that selection acts at the level of the gene (Hamilton, 1964; Maynard Smith, 1964; Williams, 1966; Cosmides and Tooby, 1981; Dawkins, 1982). The genes present in any given generation are disproportionately those that had, in preceding environments, effective "strategies" for their own propagation. The traits individuals express are present because the genes that govern their development have successful strategies of self-propagation. In other words, genes work through the individual in which they occur, and the individual's morphology and behavior embody the strategies of the genes it contains. Characteristics of groups or species are not selected or shaped *per se;* they are the result of the interactions among individuals whose behavior is controlled by proximate mechanisms whose properties correlate with genic fitness.

The genic strategies that have been identified, together with our understanding of how they interact, will be major ingredients in the conceptual model that must be constructed. Researchers now speak of organisms as "strategists," meaning that individual organisms are selected to manifest any property, behavioral or morphological, that correlates with strategies of genic reproduction—it is a convenient linguistic shorthand that bridges the gap between the level of the individual and the level of the gene. Thus, if one neglects the complications of intragenomic conflict (Cosmides and Tooby, 1981), animals will be selected to behave as if they were following strategies to promote their inclusive fitness (Hamilton, 1964).

We propose the term "strategic modeling" to cover the construction of conceptual models of primate and hominid behavior based on our understanding of 1) the genes as the unit of selection, and 2) animals as shaped to behave as strategists promoting their inclusive fitness. The premise involved is that species in the past were subject to the same fundamental evolutionary laws and ecological forces as species today, so that principles derived today are applicable throughout evolutionary history. Hence, each species is a unique expression of the same underlying principles: although no present species will correspond precisely to any past species, the principles that produced the characteristics of living species will correspond exactly to the principles that produced the characteristics of past species. By studying the present, we can discover the principles that shaped the past. The principles that shape species do not vary, only the specific parameters that govern how these principles will interact in each case.

We can estimate the parameters believed to be true of hominids at various points in their evolutionary history, from the following data:

1) our knowledge of the patterns of primate homology (investigated through behavioral, morphological, and biochemical means),

2) the characteristics present in modern humans,

3) the paleontological record,

4) the archaeological record,

5) our knowledge of ancient habitats.

The hope is that the application of evolutionary principles will constrain the range of possible hominid traits such that future discoveries about hominids will uniquely determine the answers to many of our questions about our evolutionary history.

THE PRINCIPLES OF STRATEGIC MODELING

A powerful conceptual model for reconstructing hominid evolution does not yet exist in any well-developed form. Many components of it already exist, however, and we can make some headway towards a preliminary assembly of its elements. Behavioral ecology, sociobiology, and evolutionary theory comprise the primary analytic sources for strategic modeling. Salient component theories are kin selection (Hamilton, 1964), reciprocal altruism (Trivers, 1971; Axelrod and Hamilton, 1981), parental investment, sexual selection, and mating systems (Trivers, 1972; Emlen and Oring, 1977), aggression and social dominance (Parker, 1974; Popp and DeVore, 1979), foraging theory (Charnov, 1976), defense against predation (Curio, 1976), the ecology of disease and inbreeding avoidance (Tooby, 1982), and the theory of evolutionarily stable strategies (Maynard Smith and Price, 1973; Maynard Smith, 1982).

Analytic tools for applying and combining these component theories exist in a tentative form. No good review of them exists. Therefore, a preliminary, and by no means exhaustive, list of the principles of strategic modeling may prove useful. At this stage, of course, these are nothing more than heuristic guidelines for inference (a more detailed discussion of strategic modeling in hominid evolution is planned for publication).

1) Individuals are selected to approximate inclusive fitness maximizers.

2) Interactions between individuals are to be analyzed in terms of their inclusive fitness impact on the actor.

3) Any heritable trait that increases the correlation between behavior and strategies for promoting inclusive fitness will be selected for. This correlation is all that is necessary (not any conscious pursuit or knowledge of the strategy). How strategies are incarnated differs widely, and includes morphological traits, reflexes, food and flavor preferences, complex but nonconscious learning mechanisms, and very sophisticated cognitive mechanisms. However, conscious awareness of proximate goals may have contributed to the correlation between fitness and behavior in some species; indeed, for some strategies it may have played an increasing role during hominid evolution.

4) There is no one-to-one correspondence between traits and selection pressures, and there is no fundamental distinction between behavioral and morphological traits. Selection for a trait will depend on all of the fitness components that trait impacts. To take an extreme example, a morphological change that makes locomotion extremely costly will also increase the cost of avoiding inbreeding (for example, winglessness in insects). Lowering the cost of locomotion makes it cheaper to search for less related mates, and therefore is, in part, an adaptation to inbreeding avoidance. A trait is an adaptive compromise to all of its positive and negative fitness consequences.

5) Individuals are selected to be adapted to their individual situation, not simply to their local habitat. This means that they may be facultative strategists (where appropriate) rather than inflexibly committed to the same behavior or morphology.

6) The situational specificity of adaptation depends on the selective history of similar situations. The degree of situational adaptation manifested by individuals will be a matter of a) how common in the species' evolutionary history that situation has been, b) how long (in phylogenetic terms) it has been recurring, and c) how large its fitness consequences are. Organisms will be well adapted to common, important situations, reasonably adapted to common less important conditions and uncommon highly important conditions, but not adapted to uncommon, unimportant situations.

7) To the extent made reasonable by the considerations above, behavioral variation observed within groups, and between groups of the same species initially should be presumed to be adaptive responses

to differences in individuals and local conditions, until accumulated evidence indicates otherwise.

8) Consequently, the tendency to generalize typologically to entire species from individual studies should be dispensed with in primate and hominid behavioral biology. Looking at behavior observed in individual studies as strategic adaptive responses to local conditions frees investigators from the perpetual confusion that arises from the discovery that primate behavior changes markedly at the same site when it is observed over many seasons, or from study site to study site.

9) Selection acts on all categories of individuals, and at each stage of the life cycle. No sex or age group is more "important" others; strategic modeling applies to all categories. The amount of kin and parental investment received, the age of the individual, the amount of prospective direct reproduction left to an individual, and the amount of prospective kin-directed altruism left to an individual, will all influence the intensity of selection on particular age-sex categories (Williams, 1966). However, no age-sex category whose behavior can still have consequences on kin is immune from selection. Therefore, to be complete and accurate, an account of hominid evolution must describe the special adaptations of each age-sex class, and the relation of each to the others. Any account of hominid evolution that concentrates only on males, or only on females, or suggests that any specific age-sex class is responsible for hominid evolution, is defective; both "Man the Hunter" and "Woman the Gatherer" analyses frequently suffer from this problem.

10) For certain social and reproductive behaviors, the favored strategy will depend on the distribution of other behaviors in the population. The prevailing analytic tool for dealing with this is game theory and evolutionarily stable strategies (ESS) (Maynard Smith and Price, 1973). Its application to sex ratio theory is well known (Hamilton, 1967). In hominid evolution such an analysis may be relevant to such issues as how much to hunt versus how much to gather, whether to pursue a high male investment strategy, how much intergroup male coalitional conflict there is, and so on. Hominid groups may not have had one best universally shared behavior pattern, but may have contained multiple alternative strategies over many generations. In fact, multiple strategies, such as complementary male and female foraging patterns, or dominance-subordination behaviors, may depend on each other and evolve together.

11) Despite recent attacks on the adaptationist program (Lewontin, 1979), there are many diagnostic means that can be used to identify likely adaptations. Notwithstanding naive claims to the contrary, all science uses and proceeds by "just so stories," that is, by attempting

to incorporate past events into the framework of established principle. What differs is the rigor with which this is done, how tightly constrained the predictions are, and to what extent their implications are susceptible to falsifying empirical tests. Evolutionary "just so" stories (reconstructions of adaptative patterns) can be extremely rigorous, if they are embedded in a deductive framework from which implications are deduced and tested. Predictions need not be about future events, only about data not yet gathered or analyzed. Predictions about patterns yet to be found in data relevant to hominid evolution can be a primary method of validating various hominid scenarios.

12) Moreover, the aim of reconstruction is not to test the theory of natural selection, but rather to discover past events and species characteristics using the theory of natural selection as an inferential tool. Natural selection is a well-validated theory, and does not require verification in every instance in which it is invoked. In no science is every principle tested every time it is applied. The point of potassium-argon dating is not to test theories of nuclear fission, but to date geological strata assuming the truth of the theory of radioactive decay.

13) Given that natural selection is the major constructive and ordering force in evolution, the initial presumption about a trait is that it is adaptive (i.e., promotes fitness). Some additional diagnostic indicators of adaptation include:

i) the greater the number of genes that contribute to a trait, the more likely it is to have been adaptively patterned since it is unlikely that they could all have become fixed through drift.

ii) the more uniquely derived a trait is, the more likely it is to have been created by natural selection. Such a trait is an indication that genes now present were not present ancestrally. As drift has stochastic properties that probabilistically limit the distance of departure from the ancestral genotype over time, the further away from the common ancestor the traits involved are, the stronger the evidence that the difference was driven by active selective forces.

iii) the more ordered traits are, the more likely they are to have been shaped by natural selection. Stochastic processes will tend to produce random results, not ordered ones. The cumulative probability that a large number of genes that just happen to fit together in an ordered relationship with various environmental variables all attained fixation through drift is extremely slight. Adaptation is also indicated when traits are highly interwoven or interdependent.

iv) the larger a trait's potential impact on fitness-related variables, the more likely it is to have been shaped by selective forces. It can have an effect either because it is costly, or because its consequences are large. The intensity of selection will be a function of the magnitude of a trait's consequences on the various components of fitness, and the size of its cost.

v) variation in heritable traits (or more properly, that subset of heritable variation not explained by frequency dependent selection) is evidence that selection has not been acting on those traits very intensely or for very long.

vi) convergent evolution in parallel conditions is evidence for adaptation.

Therefore, any costly and complex behavior that individuals regularly direct towards others must benefit the actor by enhancing its eventual reproduction, or the eventual reproduction of its relatives. This is particularly true of any complexly patterned, nonhomologous behavior. *The hominid lineage is notable for its large number of ordered, complex, costly, and nonhomologous traits, and the complexity of the genetic basis of these traits.*

14) Systematic deviations from inclusive fitness promotion are the result of phylogenetic lag, phylogenetically rare individual circumstances, competition with coevolving antagonistic organisms, ontogenetic constraint, or intragenomic conflict (Dawkins and Krebs, 1979; Cosmides and Tooby, 1981). Each of these possible explanations, however, has implications that are potentially falsifiable.

15) To be selected for, a trait need not be advantageous under every conceivable potential circumstance. It need only be of benefit *on balance.* This means it must be advantageous more often than not, or that the frequency with which it is advantageous, times the magnitude of the advantage, outweighs the frequency of disadvantage times the cost. Thus, selection for a trait is always against a background probability distribution of ancestral environmental conditions, and cannot be understood when abstracted from this background.

16) For the above reasons, one begins with the methodological presumption that the great majority of significant traits are or were adaptive. Using these traits one tries to construct a coherent description of the organism's system of adaptation. The investigator should attempt to trace the adaptive consequences of a feature. If a sufficient explanation for the feature is not found (and validated), and all of the significant components of adaptation are ruled out, the nonadaptive nature of the feature will become evident. In such a case, the next step is to see how the feature fits in to the larger developmental, phylogenetic, and adaptive patterns of the organism. If a behavior appears to cost the organism, but confer no benefit, the

researcher then looks for a more encompassing system of adaptation of which the feature is an inevitable concommitant. If the feature or behavior under observation appears maladaptive, one investigates to see if, under other more common conditions, the feature might be adaptive, or if under other, rarer conditions, it might be compensatorily highly adaptive. Alternatively, one can investigate for evidence of other conditions that were more prevalent in the past. Finally, one investigates to see if the feature is the product of some sort of ontogenetic or physical constraint on adaptation. Adaptive or not, any feature requires explanation. However, explanations of features through an appeal to nonadaptive aspects of the evolutionary process remain the *weakest and least testable* kinds of explanations. The alternative stochastic processes such as drift and hitch-hiking that are frequently invoked (Lewontin, 1979) are almost unfalsifiable. In any case, despite criticisms of the adaptationist program, characterizations of traits as nonadaptive cannot be supported without the application of the adaptationist program.

17) There is a strong and underemphasized relationship between the psychological (and physiological) capacities of organisms and the adaptive strategies they pursue. There is an enormous gap between knowing what habitat a species occupies, and predicting its social structure and other behaviors. Thus, species that differ in intelligence and communicative ability may also differ in how they respond to the same ecological pressure. The reason why male coalitions for intragroup conflicts are frequent in savanna baboons but absent in Hanuman langurs may be partly due to different levels of and constraints on social cognition in the two groups. Similarly, the emergence of strong male coalitions for intergroup conflict in common chimpanzees may be due in part to their expanded capacity for social cognition.

18) Therefore, as capacities increase or diminish, the fitness and availability of various strategies will change accordingly.

During hominid evolution, intelligence and the ability to communicate expanded enormously, and therefore strategies made possible by intelligence and communication would have appeared or expanded accordingly (cf. Kurland and Beckerman, 1985). This must have had a major impact on almost every dimension of social strategy. For example, if a male can only aggressively punish behavior that takes place in his presence, this will influence where he can travel and what he can prevent. If, by communication, he can discover what has happened in his absence, that behavior can become a point of negotiation. He can deliver threats about what will happen when he is away; he can punish behavior that occurred during his absence. For example, for the first time, paternity certainty can be indicated in his absence, making it possible for males to combine high investment strategies with periods of absence. A male's kin can keep watch for him, and even if they cannot prevent infidelity, the fact that they can report it may deter it. Similarly, large, regulated, and stable coalitions can be formed for intergroup aggression. Sharing in the fruits of cooperative effort can be mediated by communication. Reciprocity can be elaborated over longer periods of time, involve more individuals, and be made to apply to behaviors that take place during an individual's absence.

These new capacities allow the evolutionary elaboration of adaptively patterned behaviors to new levels of sophistication not found in other species. Although some of these behaviors are found only among hominids, they are still susceptible to evolutionary analysis. However, such an analysis will require the development of new theories of social psychology, based on the wedding of game theory to evolutionary principles (Axelrod and Hamilton, 1981; Cosmides, 1985; Tooby, 1985).

19) The interests of different individuals often will be in conflict. Therefore, larger patterns of social behavior are not necessarily optimal for any individual or group of individuals, but rather may be the emergent result of the conflicting interests of interacting individuals. Frequently, therefore, the behavior of an individual cannot be understood in isolation; its behavior will be the mutual result of its interests and the counter-strategies of those with whom the individual is associated.

20) Group processes and characteristics are not selected for in themselves (for example, by group selection), but are the emergent product of dynamic processes taking place at the individual strategic level, and must be analyzed at that level. Thus, intergroup conflict cannot be understood in terms of "benefit to the group", whatever that might mean. Instead, the costs and benefits to the individual actors must be analyzed. Thus, "intergroup hostility" may instead be hostility between different male coalitions (as in chimpanzees), or simply hostility between the dominant male of a group and outside males (as is usual in langurs). "Group" protection from predators in baboons is the defense of some individuals or sets of individuals by others (Strum, 1982). Similarly, infanticide in langurs is carried out by some individuals, in specific circumstances at the expanse of others; hypotheses of "social pathology" posed at the group level have not been productive (Hrdy, 1977). It is necessary to analyze who is acting, who is experiencing the consequences, and the relationship between the two.

21) However, although group level characteristics and processes are the consequences of strategies at the individual level, they can

also operate in feedback as general conditions individuals must adapt to. Thus, male-male hostility and competition among male gorillas has a determinative impact on female strategies, and female foraging patterns and dispersion patterns in space and time are the primary determinants of male strategies in chimpanzees and orangutans (Wrangham, 1979a, 1980). The earlier patterns of individual choices add up to a set of circumstances within which those and other individuals make subsequent choices. Consequently, a hypothesized hominid scenario must not only describe strategies for all of the age-sex classes, but must make certain that *all of the hypothesized strategies are consistent with each other.* As we will discuss, it is not clear whether they are in Lovejoy's model (1981) or the "Woman the Gatherer" models (Tanner, this volume).

22) Adaptation is not an absolute standard, but a relative one. A proposed adaptation or system of adaptations must not only work, but must work better than all identified possible alternative strategies. This is a very useful inferential tool. For example, in modern hunting-gathering peoples, there tends to be a sexual division of labor, where men hunt and women gather. Proponents of the "Woman the Gatherer" hypothesis have claimed that gathering is the major hominid adaptation, and that it is and always has been primarily the activity of women. Hunting is considered to be a minor, supplemental, and late-appearing marginal activity, rather than a major and evolutionarily significant subsistence activity. However, because women gather, we know that men have had, as an available alternative strategy, the possibility of gathering just as intensively. If gathering was the superior subsistence strategy practiced by itself, why didn't men give up the inferior practice of hunting and exclusively gather instead? The fact that they did not strongly implies that for men, hunting was a superior strategy relative to gathering. The converse also applies: if hunting is globally superior, why don't females abandon gathering and hunt instead? Any hominid scenario that posits such a sexual division of labor must explain why gathering is the best strategy for females, and hunting is the best for males. It cannot simply assert that one subsistence pattern or the other is "better", irrelevant of gender and condition. From this principle, one can strongly infer that the gathering hypothesis, for example, is defectively incomplete. In general, any proposed hominid behavioral pattern must be examined with the question *could they be doing something else* that is more adaptive?

23) This form of analysis may be termed *evolutionary psychology* (Tooby, 1985). The psychology of an organism consists of the total set of proximate mechanisms that control behavior. Natural selection, acting over evolutionary time, shapes these mechanisms so that the

behavior of the organism correlates to some degree with its fitness. However, in the lifetime of any particular animal, it is the proximate mechanisms that actually control behavior. If these can be understood, behavior can be predicted exactly; understanding fitness-promoting strategies allows only approximate prediction. Behavior correlates exactly with these proximate mechanisms, but only approximately with the fitness promoting strategies that shaped them. Evolutionary psychology relates explanations in terms of adaptive strategy to explanations in terms of proximate mechanisms. Correct characterization of adaptive strategies gives precise meaning to the concept of function for proximate mechanisms. Reciprocally, a detailed analysis of the proximate mechanisms of a species gives rich insight into the present and past selective pressures that have acted on it.

The traits of modern humans, including their innate psychology, give powerful evidence of the nature of the past. Important clues can be found in such psychological phenomena as: the conditions that foster strong male-female bonds, the potential strength of father-offspring bonds, the pattern and timing of male and female aggression, the psychology of male coalitions and group aggression.

24) The comparative method is a crucial element in strategic modeling. Living species are used as the data base to derive, test, refine, and scale the evolutionary principles that comprise the conceptual model. Although this data base allows the confirmation of deductive principles, such as kin selection, it is also the primary source for empirical principles, which are equally important in inferential research. Certain processes are so complicated that they cannot be conceptually modeled and must be measured directly. These processes involve so many interacting factors, which singly or together are so little understood, that direct observation is still the primary or only method of investigation. For example, the correlates of sexual dimorphism must be studied in this fashion. The ecological factors influencing strategies of foraging, the differential impact of mate competition, the biomechanics of bones, the energetics of locomotion, the nutritional drain of pregnancy and lactation, the possible existence of limiting nutrients, the biochemistry of the detoxification of secondary compounds, the differential impact of predation, and many other factors may all feed into the cross-specific patterns of sexual dimorphism that are observed. Clearly, present knowledge is so inadequate that these patterns are not directly derivable from any existing deductive framework, and the comparative approach is the only method for their investigation.

By following patterns of convergence and divergence among homologous and uniquely derived features, and analogous and non-analogous adaptations, the comparative approach allows some inferences to be made about functional and ontogenetic interdependence (see Wrangham, this volume). By tracing out the patterns of covariance among traits in related and unrelated species, one can tell which traits tend to form adaptive constellations, which traits are functionally incompatible and hence mutually exclusive, which traits may be developmentally linked, and which have little impact on each other. Minimally, if a series of adaptations are all present in the same species, they must be mutually compatible. Moreover, these kinds of data can occasionally allow one to scale relationships mathematically so that quantitative inferences can be made from known species to partially known (e.g., hominid) species. In addition, such studies reveal which kinds of traits are conservative, and which change more rapidly and hence track selective shifts more closely.

Although empirical principles derived from comparative data are useful, they are far from infallible. Empirically derived comparative principles are, first of all, probabilistic. They can be wrong in any specific case, because specific cases may have unique or unusual elements that can alter how functional variables operate on a specific species, making the general relationship inapplicable or misleading.

For example, some have argued (e.g., Zihlman, 1981) that the reduction in canines and canine dimorphism in the hominid line is evidence for a waning of male-male competition, because of the correlation between these two variables among cercopithicines. However, as Darwin first suggested, the functional uses of canines (attack, threat and defense) may have been supplanted by tools (Darwin, 1871). Alternatively, the shift to bipedal posture may have removed the head and mouth from close combat, with the greater striking distance of arms and hands replacing canines as weaponry. As both tool use and bipedalism are drastically increased in hominids, their functional appearance may render generalizations based on other primates inapplicable. This is an example of why, ultimately, empirically derived comparative relationships must be supplemented by (and ultimately subsumed into) functional relationships. With a functional model, the appearance of a unique element can be factored in deterministically.

25) One cannot explain hominid evolution by an appeal to factors that would have equally impinged on other species, especially if the other species had the same pre-adaptations: a theory must explain why we are not our close relatives, the chimpanzees, gorillas, or bonobos. Unique adaptations must be explained by unique factors in an evolutionary lineage. Prospective reconstructions of hominid adaptation must not only be internally coherent, but they must explain what was special about the events that produced the various unique features of hominids: bipedalism, high social and causal intelligence,

language, culture, and expanded sociality. Again, it is not clear whether Lovejoy's hypothesis (1981) or certain versions of the "woman the gatherer" approach have met this requirement.

Prime Determinants, Inference and the Hominid Trajectory

The real power of strategic modeling arises from the fact that species embody *systems of adaptation*. Because the traits of an organism co-evolved and are co-adapted, they constitute an articulated system of features that fit together in an interlocking and constrained fashion; the constrained nature of co-adaptation can provide a sound basis for inference. If some traits are known through paleontological observation, potentially some or all of the others can be worked out as the necessary concommitants of these observed traits, provided the applicable theory of co-adaptation is solidly developed.

Indeed, hominid reconstruction should be treated as a logical puzzle: One starts from what is known, then systematically applies the body of evolutionary knowledge and rules of inference to reconstruct the system of adaptations that characterize a particular hominid species at a certain point in its evolutionary trajectory. This process produces an integrated framework of specific knowledge about hominid evolution within which hypotheses about specific traits can be evaluated. Each hypothesis about a specific trait (hunting, tool use, mating patterns, child care, etc.) is a fragmentary element which, if true, would help comprise the entire scenario of hominid evolution. But such individual elements are impossible to evaluate in isolation; by gathering them together into a larger inferential web, they can be considered together, as part of the system of adaptations. By using behavioral ecology to structure relations among different features, one can investigate the combinatorial patterns that emerge among the hypothesized adaptations, and discern which proposed adaptations fit together and which do not. This process is similar to solving sets of equations (Gaussean elimination). By the simultaneous consideration of the known facts and principles, there may emerge just a single solution, or a limited number of possible alternatives. The more discoveries that are made, and the more vigorously these are milked for constraints and implications, the more unknowns will be filled in, and the range of possibilities will be narrowed.

To understand the sequence of human evolution, we need to characterize each hominid species at a given point in time by its distinctive system of adaptations, expressed in terms of the variables that vertebrate ecology suggests will be evolutionarily significant.

The set of variables necessary to characterize a hominid species is far more extensive than is commonly appreciated. The usual sketch of a few major adaptations (e.g., gathering, hunting, tool-use) is fatally incomplete.

Factors involved in a description of a species' distinctive system of adaptation include diet, foraging strategies, distribution of patch sizes, patterns of secondary compound distribution in dietary items, predation pressure, disease pressure, genetic diversity in disease resistance, locomotion system, costs of locomotion, habitat type, degree of seasonal variation in environmental determinants, weather, body size, nature and magnitude of sexual dimorphism, demographic and life history variables (e.g., age-sex class specific mortality rates, lifespan, interbirth interval, gestation time, dependency period), ranging patterns, female advertisement of fertility, forms of male investment (carrying, predator protection, feeding toleration, provisioning, protection from infanticidal males and females), forms of female investment, kinship structure, mating structure, negotiation patterns, intergroup conflict, group size, group fissioning, coalitions, communication capacities, patterns of food sharing (kin based, dominance-based, extortive, reciprocal, mate-directed), nature of the species-specific social psychology, whether groups are male or female bonded, whether social groups are closed, whether there is cooperative labor in foraging or information, reliability of paternity identification, and how all these factors differ depending on age-sex class.

Major questions that structure the assembly of these factors into a coherent system of adaptation are: In what ways can an individual, in each age-sex class, help or harm other individuals, both kin and non-kin? What age-sex classes are exposed to each other, and under what conditions? What are the nonsocial limiting resources to reproduction (e.g., food, water, sleeping sites) and how do they vary from habitat to habitat and from species to species? What are the exogenous factors (e.g., distribution of food and patch size, predator pressure, disease pressure) that influence fitness, and how does their magnitude vary for each age-sex class? What are the pay-offs for cooperative and coalitional behavior between members of each age-sex class, in relation to these exogenous and social selection pressures? What are the pay-offs for reciprocal exchange among and between members of each age-sex class?

Depending on such factors as diet, resource distribution, locomotion, season, habitat, predation pressure, and phylogenetic constraint, strategically motivated patterns of association and avoidance will produce a local population's distribution of social systems. The goal is to describe a social system in terms of the strategies of the individuals that comprise it, and not just in terms of the physical distribution of age-sex classes. A description based on strategic modeling would provide a foundation for interpreting how a species' system of adaptations can evolve from one structure into another over time and across habitats.

Such factors as those enumerated above (by no means an exhaustive list) all deserve to be considered in characterizing a primate species. Because of the interlocking nature of systems of adaptations, it is to be hoped that such factors can be weighted or separated into those that are prime determinants of a species' system of adaptations, and those that are secondarily determined by these systems. In the interpretation of the fossil record, the function of understanding the relationships of prime determinants to secondary determinants is to be able to infer those prime determinants that cannot be directly assessed from the fossil record on the basis of the measurable secondary factors that may be preserved, and which are tightly regulated by the prime determinants.

The Stages of Hominid Evolution

Before the advent of reliable radiometric dating in the 1960s, it was widely believed that human evolution took place in a brief million year span, rather than in the six to ten million year period currently estimated. Although the vast expanse of time involved in human evolution is now recognized, certain habits of thought shaped by that narrow time frame still survive implicitly in much present day discourse about hominid evolution. Many researchers still compress hominization into a single process, rather than exploring the possibility that it consisted of a large number of discrete stages characterized by sharply differentiated selective forces and adaptive complexes. Hominid models have not yet expanded to fill the time available for human evolution. Although no one seriously argues for the existence of a single "missing link", this phantom makes its covert presence felt in the structure of many other arguments. For example, arguments that attempt to minimize the importance of a factor at one stage (e.g., hunting by australopithecines) have tended to be interpreted as generalized rejections of the importance of that factor at *all* stages of hominid evolutionary history. Similarly, reconstructions of hominid evolution often draw their inspiration from one stage (e.g., Tanner's [1981] description of australopithecine life), yet are treated as generalized accounts of human evolution and modes of life, often including even modern hunter-gatherers. If one recognizes that one is actually involved in a series of reconstructions of *different animal species,* it is easy to see that such generalizations are ill-founded. A feature, such as hunting, that seems to be an inappropriate major adaptation for one chronospecies may be fully appropriate for others.

Both socioecology and the increasingly complete stratified fossil record require that hominid evolution be regarded as a discrete series of branches and stages. In the first place, the discovery that hominids were fully bipedal at 4 million years (Johanson, White, and Coppens, 1978), long before the appearance of the first detectable stone tools, has decoupled Darwin's compelling trinity of bipedalism, tool use, and brain expansion, at least in any simple form, and thereby made bipedalism the original trait requiring independent explanation. Second, the simultaneous and possibly sympatric existence of several hominid species in the 2 million year range is a fact which, by itself, destroys the linear model of human evolution. Morphologically distinguishable coexisting species must have differed in adaptive configuration, as must morphologically different species at different times. Distinct fossil forms are now known to represent species whose constellations of traits diverged sharply from each other and from those of any living animal. The huge cheek teeth, limited cranial capacity, and bipedality of australopithecines is evidence for a family of adaptive modes that are not human and not yet understood.

In response to these discoveries, many researchers view human evolution as a long corridor, where chimpanzees enter at one end and modern hunter-gatherers exit at the other. Modern hunter-gatherer traits, such as language, food-sharing and pair-bonding, are projected backwards towards the ape-hominid common ancestor, who is depicted as a slightly brainy, tool-using chimpanzee. Using these *referential* methods, ancestors are reconstructed with a combination of living ape and human traits—a "Piltdown approach" to behavioral ecology. Forms are often considered to be an intergraded series with australopithecines as a midpoint, half chimpanzee, half hunter-gatherer (e.g., Tanner, 1981). *Homo erectus* and subsequent forms are often depicted as inept or simplified versions of the !Kung San, Hadza, or Mbuti.

Strategic modeling requires a radically different approach to these issues. The landscape of hominid evolution is far richer than the linear, referential view can accommodate; interpolating between the two ends of a "corridor" is seriously misleading. The adaptations and traits of different species do not simply grade into each other, forming a smooth continuum, in which any feature is equally compatible with any other. Because a species' adaptations form a coevolved and coadapted *system*, only some clusters of traits are mutually consistent with each other and are therefore acceptable as models of or hypotheses about a particular extinct hominid or hominoid form. Thus, each extinct form corresponds to a distinct configuration of adaptations, and neither traits nor selection pressures necessarily follow a smooth trend line between earlier and later forms. Extinct hominids, both *Australopithecus* and early *Homo,* display combinations of traits that are not parallel to any living primate, including modern hunter-gatherers; these forms are not usefully analogous to any living animal. An extinct species should not be viewed as a crude, imperfect version of a living form, but as interesting in its own right, just as adapted to its own archaic present as any living animal. Each morphologically distinguishable fossil species needs to be characterized in terms of its distinctive interlocking system of adaptations. Other proposals can be winnowed out as "Piltdown" mosaics of incongruous traits.

Therefore, the task of understanding human evolution becomes the understanding of each of a number of ancestral chronospecies in terms of its habitat and its distinctive system of adaptations. It is not the reconstruction of a single pre-modern mode of life. Each chronospecies corresponds to a stage, and requires the inferential reconstruction of its unique and interlocking constellation of selection pressures, strategies, and morphological traits. Each stage represents different clusters of mutually consistent adaptations, and these in turn correspond (at least) to each morphologically distinguishable chronospecies. Moreover, there may be forms not yet discovered in the fossil record.

A list of the stages requiring characterization includes (at least):

1) the pongid-hominid common ancestor,

2) the hominid common ancestor, putatively an early australopithecine, possibly *Australopithecus afarensis,*

3) the late ancestral australopithecine,

4) the transitional form to *Homo erectus,* possibly *habilis,* or *ergaster,*

5) *Homo erectus,* (possibly divisible into early and late),

6) archaic *sapiens,* if different from late *erectus,*

7) the Neanderthal period ancestral form, and

8) anatomically modern *Homo sapiens.*

To these should be added, secondarily, the non-ancestral branching species: the robust and late gracile australopithecines, European Neanderthals, and any others that can be identified. Knowledge of these species should shed light on ecological competition, phylogenetic constraints, and a host of other factors that would assist the elucidation of the hominid lineage which produced modern humans. Of course, it is important to bear in mind that there are undoubtedly ancestral and branching forms that are yet to be uncovered in the fossil record and will need to be integrated as soon as they are discovered. The gap in the fossil record from 4 to 8 million years ago may uncover several such discrete ancestral chronospecies, which may throw light on the transition to bipedality and the causes of the hominid-pongid split. A similar mystery involves the location and characteristics of the direct precursor to modern *Homo sapiens.*

The estimate of 4 to 5 million years for the hominid-pongid common ancestor (Sarich, 1980) is discrepant with the discovery of fully developed bipedality 4 million years ago, indicating that the molecular clock may need some recalibration. In particular, the probability that a large fraction of protein polymorphism and recombination is driven by parasite pressure implies that substitution rates will differ somewhat depending on the variations in the ecological correlates of parasite load (Tooby, 1982). If this reasoning is correct, the hominid colonization of the savannah habitat and subsequent occupation of temperate areas—habitats freer of disease than forests—would have slowed substitution rates, giving a spuriously late date for the hominid-pongid divergence. Depending on the magnitude of this correction factor (perhaps back to 10 million years), there may well be additional room in the hominid ancestral line for additional chronospecies. Aside from uncertainties in dating the hominid-pongid split, confusion remains about how the split should be treated. The premise that the split was driven by some major new selection pressure is not necessary. The most common kind of speciation is created simply by geographical isolation (Mayr, 1963), and the early phases of hominid evolution may not have been fundamentally different from the early hominoid branches.

The explicit recognition of the existence of numerous stages of hominid evolution opens inquiry into a number of possibilities not usually addressed. In the first place, there may have been many abrupt reversals in adaptive patterns along the hominid lineage. The tacit assumption of continuity between different stages, especially those distantly separated in time, becomes suspect. To look at a chimpanzee diet (as an analog for the hominid-pongid common ancestor) and compare it to a San diet also rich in plant foods, and to infer continuity in dietary constituents in hominid diet is completely unwarranted. Hominid diet may have been initially rich in plant foods, then switched to long periods of intense meat consumption, and then returned to increased plant exploitation, as changing variables shifted the relative value of doing so. Any substantial change in a major socioecological variable may reorganize the relationship of many of the others, causing the pay-offs of other activities to change markedly, and the labile components of adaptive configurations to alter abruptly. For trends to continue, the underlying forces that drive them must also continue. This is not just a logical possibility. In the case of the relative pay-offs of plant foods versus meat, there are a number of changes in underlying determinative variables that are known to have occurred, and are surely relevant. Cooking denatures plant secondary compounds (Rhoades and Cates, 1976), making them more digestible, and so the systematic use of fire (starting at least 500 thousand years ago) would have substantially altered the pay-offs of alternative dietary constituents and foraging efforts, opening up a far broader variety of plant foods to human exploitation. The disappearance of the Pleistocene megafauna would also have changed hunting pay-offs, again possibly dramatically altering diets.

Many such variables have changed over the course of hominid evolution, so that it is to be expected that hominids at various stages would be very different animals, sharply differentiated in at least some of their adaptations even from their direct precursors and successors. Sewall Wright's idea of separate peaks on an adaptive topography (Wright, 1951) helps one conceptualize the trajectory of hominid evolution: a single change in pay-offs or in other variables can make two previously compatible elements incompatible, pushing the whole matrix of adaptations rapidly into a different configuration or adaptive peak, potentially reversing earlier trends, perhaps several times in succession. For this reason (considering the large number of variables regulating adaptation that are known to be different), it is unlikely that *Homo erectus* and even archaic *sapiens* were merely simplified versions of modern hunter-gatherers. For example, the vast expansion in learning and culture changed pay-offs of a whole range of activities and behaviors, and it is surely unlikely that diet and social organization remained uninfluenced by these changes.

The value of adaptations is always specific to their context, and the context of each stage in the hominid lineage, on the basis of known differences in behavioral-ecological variables, is different enough that specific adaptive hypotheses concerning the importance of a given factor in hominization must be evaluated separately for each specific stage. Hypotheses must be linked to discrete stages. Consequently, given this expanded trajectory of hominid evolution, hypotheses (e.g., hunting, gathering) that are often treated as logical alternatives may, in fact, both be correct, but simply apply at different time periods.

All traits present in modern humans must have appeared during some specific ancestral stage, and each trait must be correctly assigned to a stage. We thus know something very powerful about ancestral hominids which the fossil record alone cannot tell us: all innate traits characterizing modern humans evolved sometime in the past, in association with the morphological traits that we can directly observe. One profitable inferential exercise would be to take a trait known to characterize modern humans, hypothetically assign it to a particular ancestral stage, and then reason what consequences that introduced trait would have on the system of adaptations of that ancestral stage.

ANALYZING ZOOLOGICALLY UNUSUAL FEATURES OF HOMINID ADAPTATION

The zoologically unprecedented characteristics of humans require explanation consistent with modern evolutionary biology. These unique features of human life are not minor and incidental, but lie at the heart of our adaptive system. Consequently, the most telling test of hypotheses about hominid evolution is whether they provide an explanation for these divergent properties. Explaining how hominid systems of adaptation propelled the emergence of evolutionary novelty rests on interrelating the prime determinants of primate behavioral ecology to our unusual traits. To deal with human uniqueness in a principled way, these elements must be fitted together into novel but lawful patterns.

Such explanations should not be post hoc: novel features should emerge naturally as an inextricable part of the process of hominization rather than as forced adjuncts of a scenario. Powerful selection pressures were required to drive the hominid lineage along so differentiated an adaptive path: any analysis that makes us appear just like other animals is unlikely to have addressed the biological reality underlying our unusual trajectory. Close strategic analysis of these divergent features in terms of their socioecological meaning and consequences should transform the problem of human uniqueness from an imponderable mystery to a sophisticated but straightforward problem in evolutionary biology.

Zoologically unique hominid divergences include the following properties:

1) the ability to attain fitness goals through complexly organized, situationally-tailored, instrumental sequences of behavior;

2) unparalleled cognitive models of changing aspects of the world (high causal intelligence);

3) the ability to communicate these models of the world through language;

4) unmatched learning abilities, including skill acquisition;

5) an unparalleled degree of tool manufacture, variety, and use;

6) a vast expansion in cultural transmission and interindividual involvement in the creation and maintenance of information;

7) unprecedented development in the frequency and degree of reciprocity and the variety of its manifestations;

8) unparalleled degree of negotiation, intercontingent behavior, and social exchange;

9) quantitatively and qualitatively divergent patterns of food manipulation, including collection and transport, extensive processing and preparation, storage and sharing;

10) an increased division of labor between sexes;

11) far larger and more structured coalitions, including bisexual, female, and especially male coalitions;

12) a high degree of male coalitional intergroup aggression (war);

13) the controlled use of fire;

14) a set of psychological mechanisms regulating an expanded system of kin-directed behavior, manifesting situation-appropriate kinship systems:

15) mating negotiation and exchange, probably consisting of wife exchange among groups, or at least kin involvement in mate selection and the attendant intercontingent sequelae.

Hominid divergences from the apes include the following zoologically nonunique features:

1) bipedality;

2) situation-appropriate, intensive male parental investment and an increase in female parental investment;

3) a unparalleled degree of hunting and meat consumption;

4) a change in life history correlates: an extension of lifespan, an increase in the period of investment in offspring, a marked increase in the altriciality of human young;

5) an expansion of ecozones occupied, from tropical woodland and forest into savannah areas, but eventually including every other terrestrial ecozone;

6) concealed ovulation coupled with continuous sexual receptivity.

The Human Penetration of the Cognitive Niche

The following section considers the hominid trajectory by exploring how these divergent features interact with the prime determinants of primate adaptation.

A significant fraction of any species' environment consists of constantly coevolving organisms; fitness gains by one species frequently occur at the expense of other species that are preyed upon, defended against, or parasitized (Van Valen, 1973). This is the Red Queen view of adaptation: species coevolve in antagonistic dynamic relationships. All food items (except such items as fruits whose seeds reqire dispersal) are parts of organisms whose fitness is antagonistically related to that of the forager. In order to survive, both plants and prey animals depend on an array of defenses to inhibit or prevent consumption. Because these defenses are genetically based, the rate at which they can change is relatively slow: within a lifetime, they are fixed defenses. Any balance that is maintained occurs because both attack and defense take place in evolutionary time; moreover, attacks are limited in innovation by the fact that every intervening increment must be advantageous to the attacker.

Humans have made a unique and major innovation in this co-evolutionary relationship—an innovation that is our most distinctive characteristic. The defenses of plant and animal prey species can be circumvented by "surprise" attacks, attacks that consist of many novel and discrete manipulations, evolutionarily unprecedented actions that prey defenses are not equipped to repel. Goal-oriented actions by humans, shaped to suit the particular situation, constitute surprise attacks. We accomplish this by conceptually abstracting from a situation a model of what manipulations are necessary to achieve proximate goals that correlate with fitness. These highly orchestrated and intricate situation-specific sequences of behavior are cognitively organized.

The core of our zoological distinctiveness is our entry into this *cognitive niche*. By entering it, humans have made available to themselves thousands of new plant and animal prey species. Burrowing animals, underground storage organs, nuts, seeds, bone marrow, birds, fish, mollusks, tool accessible nests, plant foods whose toxins or other inhibiting secondary compounds can be neutralized through processing or cooking, quick animals that must be ambushed, animals whose capture requires close cooperation, tools, or intelligent trickery—all are made accessible by the ability to perform appropriate learned or invented manipulations. The rapidity with which cognitively guided manipulations can circumvent genetically fixed defenses in prey species accounts for the surge in extinctions that have accompanied the evolution and spread of humans into new habitats.

Not only are thousands of new items opened by cognitively guided manipulations, but expanded cognitive abilities also allow humans to adopt flexible solutions to a wide array of other adaptive problems. At the core of this lies a causal or instrumental intelligence: the ability to create and maintain cause-effect models of the world as guides for prejudging which courses of action will lead to which results. Because there are an infinitely large number of possible sequences of behavior (of which the overwhelming majority are maladaptive) "behavioral flexibility" is an insufficient characterization of our innovative adaptive pattern. Our cognitive system is knowledge or information driven, and its models filter potential responses so that newly generated behavioral sequences are appropriate to bring about the desired end. Of course, exploration, trial and error, and feedback are essential to the system, but, by themselves, they are inadequate to construct or maintain it.

Viewed this way, many other zoologically anomalous features reveal themselves to be aspects of the cognitive niche. Tool use is manipulation of objects instrumentally; skill acquisition is the perfecting of the cognitive tools necessary to bring about successful, situation-specific manipulations. It is no accident that language coevolved with or followed upon these cognitive innovations; language is different from other animal communication systems in that it allows the exchange of model-based information referring to cause-and-effect categories. This vastly increases the efficiency of occupying the cognitive niche, by drastically reducing the costs of information. The individual is no longer limited by the models he can construct himself, or the information he directly observes. This also means that a social animal occupying the cognitive niche is greatly favored: a useful piece of knowledge or a model innovation can benefit not just the individual, but all of its kin and descendants for generations, adding a huge pay-off to counterbalance the risks and costs of exploration. This social dimension to the cognitive niche constitutes the basis for culture, which is the transmission between individuals and generations of the information necessary to pursue fitness in a particular social and ecological habitat. Finally, the radiation of humans into all terrestrial habitats is also a product of entering the cognitive niche. The liberation of fitness goals from environment-specific, behavior-controlling cues means that novel manipulations can be manufactured to promote fitness in new and differing habitats. Human evolution involved the selection of psychological mechanisms that turned out to be general solutions to local adaptive problems, allowing us to spread beyond our habitat of origin.

Since such abilities would be favored for many kinds of organisms, why did hominids evolve them and not others? First, an animal must not only know what manipulations to make, it must also be able to make them. The existence of hands that are dexterous in their manipulation of objects is a necessary precondition, limiting the possibilities to certain primates, especially the great apes. Numerous other factors, such as binocular color vision and a certain minimum body size are also probably important. Certain neural preadaptations are necessary, no doubt, but at the present state of neuroscience, such assertions remain vague and unhelpful.

Since the great apes have all of these preadaptations, why did they not develop along hominid lines? Chimpanzees, and probably all of the great apes, have significant cause-and-effect-oriented cognitive abilities that parallel in embryonic form those that developed in the hominid lineage. One possible answer is bipedalism; more sophisticated manipulations are possible if the animal can assemble in one place materials from different locations. Moreover, the results of such manipulations are more useful if they can be removed from the site of manipulation (for many reasons: safety, sharing, access to other nonmoveable things such as water, further processing, etc.). If bipedality evolved in the hominid line for some independent purpose (such as monitoring predators on the open savannah), then it would provide a factor that differentiated us from the apes.

Life in a social group greatly enhances the pay-offs and reduces the cost of information seeking. This could explain why gibbons, siamangs, and orangutans—solitary primates— did not more fully enter the cognitive niche. A third possibility involves the ratio of the costs of added cognitive abilities versus the increased pay-offs. The brain is a nutritionally and metabolically costly organ (Martin, 1983). To justify the marginal cost of increasing its size, the marginal benefit must be correspondingly high. It may be that for brain expansion to pay off, it must increase access to very nutritionally rich sources of food, such as meat. Open habitats are far more meat productive than tropical forests, and it may be that occupation of the meat-rich savannah is what differentiated hominids from the forest-bound apes. The role of meat may go beyond its production of calories: the constituents of the brain require essential fatty acids, which may prove to be the real limiting factor made available by meat.

Entering the cognitive niche is a matter of degree: reaching our present level of cognitive abilities and flexibility of behavior required several million years. As cognitive abilities grow, broadening the range of possible food sources and habitats, radiation into the range of newly opened niches is to be expected. Modification and perhaps specialization of the digestive tract and dentition to take advantage of these new food sources provides an explanation for the hominid radiation that took place two to three million years ago separating hominids into several different "specialists" (e.g., meat specialists, underground storage organ specialists, or perhaps "habitat specialists"). This intermediate hominid radiation would have been ended when one diverging branch advanced far enough into the cognitive niche that its general solution to local adaptive problems proved superior to the specialists.

PRIMATE MODELS FOR HOMINID EVOLUTION: THE STATE OF THE ART

The articles in this volume provide an excellent cross-section of the state of hominid modeling. It appears that most (though not all) of the ingredients required to reconstruct hominid behavioral evolution are at hand, and that cooperative efforts towards their integration would bring substantial results. In what follows, we will attempt to show how the injection of even a few considerations drawn from strategic modeling can assist evaluation of the contributions in this volume, as well as of several prominent scenarios of hominid evolution drawn from other sources.

The State of Hominid scenarios

Woman the Gatherer. The advocacy of the "woman the gatherer" model by Tanner, Zihlman, and others (Tanner and Zihlman, 1976a; Tanner, 1981; Zihlman, 1981; Tanner, this volume) has offered a healthy corrective on key issues in hominid evolution. The model proposes that the key element in the pongid-hominid split, and the prime mover in the process of hominization, was the gathering of plant foods with tools—then as now, predominantly a female activity. Facts and beliefs that have lent weight to this hypothesis are:

1) the diet of our primate relatives (and hence presumably that of our pre-hominid ancestors) consists very largely of foraged plant foods;

2) early quantitative reports on the San and several other relict tropical hunter-gatherer groups indicate that 50–70% of the diet comes from gathered plant foods (Lee and DeVore, 1968);

3) hominid bipedality significantly antedates the first identifiable stone tools;

4) in evolutionary terms, all members of the population are important, and that in terms of their "contributions" or participation in the evolutionary process, females are as important as males; and finally;

5) the model is congruent with the social and intellectual climate engendered by feminism, with its vigorous advocacy of the importance of women in all areas, and its emphasis on the ubiquity of male biases and pretensions.

The emergence of this viewpoint has had widespread effects on paleoanthropology. It has not only contributed to the growing trend towards the balanced investigation of both sexes, which is essential to the creation of an accurate picture of hominid adaptation, it has also added impetus to the movement toward quantitative analysis of hunter-gatherer foraging and the role of gathered foods, as well as increased scrutiny of diet as a prime determinant in hominid evolution (see also Sussman, this volume).

Despite these valuable contributions, strategic modeling of the primary elements involved indicates serious problems with the gathering hypothesis, at least as articulated. Its premises and implications do not cleanly mesh with the principles of behavioral ecology. First, it fails genuinely to confront optimal foraging theory with the reality that males do, in fact, hunt. Given that members of each sex would pursue strategies that are the most productive, and if gathering is the most productive activity, why don't males gather (more than they do)? There is no constraint whatsoever on their doing so. On the other hand, the reciprocal question, *why don't females hunt* (more than they do), has a ready answer. Throughout most adult hunter-gatherer females' lifetimes, they are pregnant, lactating, and/ or burdened with dependent offspring. Although there are situations in which they could (and do) hunt (Estioko-Griffin and Griffin, 1981), their ability to engage in the behavior, and profit from learning and maintaining the necessary skills is far less. Also, because of male-male competition, males are larger and stronger than females, and more experienced in aggression and weapon use. Other things being equal, many aspects of hunting are less costly for males to engage in than females. Conversely, it should be more advantageous for frequently burdened females to acquire the skills to allow them to exploit sessile and harmless food resources. Such division of labor exploits both dimensions of the same terrain, allows for complementarity of nutrition between plant and animal sources, and smooths out the risk that complete dependence on irregularly captured game animals, or seasonal plant foods produces (Lee, 1979). Regardless, to be coherent, a theory of hunter-gatherers must account for why it is optimal for males to hunt and females to gather.

There are numerous other major zoological features of the human system of adaptations that "woman the gatherer" models do not predict or account for. Because plant collecting by females is so continuous with great ape behavior, there is little in such a model to explain differences between humans and the great apes. Among the great apes (and other primates), females forage for plant foods with their dependent offspring. Although tools and carrying devices make foraging easier, this improvement seems insufficient to be the major cause of changes in the hominid lineage (or, indeed, explain why the great apes did not follow the hominid trajectory). There is no explanation for increased male parental investment (MPI), for human altriciality, for the readiness with which males form male coalitions, for the frequency of agnatic kin-based coalitions, or for the ease with which humans penetrate habitats without substantial exploitable plant resources. Such models provide no persuasive selective advantage for why females would bring plant foods back to feed parasitic males. There is little to explain the hypertrophy of reciprocity and sharing. Other primates rarely share plant foods, because: 1) it is unlikely that many plant foods aside from nuts could, before the advent of cooking, repay the bioenergetic costs of collecting and carrying; 2) the realities of differing aggressiveness and formidability lead to the frequent expropriation of laboriously acquired foods (such as tubers), causing labor inputs to be limited to what can be readily consumed by the laborer; 3) extra high quality plant foods rarely occur in quantities that are substantially greater than can be consumed by the foraging group—when they do, it is more efficient (and less burdensome) to carry information about the location back to others.

Woman the gatherer models have offered no cogent treatment of male competition for mates. In systems where males associate with females in groups, and where males invest little in offspring, selection pressures act to create intense male-male competition and sizeable sexual dimorphism. The reduction in sexual dimorphism observed across the hominid lineage undermines the assumption that MPI is low. The assumption of low MPI contradicts the conclusion that social relations are gentle and egalitarian within and between sexes. Taking the two cases of common chimpanzees and gorillas, where male investment (except perhaps in the form of protection from other males) is minimal, one finds them anything but peaceful or egalitarian (Wrangham, 1979a, this volume). Chimpanzees sexually compete through aggressive male coalitions, and in gorillas, infanticide and protection from it are pervasive features of the social system. Suggestions of male kin remaining with female kin (e.g., Tanner, this volume) contradict knowledge that inbreeding avoidance reduces intersexual kinship associations through forcing transfer, especially among long-lived animals (Tooby, 1982). There is no recognition of the nature and impact of intersexual negotiation (except female choice): of the threat of infanticide (as in gorillas or bonobos, [Wrangham, this volume]), of the possibility of meat provisioning, of the possibility of special relationships (as in baboons, [Smuts, 1983; Strum and Mitchell, this volume]), or even of the effects on females of intergroup male aggression (as in chimpanzees). In short, although females (and males) undoubtedly have gathered plant foods from the earliest times, this single component of hominid behavior seems wholly insufficient to account for the major features of hominid evolution, certainly in its later phases. Many of its proposed correlates do not make sense in terms of the basic elements of behavioral ecology.

If the "gathering hypothesis" characterization of the social life of hominids is modified to be brought in line with ecological principles, the great sexual dimorphism of the australopithecines is consistent with some of its major tenets. It is possible that *A. robustus* is an exemplar of "woman the gatherer" (but if so, its social system would more likely resemble that of gorillas). It is unlikely that *H. erectus* or any known variant of *H. sapiens* is such an exemplar.

Pair-bonding and the Lovejoy hypothesis. Lovejoy (1981; Johanson and Edey, 1981) has recently advanced a scenario for hominid-pongid divergence that invokes pair-bonding and male provisioning as the prime movers. He argues that the key hominid innovation was a discontinuous increase in MPI in the form of males provisioning their mates and young with collected plant foods. The associated mating system was monogamous, and carrying and provisioning behavior brought about the transition to bipedality. Lovejoy's effort is valuable for two reasons: 1) its attempt to introduce principles from evolutionary ecology to organize our understanding of hominid evolution, and 2) its focus on behavioral innovation (in this case) MPI as an important factor in human social life. Unfortunately, Lovejoy's analysis is inconsistent with several branches of modern behavioral ecology including life history theory, mating theory and the modern understanding of levels of selection (he implicitly invokes group selection). Although he has borrowed some key concepts from ecology (most notably the concepts of r and K selection (MacArthur and Wilson, 1967; Pianka, 1970), his application of them is seriously at variance with their valid use and meaning. He argues that the apes are somehow caught in an orthogenetically driven K-strategist cul-de-sac, from which hominids escaped by their innovation of monogamous MPI through bipedal carrying of collected plant foods. Supposedly, this increased "reproductive rates".

Fundamentally, Lovejoy appears to confuse issues at the heart of the r and K strategy distinction: net reproductive rate versus maximal intrinsic rate of increase in a competitive vacuum. The very long term net reproductive rate of any persisting species, r-strategist or K-strategist, must be very close to 1 (otherwise it will either become extinct or fill the universe), so a position on the r-K spectrum does not refer to how successful a population is at expanding its numbers, except locally. Instead, the r-K spectrum refers to how much evolutionary time a population spends either far below or near K, the carrying capacity of the environment. In r-selected species, the population fluctuates sharply, whereas in K-selected species the population is relatively stable. As concepts, r and K selection are used to make sense of certain types of correlated life history variables: r-selected species are species that are subjected to repeated and intense pulses of density independent mortality, and so are often well below the carrying capacity of the environment. The correlates of r strategy are lax or reduced intraspecific competition, rapid development, early reproduction, high rate of increase, small body size, and short lifespan. K-selected species tend to hover near carrying capacity, and mortality is accordingly mostly density dependent. As a result, the major selection pressures tend to be the results of intraspecific competition, resulting in slower development, delayed reproduction, larger body size, repeated reproductions, and greater parental care (Pianka, 1970). Such distinctions are more meaningful when applied to species that are more sharply differentiated in terms of life history variables than are apes and humans. Lovejoy presents no basis for believing that density independent mortality struck hominids more frequently than other hominoids, and judging by the correlated attributes listed above, humans and hominoids appear very similar, with humans being, if anything, the greater K-strategists. Finally, once all exogenous limiting factors are removed, there is little evidence on whether apes and humans do have different maximum intrinsic rates of increase. Many of Lovejoy's other assertions about life history are also inconsistent with current life history theory (Stearns, 1976).

Leaving such issues aside, however, the major inadequacy of Lovejoy's formulation involves his treatment of mating systems. He correctly relates monogamy and MPI, and the existence of extensive MPI among modern humans does argue for its emergence at some stage in hominid evolution. However, mating systems are best treated as dependent variables, driven by other ecological factors, rather than as independent determinants themselves. The onset of substantial MPI would require some combination of the following: 1) a reduction in the relative profitability of investing energy in competition for additional females (which argues for the absence of a female-based social group); 2) certainity of paternity (which argues for males and females foraging together); and 3) an increase in the efficacy of MPI (which argues for some new and concentrated food source, not utilized previously, with which males can efficiently provision the mother or feed the offspring). Lovejoy's model does not deal convincingly with any of these issues. He explicitly rejects provisioning with meat, the only type of food that mammals regularly use to provision young. Carnivore provisioning of females and/or young is widespread, and meat is one of the few foods primates share (Strum, this volume). Although other forms of food investment are logically possible, they must fit the requirement that they be energetically efficient, as compared to the costs and benefits of competing for females. It is unclear what vegetable foods meet these criteria, although very large underground storage organs are a possibility. However, even among modern hunter-gatherers, small quantities of favored food items are usually consumed on the spot; only large quantities of food (meat or items such as mongongo nuts among the !Kung in season) are brought back to be shared. It seems likely from these considerations that intense male parental investment through provisioning awaited the onset of more intensive hunting practices.

Finally, Lovejoy's assignment of monogamy to the earliest phases of hominid evolution is inconsistent with the realities of australopithecine sexual dimorphism (see also Crockett, this volume). Gibbons and other monogamous species exhibit the least sexual dimorphism (there are also primates, such as *Brachyteles*, that are monomorphic but not monogamous [Milton, 1985]). Moreover, although not impossible, the existence of social groups within which there are stable monogamous pairs is very rare in the primate world (Kinzey, this volume). When females gather into social groups, selection pressures for intense male-male competition become great. Gibbons are monogamous, but manage this sexual exclusivity through the absence of a larger social group. However, even solitary females are no guarantee of male investment, as the case of organutans demonstrates.

Home bases, food sharing, and scavenging. Isaac (1978a, b) has been the most eloquent advocate of what might be called the dual foraging and exchange model of hominid evolution. He and others originally interpreted finds from the rich East African fossil and archaeological sites of Plio-Pleistocene hominid activities as evidence for 1) food sharing; 2) home bases as centers for food exchange and processing; 3) tool use; 4) meat consumption based on some combination of hunting and scavenging; and 5) bipedal transport. Females were assumed to have gathered plant and other collectable foods, males to have acquired meat; individuals met at home bases for the exchange of food items in a sex-based division of labor and reciprocal exchange that is similar to the practices of modern hunter-gatherers. The lack of evidence for plant foods and plant collecting tools is, as is customary, attributed to preservational bias in the fossil record.

More recently Isaac and others have begun to entertain a wide range of alternative hypotheses about the accumulations of tools and bones in these early sites; some of these alternate scenarios bear little resemblance to the campsites of living hunter-gatherers (e.g., Isaac 1983a, 1983b, 1984; Potts, this volume). Indeed, one of the problems with the earlier formulations was that they hypothesized behavior so similar to that of contemporary hunter-gatherers that it left unexplained the rise of many distinctively human traits, traits which (in this view) took place during stages that preceded the period the model depicts. Additional models of earlier stages must be added. Also, this approach is more a description of behavior than an analysis of the selection pressures that shaped it. These pressures require more precise characterization.

Food collection and sharing is not, *per se,* advantageous. In fact, it is rarely practiced in the animal world. Food sharing requires explanation because the forager is laboring to collect and transport food he or she will not consume: for this to be advantageous, the return must exceed the cost. Either other food or equal value must be returned at the time (exchange) or later (reciprocity), something else of equal or greater value must be provided (e.g., protection or sexual access), or sharing must sufficiently benefit offspring (provisioning) or kin.

Why share food? Each type of answer imposes certain assumptions about the nature of the social system, which should be spelled out. In a richly negotiative social life, collected and transported food represents one kind of good that can be used in a large variety of ways. Provisioning of young is not exactly food sharing, and does not bring adults together (except mates or kin). If the force involved is kin selection, cross-sex food sharing will be more limited, since adult members of different sexes are pulled apart by inbreeding avoidance and transfer. Adults will most often maintain relations with kin of the same sex, and if the sex ratio of transfer is heavily biased, one sex may be frequently separated from most of the close kin of both sexes. As a result, one would expect one sex to be more cooperative than the other. Food provisioning based on males bargaining for mating opportunities from females is possible, but does not explain female food sharing with males (if any). Within and between sex reciprocation constitutes another kind of force: in this case, exchange is based on shifting marginal values of different kinds of food to different individuals at different times. However, in this case, one must explain why other primates do not engage in such exchanges. Perhaps a diet based on both animal and plant foods is superior to a diet based on either alone. Additional reasons for "sharing" involve the avoidance of aggression, and extortion (Moore, 1984). However, such expropriation, if widespread, selects against foraging for more than the forager can consume himself. In short, although the elements proposed are plausible, they need to be assembled into a strategic model of an entire social structure, and questions about what forces shaped food sharing and exchange need to be more fully addressed: how do males compete for mates? do they invest? how would females gain sufficient resources for reproduction? why would they gather more than they needed? An account of how hominids evolved to such a stage must also be provided.

We entirely agree with Potts' (this volume) lucid and cautionary arguments about the possible misuse of analogies between individual modern primate species or modern hunter-gatherers and extinct hominid species. He argues that there is evidence indicating that extinct forms were morphologically unlike any living primate, therefore many adaptations of archaic hominids were also undoubtedly unique. He also points out that many widely accepted parallels between modern hunter-gatherers and archaic hominids may fail to capture the unique adaptive syustems of those extinct animals. In support of this contention, he advances an imaginative alternative interpretation of the Plio-Pleistocene archeological sites that for the main evidential base for the home base and food sharing scenario. Potts (1984b, this volume) proposes that instead of home bases, the early Olduvai sites functioned as "stone caches", that is, storage locations where stone tools and tool making materials too heavy for regular transport were deposited, brought from more distant sources of raw materials. Parts of animal carcasses, either scavenged or from hunts, were transported to these stone caches, where they were slaughtered or otherwise processed. According to this view, an individual hominid or hominid group established many such caches within its range, so that when they opportunistically acquired animal tissues, they could bring them to the tools for processing. Therefore, "home base" is not a necessary conclusion based on the presently available evidence. Moreover, the evidence for frequent carnivore exploitation of these faunal remains makes it unlikely that the more vulnerable members of hominid groups (i.e., children, females, the sick and old) occupied these locations as home bases.

The most valuable aspect of Potts' discussion is his recognition that if Plio-Pleistocene hominids were hunting and/or scavenging, they would be engaged in intensive direct and indirect competition with carnivores, and that if the processing sites were also home bases they would be very unsafe ones, particularly for dependent young. The evidence for repeated attraction of carnivores to these sites argues that they are not home bases. However, this does not mean that there were no home bases, that is, occupation sites where a social group can rejoin and exchange provisions. In fact, the threat that attraction of large predators creates provides a rationale for separate processing sites. As Potts points out, these sites would serve as processing centers where stone tools and associated materials too heavy to be continually carried could be cached. When animal tissues are acquired, they can be transported to the tools required for their processing. These sites would also function as garbage dumps, where the residue that attracts carnivores can be abandoned. The home base or core social group would be located some safe distance away (upwind). As Potts points out, modern hunter-gatherers, defended by fire and better weapons, have the leisure for more efficient and more complete processing of large kills. Earlier less formidable hominids may have been forced to more hit and run hunting and slaughtering tactics. If carnivores provided a significant threat to such hominids, group size might have been at a premium, not only for social hunting but also for social defense of successful kills and social transport of larger kills to rapidly vacated processing sites. Finally, Potts' hypothesis needs to be considered in the light of a completed social structure: in this case, that of intergroup relations. If stone tools and materials are scarce and valued resources, how can this be reconciled with the possibility of intergroup conflict, or even of overlapping ranges? The question of how members of such a social group would protect their labor and effort needs to be addressed.

The discovery of these sites has raised an important issue: What proportion of hunting versus scavenging did Plio-Pleistocene hominids engage in? Perhaps spurred by the increasing popularity of the gathering hypothesis, some researchers are skeptical that the Plio-Pleistocene archaeological and faunal assemblages do, in fact, indicate hunting. They propose scavenging as the major source of whatever animal tissues were in the early hominid diet (e.g., Shipman, 1985).

This hypothesis can be evaluated by subjecting it to ecological principle. The ecology of predation and scavenging makes it unlikely that "scavenging" is an adequate characterization of our ancestors' major subsistence patterns. In the first place, due to their position on the food chain, large ranges are required to support predators, and consequently, in any specific area kills by large predators are rare. Scavenging as a form of subsistence is dependent on what is left over (often, very little) from such rare kills after the predator has finished. Add to this intense competition with micro-organisms, insects, avians, and mammalian carnivores and scavengers (not to mention the returning predator or its kin). The ability of avian scavengers to scan large areas from a great height, and to escape readily when threatened, make scavenging a feasible mode of subsistence for them. Micro-organisms have their own defenses (Janzen 1979), which rapidly render carcasses toxic, disease-ridden, or otherwise dangerous to vertebrate competitors. Specialized vertebrate scavengers have dietary adaptations which, to some extent, counteract these dangerous aspects of rotting meat. Moreover, hominid competition for such remains would be actively dangerous: most mammalian scavengers are themselves predators. Active scavenging would continuously lead hominids to converge on the same resources as those dangerous animals. To compete for meat against the formidable predators who killed it, and the large and/or social scavengers who otherwise exploit such resources indicates a substantial measure of aggressive formidability not well captured by the phrase "timid". Even if scavenging opportunities are imagined to be limited to the even rarer occasions when kills have been abandoned by the predator(s) and have not yet been discovered by other scavengers, such behavior continually courts danger. The older the meat, the more dangerous and unwelcome it would be to the less well defended members of hominid groups. Given the possible costs, avoidance rather than exploitation might be the expected behavior.

Scavenging as a niche is a specialized and competitive one. Observed primate behavior testifies to this: many kinds of primates have been exposed to abandoned kills throughout their evolutionary history as an occasional opportunity, but they very rarely avail themselves of dead carcasses (DeVore and Hall, 1965; Strum, 1981). Instead, they tend to limit their meat consumption, with few exceptions, to animals that they themselves have killed. Even modern humans do not seem to scavenge much, despite the fact that the dangers posed by parasites and toxins can be neutralized by cooking. Modern hunter-gatherer practices would seem to set an upper boundary on scavenging as a hominid activity.

In short, those who propose that hominids acquired most of their meat through scavenging are confronted with a number of problems and a major contradiction: if hominids were formidable enough to scavenge, hunting itself was open to them as an option. Why not also hunt, or solely hunt? Hunting only opposes the hunter to game animals, which are intrinsically far less dangerous than predators. The fact that mammals that scavenge also tend to hunt indicates that scavenging without hunting is not a realistic mode of subsistence. Cooperative and manual or tool-based hunting seems far less dangerous, given the possibilities of game driving, ambush, and weaponry. Moreover, slaughtering the freshly killed animal and carrying off the richest and most rapidly consumable parts is far less conspicuous to scavengers who search by scent, and would be less likely to draw them to vulnerable hominids at their home bases. Instead of the opposed concepts of the timid scavenger and the fearless hunter, a fairer characterization would be the timid hunter and the fearless scavenger.

Finally, the archeological finds indicate that meat and bone handling were major activities. For hominids to develop the practice of stone tool manufacture, stone transport over large distances from the sources of raw materials, and localization of recurrent animal processing sites—and that evidence of these activities and the attendant heavy bone accumulation is rich enough to have survived across 2 million years—indicates that these activities were neither marginal nor occasional. Opportunistic scavenging alone with its rarity and risks would not justify the expenditure of the efforts the archeological record indicates. The skills this requires would have also opened the far richer (and less dangerous) food source of direct hunting.

From the evidence of cut marks on large bones (from animals that were presumably too large to have been killed by early hominids), most observers would agree that some opportunistic scavenging of meat occurred. (It is equally true that the remains of smaller, hunted game will have been lost from the fossil record). From the evidence of large, broken bones in association with battering stones, it seems equally clear that scavenged bones were exploited for their marrow content (Isaac 1983b; Binford 1983, 1984). What remains at issue is the frequency and importance of scavenging behavior at the various stages of hominid evolution.

The hunting hypothesis. Numerous authors, beginning with Darwin, have argued for the primacy of hunting in human evolution (Darwin, 1871). The hunting hypothesis was advanced in both sophisticated (Washburn, 1958; Washburn and Lancaster, 1968) and sensational forms (Ardrey, 1961, 1976; Dart, 1953), but has since fallen from favor for cultural reasons (feminist revisionism) and because quantitative analysis of certain modern hunter-gatherer diets indicates that plant foods provide the majority of the calories. The refutation of the hunting hypothesis in its extreme and unsophisticated forms has been regarded by many (Lovejoy, 1981; Zihlman, 1981; Shipman, 1985; Tanner, this volume) as definitive, and with only a few notable exceptions (see especially Hill, 1982), the role of hunting has been discarded or downplayed in recent discussions of human origins. However, the application of strategic modeling to the issue of the role of hunting indicates that, when considered in the context of an integrated social structure, hunting offers certain compelling features that make a reassessment of its role necessary.

Although only a cursory analysis is possible here, the major conclusions are clear: if hunting were a major part of hominid foraging, it would elegantly and economically explain a large number of the unusual aspects of hominid evolution:

Male parental investment: Meat is a richly concentrated food source, well worth transporting and effective for provisioning. The major cost of acquisition and transport can be accomplished by males, making MPI an attractive alternative to additional competition for females Hunting provides a ready explanation for MPI, which gathering vegetable foods cannot plausibly match; it is not efficient to carry low calorie foods large distances. High MPI through food provisioning among mammals is very rare in the absence of carnivory. If MPI is considered to be a major feature of human adaptation, hunting is the most likely explanation for it.

Sexual dimorphism: The reduction in sexual dimorphism across the hominid lineage may be explained through increased male parental investment. As noted, the most bioenergetically plausible form of investment is the provisioning of females and young through the capture and transport of animals.

Male coalitions: As Eisenberg (1981) and others have pointed out, the availability of large game animals has selected, among the carnivores, for social hunting. The degree of human coalitional behavior and capacity for extended cooperation represents a phenomenon requiring explanation, and social hunting provides one major plausible explanation. Any explanation of the elaboration of the cognitive and motivational substrate for cooperation and coalitions must posit recurring situations with major economies of scale and returns to cooperation of additional individuals. The only alternative (but not mutually exclusive) explanation is intergroup aggression and defense, as in chimpanzees.

Reciprocity, sharing, and social exchange: There is little limiting nonhuman primates from engaging in extensive reciprocal relations except the relative rarity of items and actions for exchange. Reciprocal altruism is far greater in humans than in any other animal. Meat, unlike vegetable foods, comes in discrete quantities: an entire animal is either captured or lost. Moreover, the size of the animal pursued depends more on what opportunities present themselves than on the degree of hunger of the hunters. Vegetable foods, on the other hand, come in more continuously graded quantities, and the quantity gathered is more directly related to the energy expended and the amount needed. As is well recognized, the variability in hunting success, and the fact that meat comes in chunked quantities often in excess of what the capturers can readily consume, provides a ready explanation for food sharing, food exchange and risk sharing through deferred reciprocation among the larger social group. It is difficult to find in plant foods plausible attendant selection pressures that could explain these unique hominid psychological capacities. Strum and Mitchell (this volume) report that extensive hunting among baboons in their study has led to occasional meat sharing, a behavior notably unlike the usual reluctance of baboons to share food.

Sexual division of labor: Among primates, males differentially engage in hunting, no doubt because of their greater size and because females are so often encumbered with dependent offspring. As noted, successful hunts frequently leave the hunters with more meat than they can readily consume, and this provides an explanation for food sharing and reciprocation between the sexes. Extreme differentiation of foraging is not feasible without food exchange between males and females. If males changed from occasional to intensive hunting, one consequence would be the extreme sexual division of labor found among humans, with females exploiting the more sessile food sources. Male parental investment through provisioning, exchange of hunted for collected food, and exchange of meat for sexual access all provide possible and mutually compatible avenues for the extreme development of the sexual division of labor characteristic of modern humans. The evolution of this behavior requires no qualitative leaps from other primates: in chimpanzees (Teleki, 1973) and baboons (Strum, 1981; Strum and Mitchell, this volume) estrous females receive disproportionate shares of meat from hunts made by males.

Home bases: For food exchange and meat provisioning to take place between independently foraging subgroups, there must be a home base. Such a meeting area to exchange food makes sense if the supply is irregular: either more (in the case of success) or less (in the case of failure) than the hunters would need for themselves. It is harder to create a plausible model of selective forces that would make this novel behavior pattern adaptive if the only food exchanged is collected plant foods. Other primates, foraging on vegetable foods, have never engaged in extensive (non-meat) sharing, or met regularly at any location to share foods. In contrast, male *anubis* baboons do return to the social group with kills (Strum and Mitchell, this volume).

Stone tool use: The major function of stone tool use appears to be for the slaughter of game animals. The earliest hominid archaeological evidence, dating from over 2 mya, is of slaughter sites and game butchery. Unambiguous evidence of plant processing does not appear until far later, though preservational bias could wholly explain this difference (Isaac 1978a, b).

Brain size: The human brain is an extremely metabolically costly organ (Martin, 1983). It may well be that this cost can only be justified if this expanding hominid brain, in turn, also makes rich new sources of food possible. We know that all carnivores have significantly higher encephalization quotients than do non-predators (Jerison, 1973), that some nutrients found in meat are particularly important to brain tissues, and that these are hard to obtain and metabolically process from plant foods (Crawford and Crawford, 1972).

Pongid-hominid divergence: Many scenarios invoke selection pressures that would have impinged equally on other hominoids, and hence fail to explain the pongid-hominid split. However, open country habitats support far more game animals, so that the opportunities and payoffs of shifting to increased predation are highest on the savannah. The forest dwelling pongids, on the other hand, would have had more fruit and much less game available. Hominids penetrating the savannah would have had increased opportunities and payoffs for hunting, and the requisite size and strength to exploit them. It is notable that the largest open country primates, savannah baboons, have been reported to have the highest rates of hunting for any nonhuman primate (Strum, 1981; Strum and Mitchell, this volume).

Geographical distribution: Human predation as a major component of a flexible subsistence strategy explains in part the ease with which humans have been able to penetrate temperate and even periglacial habitats where plant foods would be scarce during the winter.

The observation that modern tropical hunter-gatherer groups derive only about 40% of their calories from meat has been considered to undermine severely the hunting hypothesis. However, this is a *non sequitur*, unless one implicitly employs typological thinking (humans as either "hunters" or "gatherers") rather than quantitative analysis. Such findings only undermine the naive early view that humans were nearly exclusive hunters. Recent discussions of primates as general "omnivores" have similarly obscured vital distinctions in diet among different primate species (Harding and Teleki, 1981). Even if it were true that throughout human evolutionary history (and not just among modern relict populations living in unproductive habitats) humans derived no more than 40% of their calories from meat, hunting would still have played a crucial role in hominid differentiation. Such a major fraction of the diet is far from selectively insignificant, and such a proportion is far greater than that of any other primate (Harding and Teleki, 1981; Hill, 1982).

The issue is not whether humans eat nothing but meat, or even whether they derive more from vegetable foods than from meat (if this is true), but rather, how much more meat humans eat than does any other primate. In the search for divergent selection pressures on hominids, proportions relative to other primates are what are important. Even fire-using modern human hunter-gatherers eat a large amount of meat. The lowest estimates are far higher than that of any other primate, and most temperate and high latitude human groups live almost exclusively on animal products for most or all of the year. Moreover, total caloric content is far from the sole measure of nutritional importance: the metabolic costs of synthesis and the existence of rate limiting nutrients may make calories the least important factor in optimal health or successful reproduction. To gauge accurately the relative importance of animal foods in the hominid diet, vitamins, trace minerals, essential fatty acids, calcium, and the necessity to balance amino acid proportions all need to be examined by contrasting plant foods with animal foods. Nutritional analysis needs to extend beyond muscle tissues to include the nutritional value of internal organs and blood. At the grossest level, it is impossible for modern humans to live exclusively on uncooked plant foods (e.g., cyanocobolamine deficiency).

The view that plant foods were predominent in tropical hunter-gatherer diet was based largely on the work of Lee and Tanaka (Lee, 1969, 1979, 1984; Tanaka, 1980). Although this view has gained nearly universal acceptance, it must now be revised in the light of new data. Draper's (in press.) report on the !Kung at /Du/da, who do not have access to the copious supplies of mongongo nuts available to the !Kung at Dobe (studied by Lee) indicates that the men at /Du/da invest far more time and effort in hunting, and have far more success. Similarly, Silberbauer's (1981) study of the G/wi, undertaken just prior to Tanaka's study of the same population, reports a much higher rate of hunting success and a far greater dependence on meat. The reports by Draper and Silberbauer are much nearer the qualitative estimates of hunting and meat eating made by the Marshalls among !Kung at Nyae Nyae in the 1950's (Marshall, 1976).

By considering the strategic ramifications of hunting on hominid adaptations in systematic combination, its explanatory power becomes clear. Although there has only been space to sketch in a few major relationships here, even such cursory examination shows that hunting has features that are not only fully compatible with the known outlines of human evolution, but the distinctive properties of hunting predict or account for many (though not all) of the unique features of hominid sociality.

The state of primate-derived models

Although the use of particular primate species as direct analogies for extinct hominids is fraught with problems, primates remain the major source of data from which to derive and test evolutionary principles, explore comparative relationships, and discover the patterns of homology and phylogenetic constraint relevant to human evolution. Moreover, they provide important heuristic examples for the partial exploration of certain issues which cannot be confidently assessed on theoretical grounds alone.

Shared features of African apes. Wrangham (this volume) uses phylogenetic comparison to identify possible conservative features in social organization in an attempt to characterize the hominid-pongid common ancestor. According to this approach, shared features of social organization among humans, gorillas, chimpanzees, and bonobos are likely to have been present in the common ancestor, and can be viewed as part of an "ancestral suite" of behaviors likely to have characterized hominids (and pongids) at any point in their evolutionary history. After reviewing the available data, he concludes that the hominid-pongid common ancestor probably had closed social networks, male-dominated intergroup aggression, female transfer, a lack of alliances among females, and males mating with more than one female.

Wrangham's study constitutes an innovative contribution, and can provide important supplementary evidence to guide hominid behavioral reconstruction. However, as Wrangham himself notes, this approach as applied to these hominoids is in its infancy and adequate data are presently lacking, especially on lowland gorillas, open country chimpanzees, and bonobos. Also, there are a number of pitfalls that must be kept in mind. The first is simply statistical or probabilistic. A clear model of the number of alternatives for a given behavioral category needs to be developed, and the relative independent probabilities of each estimated. Since the number of "independent" taxa compared is small, (four), and the number of possible features that might be held in common are large, the process of exhaustively searching for common features will inevitably produce commonalities, even if features vary rapidly along lineages, and commonalities are produced entirely by chance rather than common ancestry. In Wrangham's list of fourteen characteristics, eight were considered to be similar, whereas six varied. If one simply searched for all possible similarities among, say olive baboons, Japanese macaques, howlers, and humans, one might also generate a list of identified behavioral "homologies", especially if the search list was extensive. Because these probabilities are difficult to quantify, one type of control might be to select several sets of well-studied primate species randomly, and see how many features from the same master list are held in common among each set. Although it is likely that many of the common features Wrangham identified are genuinely produced by phylogenetic factors, and there are independent reasons to believe they constitute accurate characterizations, the cladistic method of demonstrating behavioral homologies would appear more powerful if some kind of control were incorporated.

A second dimension that needs to be closely scrutinized is the method of behavioral categorization. Behavioral categories in primatology have been fluid and often unreliable, and one wants to be certain that behaviors categorized as similar are genuinely unitary phenomena, rather than simply superficially similar. For example, common chimpanzees engage in male coalitional intergroup aggression (Wrangham, 1979a, 1980), whereas intermale aggression among gorillas, usually not coalitional, tends to occur between single males living in single male groups (with rarely more than two breeding males). It is not clear whether gorillas and chimpanzees are equally well categorized as engaging in "intergroup" aggression. To decide such questions, arguments about the appropriate categories for behavioral homology must ultimately be grounded in their functional explanation and evolutionary source: Are they adaptively the same behaviors, shaped by the same selection pressures? Alternatively, are they the consequence of the same ancestrally derived psychological or physiological mechanisms? As powerful a tool as phylogenetic inference is, it must be complemented by a comprehensive strategic model: even the successful reconstruction of the hominid-pongid common ancestor, useful as it is, will leave unanswered one of the most crucial questions of human evolution, *why are we so different from our near relatives?*

The pygmy chimpanzee. Susman's review (this volume) of the behavior and ecology of the pygmy chimpanzee or bonobo (*Pan paniscus*) contains several features relevant to the formulation of a strategic model. Compared to common chimpanzees, bonobos appear to mainfest increased arboreal feeding, smaller day ranges, less time spent feeding, lower levels of aggression, less sexual dimorphism, and higher male-female and female-female affinities. Susman interprets many of the differences between common chimpanzees and bonobos as consequences of differential occupation of open country vs. forest habitats. Morphological differences are attributed to the increased adaptation of bonobos to arboreal feeding, involving modifications for climbing and suspensory activities. Such adaptations may, in fact, preadapt hominoid morphology more closely for the transition to bipedalism. As Susman points out, research on bonobos may help us judge the probability that the earliest hominids were more forest than open country dwelling.

Bonobos are the least well known of any ape, and data from bonobo studies are only beginning to be organized into a picture of bonobo social life. Some morphological and behavioral features have prompted the proposal that they are yet another "best" model of early hominids (Zihlman et al., 1978). Regardless of their use as a single species model, however, bonobos do have features that may prove pivotal in discovering the principles governing male-female relations among hominoids, by providing yet another distinctive configuration of evolutionary variables. These features include nearly continuous sexual receptivity, the resumption of cycling within 1 year of giving birth, semipermanent male-female associations, food sharing, differential male hunting, meat sharing contingent on copulation, and cohesive mixed sex groups. Bonobos provide another case of extended male-female associations developing within the context of a larger social community. From the point of view of modern human sociality, these features are especially striking, and a principled understanding of what forces shaped them in bonobos would go a long way towards explaining many related features in humans. Close comparison between bonobos and common chimpanzees with repsect to social organization may prove to be especially illuminating (see Wrangham, 1985), especially with respect to the strategic structuring of male coalitions, intercommunity relations, and male-female associations.

Baboons.   Strum and Mitchell (this volume) have made an outstanding contribution both in their general remarks about the limitations of direct anaalogies between hominids and living primates, and more especially concerning the use of their baboon studies (*Papio anubis*) to explore a number of crucial issues in hominid behavior. First, reports on hunting by baboons under study, and leading to the highest predation rate recorded for any nonhuman primate. The relative absence of carnivores has two types of consequences: 1) the opportunities for predation among open-country forms are substantial, so that hominid penetration of the savannah markedly changed the possibilities for predation; 2) as far as hunting is concerned, phylogenetic constraint is not an insurmountable pressure: the baboons responded to the direct effects of changed ecological conditions within the short time span of the study by major alterations in the frequency and kinds of hunting practiced; 3) when carnivores are present, the risk to the baboons is significant enough to deter temporary departures from the social group; therefore, anything that reduces the risk of being preyed upon (increased body size, effective coalition formation, improvements in morphological or tool-based weaponry) increases the advantages of hunting; 4) the upper boundary on prey sizes is determined, before the advent of weapons, by the body size of the primate predator; and 5) male-female relations are indeed influenced by hunting: males differentially do the hunting, and they share the kills differentially with estrous females, and/or with females with whom they have special long term relationships.

Strum and Mitchell's chapter also documents their careful construction of a more sophisticated picture of baboon social life, involving the increasing recognition that baboons are sophisticated social strategists, and that aggression is only one dimension of the intricate social negotiation that goes on. Additional dimensions include "friendships" between individual females and males, female buffering of male aggression, meat sharing between males and females, and the importance of social knowledge, social skills, the length of residency, cooperation, and manipulation in the web of intercontingent negotiation that dominates baboon social life. Their valuable observations and interpretations provoke a flood of questions, indicating the need for a surer analytic understanding of social interaction. For example, if prospectively delivered assistance from males towards females is "paid" for by copulations or female consortship, what protects the male from a female cheater? How are such exchanges structured? How can male investment antedate direct female reciprocity by months or years? The answers to such questions will prove vital to hominid behavioral reconstruction, because the true evolutionary parallel for hominid "monogamy" might be found in incipient form in such male-female friendships existing in a larger social context, rather than in the sexually exclusive relationships found among more solitary primates such as gibbons.

Monogamous primates.   There is no issue more central to the reconstruction of hominid social systems than that of the role of monogamy, and Kinzey (this volume) addresses an array of questions that throw light on this issue. Kinzey outlines the central features of monogamous mating and breeding systems, and stresses the social poverty (or simplicity) of nonhuman primate monogamy, possibly resulting from its evolution out of solitary ancestral conditions. This naturally raises the question: Did hominid monogamy precipitate out of a larger social group and social system (like long term associations and consortships among baboons or bonobos), or did, as Kinzey asks, "a monogamous primate augment its social system to include other members into the social group?" If hominid monogamy originated inside a larger social group, the dynamics structuring male-female relationships would have been considerably different from those governing mating among initially solitary primates that became monogamous through the recruitment of the male to the mother-infant dyad, and whose social group grew in size through retaining "helpers at the nest".

There are a number of dimensions relevant to human and non-human male-female relations and the question of monogamy. They can be inventoried with the following series of questions:
—does a specific female mate exclusively with a single male?
—does a specific male mate exclusively with a single female?
—do males invest in their offspring or assist their mates or both?
—how successfully can unassisted females raise offspring?
—is there only one breeding female in the social group?
—is there only one breeding male in the social group?
—if the two mates practice sexual exclusivity, what is the duration of their relationship?
—are members of the species facultative in their selection of mating strategy?

Among primates, humans are unique in simultaneously practicing (on a facultative basis): high MPI, multiple breeding males and females in the same social group, and sexual exclusivity (of at least limited duration) of individual females for males and males for females, frequently simultaneous and reciprocal. The features of this unique mating system are not directly paralleled by any other primate, and are not well captured by the term "monogamy", especially given the statistical distribution of deviations on most of these practices. To construct an image of the selection pressures constituting these unusual behaviors, one must look to many different primate mating systems to find the component parallels, and it requires behavioral ecological principles to analyze how they all work in combination. Common chimpanzees, bonobos and savannah baboons manifest extended relationships between individual males and females among larger social groups. Gibbons and a few New World primates practice monogamous sexual exclusivity. Hamadryas baboons and gorillas have females exclusively attached to a single male, while certain tamarins and marmosets, formerly thought to be monogamous, now appear polyandrously to have several males attached to and mating with a single female (Sussman and Kinzey, 1984; Kinzey, this volume). Although many aspects of mating systems and their consequences are beginning to be understood (e.g., the reduction of sexual dimorphism in monogamous species, the relationship between paternity certainty and MPI), many still need to be sorted out. These puzzles include the determinants of female-female tolerance and intolerance (an important factor in neotropical monogamous and polyandrous species), female dominance and the inhibition of ovulation, and the determinants that lead to low female reproductive success in the absence of male assistance. However, perhaps the single major question facing hominid social theory is the reconciliation of group life with high MPI and sexual exclusivity. What role intergroup conflict (as in lions and chimpanzees) may have played in this process is another crucial question.

Howler Monkeys. Beginning with Carpenter's pioneering work in 1934, howler monkeys have been the object of systematic study longer than any other primate. Because many of these studies have been based on Barro Colorado Island, there are now more long-term data on the BCI population than for any other monkey or ape. Howlers have also been studied in a greater variety of habitats than other primate genera, and provide a New World counterpart to the numerous studies of macaques and baboons.

By virtue of their phylogenetic distance from the Old World primates, no one, including Crockett (this volume) has yet been tempted to propose a "howler model" of hominid evolution. Instead, Crockett's approach is very much in the spirit of the strategy urged in this essay, namely, the development of principles of behavioral ecology that apply across taxonomic groups, and hence can be used to reconstruct aspects of hominid behavior. As she points out, the observation of sexually selected infanticide among red and mantled howlers provides additional confirmation of at least one evolutionary principle that applies systematically across highly diverse taxa, raising the question of what role, if any, sexually selected infanticide played in human evolution. Her documentation of female emigration, a rare occurrence in mammals (but present in the African apes and humans), is a welcome addition to our principled understanding of this feature of primate social organization.

Because her report includes behavioral ecological comparisons of six howler species occupying a broad range of habitats, it is now clear that the feeding strategy in this folivore-frugivore is anything but simple. While howlers can be said to occupy a "single" feeding niche, it is obvious that their foraging and activity patterns are enormously affected by environmental variation, both in habitat and in seasonal differences. Such observations suggest the perils of relying on the purported implications of a "single" feeding strategy, whenever this is advanced for a particular stage of hominid evolution. Finally, her discussion of sexual dichromatism is a healthy reminder that many features of sexual dimorphism (including important secondary sexual characteristics of humans) will not be preserved in the fossil record, and that natural selection may operate very differently on the two sexes.

The state of paleoecological methods

Paleoecological reconstruction depends on the mutual development of evolutionary principles and the methods that supply the data necessary for inferential reconstruction. Evidence is only interpretable or made meaningful by validated theory; without coherent theory, one is unable to recognize evidence, categorize it, relate it, or make valid inferences from it. Precisely because hominids are so remote from direct observation, methods (and the models that make them possible) play a central role in hominid reconstruction. Both Marks (this volume) and Sussman (this volume) suggest what may become important new methods for paleoecology, methods that use the features of living animals comparatively to assess ancestral conditions.

Cytogenetic Methods.   Marks proposes an ingenious new approach to the determination of ancestral hominid and pongid social structure. By searching for the social and ecological correlates of recognizable cytogenetic patterns, and examining humans and pongids for these patterns, Marks suggests that the long term average mating structure along lineages can be inferred. According to this method, the rate of karyotypic changes indicates the degree to which a lineage's mean mating system favors genetic drift and lineage fixation of neutral chromosomal variants. Small group size, monogamy, arboreality and small range size are factors that may inhibit gene flow, whereas polygyny, high rates of transfer and large social groups are the sorts of factors that retard the establishment of chromosomal variations among populations. Because Marks estimates that the number of chromosomal variations along the human lineage is approximately comparable to those among chimpanzees and gorillas, he infers that in terms of social structure, humans more closely resembled chimpanzees and gorillas than they did the social structure of either gibbons or baboons. He is properly cautious about the reliability of the results, and fully cognizant of the work that remains to be done to establish the validity of the method.

The prospect of assessing, even approximately, average parameters of a lineage's social structure is very intriguing. Certainly the direction taken needs to be developed as fully as possible. Relating observed cytogenetic patterns to observed social systems is the first step, but further elucidation of the causes of the relationships will allow the interpretation to become more detailed and reliable. There is good reason to believe that many aspects of the genome are shaped by the interaction between parasite pressures, ecological factors, and social organization (Tooby, 1982), including the degree of polymorphism, the rate of protein evolution, and chromosome number and conformation. Some of the relationships between social organization and chromosomal evolution may not be due simply to their effects on fixation of neutral variants, but might be driven by parasite pressure instead. If so, the estimates drawn from the observed rate of changes may need to be somewhat recalibrated to take into account differing degrees of parasite pressure. However, this in itself may provide interesting data about ancestral habitat.

Morpho-behavioral Analysis of Primate Diets. Sussman (this volume) proposes that ancestral diet can be inferred on the basis of conservative features of the digestive tract. On the basis of a preliminary, allometrically corrected, comparative analysis of the proportionate potential areas of absorption in gastrointestinal compartments, Sussman found that his sample of modern humans clustered with other faunivorous mammals. This is consistent with the results of Martin *et al* (1985). However, Sussman cautions that the factors he has chosen to study may unfortunately be environmentally malleable, and so may not after all tell us about ancestral diets.

Regardless of the specific merits of Sussman's method, the general direction of study has much to commend it. Diet is the primary factor allowing or constraining the rest of a species' system of adaptations. If it could be ascertained what a given ancestor's diet was, (i.e., 40% meat, or 90% fruit, etc., many of the constraints necessary for the inference of its system of adaptations would be present. The inference of ancestral diets from modern humans is an effort that has scarcely begun, and the scrutiny of conservative aspects of our dietary physiology and biochemistry may ultimately reveal a great deal. Species-specific nutritional requirements provide an entry point: the patterns involved in what must be supplied in the diet, what can be synthesized, and what must be present to effect cross-synthesis all constitute an unmined vein of information on ancestral diets. An animal can afford to lose the ability to synthesize a nutrient if it is reliably present in the diet. An animal must be able to synthesize out of available dietary substrates what is essential but always lacking in the diet. The hierarchy of absorption and cross-synthesis can potentially reveal considerable information on the relative abundances of different nutrients in the diet. Vitamins, essential fatty acids and structural fats, minerals (especially calcium), and amino acids all provide a starting point. The biochemistry of digestion, absorption, and detoxification may also prove to be highly revealing: special function digestive enzymes all provide compelling evidence that a specific protein, sugar, or toxin was abundant in the diet. Various amino acids are differentially absorbed, and can displace each other in a hierarchy. Presumably, the scarcer and more important the amino acid is, the more the digestive system is selected to absorb it efficiently. The profile of amino acids in ancestral diets might be inferred from such a hierarchy. Examining the physiology and biochemistry of human digestion and matching it against the nutritional profiles of various foods (cooked and uncooked fruits, tubers, nuts, shoots, leaves, bulbs, seeds, meat, liver, heart, brain, blood, marrow, etc.) can settle debates about recent hominid diet.

Discussion and Conclusions

Strategic modeling has the potential for resolving a number of the thorniest issues concerning human evolution. For example, many social scientists (e.g., Geertz, 1973; Sahlins, 1976; Harris, 1979) have defended the notion that, due to intelligence and the capacity for culture, human behavior has become independent of evolutionary forces. They argue that in the transition from simpler primate behavioral mechanisms to the more elaborated and powerful ones present in modern humans, a crucial boundary was crossed. Many regard this, almost mystically, as a watershed transition that places human phenomena in another category entirely, beyond the capacity of evolutionary and ethological methods to study, model or understand. They take the uniqueness of humanity to mean that human behavior is incomprehensible in evolutionary terms.

The immense difference in the complexity and variation of behavior among primates, protohumans and humans is tractable to strategic modeling. Essential to strategic modeling is the distinction between proximate means and evolutionary ends. Proximate mechanisms are selected ("designed") to accomplish the promotion of inclusive fitness. This end is fixed; it is intrinsic to the evolutionary process. However, the proximate mechanisms by which fitness is promoted change over evolutionary time, depending on factors such as the previous adaptive constellation of the species, what mutations have occurred, ontogenetic constraints, and the existence of preadaptations (exaptations [Gould and Vrba, 1982]). The elaboration of mechanisms from the simple into the complex changes only the proximate means, not the evolutionary ends. In fact, such changes will occur only when they increase inclusive fitness—only when they better promote the same evolutionary ends.

Humans are characterized by a remarkable expansion in intelligence, consciousness (however defined), complex learning, and culture transmission mechanisms—all interpenetrated by a sophisticated coevolved motivational system. Strategic modeling is uniquely suited to the analysis of these mechanisms, precisely because it analyzes mechanisms in terms of evolutionary ends, which do not change. As intelligence, learning, consciousness and motivational systems progressively become more sophisticated, they still serve the same strategic ends according to the same evolutionary principles. To methods of analysis that focus only on proximate mechanisms, unprecedented capacities are discontinuities, difficult to investigate. But to strategic modeling, they are not discontinuities at all; they are new (and gradually complexifying) expressions of the same adaptive processes. For rapidly changing proximate mechanisms, invariances exist only at the strategic level. Hence, strategic modeling is the method most suited to the investigation of hominid evolution and human behavior—it is the method least thwarted or confused by hominid singularity.

In fact, instead of being divergent from evolutionary principles, sophisticated hominid mechanisms may more purely incarnate adaptive strategies. Hominids' more intelligent, flexible and conscious systems are less limited by mechanistic and informational constraints; they can more sensitively track special environmental, historical, and situational factors and modify their behavior in adaptively appropriate ways. Evolutionary processes select for any behavioral mechanism, no matter how flexible or automatic, that increases fitness. Although the invocation of strategies does not imply that the actor is conscious of what he is doing or why, it may in fact be true that humans are more aware of their strategies for pursuing proximate motivational goals (goals that correlate with fitness).

Those who continue to assert that humans became immune to the evolutionary process must somehow reason their way past the following fatal objection to their position: the innate characteristics that have become incorporated into the human genome were incorporated because they increased inclusive fitness, and therefore they are adaptively patterned. To assert anything else is to maintain that somehow a large number of less fit innate characteristics (ones that did not correlate with fitness) displaced those that were more fit. In other words, advocates of this position must explain how evolutionary processes systematically produced maladaptive traits.

Twenty years ago, evolutionary theory and behavioral ecology did not have sufficient definition to be very helpful in research on human origins, but their present maturity and accelerating progress mean that they have the potential to become an essential tool in paleoanthropology. Even in its present form, behavioral ecology is largely neglected as a resource for paleontological interpretation. However, it is no longer possible to treat a proposed scenario as if one hypothesis is as good as another. We know that certain hypotheses, such as Lovejoy's (1981) and Zihlman and Tanner's (1978), cannot be true, because they violate validated principles of evolutionary biology. To construct hypotheses about extinct hominids seriously, a researcher must now be cognizant of an entire armamentarium of principles and analytic tools. To progress, paleoanthropologists must be prepared to discard prime mover and single-primate-species models of human evolution, and recognize that evolutionary biology can provide the conceptual model that will organize our understanding of hominids. The central labor in paleoanthropology is the development of this set of inferential procedures (the principles of strategic modeling), deduced from evolutionary theory, refined with empirically validated evolutionary biology, phylogenetically honed by primate studies, and fitted with specific evidence about hominids deduced from traces left in their living descendants, their fossils, the archeological record, and the reconstruction of paleoenvironments. The trajectory of hominid evolution can eventually be deduced by applying these inferential procedures to the available data. This set of tools is far from complete, but at least we now can begin to outline what, at minimum, a serious effort at hominid behavioral reconstruction should encompass. We can now target the specific knowledge we will need to recover about hominids to discover how these evolutionary principles uniquely express themselves in the hominid lineage. By this process the enterprise of understanding hominids will eventually be transformed from a historical and descriptive enterprise into a fully scientific one: of theory, hypothesis testing, reduction of uncertainty, and the explanation of many facts by a few central features.

ACKNOWLEDGEMENTS

We deeply appreciate the assistance of many persons in the preparation of this manuscript. Peter Jones, John Noss, David Pilbeam, Pat Shipman, and Steven Ward commented on portions of the draft. For unstinting assistance and detailed comments we are especially grateful to Stephen Bartz, Martin Daly, Nancy DeVore, Martin Etter, Glynn Isaac, Warren Kinzey, Karen Strier, and Margo Wilson. As the reader will quickly discover, the resulting essay cannot be interpreted as a consensus of these commentator's views.

For patient and cheerful manuscript preparation we thank Julie C. Benyo, Nancy Black and Mark Jenike. NSF grant number BNS–83–19629 provided partial support for this research.

Finally, we express our special gratitude to Leda Cosmides, without whose ideas and tireless labor this article would never have been completed.

References

Abrahamson, D.
1985 Tamarins in the Amazon. *Science 85* 6(7):58–63.

Aldrich-Blake, F.P.G.
1980 Long-tailed macaques. In *Malayan Forest Primates: Ten Years' Study in Tropical Rain Forest*, ed. D.J. Chivers, pp. 147–165. New York: Plenum Press.

Alexander, R.D.; Hoogland, J.L.; Howard, R.D.; Noonan, K.M.; and Sherman, P.W.
1979 Sexual dimorphisms and breeding systems in pinnipeds, ungulates, primates and humans. In *Evolutionary Biology and Human Social Behavior: An Anthropological Perspective*, eds. N.A. Chagnon and W. Irons, pp. 402–435. North Scituate, MA: Duxbury Press.

Alexander, R.D., and Noonan, K.M.
1979 Concealment of ovulation, parental care, and human social evolution. In *Evolutionary Biology and Human Social Behavior: An Anthropological Perspective*, pp. 436–453. North Scituate, MA: Duxbury Press.

Allen, L.L.; Bridges, P.S.; Evon, D.L.; Rosenberg, K.R.; Russell, M.D.; Schepartz, L.A.; Vitzthum, V.J.; and Wolpoff, M.H.
1982 Demography and human origins. *Amer. Anthro.* 84(4):888–896.

Altmann, Jeanne
1974 Observational study of behavior: sampling methods. *Behaviour* 49:227–267.

Altmann, Stuart A.
1974 Baboons, space, time, and energy. *Am. Zool.* 14:221–248.

Altmann, Stuart A., and Altmann, Jeanne
1979 Demographic constraints on behavior and social organization. In *Primate Ecology and Human Origins: Ecological Influences on Social Organization*, eds. I.S. Bernstein and E.O. Smith, pp. 47–63, New York: Garland STPM Press.

Amerasinghe, F.P.; Van Cuylenberg, B.W.B.; and Hladik, C.M.
1971 Comparative histology of the alimentary tract of Ceylon primates in correlation with diet. *Ceylon J. Sci. Biol.* 9:75–87.

Anderson, C.O., and Mason, William A.
1974 Early experience and complexity of social organization in groups of young rhesus monkeys (*Macaca mulatta*). *J. Comp. Physiol. Psychol.* 87:681–690.

Andrews, P., and Cronin, J.E.
1982 The relationships of *Sivapithecus* and *Ramapithecus* and the evolution of the orang-utan. *Nature* 297:541–546.

Ardrey, R.
1961 *African Genesis*. New York: Dell Publishing Co.
1969 Introduction. In *The Soul of the Ape* by Eugene Marias, pp. 1–55. New York: Atheneum.
1970 *The Territorial Imperative*. New York: Atheneum.
1976 *The Hunting Hypothesis*. New York: Bantam Books.

Arnason, U.
1972 The role of chromosomal rearrangement in mammalian speciation with special reference to Cetacea and Pinnipedia. *Hereditas* 70:113–118.

Axelrod, R.T., and Hamilton, W.D.
1981 The evolution of cooperation. *Science* 211:1390–1396.

Azen, E.A., Leutenegger, Walter; and Peters, Erwin
1978 Evolutionary and dietary aspects of salivary basic (Pb) and post Pb (PPb) proteins in anthropid primates. *Nature* 273:775–778.

Badrian, A., and Badrian, N.
1984 Social organization of *Pan paniscus* in the Lomako Forest, Zaire. In *The Pygmy Chimpanzee, Evolutionary Morphology and Behavior*, ed. R.L. Susman, pp. 325–346. New York: Plenum Press.

Badrian, N.; Badrian, A.; and Susman, R.L.
1981 Preliminary observations on the feeding behavior of *Pan paniscus* in the Lomako Forest of Central Zaire. *Primates* 22:173–181.

Badrian, N., and Malenky, R.K.
1984 Feeding ecology of *Pan paniscus* in the Lomako Forest, Zaire. In *The Pygmy Chimpanzee, Evolutionary Biology and Behavior*, ed. R.L. Susman, pp. 275–299. New York: Plenum Press.

Baer, D., and McEachron, D.L.
1982 A review of selected sociobiological principles: application to hominid evolution. I. The development of group social structure. *J. Social Biol. Struct.* 5:69–90.

Baldwin, P.J.; McGrew, W.C.; and Tutin, C.E.G.
1982 Wide-ranging chimpanzees at Mt. Assirik, Senegal. *Int. J. Primatol.* 3:367–385.

Barnard, A.
1983 Contemporary hunter-gatherrers: current theoretical issues in ecology and social organization. *Ann. Rev. Anthro.* 12:193–214.

Bartholomew, G.A., and Birdsell, J.P.
1953 Ecology and the protohominids. *Amer. Anthro.* 55:481–498.

Baumgartel, W.
1976 *Up Among the Mountain Gorillas*. New York: Hawthorn Books.

Beer, F.A.

1981 *Peace Against War: The Ecology of International Violence.* San Francisco: W.H. Freeman.

Behrensmeyer, A.K.

1982 Time resolution in fluvial vertebrate assemblages. *Paleobiology* 8:211–227.

Behrensmeyer, A.K., and Hill, A., eds.

1980 *Fossils in the Making.* Chicago: University of Chicago Press.

Bengtsson, B.O.

1980 Rates of karyotype evolution in placental mammals. *Hereditas* 92:37–47.

Benirschke, K.; Kumamoto, A.T.; Esra, G.N.; and Woods, F.

1982 The chromosomes of the emperor tamarin, *Saguinus imperator* Goeldi, 1907. *Zool. Garten* N.F. 52:168–174.

Benveniste, R.E., and Todaro, G.J.

1976 Evolution of type C viral genes: evidence for an Asian origin of man. *Nature* 261:101–108.

Bernstein, I., and Smith, E., eds.

1979 *Primate Ecology and Human Origins.* New York: Garland STPM Press.

Bernstein, R.; Pinto, M.; Mrcom, G.; and Bielert, C.

1980 A reassessment of the karyotype of *Papio ursinus:* homoeology between human chromosome 15 and 22 and a characteristic submetacentric baboon chromosome. *Cytogenet. Cell Genet.* 28:55–63.

Binford, L.R.

1981 *Bones: Ancient Men and Modern Myths.* New York: Academic Press.

1983 *In Pursuit of the Past: Decoding the Archaeological Record.* London: Thames and Hudson.

1984 *Faunal remains from Klasies River Mouth.* New York: Academic Press.

Birdsell, J.B.

1972 *Human Evolution: An Introduction to the New Physical Anthropology.* Chicago: Rand McNally College Publishing Co.

Bodmer, W.F.

1981 Gene clusters, genome organization and complex phenotypes: when the sequence is known, what will it mean? *Am. J. Hum. Genet.* 33:664–682.

Boesch, Christophe, and Boesch, Hedwige

1981 Sex differences in the use of natural hammers by wild chimpanzees: a preliminary report. *J. Human Evolution* 10:565–583.

1983 Optimisation of nut-cracking with natural hammers by wild chimpanzees. *Behaviour* 83:265–286.

1984 Possible causes of sex differences in the use of natural hammers by wild chimpanzees. *J. Human Evolution* 13:415–440.

Bonnefille, R.

1979 Methode palynologique et reconstitutions paleoclimatiques au Cenozoique dans le Rift Est Africain. *Bull. Soc. Geol. France* 12:331–342.

Bourliere, F.
  1961 Patterns of social grouping among wild primates. In *Social Life of Early Man*, ed. S.L. Washburn, pp. 1–10. New York: Wenner-Gren Foundation for Anthropological Research, Inc.
Brace, C.L.
  1979 Biological parameters and Pleistocene hominid lifeways. In *Primate Ecology and Human Origins*, ed. I. Bernstein and E. Smith, pp. 262–289. New York: Garland STPM Press.
Brain, C.K.
  1970 New finds at the Swartkrans australopithecine site. *Nature* 225:1112–1119.
  1972 An attempt to reconstruct the behaviour of australopithecines: the evidence for interpersonal violence. *Zool. Afr.* 7:379–401.
Brown, Wesley M.; Prager, Ellen M.; Wang, Alice; and Wilson, Allan C.
  1982 Mitochondrial DNA sequences of primates: tempo and mode of evolution. *Journal of Molecular Evolution* 18:225–239.
Bruce, Elizabeth J., and Ayala, Francisco J.
  1978 Humans and apes are genetically very similar. *Nature* 276:264–265.
  1979 Phylogenetic relationships between man and the apes: electrophoretic evidence. *Evolution* 33:1040–1056.
Buchanan, D.B.; Mittermeier, R.A.; and van Roosmalen, M.G.M.
  1981 The saki monkeys, Genus *Pithecia*. In *Ecology and Behavior of Neotropical Primates, Vol. 1*, eds. A.F.Coimbra-Filho and R.A.Mittermeier, pp. 391–417. Rio de Janeiro: Academia Brasileirade Ciencias.
Buettner-Janusch, J., and Hamilton, A.E.
  1979 Chromosomes and Lemuriformes. IV. Karyotype evolution in *Lemur fulvus collaris* (E. Geoffroy 1812). *Am. J. Phys. Anthro.* 50:363–366.
Bunn, H.T.
  1981 Archaeological evidence for meat-eating by Plio-Pleistocene hominids from Koobi Fora and Olduvai Gorge. *Nature* 292:574–577.
  1982 "Meat-eating and human evolution." Ph.D. dissertation, University of California, Berkeley.
Bush, G.L.; Case, S.M.; A.C.; and Patton, J.L.
  1977 Rapid speciation and chromosomal evolution in mammals. *Proc. Natl. Acad. Sci.* 74:3942–3946.
Bygott, J.D.
  1979 Agonistic behavior, dominance, and social structure in wild chimpanzees of the Gombe National Park. In *The Great Apes*, eds. D.A. Hamburg and E.R. McCrown, pp. 405–427. Menlo Park, CA: Benjamin/Cummings.
Caballin, M.R.; Miro, R.; Ponsa, M.; Florit, F.; Massa, C.; and Egozcue, J.
  1980 Banding patterns of the chromosomes of *Cercopithecus petaurista* (Schreber, 1775): comparison with other primate species. *Folia primatol.* 34:278–285.
Cachel, S.M.
  1975 A new view of speciation in *Australopithecus*. In *Paleoanthropology, Morphology and Paleoecology*, ed. R.H. Tuttle, pp. 183–201. The Hague: Mouton Press.

Callow, M.H.; Boon, A.R.; and Davison, E.V.
1979 Translocation C:D involving chromosomes 11 and 14. *Hum. Genet.* 46:149–153.

Cambefort, Y.; Mounie, C.; and Colombies, P.
1976 Topographies des bandes chromosomiques chez Papio hamadryas. *Ann. Génêt.* 19:269–272.

Campbell, B.
1966 *Human Evolution: An Introduction to Man's Adaptations.* Chicago: Aldine.
1979 Ecological factors and social organization in human evolution. In: *Primate Ecology and Human Origins: Ecological Influences on Social Organization,* eds. I.S. Bernstein and E.O. Smith, pp. 291–312. New York: Garland STPM Press.
1982 *Humankind Emerging.* Boston: Little, Brown.

Carpenter, C.R.
1934 A field study of the behavior and social relations of howling monkeys (*Alouatta palliata*). *Comparative Psychology Monographs* 10:1–168.
1940 Field study in Siam of the behavior and social relations of the gibbon (*Hylobates lar*). *Comparative Psychology Monographs* 16:1–212.
1942 Societies of monkeys and apes. *Biological Symposia* 8:177–204.
1965 The howlers of Barro Colorado Island. In *Primate Behavior: Field Studies of Monkeys and Apes,* ed. I. DeVore, pp. 250–291. New York: Holt, Rinehart and Winston.

Casimir, M.J., and Butenandt, E.
1973 Migration and core area shifting in relation to some ecological factors in a mountain gorilla group (*Gorilla gorilla beringei*) in the Mt. Kahuzi region (Republique du Zaire). *Z. Tierpsychol.* 33:514–522.

Cerling, T.E.; Hay, R.; and O'Neil, J.R.
1977 Isotopic evidence for dramatic climatic changes in East Africa during the Pleistocene. *Nature* 267:137–138.

Chagnon, N.A.
1980 Kin-selection theory, kinship, marriage and fitness among the Yanomamo Indians. In *Sociobiology: Beyond Nature/Nurture?,* eds. G.W. Barlow and J. Silverberg, pp. 545–571. Boulder: Westview Press.

Chang, L.Y., and Slightom, Jerry L.
1984 Isolation and nucleotide sequence analysis of the B-type globin pseudogene from human, gorilla, and chimpanzee. *Journal of Molecular Biology* 180:767–784.

Charles-Dominique, P.
1975 Nocturnality and diurnality: an ecological interpretation of these two modes of life by an analysis of the higher vertebrate fauna in tropical forest ecosystems. In *Phylogeny of the Primates: A Multidisciplinary Approach,* eds. W.P. Luckett and F.S. Szalay, pp. 69–88, New York: Plenum Press.

Charnov, E.L.
  1976   Optimal foraging: the marginal value theorum. *Theoretical Popu-
         lation Biology* 9:129–136.
Cheney, D.L.
  1983   Intergroup encounters among Old World Monkeys. In *Primate Social
         Relationships,* ed. R. Hinde, pp. 233–241. Oxford: Blackwell.
Cheney, D.L., and Seyfarth, R.M.
  1983   Nonrandom dispersal in free-ranging vervet monkeys: social and
         genetic consequences. *Am. Nat.* 122:392–412.
Chevalier-Skolnikoff, Suzanne; Galdikas, B.M.F.; and Skolnikoff, A.Z.
  1982   The adaptive significance of higher intelligence in wild orang-utans:
         a preliminary report. *J. Human Evolution* 11:639–652.
Chiarelli, A.B.
  1966   Karyology and taxonomy of the catarrhine monkeys. *Am. J. Phys.
         Anth.* 24:155–169.
  1972   Comparative chromosome analysis between man and chimpanzee.
         J. Human Evolution 1:389–393.
  1975   The study of primate chromosomes. In *Primate Functional Mor-
         phology and Evolution,* ed. R.H. Tuttle, pp. 103–134. Mouton: The
         Hague.
  1982   Karyological individualities in nonhuman primates and their po-
         tential inheritance. *Cytogenet. Cell Genet.* 34:43–47.
Chitolina, O.P., and Sander, M.
  1981   Contribuição ao conhecimento da alimentação de *Alouatta guariba
         clamitans* Cabrera, 1940 em habitat natural no Rio Grande do Sul
         (Cebidae, Alouattinae). *Inheringia Sér. Zool.,* Pôrto Alegre 59:37–44.
Chivers, David J.
  1972   The siamang and the gibbon in the Malay peninsula. In *Gibbon
         and Siamang, Volume 1: Evolution, Ecology, Behavior, and Captive
         maintenance,* ed. D.M. Rumbaugh. Basel: S. Karger.
  1984   Feeding and ranging in gibbons, a summary. In *The Lesser Apes,
         Evolutionary and Behavioral Biology,* eds. H. Preuschoft, D.J. Chiv-
         ers, W.Y. Brockelman, and N. Creel, pp. 267–281. Edinburgh: Uni-
         versity Press.
Chivers, David J., and Hladik, C.M.
  1980   Morphology of the gastrointestinal tract in primates: comparisons
         with other mammals in relation to diet. *J. Morphology* 166:337–386.
  1984   Diet and gut morphology in primates. In *Food Acquisition and
         Processing in Primates,* eds. D.J. Chivers, B.A. Wood and A. Bils-
         borough, p. 213–230. New York:Plenum Press.
Ciochon, R.L.
  1983   Hominoid cladistics and the ancestry of modern apes and humans:
         a summary statement. In *New Interpretations of Ape and Human
         Ancestry,* eds. R.L. Ciochon and R.S. Corrucini, pp. 783–843. New
         York: Plenum Press.
Clarke, M.R.
  1983   Infant-killing and infant disappearance following male takeovers in
         a group of free-ranging howling monkeys *(Alouatta palliata)* in
         Costa Rica. *Am. J. Primatol.* 5:241–247.

Clarke, M.R., and Glander, K.E.
1984   Female reproductive success in a group of free-ranging howling monkeys *(Alouatta palliata)* in Costa Rica. In *Female Primates: Studies by Women Primatologists,* ed. M. Small, pp. 111–126. New York: Alan R. Liss.

Clutton-Brock, T.H.
1972   "Feeding and ranging behavior in the red colobus monkey." Ph.D. dissertation, Cambridge University.
1975   Feeding behavior of red colobus and black and white colobus in East Africa. *Folia primatol.* 23:165–207.

Clutton-Brock, T.H., and Harvey, P.H.
1977a   Primate ecology and social organisation. *J. Zool., London* 183:1–39.
1977b   Species differences in feeding and ranging behaviour in primates. In *Primate Ecology: Studies in Feeding and Ranging Behavior in Lemurs, Monkeys and Apes,* ed. T.H. Clutton-Brock, pp. 557–584. London: Academic Press.

Comings, D.E.
1978   Mechanisms of chromosome banding and implications for chromosome structure. *Ann. Rev. Genet.* 12:25–46.

Coolidge, H.J.
1933   *Pan paniscus:* pigmy chimpanzee from south of the Congo river. *Am. J. Phys. Anth.* 18:1–57.

Coon, C.S.
1948   *A Reader in General Anthropology.* New York: Holt.

Cosmides, L.
1985   "Deduction or Darwinian algorithms? An explanation of the elusive content effect on the Wason selection task." Ph.D. dissertation, Harvard University.

Cosmides, L., and Tooby, J.
1981   Cytoplasmic inheritance and intragenomic conflict. *J. Theoretical Biology* 89:83–129.

Coult, A.D., and Habenstein, R.W.
1965   *Cross Tabulations of Murdock's World Ethnographic Sample.* Columbia: University of Missouri Press.

Couturier, J.; Dutrillaux, B.; Turleau, C.; and de Grouchy, J.
1982   Comparaisons chromosomiques chez quatre espèces ou sous-espèces de gibbons. *Ann. Génét.* 25:5–10.

Cramer, D.L.
1977   Craniofacial morphology of *Pan paniscus.* A morphometric and evolutionary appraisal. *Contrib. to Primatol.* 10:1–64.

Crawford, M., and Crawford, S.
1972   *What We Eat Today.* London: Spearman.

Crespo, J.A.
1982   Ecología de la comunidad de mamíferos del Parque National Iguazu, Misiones. *Revista de Museo Argentino de Ciencias naturales 'Bernadino Rivadavia', Inst. National de Investigacion de las Ciencias Naturales.*

Crockett, C.M.
1984 Emigration by female red howler monkeys and the case for female competition. In *Female Primates: Studies by Women Primatologists,* ed. M. Small, pp. 159–173. New York: Alan R. Liss.
1985 Population studies of red howler monkeys *(Alouatta seniculus). Natl. Geo. Research* 1:264–273.
In prep. *The Red Howler Monkey: Behavior and Ecology in Two Habitats.*
Crockett, C.M., and Eisenberg, J.F.
1986 Howlers: variations in group size and demography. In *Primate Societies,* eds. B.B. Smuts, D.L. Cheney, R.M. Seyfarth, R.W. Wrangham and T.T. Struhsaker. Chicago: Univ. of Chicago Press.
Crockett, C.M., and Sekulic, R.
1984 Infanticide in red howler monkeys *(Alouatta seniculus).* In *Infanticide: Comparative and Evolutionary Perspectives,* eds. G. Hausfater and S.B. Hrdy, pp. 173–191. Hawthorne, NY: Aldine.
Cronin, John E.
1975 Molecular systemics of the order primates. Doctoral dissertation, genetics and anthropology: University of California, Berkeley.
1983 Apes, humans and molecular clocks: a reappraisal. Appendix: Retrospective on hominoid macromolecular systematics, by V.M. Sarich *New Interpretations of Ape and Human Ancestry,* eds. R.L. Ciochon and R.S. Corruccini, pp. 115–150. New York: Plenum.
Crook, J.H.
1970 The socio-ecology of primates. In *Social Behavior in Birds and Mammals,* ed. J.H. Crook. London: Academic Press.
Crook, J.H. and Gartlan, J.S.
1966 Evolution of primate societies. *Nature* 210:1200–1203.
Curio, E.
1976 *The Ethology of Predation.* Berlin: Springer-Verlag.
Dahlberg, Frances, Ed.
1981 *Woman the Gatherer.* New Haven and London: Yale University Press.
Dart, R.A.
1925 *Australopithecus africanus:* the man-ape of South Africa. *Nature* 115:195–199.
1926 Taung and its significance. *Natural History* 26:315–327.
1953 The predatory transition from ape to man. *Int. Anthro. Ling. Rev.* 1:201–218.
1957 The osteodontokeratic culture of *Australopithecus prometheus. Trans. Mus. Mem.* 10:1–105.
1959 Further light on australopithecine humeral and femoral weapons. *Am. J. Phys. Anth.* 17:87–94.
1963 Carnivorous propensity of baboons. *Symp. Zool. Soc. Lond.* 10:49–56.
Darwin, Charles
1871 *The Descent of Man and Selection in Relation to Sex.* The Modern Library edition, 1936. New York: Random House.
Dawkins, R.
1982 *The Extended Phenotype.* San Francisco: W.H. Freeman.

Dawkins, R., and Krebs, J.R.
1979   Arms races between and within species. *Proc. Roy. Soc. Lond. B.* 205:489–511.

Dawson, G.A.
1977   Composition and stability of social groups of the tamarin, *Saguinus oedipus geoffroyi*, in Panama: ecological and behavioral implications. In *The Biology and Conversation of the Callitrichidae*, ed. D.G. Kleiman, pp. 23–37. Washington, D.C.: Smithsonian Institution Press.

de Bonis, L.
1983   Phyletic relationships of Miocene hominoids and higher primate classification. In *New Interpretations of Ape and Human Ancestry*, eds. R.L. Ciochon and R.S. Corrucini, pp. 625–649. New York: Plenum Press.

de Vries, G.F.; de France, H.F.; and Schevers, J.A.M.
1975   Identical giemsa banding patterns of two *Macaca* species: *Macaca mulatta* and *M. fascicularis*. *Cytogenet. Cell Genet.* 14:26–33.

de Waal, Francis
1982   *Chimpanzee Politics.* London: Jonathan Cape.

Deag, J.
1974   "A study of the social behavior and ecology of the wild Barbary macaque." Ph. D. dissertation, Univ. of Bristol, England.

Dene, H.T.; Goodman, M.; and Prychodko, W.
1976   Immunodiffusion evidence on the phylogeny of the primates. In *Molecular Anthropology*, eds. M. Goodman and R.H. Tashian, pp. 171–194. New York: Plenum.

Denham, W.W.
1971   Energy relations and some basic properties of primate social organization. *Am. Anthro.* 73:77–95.

DeVore, I., and Hall, K.R.L.
1965   Baboon ecology. In *Primate Behavior: Field Studies of Monkeys and Apes*, ed. I. DeVore, pp. 20–52. New York: Holt, Rinehart and Winston.

DeVore, I., and Washburn, S.L.
1963   Baboon ecology and human evolution. In *African Ecology and Human Evolution*, eds. F.C. Howell and F. Bourliere, pp. 335–367. Chicago: Aldine.

Dickemann, M.
1984   Concepts and classification in the study of human infanticide: sectional introduction and some cautionary notes. In *Infanticide: Comparative and Evolutionary Perspectives*, eds. G. Hausfater and S.B. Hrdy, pp. 427–437. Hawthorne, NY: Aldine.

Dittus, W.P.J.
1974   "The ecology and behavior of the toque monkey, *Macaca sinica*" Ph.D. dissertation, University of Maryland.

Dobzhansky, T.; Ayala, F.J.; Stebbins, G.L.; and Valentine, J.W.
1977   *Evolution.* San Francisco: W.H. Freeman.

Dodson, P.
   1973   The significance of small bones in paleoecological interpretation. *Contrib. Geol.* 12:15–19.
Dolhinow, Phyllis
   1972   *Primate Patterns.* New York: Holt.
Doolittle, Russel F.
   1971   Hominoid evolution as judged by fibrinopeptide structures. *Journal of Molecular Evolution* 1:74–83.
Dorfman, Andrea
   1984   Quest for the missing link. *Science Digest,* March, p.22.
Dover, G.
   1982   Molecular drive: a cohesive model of species evolution. *Nature* 299:111–117.
Draper, P.
   (In press) !Kung work: a southern perspective. Human Biology
Dresser, M.E., and Hamilton, A.E.
   1979   Chromosomes of Lemuriformes. V. A comparison of the karyotype of *Cheirogaleus medius* and *Lemur fulvus fulvus. Cytogenet. Cell Genet.* 24:160–167.
Dugoujon, J.M.; Moro, F.; and Larrouy, G.
   1982a Cytogenetic study of a *Cercopithecus pogonias grayi* X *Cercopithecus mona mona* hybrid. *Folia primatol.* 38:130–135.
   1982b Cytogenetic study of *Cercopithecus pogonias grayi* X *Cercopithecus ascanius katangae* hybrids. *Folia primat.* 38:269–274.
Dunbar, R.
   1983   Relationships and social structure in gelada and hamadryas baboons. In *Primate Social Relationships* ed. R. Hinde, pp. 299–307. Sunderland: Sinauer.
Dunbar, R., and Dunbar, E.
   1975   *Social Dynamics of Gelada Baboons.* Karger: Basel.
Dunnette, J.H., and Weinshilboum, R.M.
   1983   Serum dopamine beta hydroxylase EC-1.14.17.1 Activity in non-human primates phylogenetic and genetic implications. *Comp.Biochem.Physiol. C. Comp. Pharmacol.* 75(1):85–92.
Durham, W.H.
   1976   Resource competition and human aggression, Part I: a review of primitive war. *Qrt. Rev. Biol.* 51:385–415.
Dutrillaux, B.
   1979   Chromosomal evolution in primates: tentative phylogeny from *Microcebus murinis* (Prosimian) to man. *Hum. Genet.* 48:251–314.
   1980   Chromosomal evolution of the great apes and man. *J. Reproduction Fertility, Supplement* 28:105–111.
Dutrillaux, B.; Biemont, M.C.; Viegas-Pequignot, E.; and Laurent, C.
   1979   Comparison of the karyotypes of four Cercopithecoidae (sic): *Papio papio, P. anubis, Macaca mulatta* and *M. fascicularis. Cytogenet. Cell Genet.* 23:77–83.

Dutrillaux, B.; Couturier, J.; and Chauvier, G.
1980 Chromosomal evolution of 19 species or sub-species of Cercopithecinae. *Ann. Génét.* 23:133–143.
Dutrillaux, B.; Couturier, J.; Muleris, M.; Lombard, M.; and Chauvier, G.
1982 Chromosomal phylogeny of forty-two species or subspecies of cercopithecoids (Primate Catarrhini). *Ann. Génét.* 25:96–109.
Dutrillaux, B.; Couturier, J.; and Ruedi, D.
1981 Le caryotype de *Colobus vellerosus* et de *C. palliatus.* Comparison avec les Cercopithecidae et l'Homme. *Ann. Génét.* 24:78–81.
Dutrillaux, B.; Fosse, A.M.; and Chauvier, G.
1979 Étude cytogénétique de six espèces ou sous-espèces de mangabeys (Papiinae, Cercopithecidae). *Ann. Génét.* 22:88–92.
Dutrillaux, B.; Rethore, M.O.; Aurias, A.; Goustard, M.
1975 Analysis of the karyotype of two species of gibbons (*Hylobates lar* and *H. concolor*) by various banding techniques. *Cytogenet. Cell Genet.* 15:81–91.
Dutrillaux, B., and Rumpler, Y.
1977 Chromosomal evolution in Malagasy lemurs. II. Meiosis in intra- and interspecific hybrids in the genus *Lemur. Cytogenet. Cell Genet.* 18:197–211.
Dyson-Hudson, R., and Smith, E.A.
1978 Human territoriality: an ecological reassessment. *Amer. Anthro.* 80:21–42.
Eaton, S.B., and Konner, M.
1985 Paleolithic Nutrition: A Consideration of its Nature and Current Implications. *New England J. Medicine* 312:283–289.
Eisenberg, J.F.
1977 The evolution of the reproductive unit in the class Mammalia. In *Reproductive Behavior and Evolution,* eds. J.S. Rosenblatt and B. Komisaruk, pp. 39–71. New York: Plenum Press.
1981 *The Mammalian Radiations, An analysis of Trends in Evolution, Adaptation, and Behavior.* Chicago: University Press.
Eisenberg, J.F.; Muckenhirn, N.A.; and Rudran, R.
1972 The relation between ecology and social structure in Primates. *Science* 176:863–874.
Ellefson, J.D.
1968 Territorial behavior in the common white-handed gibbon, *Hylobates lar* Linn. In *Primates: Studies in Adaptation and Variability,* ed. P. C. Jay, pp. 180–199. New York: Hold Rinehart, and Winston.
Ember, C.R.
1978 Myths about hunter-gatherers. *Ethnology* 17:439–448.
Emlen, S.T., and Oring, L.W.
1977 Ecology, sexual selection and the evolution of mating systems. *Science* 197:215–223.
Estioko-Griffin, A., and Griffin, P.B.
1981 Woman the hunter: the Agta. In *Woman the Gatherer,* ed. F. Dahlberg, pp. 121–152. New Haven: Yale Univ. Press.

Estrada, A.
   1984   Resource use by howler monkeys (*Alouatta seniculus*) in the rain
          forest of Los Tuxtlas, Veracruz, Mexico. *Int. J. Primatol.* 5:105–131.
Ewel, J.J.; Madriz, A.; and Tosi, J.A. Jr.
   1976   *Zonas de vida de Venezuela.* Caracas: Ministerio de Agricultura y
          Cría, Fondo Nacional de Investigaciones Agropecuarias.
Fagan, B.
   1983   *People of the Earth.* Boston: Little, Brown
Falk, D.
   1985   Hadar AL 162-28 Endocast as evidence that brain enlargement
          preceded cortical reorganization in hominid evolution. *Nature* 313
          (5997):45–47.
Fenart, R., and Deblock, R.
   1973   *Pan paniscus* et *Pan troglodytes* craniometrie. Étude comparative et
          ontogenique selon les methodes classiques et vestibulaires. *Ann.
          Mus. Royal de l'Afrique Centrale Sci. Zool.* 204.
Ferguson, Walter F.
   1983   An alternative interpretation of *Australopithecus afarensis* fossil ma-
          terial. *Primates* 24(3):397–409.
Ferris, S.D.; Wilson, A.C.; and Brown, W.M.
   1981   Evolutionary tree of apes and humans based on mitochondrial DNA.
          Proc. Natl. Acad. Sci. 78: 2432–2436.
Finney, Ben R., and Jones, Eric M., eds.
   1985   *Interstellar Migration and the Human Experience.* Berkeley, Los An-
          geles, and London: University of California Press.
Fisher, Helen E.
   1984   Origin of the human female dual reproductive strategy. Paper pre-
          sented at American Anthropological Association meeting, Denver,
          CO, Nov. 17, 1984.
   ms.   Origin of human female sexual behavior.
Flinn, M.
   1981   Uterine vs. agnatic kinship variability and associated cousin marriage
          preference. In *Natural Selection and Social Behavior*, eds. R.D. Alex-
          ander and D.W. Twinkle, pp. 439–475. Concord, MA: Chiron.
Forde, C.D.
   1934   *Habitat, Economy and Society.* London: Methuen.
Fossey, Dian
   1979   Development of the mountain gorilla (*Gorilla gorilla beringei*): the
          first thirty-six months. In *The Great Apes*, eds. David A. Hamburg
          and Elizabeth R. McCown, pp. 139–184. Menlo Park, CA: Benjamin/
          Cummings.
   1981   The imperial mountain gorilla. *Nat. Geogr.* 159:501–523.
   1982   Reproduction among free-living mountain gorillas. *Am. J. Primatol.*
          1:97–104.
   1983   *Gorillas in the Mist.* Boston: Houghton Mifflin.

Fossey, Dian, and Harcourt, A.H.
1977 Feeding-ecology of free-ranging mountain gorilla *(Gorilla gorilla beringei)*. In *Primate Ecology,* ed. T.H. Clutton-Brock, pp. 415–447. London: Academic Press.
Fragaszy, D.M., and Mason, W.A.
1983 Comparisons of feeding behavior in captive squirrel and titi monkeys *Saimiri sciureus* and *Callicebus moloch. J. Comparative Psychology* 97:310–326.
Frisch, J.E.
1968 Individual behavior and intertroop variability in Japanese macaques. In *Primates,* ed. P. Jay, pp. 243–252. New York: Holt, Rinehart and Winston.
Galdikas, Biruté M.F.
1979 Orangutan adaptation at Tanjung Puting Reserve: mating and ecology. In *The Great Apes,* eds. D.A. Hamburg and E.R. McCown, pp. 195–233. Menlo Park CA: Benjamin/Cummings.
Galdikas, Biruté M.F., and Teleki, Geza
1981 Variations in subsistence activities of female and male pongids: new perspectives on the origins of hominid labor division. *Current Anthropology* 22:241–256, 316–320.
Gale, Fay
1974 *Women's Role in Aboriginal Society.* Canberra: Australian Institute of Aboriginal Studies.
Gallup, Gordon G. Jr.
1970 Chimpanzees: self recognition. *Science* 167:86–87.
Gantt, D. G.
1983 The enamel of Neogene hominoids: structural and phyletic implications. In *New Interpretations of Ape and Human Ancestry,* eds. R. L. Ciochon and R. S. Corrucini, pp. 249–268. New York: Plenum Press.
Gardner, R. Allan, and Gardner, Beatrice T.
1978 Comparative psychology and language acquisition. *Annals New York Academy of Sciences* 309:37–76.
Gartlan, J. S.
1964 Dominance in east African monkeys, *Proc. E. A. Acad.* 2:75–79.
1968 Structure and function in primate society. *Folia Primatol.* 8:89–120.
Gaulin, S. J. C., and FitzGerald, R. W.
1986 Sex differences in spatial ability: an evolutionary hypothesis and test. *The American Naturalist* 127:74–88.
Gaulin, S. J. C., and Gaulin, C. K.
1982 Behavioral ecology of *Alouatta seniculus* in Andean cloud forest. *Int. J. Primatol.* 3:1–32.
Gaulin, S. J. C., and Kurland, J. A.
ms. Ecological tactics in monogamy: mating system, body weight, and diet among primates.
Gaulin, S. J. C. and Sailer, L. D.
1984 Sexual dimorphism in weight among the primates: the relative impact of allometry and sexual selection. *Int. J. Primatol.* 5:515–535.

Gautier-Hion, A., and Gautier, J. P.
1978 Le singe de Brazza: une strategie originale. *Z. Tierpsychologie* 46:84–104.

Geertz, C.
1973 *The Interpretation of Cultures.* New York: Basic Books.

Ghiglieri, M. P.
1984 *The Chimpanzees of Kibale Forest: A Field Study of Ecology and Social Structure.* New York: Columbia Univ. Press.

Gillespie, David
1977 Newly evolved repeated DNA sequences in primates. *Science* 196:889–891.

Gittins, S. P.
1980 Territorial behavior in the agile gibbon. *Int. J. Primatol.* 1(4):381–399.

Gittins, S. P., and Raemaekers, J. J.
1980 Siamang, lar, and agile gibbons. In: *Malayan Forest Primates,* ed. D. J. Chivers, pp. 63–105. New York: Plenum Press.

Glander, K. E.
1978 Howling monkey feeding behavior and plant secondary compounds: a study of strategies. In *The Ecology of Arboreal Folivores,* ed. G. G. Montgomery, pp. 561–574. Washington, DC: Smithsonian Institution Press.
1981 Feeding patterns in mantled howling monkeys. In *Foraging Behavior: Ecological, Ethological and Psychological Approaches,* eds. A. C. Kamil and T. D. Sargent, pp. 231–257. New York: Garland STPM Press.

Goldizen, A.
1986 Tamarins and marmosets: communal care of offspring. In *Primate Societies,* eds. Barbara B. Smuts, D. L. Cheney, R. M. Seyfarth, R. W. Wrangham, and T. T. Struhsaker. Chicago: University of Chicago Press.

Goodall, A. G., and Groves, C. P.
1977 The conservation of Eastern gorillas. In *Primate Conservation,* eds. H. S. H. Prince Rainier III and G. H. Bourne, pp. 599–637. New York: Academic Press.

Goodall, Jane van Lawick-
1963 Feeding behavior of wild chimpanzees. *Symp. Zool. Soc. Lond.* 10:39–47.
1965 Chimpanzees of the Gombe Stream Reserve. In *Primate Behavior: Field Studies of Monkeys and Apes,* ed. I. DeVore, pp. 425–473. New York: Holt, Rinehart and Winston.
1967 *My Friends the Wild Chimpanzees.* Washington, DC: The National Geographic Society.
1968a *In the Shadow of Man.* Boston: Houghton Mifflin.
1968b The behavior of free-living chimpanzees in the Gombe stream reserve. *Animal Behavior Monographs* 1:165–311.
1968c A preliminary report on expressive moments and communication in the Gombe Stream chimpanzee. In *Primates, Studies in Adaptation and Variability,* ed. Phyllis C. Jay, pp. 313–374. New York: Holt, Rinehart and Winston.

1973a The behavior of the chimpanzees in their natural habitat. *Am. J. Psychiatry* 130:1–12.

1973b Cultural elements in a chimpanzee community. In *Precultural Primate Behavior,* ed. E. W. Menzel, pp. 144–184. Basel: S. Karger.

1975 The behavior of the chimpanzee. In *Hominisation und Verhalten,* eds. G. Kurth and I. Eibl-Eibesfeldt, pp. 74–136. Stuttgart: Gustav Fischer.

1977 Infant killing and cannibalism in free-living chimpanzees. *Folia Primatol.* 28:259–282.

1979 Life and death at Gombe. *Natl. Geographic* 155:593–621.

1983 Population dynamics during a 15 year period in one community of free-living chimpanzees in the Gombe National Park, Tanzania. *Z. Tierpsychology* 61:1–60.

Goodall, Jane; Bandora, A.; Bergmann, C.; Busse, C.; Matama, H.; Mpongo, E.; Pierce, A.; and Riss, D.

1979 Intercommunity interactions in the chimpanzee population of the Gombe National Park. In *The Great Apes,* eds. D. A. Hamburg and E. R. McCown, pp. 12–53. Menlo Park CA: Benjamin/Cummings.

Goodall, Jane, and Hamburg, David A.

1975 Chimpanzee behavior as a model for the behavior of man. In *New Psychiatric Frontiers,* eds. D. A. Hamburg and H. K. Brodie, pp. 14–43. New York: Basic Books.

Goodman, Morris

1962a Immunochemistry of the primates and primate evolution. *Annals of the New York Academy of Science* 102:219–234.

1962b Evolution of the immunologic species specificity of human serum proteins. *Human Biology* 34:104–150.

1963a Serological analysis of recent hominoids. *Human Biology* 35:377–436.

1963b Man's place in the phylogeny of the primates as reflected in serum proteins. *Classification and Evolution,* ed. S. L. Washburn. pp. 204–234. Viking Fund Publications in Anthropology 37.

1976 Toward a genealogical description of the primates. *Molecular Anthropology,* M. Goodman, R.E. Tashian, and J.H. Tashian eds., pp. 321–352. New York: Plenum Press.

1982 Biomolecular evidence on human origins from the standpoint of Darwinian theory. *Human Biology* 54(2):247–264.

Goodman, Morris; Baba, M. L.; and Darga, L. L.

1983 The bearings of molecular data on the cladograms and times of divergence of hominoid lineages. *New Interpretations of Ape and Human Ancestry,* ed. Russell L. Ciochon and Robert S. Corruccini, pp. 67–87. New York: Plenum Press.

Goodman, Morris; Braunitzer, G.; Stangl, A.; and Schrank, B.

1983 Evidence on human origins from haemoglobins of African apes. *Nature* 303:546–548.

Goodman, Morris; Koop, Ben F.; Czelusniak, John; and Weiss, Mark L.

1984 The n-globin gene: its long evolutionary history in the B-globin gene family of mammals. *Journal of Molecular Biology* 180:803–823.

Goss-Custard, J.; Dunbar, R.; and Aldrich-Blake, F.
1972 Survival, mating and rearing strategies in the evolution of primate social structure. *Folia Primatol.* 17:1–19.
Gould, S. J., and Vrba, E. S.
1982 Exaptation—a missing term in the science of form. *Paleobiology* 8:4–15.
Gowlett, J.
1984 *Ascent to Civilization: The Archaeology of Early Man.* New York: Alfred A. Knopf.
Grine, F.
1981 Trophic differences between 'gracile' and 'robust' australopithecines. *S. Afr. J. Sci.* 77:203–230.
1984 Deciduous molar microwear of South African australopithecines. In *Food Acquisition and Processing in Primates,* eds. D. J. Chivers, B. A. Wood, and A. Bilsborough, pp. 525–534. New York: Plenum.
Groves, C. P.
1970 Gigantopithecus and the mountain gorilla. *Nature* 226:973–974.
Haeckel, E.
1896 *The Evolution of Man.* New York: D. Appleton and Co.
Hall, K. R. L.
1965a Social organization of the old-world monkeys and apes. *Symp. Zool. Soc. London* 14:265–289.
1965b Behavior and ecology of the wild patas monkey, *Erythrocebus patas,* in Uganda. *J. Zool.* 148:15–87.
Hall, K. R. L., and DeVore, I.
1965 Baboon social behavior. In *Primate Behavior: Field Studies in Monkeys and Apes,* ed. I. DeVore, pp. 53–110. New York: Holt, Rinehart and Winston.
Hamilton, A. E., and Buettner-Janusch, J.
1977 Karyotypes of Lemuriformes. III. The genus *Lemur*: karyotypes of species, subspecies, and hybrids. *Ann. N.Y. Acad. Sci.* 239:125–159.
Hamilton, A. E.; Buettner-Janusch, J.; and Chu, E. H. Y.
1977 Chromosomes of Lemuriformes. II. Chromosome polymorphism in *Lemur fulvus collaris* (E. Geoffroy 1812). *Am. J. Phys. Anthro.* 46:395–406.
Hamilton, W. D.
1964 The genetical evolution of social behavior: Parts I and II. *J. Theoretical Biology* 7:1–52.
1967 Extraordinary sex ratios. *Science* 156:477–488.
Hamilton, W. J. III, Buskirk, R. E., and Buskirk, W. H.
1976 Defense of space and resources of chacma (*Papio ursinus*) baboons in an African desert and swamp. *Ecology* 57:1264–1272.
Hanif, G.
1967 Notes on breeding the white-faced saki *Pithecia pithecia* at Georgetown Zoo. *Int. Zoo. Yearbook* 7:81–82.
Haraway, Donna
1978a Animal sociology and a natural economy of the body politic, Part I: A political physiology of dominnce. *Signs* 4(1):21–36.

1978b Animal sociology and a natural economy of the body politic, Part II: The past is the contested zone: human nature and theories of production and reproduction in primate behavior stsudies. *Signs* 4(1):37–60.

Harcourt, A. H.

1978 Strategies of emigration and transer by primates, with particular reference to gorilla. *Z. Tier.* 48:401–420.

1979a Social relationships among adult female mountain gorillas in the wild. *Animal Behav.* 27:251–261.

1979b Social relationships between adult male and female mountain gorillas in the wild. *Animal Behav.* 27:325–342.

Harcourt, A. H.; Fossey, D.; and Sabater Pi, J.

1981 Demography of *Gorilla gorilla. J. Zool. London* 195:215–233.

Harcourt, A. H.; Fossey, D.; Stewart, K. J.; and Watts, D. P.

1980 Reproduction in wild gorilla and some comparisons with chimpanzees. *J. Reproduction Fertility,* Supplement 28:59–70.

Harcourt, A. H., and Stewart, K. J.

1977 Apes, sex and society. *New Science* 20:160–162.

1983 Interactions, relationships and social structure: the great apes. In *Primate Social Relationships,* ed. R. Hinde, pp. 307–314. Oxford: Blackwell.

Harding, R. S. O.

1981 An order of omnivores: nonhuman primate diets in the wild. In *Omnivorous Primates: Gathering and Hunting in Human Evolution,* eds. R. S. O. Harding and G. Teleki, pp. 191–214. New York: Columbia Univ. Press.

Harding, R. S. O., and Teleki, G.

1981 Introduction. In *Omnivorous Primates: Gathering and Hunting in Human Evolution,* eds. R. S. O. Harding and G. Teleki, pp. 1–9. New York: Columbia Univ. Press.

Harrington, J. E.

1978 Development of behavior in *Lemur macaco* in the first nineteen weeks. *Folia primatol.* 29:107–128.

Harris, J. W. K., and Johanson, D. C.

1983 Cultural beginnings: Plio-Pleistocene archaeological occurrences from the Afar, Ethopia. *Afr. Archeol. Review.* 1:3–31.

Harris, M.

1979 *Cultural Materialism: The Struggle for a Science of Culture.* New York: Vintage.

Harris, Stephen; Barrie, Paul A.; Weiss, Mark L.; and Jeffreys, Alec J.

1984 The primate ΨBl gene: an ancient B-globin pseudogene. *Journal of Molecular Biology.* 180:785–801.

Harrison, M. J. S.

1984 Optimal foraging strategies in the diet of the green monkey, *Cercopithecus sabaeus,* at Mt. Assirik, Senegal. *Int. J. Primatol.* 5:435–471.

Hasegawa, Masami; Kishino, Hirohisa; and Yano, Taka-aki

1985 Dating of the human-ape splitting by a molecular clock of mitochondrial DNA. *Journal of Molecular Evolution* 22:160–174.

Hasegawa, M., and Yano, T.
1984 Phylogeny and classification of hominoidea as inferred from DNA sequence data. *Proc. Jpn. Acad.* 60B:389–392.
Hasegawa, T., and Hiraiwa-Hasegawa, M.
1983 Opportunistic and restrictive matings among wild chimpanzees in the Mahale Mountains, Tanzania. *J. Ethol.* 1:75–85.
Hausfater, G.
1984 Infanticide in nonhuman primates: an introduction and perspective. In *Infanticide: Comparative and Evolutionary Perspectives,* eds. G. Hausfater and S. B. Hrdy, pp. 145–150. Hawthorne, NY: Aldine.
Hausfater, G., and Hrdy, S. B.
1984 *Infanticide: Comparative and Evolutionary Perspectives.* Hawthorne, NY: Aldine.
Hay, R.
1976 *Geology of the Olduvai Gorge.* Berkeley: University of California Press.
Heisenberg, W.
1971 *Physics and Beyond.* New York: Harper and Row.
Hernández-Camacho, J. and Cooper, R. W.
1976 The nonhuman primates of Colombia. In *Neotropical Primates: Field Studies and Conservation,* eds. R. W. Thorington, Jr. and P. G. Heltne, pp. 35–69. Washington, DC: Natl. Acad. of Sciences.
Hershkovitz, P.
1977 *Living New World Monkeys (Platyrrhini): Vol. 1.* Chicago: University of Chicago Press.
1979 The species of sakis, genus *Pithecia* (Cebidae, Primates) with notes on sexual dichromatism. *Folia Primatol.* 31:1–22.
Hewes, Gordon W.
1961 Food transport and the origin of hominid bipedalism. *Amer. Anthrop.* 63:687–710.
1964 Hominid bipedalism: Independent evidence for the food-carrying theory. *Science* 146:416–418.
1983a Cerebral brain endocast pattern of *Australopithecus afarensis* hominid. *Nature.* 303:420–422.
1983b Human brain evolution: A search for units, models, and synthesis. *Canadian Journal of Anthropology* 3(2):215–230.
Hiatt, Betty
1974 Woman the gatherer. In *Woman's Role in Aboriginal Society,* ed. Fay Gale, pp. 4–15. Canberra: Australian Institute of Aboriginal Studies.
Hill, K.
1982 Hunting and human evolution. *J. Human Evolution* 11:521–544.
Hill, W. C. O.
1972 *Evolutionary Biology of Primates.* New York: Academic Press.
Hinde, R. A., ed.
1983 *Primate Social Relationships.* Oxford: Blackwell.
Hladik, A., and Hladik, C.-M.
1969 Rapports trophiques entre végétation et primates: dans la forêt de Barro Colorodo (Panama). *Terre et Vie* 23:25–117.

Hladik, Claude-Marcel
1967 Surface relatives au tractus digestif de quelques primates: morphologie des villosités intestinales et correlations avec le régime alimentaire. *Mammalia* 31:120–147.
1977 A comparative study of the feeding strategies of two sympatric species of leaf monkeys: *Presbytis senex* and *Presbytis entellus*. In *Primate Ecology: Studies of Feeding and Ranging Behavior in Lemurs, Monkeys, and Apes*, ed. T. H. Clutton-Brock, pp. 323–353. London: Academic Press.
1981 Diet and the evolution of feeding strategies among forest primates. In *Omnivorous Primates: Gathering and Hunting in Human Evolution*, eds. R. S. O. Harding and G. Teleki, pp. 215–254. New York: Columbia Univ. Press.
Hladik, Claude-Marcel; Charles-Dominique, P.; Valdebouze, P.; Delort-Laval, J.; and Fanzy, J.
1971 La caecotrophie chez un primate phyllophage du genre *Lepilemur* et les corrélations avec les particularités de son appareil digestif. *C.R. Acad. Sci. Paris* 272:3191–3194.
Hladik, Claude-Marcel, and Hladik, A.
1972 Disponibilités alimentaires et domaines vitaux des Primates à Ceylan. *Terre et Vie* 26:149–215.
Hoebel, E. A., and Weaver, T.
1979 *Anthropology and the Human Experience*. 5th ed. New York. McGraw Hill.
Holdridge, L. R.
1967 Life Zone Ecology. Tropical Science Center, San Jose, Costa Rica.
Holloway, Ralph
1983 Cerebral brain endocast pattern of *Australopithecus afarensis* hominid. *Nature* 303:420–422.
Homewood, K.
1978 Feeding strategy of the Tana mangabey (*Cercocebus galeritus galeritus*) (Mammalia: Primates) *J. Zool. London* 186:375–391.
Horn, A.
1980 Some observations on the ecology of the bonobo chimpanzee (*Pan paniscus* Schwartz) near Lake Tumba, Zaire. *Folia primatol.* 34:145–169.
Hoyer, B. H.; Van de Velde, N. W.; Goodman, M.; and Roberts, B.
1972 Examination of hominid evolution by DNA sequence homology. *J. Human Evolution* 1:645–649.
Hrdy, S. B.
1977 *The Langurs of Abu*. Cambridge: Harvard University Press.
1981 *The Woman That Never Evolved*. Cambridge: Harvard University Press.
Hrdy, S. B., and Hausfater, G.
1984 Comparative and evolutionary perspectives on infanticide: introduction and overview. In *Infanticide: Comparative and Evolutionary Perspectives*, eds. G. Hausfater and S. B. Hrdy. Hawthorne, NY: Aldine.

Hubrecht, R. C.
1984 Field observations on group size and composition of the common marmoset (*Callithrix jacchus jacchus*) at Tapacura, Brazil. *Primates* 25:13–21.

Huxley, T. H.
1863 *Evidence as to Man's Place in Nature.* London: Williams and Norgate.

Hylander, W. L.
1975 Incisor size and diet in anthropoids with special reference to Cercopithecidae. *Science* 189:1095–1098.

Imai, H. T., and Crozier, R. H.
1980 Quantitative analysis of directionality in mammalian karyotype evolution. *Am. Nat.* 116:537–569.

Imai, H. T.; Maruyama, T.; and Crozier, R. H.
1983 Rates of mammalian karyotype evolution by the karyograph method. *Am. Nat.* 121:477–488.

Irons, W.
1983 Human female reproductive strategies. In *Social Behavior of Female Vertebrates,* ed. S. K. Wasser, pp. 169–214. New York: Academic Press.

Isaac, G.
1976 The activities of early African hominids. In *Human Origins,* eds. G. Isaac and E. McCown. pp. 483–514. Menlo Park, CA: Benjamin/Cummings.

1978a The food-sharing behavior of protohuman hominids *Sci. Amer.* 238(4):90–108.

1978b Food sharing and human evolution: archaelogical evidence from the Pio-Pleistocene of East Africa. *J. Anthropological Research* 34:311–325.

1980 Casting the net wide: a review of archaeological evidence for early hominid land-use and ecological relations. In *Current Argument on Early Man,* ed. L. K. Konigsson. pp. 227–251. New York: Pergamon Press.

1981 Archaeological tests of alternative models of early hominid behavior: excavation and experiments. In *The Emergence of Man,* eds. J. Z. Young, E. M. Jope, and K. P. Oakley. Phil. Trans. Roy. Soc. London 292:177–188.

1982 Models of human evolution. *Science* 217:295–304.

1983a Bones in contention: competing explanations for the juxtaposition of early Pleistocene artifacts and faunal remains. In *Animals and Archaeology,* vol. 1, ed. J. Clutton-Brock and C. Grigson, pp. 3–19. Brit. Arch. Report.

1983b Some archaeological contributions towards understanding human evolution. *Canadian J. Anthropology* 3:233–243.

1984 The archaeology of human origins: studies of the lower Pleistocene in East Africa 1971–1981. Chapter 1. In *Advances in World Archaeology,* Vol. 3, pp. 1–89. New York: Academic Press.

Isaac, G., and Crader, D.
1981 To what extent were early hominids carnivorous? In *Omnivorous Primates*, eds. R. Harding and G. Teleki, pp. 37–103. New York: Columbia University Press.

Itani, J.
1977 Evolution of primate social structure. *J. Human Evolution* 6:235–243.
1979 Distribution and adaptation of chimpanzees in an arid area. In *The Great Apes*, eds. D. A. Hamburg and E. R. McCown, pp. 55–71. Menlo Park, CA: Benjamin/Cummings.

Janzen, D. H.
1979 Why fruit rots. *Natl. Hist. Mag.* 88:60–64.

Jarmon, P. J.
1974 The social organization of antelope in relation to their ecology. *Behaviour* 48:215–267.

Jay, Phyllis C.
1965 The common langur of North India. In *Primate Behavior: Field Studies of Monkeys and Apes*, ed. I. DeVore, pp. 197–249. New York: Holt, Rinehart and Winston.
1968a *Primates: Studies in Adaptation and Variability*. New York: Holt, Rinehart and Winston.
1968b Primate field studies and human evolution. In *Primates*, ed. P. C. Jay, pp. 487–503. New York: Holt, Rinehart and Winston.

Jerison, H. J.
1973 *Evolution of the Brain and Intelligence*. New York: Academic Press.

Johanson, D. C.
1974 "An odontological study of the chimpanzee with some implications for hominid evolution." Ph. D. Dissertation, Univ. of Chicago.

Johanson, D. C., and Edey, M.
1981 *Lucy: the Beginnings of Humankind*. New York: Simon and Schuster.

Johanson, D. C.; White, T.; and Coppens, Y.
1978 A new species of the Genus *Australopithecus* (Primates: Hominidae) from the Pliocene of Eastern Africa. *Kirtlandia* 28:1–14.

Johanson, Donald C.; Taieb, Maurice; Coppens, Yves; and Roche, Helene
1980 New discoveries of pliocene hominids and artifacts in hadar: International Afar Research Expedition to Ethiopia (Fourth and Fifth Field Seasons, 1975–1977). *Journal of Human Evolution* 9(8):583–585.

Johanson, Donald C.; Taieb, Maurice; Gray, B.T.; and Coppens, Yves
1978 Geological framework of the Pliocene Hadar formation (Afar, Ethiopia) with notes on paleontology, including hominids. *Geological Background to Fossil Man*, ed. Walter W. Bishop, pp. 549–564.

Johanson, Donald C., and White, Tim D.
1979 A systematic assessment of early african hominids. *Science* 203:321–330.

Johnson, Steven C.
1981 Bonobos: generalized hominid prototypes or specialized insular dwarfs? *Current Anthropology* 22(4):363–375.

Jolly, A.
  1966 *Lemur Behavior.* Chicago: University of Chicago Press.
  1972 *The Evolution of Primate Behavior.* New York: Macmillan.
Jolly, C. J.
  1970 The seed-eaters: a new model of hominid differentiation based on a baboon analogy. *Man* 5:6–26.
  1973 Changing views of hominid origins. *Yearbook of Physical Anthropology* 16:1–17.
Jones, C., and Sabater Pi, J.
  1971 Comparative ecology of *Gorilla gorilla* (Savage and Wyman) and *Pan troglodytes* (Blumenbach) in Rio Muni, West Africa. *Bibliotheca Primatologica* 13, Basel: S. Karger.
Jones, K. C.
  1983 Inter-troop transfer of *Lemur catta* males at Berenty, Madagascar. *Folia primatol.* 40:145–160.
Jones, K. W.
  1976 Comparative aspects of DNA in higher primates. In: *Molecular Anthropology*, eds. M. Goodman, R. Tashian, and J. Tashian, pp. 357–368. New York: Plenum Press.
Jones, N. G. B.
  1984 A selfish origin for human food sharing: tolerated theft. *Ethology and Sociobiology* 5:1–4.
Jungers, W. L.
  1982 Lucy's limbs: skeletal allometry and locomotion in *Australopithecus afarensis. Nature:* 297:676–678.
Jungers, W. L., and Susman, R. L.
  1984 Body size and skeletal allometry in African apes. In *The Pygmy Chimpanzee: Evolutionary Morphology and Behavior*, ed. R. L. Susman, pp. 131–177. New York: Plenum.
Kano, T.
  1980 Social behavior of wild pygmy chimpanzees (*Pan paniscus*) of Wamba. *J. Human Evolution* 9:243–260.
  1982 The social group of pygmy chimpanzees (*Pan paniscus*) of Wamba. *Primates* 23:171–188.
  1983 An ecological study of pygmy chimpanzees (*Pan paniscus*) of Yalosidi, Republic of Zaire. *Int. J. Primatol.* 4:1–31.
  1984 Reproductive behavior of the pygmy chimpanzee, *Pan paniscus*, of Wamba, Republic du Zaire. In *Sexuality of the Primates*, eds. T. Maple and R. D. Nadler. New York: Van Nostrand Reinhold.
Kano, T., and Mulavwa, M.
  1984 Feeding ecology of pygmy chimpanzees (*Pan paniscus*) of Wamba. In *The Pygmy Chimpanzee: Evolutionary Biology and Behavior*, ed. R. L. Susman, pp. 233–274. New York: Plenum.
Kavanagh, M.
  1978 The diet and feeding behavior of *Cercopithecus aethiops tantalus. Folia Primatol.* 30:30–63.

Kawanaka, K.
  1981 Infanticide and cannibalism in chimpanzees with special reference to the newly observed case in the Mahale Mountains. *Afr. Stud. Monogr.* 1:69–100.
  1982 A case of inter-unit-group encounter in chimpanzees of the Mahale Mountains. *Primates* 23:558–562.
Kay, Richard F.
  1975 The functional adaptations of primate molar teeth. *Am. J. Phys. Anthro.* 43:195–216.
  1978 Molar structure and diet in extant Cercopithecidae. In *Development, Function and Evolution of Teeth*, eds. P. M. Butler and K. A. Joysey, pp. 309–339. New York: Academic Press.
  1981 The nut-crackers: a new theory of the adaptations of the ramapithecines. *Am. J. Phys. Anthro.* 55:141–152.
  1984 On the use of anatomical features to infer foraging behavior in extinct primates. In *Adaptations for Foraging in Nonhuman Primates: Contributions to an Organismal Biology of Prosimians, Monkeys, and Apes*, eds. Peter S. Rodman and John G. H. Cant, pp. 21–53. New York: Columbia University Press.
  1985 Dental evidence for the diet of *Australopithecus*. Ann. Rev. Anthropol. 14:315–341.
Kay, Richard F., and Hylander, W. L.
  1978 The dental structure of arboreal folivores with special reference to primates and Philangeroidea (Marsupialia). In *The Ecology of Arboreal Folivores*, ed. G. G. Montgomery, pp. 173–191. Washington, DC: Smithsonian Institution Press.
Kay, Richard F.; Sussman, R. W.; and Tattersall, I.
  1978 Dietary and dental variations in the genus *Lemur*, with comments concerning dietary-dental correlations among Malagasy primates. *Am. J. Phys. Anthro.* 49:119–127.
Keeley, L. and Toth, N.
  1981 Microwear polishes on early stone tools from Koobi Fora, Kenya. *Nature* 293:464–465.
Kimbel, William H.
  1984 Variation in the pattern of cranial venous sinuses and hominid phylogeny. *American Journal of Physical Anthropology* 63:243–263.
King, G.E.
  1975 Socioterritorial units among carnivores and early hominids. *J. Anth. Res.* 31:69–87.
  1980 Alternative uses of primates and carnivores in the reconstruction of early hominid behavior. *Ethol. Sociobio.* 1:99–109.
King, M. C., and Wilson, A. C.
  1975 Evolution at two levels in humans and chimpanzees. *Science* 188:107–118.
Kinzey, Warren G.
  1974 Ceboid models for the evolution of the hominoid dentition. *J. Human Evolution* 3:193–203.

1978 Feeding behavior and molar features in two species of titi monkey. In *Recent Advances in Primatology, Vol. 1, Behavior,* eds. D. J. Chivers and J. Herbert, pp. 373–385. London: Academic Press.

1981 The titi monkeys, Genus *Callicebus.* In *Ecology and Behavior of Neotropical Primates, Vol. 1,* eds. A. F. Coimbra-Filho and R. A. Mittermeier, pp. 241–276. Rio de Janeiro: Academia Brasileira de Ciências.

1982 Distribution of primates and forest refuges. In *Biological Diversification in the Tropics,* ed. G. T. Prance, pp. 455—482. New York: Columbia University Press.

1984 The dentition of the pygmy chimpanzee, *Pan paniscus.* In *The Pygmy Chimpanzee: Evolutionary Biology and Behavior,* ed. R. L. Susman, pp. 65–88. New York: Plenum.

Kinzey, Warren G., and Becker, M.
1983 Activity pattern of the masked titi monkey, *Callicebus personatus. Primates* 24:337–343.

Kinzey, Warren G., and Gentry, A. H.
1979 Habitat utilization in two species of *Callicebus.* In *Primate Ecology: Problem-Oriented Field Studies,* ed. R. W. Sussman, pp. 89–100. New York: Wiley.

Kitamura, Koji
1983 Pygmy chimpanzee association patterns in ranging. *Primates* 24:1–12.

Kleiman, D. G.
1977 Monogamy in mammals. *Qrt. Rev. Biol.* 52:39–69.

Kleiman, D. G., and Eisenberg, J. F.
1973 Comparisons of canid and felid social systems from an evolutionary perspective. *Animal Behav.* 21:637–659.

Klein, R.
1982 Age (mortality) profiles as a means of distinguishing hunted species from scavenged ones in Stone Age archaeological sites. *Paleobiology* 8:151–158.

Klinger, Harold P.; Hamerton, John L.; Mutton, David; and Lang, Ernst M.
1963 The chromosomes of the hominoidea. *Classification and Human Evolution.* ed. Sherwood L. Washburn. New York: Viking Fund Publications in Anthropology.

Kluge, A. G.
1983 Cladistics and the classification of the great apes. In *New Interpretations of Ape and Human Ancestry,* eds. R. L. Ciochon and R. S. Corruccini, pp. 151–177. New York: Plenum.

Kohne, Davie E.; Chiscon, J. A.; and Hoyer, B. H.
1972 Evolution of primate DNA sequences. *J. Human Evolution* 1:627–644.

Konner, Melvin
1986 Social subsistence and dietary adaptations of modern hunter-gatherers. Leaky symposium: diet and human evolution: from foraging to fast foods. Feb. 9, 1986, Berkeley, California.

Koop, Ben F.; Goodman, Morris; Xu, Peilin; Chan, Keith; and Slightom, Jerry
1986 Primate n-globin DNA sequences and man's place among the great apes. *Nature* 319(6050):234–238.

Krantz, G.
 1968 Brain size and hunting ability in earliest man. *Cur. Anthro.* 9:450–451.
Krebs, J. R. and Davies, N. B., eds.
 1978 *Behavioural Ecology: An Evolutionary Approach.* Oxford: Blackwell.
 1984 *Behavioural Ecology: An Evolutionary Approach,* 2nd ed. Oxford: Blackwell.
Kruuk, H.
 1972 *The Spotted Hyaena: a Study of Predation and Social Behvior.* Chicago: University of Chicago Press.
Kummer, H.
 1968 *Social Organization of Hamadryas Baboons: A Field Study.* Chicago: University of Chicago Press.
 1971 *Primate Societies.* Chicago: Aldine-Atherton.
 1978a Hamadryas research: a bias and a heuristic scheme. Paper presented at Wenner-Gren Conference: Baboon field research: myths and models, New York, June, 1978.
 1978b On the value of social relationships to nonhuman primates: a heuristic scheme. *Soc. Sci. Info.* 1:689–705.
Kummer, H.; Abegglen, J.; Bachman, C.; Falett, J.; and Sigg, H.
 1978 Grooming relationship and object competition among hamadryas baboons. In *Recent Advances in Primatology,* eds. D. Chivers and J. Herbert. London: Academic Press.
Kummer, H.; Goetz, W.; and Angst, W.
 1970 Cross species modificatiions of social behavior in baboons. In *Old World Monkeys,* eds. J. Napier and P. Napier. New York: Academic Press.
Kurland, J. A., and Beckerman, S. J.
 1985 Optimal foraging and hominid evolution: labor and reciprocity. *Am. Anthrop.* 87:73–93.
Kuroda, S.
 1979 Grouping of the pygmy chimpanzees. *Primates* 20:161–183.
 1980 Social behavior of the pygmy chimpanzees. *Primates* 21:181–197.
 1984 Interaction over food among pygmy chimpanzees. In *The Pygmy Chimpanzee: Evolutionary Biology and Behavior,* ed. R. L. Susman, pp. 301–324. New York: Plenum Press.
Lack, D.
 1968 *Ecological Adaptations for Breeding in Birds.* London: Methuen.
Lancaster, Jane
 1968 On the evolution of tool-using behavior. *Amer. Anthrop.* 70:56–66.
 1975 *Primate Behavior and the Emergence of Human Culture.*New York: Holt, Rinehart and Winston.
 1978 Carrying and sharing in human evolution. *Human Nature* 4:82–89.
Landau, M.; Pilbeam, D.; and Richard, A.
 1982 Human origins a century after Darwin. *Bioscience* 32(6):507–512.
Laporte, L.F., and Zihlman, A.L.
 1983 Plates, climate and hominid evolution. *S. Afr. J. Sci.* 79:96–110.

Latimer, B.M.; White, T.D.; Kimbel, W.H.; Johanson, D.C.; and Lovejoy, C.O.
 1981 The pygmy chimpanzee is not a living missing link in human evolution. *J. Human Evolution* 10:475–488.
Latour, Bruno, and Strum, S.C.
 (in press) Human social origins. *J. Biol. Soc. Structures.*
Latour, Bruno and Woolgar, S.
 1979 *Laboratory Life.* Beverly Hills, CA: Sage.
Leakey, M.D.
 1971 *Olduvai Gorge.* Vol. 3. London: Cambridge University Press.
Leakey, M.D., and Hay, R.L.
 1979 Pliocene footprints in the Laetolil beds at Laetoli, North Tanzania. *Nature* 278:317–323.
Leakey, R.E., and Lewin, R.
 1977 *Origins.* New York: E.P. Dutton.
Lee, Richard B.
 1968 What hunters do for a living, or, how to make out on scarce resources. In *Man the Hunter,* eds. Richard B. Lee and Irven DeVore, pp. 30–48. Chicago: Aldine.
 1969 !Kung bushman subsistence: an input-output analysis. In *Environment and Cultural Behavior,* ed. A.P. Vayda, pp. 47–79. New York: Natural History Press.
 1979 *The !Kung San: Men, Women, and Working in a Foraging Society.* New York: Cambridge University Press.
 1984 *Te Dobe !Kung.* New York: Holt, Rinehart and Winston.
Lee, Richard B., and DeVore, I.
 1968 *Man the Hunter.* Chicago: Aldine.
Leibowitz, Lila
 1978 *Females, Males, Families: A Biosocial Approach.* Belmont, CA: Wadsworth.
Leutenegger, Walter
 1980 Monogamy in callitrichids: a consequence of phyletic dwarfism? *Int. J. primatol.* 1:95–98.
Levins, R.
 1966 The strategy of model building in population biology. *American Scientist* 54:421–431.
 1968 *Evolution in Changing Environments.* Cambridge: Harvard University Press.
Lewin, Roger
 1984 DNA reveals surprises in human family tree: the application of DNA-DNA hybridization to relationships among hominoids places humans with chimps, while gorillas are separate. *Science* 226:1179–1182.
Lewontin, R.C.
 1979 Sociobiology as an adaptationist program. *Behavioral Science* 24:5–14.
Lindburg, Donald G.
 1969 Rhesus monkeys: mating season mobility of adult males. *Science* 166:1176–1178.

Linton, Sally
1971 Woman the gatherer: male bias in anthropology. *Woman in Cross-Cultural Perspective: a Preliminary Sourcebook,* ed. Sue-Ellen Jacobs, pp. 9–21. Urbana: University of Illinois Press.

Lorenz, K.
1967 *On Aggression.* New York: Bantam Books.

Lovejoy, C. Owen
1975 Biomechanical perspectives on the lower limb of early hominids. In *Primate Functional Morphology and Evolution,* ed. R.H. Tuttle, pp. 291–326. The Hague: Mouton.
1978 A biochemical review of the locomotor diversity of early hominids. In *Early Hominids of Africa,* ed. C. Jolly, pp. 403–429. New York: St. Martin's Press.
1979 Hominid origins: the role of bipedalism. *Am. J. Phys. Anth.* 52:250.
1981 The origin of man. *Science* 211:341–350.
1982 Models of human evolution. *Science* 217:304–305.

Lovejoy, C. Owen; Heiple, K.; and Burnstein, A.
1973 The gait of *Australopithecus. Am. J. Phys. Anth.* 38:757–780.

MacArthur, R.H., and Wilson, E.O.
1967 *The Theory of Island Biogeography.* Princeton: Princeton University Press.

Macdonald, D., ed.
1984 *The Encyclopedia of Mammals.* New York: Facts on File Publications.

MacKinnon, J.R.
1974 The behavior and ecology of wild orang-utans (*Pongo pygmaeus*). *Anim. Behav.* 22:3–74.

MacKinnon, J.R. and MacKinnon, K.S.
1980 Niche differentiation in a primate community. In *Malayan Forest Primates: Ten Years' Study in Tropical Rain Forest,* ed. D.J. Chivers, pp. 167–190. New York: Plenum.

Marias, Eugene
1940 *My Friends the Baboons.* New York: McBride.
1969 *The Soul of the Ape.* New York: Atheneum.

Markowitz, J.
1979 Environmental enrichment and behavioral engineering for captive primates. In *Captivity and Behavior.* eds. J. Erwin, T. Maple and G. Mitchell. New York: Van Nostrand.

Marks, Jon
1983a Hominoid cytogenetics and evolution. *Yearbook Phys. Anthrop.* 25:125–153.
1983b Rates of karyotype evolution. *Syst. Zool.* 38:207–209.

Marshall, L.
1976 *The !Kung of Nyae Nyae.* Cambridge: Harvard University Press.

Martin, D.E.; Gould, K.G.; and Warner, H.
1975 Comparative morphology of primate spermatozoa using scanning electron microscopy. I. Families hominidae, pongidae, cercopithecidae, and cebidae. *Journal of Human Evolution* 4:287–292.

Martin, M.K. and Voorhies, B.
1975 *Female of the Species.* New York: Columbia University Press.

Martin, R.D.
1978 Major features of prosimian evolution: a discussion in light of chromosomal evidence. In *Recent Advances in Primatology, Vol. 3,* eds. D.J. Chivers and K.A. Joysey, pp. 3–26. London: Academic Press.

1983 *Human Brain Evolution in an Ecological Context.* Fifty-Second James Arthur Lecture on the Evolution of the Human Brain. New York: American Museum of Natural History.

Martin, R.D.; Chivers, D.J.; MacLarnon, A.M.; and Hladik, C.M.
1985 Gastrointestinal allometry in primates and other mammals. In *Size and Scaling in Primate Biology,* ed. W.L. Jungers, pp. 61–90. New York: Plenum Press.

Maynard Smith, J.
1964 Group selection and kin selection. *Nature* 201:1145–1147.

1982 *Evolution and the Theory of Games.* Cambridge: Cambridge University Press.

Maynard Smith, J., and Price, G.R.
1973 The logic of animal conflict. *Nature* 246:15–18.

Mayr, E.
1963 *Animal Species and Evolution.* Cambridge: Harvard University Press.

McGrew, W.
1979 Evolutionary implications of sex differences in chimpanzee predation and tool-use. In *The Great Apes.* Perspectives on Human Evolution, vol. 5, eds. David A. Hamburg and Elizabeth R. McCown, pp. 441–463. Menlo Park, CA:Benjamin/Cummings.

1981 The female chimpanzee as a female evolutionary prototype. *Woman the Gatherer,* ed. F. Dahlberg, pp. 35–73. New Haven: Yale University Press.

McGrew, W.; Baldwin, P.J.; and Tutin, C.E.G.
1981 Chimpanzees in a hot, dry and open habitat: Mt. Assirik, Senegal, West Africa. *J. Hum. Evol.* 10:227–244.

McGrew, W.; Tutin, C.I.G.; and Baldwin, P.J.
1979 Chimpanzees, tools, and termites: cross-cultural comparisons of Senegal, Tanzania and Rio Muni. *Man* 14:185–214.

McHenry, Henry M.
1975 Fossils and the mosaic nature of human evolution. *Science* 190:425–431.

McHenry, Henry M., and Corruccini, R.S.
1981 *Pan paniscus* and human evolution. *Am. J. Phys. Anth.* 54:355–376.

McKenna, J.J.

1982 The evolution of primate societies, reproduction, and parenting. In *Primate Behavior,* eds. J.L. Fobes and J.E. King, pp. 87–133. New York: Academic Press.

Mead, M.

1982 *Coming of Age in Samoa.* New York: American Museum of Natural History.

Mech, D.L.

1970 *The Wolf.* New York: Doubleday.

Menzel, Emil W. Jr.

1973 Chimpanzee spatial memory organization. *Science* 19:450–457.

1974 A group of young chimpanzees in a one acre field. *Behavior of Nonhuman primates: Modern Research Trends,* vol. 5, eds. A.M. Schrier and F. Stollnitz, pp. 83–153. New York: Academic Press.

Menzel, Emil W. Jr., and Halperin, Stewart

1975 Purposive behavior as a basis for objective communication between chimpanzees. *Science* 189:652–654.

Miller, Dorothy A.

1977 Evolution of primate chromosomes: man's closest relatives may be the gorilla not the chimpanzee. *Science* 198:1116–1124.

Miller, Dorothy A.; Choi, Y.-C.; and Miller, O.J.

1983 Chromosome localization of highly repetitive human DNA's and amplified ribosomal DNA with restriction enzymes. *Science* 219:395–397.

Milton, K.

1980 *The Foraging Strategy of Howler Monkeys.* New York: Columbia University Press.

1985 Multimale mating and absence of canine tooth dimorphism in woolly spider monkeys (*Brachyteles arachnoides*). *Am. J. Phys. Anth.* 68:519–523.

Mintz, K.P.; Weinshilboum, R.M.; and Brimijoin, W.S.

1984 Evolution of butyrylcholinesterase in higher primates: an immunochemical study. *Comp. Biochem. Physiol.* 79C(1):35–37.

Mittermeier, R.A., and van Roosmalen, M.G.M.

1981 Preliminary observations on habitat utilization and diet in eight Surinam monkeys. *Folia primatol.* 36:1–39.

Moore, J.

1984 The evolution of reciprocal sharing. *Ethology and Sociobiology* 5:5–14.

Morgan, E.

1972 *The Descent of Woman.* New York: Stein and Day.

Morris, D.

1967 *The Naked Ape.* New York: McGraw-Hill.

Murdock, George P.
  1949   *Social Structure.* New York: Macmillan.
  1957   World ethnographic sample. *Am. Anthrop.* 59:664–687.
Myers, R.H., and Shafer, D.A.
  1979   Hybrid ape offspring of a mating of gibbon and siamang. *Science* 205:308–310.
Napier, J.
  1962   Fossil hand bones from Olduvai Gorge. *Nature* 196:409–411.
Neyman, P.F.
  1977   Aspects of the ecology and social organization of free-ranging cotton-top tamarins *Saguinus oedipus* and the conservation status of the species. In *The Biology and Conservation of the Callitrichidae,* ed. D.G. Kleiman, pp. 39–71. Washington, D.C.: Smithsonian Institution Press.
Nimkoff, M.F., and R. Middleton
  1960   Types of family and types of economy. *Am. J. Sociology* 66:215–224.
Nishida, Toshisada
  1979   The social structure of the chimpanzees of the Mahale Mountains. In *The Great Apes.* Perspectives on Human Evolution, vol. 5, eds. David A. Hamburg and Elizabeth R. McCown, pp. 72–121. Menlo Park, CA: Benjamin/Cummings.
  1983a Alpha status and agnostic alliance in wild chimpanzees (*Pan troglodytes schweinfurthii*). *Primates* 24(3):318–336.
  1983b Alloparental behavior in wild chimpanzees of the Mahale Mountains, Tanzania. *Folia Primatol.* 41:1–33.
Nishida, Toshisada, and Kawanaka, Kenji
  1972   Inter-unit-group relationships among wild chimpanzees of the Mahali Mountains. *Kyoto University African Studies* 7:131–169.
Oakley, K.
  1961a *Man the Tool-Maker.* Chicago: University of Chicago Press.
  1961b On man's use of fire, with comments on tool-making and hunting. In *Social Life of Early Man,* ed. S.L. Washburn. Chicago: Aldine.
Ohno, S.
  1982   The common ancestry of genes and spacers in the euchromatic region: *Omnis ordinis hereditarium a ordinis priscum minutum. Cytogenet. Cell Genet.* 34:102–111.
Oppenheimer, J.R.
  1968   "Behavior and Ecology of the White-faced Monkey, *Cebus capucinus,* on Barro Colorado Island, Canal Zone." Ph.D. dissertation, University of Illinois.
Orlove, B.S.
  1980   Ecological anthropology. *Ann. Rev. Anthro.* 9:235–273.
Otterbein, K.F.
  1974   The Anthropology of War. In *Handbook of Social and Cultural Anthropology,* ed. J.J. Honigmann, pp. 923–958. New York: Rand McNally.

Oxnard, Charles E.
1975 *Uniqueness and Diversity in Human Evolution.* Chicago: Chicago University Press.
1981 The place of man among the primates: anatomical, molecular, and morphometric evidence. *Homo* 32(3–4):149–176.
1984 *The Order of Man.* New Haven: Yale University Press.

Packer, C.
1975 Male transfer in olive baboons. *Nature 255:219–220.*
1979 Inter-troop transfer and inbreeding avoidance in *Papio anubis. Anim. Behav.* 27:1–36.

Packer, C. and Pusey, A.E.
1983 Adaptations of female lions to infanticide by incoming males. *Am. Naturalist* 121:716–728.
1984 Infanticide in carnivores. In *Infanticide: Comparative and Evolutionary Perspectives,* eds. G. Hausfater and S.B. Hrdy, pp. 31–42. Hawthorne, NY: Aldine.

Paris Conference (1971); Supplement (1975)
1975 Standardization in human cytogenetics. *Birth Defects: Original Article Series* vol. 11, no. 9. New York: The National Foundation— March of Dimes.

Parker, C.A.
1974 Assessment strategy and the evolution of fighting behavior. *J. Theoretical Biology* 47:223–243.

Petter, J.-J.
1962 Recherches sur l'écologie et l'éthologie des lémuriens malgaches. *Mém. Mus. Natl. Hist. Paris* 27A:1–146.

Pfeiffer, J.E.
1972 *The Emergence of Man.* New York: Harper and Row.

Pianka, E.R.
1969 Sympatry of desert lizards (*Ctenotus*) in western Australia. *Ecology* 50:1012–1030.
1970 On r- and K- selection. *Am. Naturalist* 104:592–597.
1973 The structure of lizard communities. *Annual Review of Ecology and Systematics* 4:53–74.

Pilbeam, David R.
1983 New hominoid skull material from the Miocene of Pakistan. *Nature* 295:232–234.
1984 The descent of hominoids and hominids. *Scientific American* 250(3):84–97.

Pilbeam, D.R.; Behrensmeyer, A.K.; Barry, J.; and Shah, S.I.
1979 Miocene sediments and faunas of Pakistan. *Postilla* vol. 179:1–45.

Pollock, J.I.
1977 The ecology and sociology of feeding in *Indri indri.* In *Primate Ecology: Studies of Feeding and Ranging Behavior in Lemurs, Monkeys and Apes,* ed. T.H. Clutton-Brock, pp. 38–69. London: Academic Press.

1979   Spatial distribution and ranging behavior in lemurs. In *The Study of Prosimian Behavior,* eds. G.A. Doyle and R.D. Martin, pp. 359–409. New York: Academic Press.

Popp, J.L.
1978   Kidnapping among male anubis baboons in Masai Mara Resserve. Paper presented at Wenner-Gren conference, Baboon Field Research: Myths and Models. New York, June, 1978.

Popp, J.L., and DeVore, I.
1979   Aggressive competition and social dominance theory: Synopsis. In *The Great Apes.* Perspectives on Human Evolution, vol. 5, eds. David A. Hamburg and Elizabeth R. McCown, pp. 317–338. Menlo Park, CA: Benjamin/Cummings.

Popper, K.R.
1959   *The Logic of Scientific Discovery.* New York: Harper and Row.
1972   *Objective Knowledge: An Evolutionary Approach.* London: Oxford University Press.

Potts, Richard
1982   "Lower Pleistocene site formation and hominid activities at Olduvai Gorge, Tanzania." Ph.D. dissertation, Harvard University.
1983   Foraging for faunal resources by early hominids at Olduvai Gorge, Tanzania. In *Animals and Archaeology,* eds. J. Clutton-Brock and C. Grigson, pp. 51–62. Brit. Arch. Rep.
1984a   Hominid hunters? Problems of identifying the earliest hunter/gatherers. In *Hominid Evolution and Community Ecology: prehistoric human adaptation in biological perspective,* ed. Robert Foley, pp. 129–166. London: Academic Press.
1984b   Home bases and early hominids. *American Scientist* 72:338–347.

Potts, Richard, and Shipman, P.
1981   Cutmarks made by stone tools on bones from Olduvai Gorge, Tanzania. *Nature* 291:577–580.

Preuschoft, H.
1971   Body posture and mode of locomotion in early Pleistocene hominids. *Folia Primatologica* 14:209–240.

Prouty, L.A.; Buchanan, P.D.; Pollitzer, W.S.; and Mootnick, A.R.
1983   A presumptive new hylobatid subgenus with 38 chromosomes. *Cytogenet. Cell Genet.* 35:141–142.

Pusey, Anne
1979   Intercommunity transfer of chimpanzees in Gombe National Park. In *The Great Apes.* Perspectives on Human Evolution, vol. 5, eds. David A. Hamburg and Elizabeth R. McCown, pp. 465–479. Menlo Park, CA: Benjamin/Cummings.

Quris, R.
1975   Ecologie et organisation sociale de *Cercocebus galeritus agilis* dans le Nord-est du Gabon. *Terre et Vie* 29:337–398.

Raemaekers, J.
1979   Ecology of sympatric gibbons. *Folia primatol.* 31:227–245.

Ransom, T.W.
1971 "Ecology and social behavior of baboons at the Gombe National Park." Ph.D. dissertation, University of California, Berkeley.
Ransom, T.W. and Ransom, B.S.
1971 Adult male-infant relations among baboons (*Papio anubis*). *Folia Primatol.* 16:179–195.
Redican, William K.
1976 Adult male-infant interactions in nonhuman primates. In *The Role of the Father in Child Development,* ed. Michael E. Lamb, pp. 345–385. New York: Wiley.
Redican, William K., & David M. Taub
1981 Male parental care in monkeys and apes. In *The Role of the Father in Child Development,* 2nd edition, ed. Michael E. Lamb, pp. 203–258. New York: Wiley.
Reynolds, P.C.
1976 The emergence of early hominid social organizations: I. The attachment systems. *Yrbk. Phys. Anthro.* 20:73–95.
Reynolds, Vernon
1965 *Budongo: An African Forest and its Chimpanzees.* New York: Natural History Press.
1966 Open groups in hominid evolution. *Man* 1:441–452.
1975 How wild are the Gombe Chimpanzees? *Man* 10 (1):123–126.
Reynolds, Vernon, and Reynolds, Frances
1965 Chimpanzees of the Budongo Forest. In *Primate Behavior: Field Studies of Monkeys and Apes,* ed. I. DeVore, pp. 368–424. New York: Holt, Rinehart and Winston.
Rhoades, D.F., and Cates, R.G.
1976 A general theory of plant antiherbivore chemistry. *Recent Advances in Phytochemistry* 10:168–213.
Riccardi, V.M., and Holmquist, G.P.
1979 De novo 13p paracentric inversion in a boy with cleft palate and mental retardation. *Hum. Genet.* 52:211–215.
Richard, A.
1978 Variability in the feeding behavior of a Malagasy prosimian, *Propithecus verreauxi.* In *The Ecology of Arboreal Folivores,* ed. G.G. Montgomery, pp. 519–533. Washington D.C.: Smithsonian Institution.
1981 Changing assumptions in primate ecology. *Am. Anthro.* 83:517–533.
1985 *Primates in Nature.* San Francisco: Freeman.
Ricklefs, R.E.
1973 *Ecology.* Portland, OR: Chiron Press.
Rijksen, H.D.
1978 A field study on Sumatran orang utans (*Pongo pygmaeus abeli* Lesson 1827). Wageningen: H. Veenman and Zonen.
Ripley, S.
1984 Environmental grain, niche diversification and feeding behaviour in primates. In *Food Acquisition and Processing in Primates,* eds. D.J.

Chivers, B.A. Wood and A. Bilsborough, pp. 33–72. New York: Plenum Press.

Riss, David C., and Busse, Curt D.
1977 Fifty day observation of a free-ranging adult male chimpanzee. *Folia Primat.* 28:283–297.

Robinson, John G.
1982 Intrasexual competition and mate choice in primates. *Am. J. Primatol.*, Supplement 1:131–144.

Robinson, John G.; Wright, P.C.; and Kinzey, W.G.
1986 Monogamous cebids and their relatives: intergroup calls and spacing. In *Primate Societies,* eds. B. Smuts, D.L. Cheney, R.M. Seyfarth, R.W. Wrangham, and T.T. Struhsaker. Chicago: University of Chicago Press.

Robinson, John T.
1972 *Early Hominid Posture and Locomotion.* Chicago: University Chicago Press.

Robinson, P.A.; Hawkey, C.; and Hammond, G.L.
1985 A phylogenetic study of the structural and functional characteristics of corticosteroid binding globulin in primates. *Journal of Endocrinology* 104:251–257.

Rodman, Peter S.
1977 Feeding behavior of orang-utans of the Kutai reserve. In *Primate Ecology: Studies of Feeding and Ranging Behaviour in Lemurs, Monkeys and Apes,* ed. T.H. Clutton-Brock, pp. 384–413. London: Academic Press.
1979 Individual activity patterns and the solitary nature of orangutans. In *The Great Apes.* Perspectives on Human Evolution, vol. 5, eds. David A. Hamburg and Elizabeth R. McCown, pp. 235–255. Menlo Park, CA: Benjamin/Cummings.
1984 Foraging and social systems of orangutans and chimpanzees. In *Adaptations for Foraging in Non-Human Primates,* eds. P.S. Rodman and J.G.H. Cant, pp. 134–160. New York: Columbia University Press.

Rodman, Peter S., and Wrangham, Richard W.
1979 Sexual dimorphism and comparative socioecology of orang-utans and chimpanzees. *Am. J. Phys. Anth.* 50(3):475–476.

Romero-Herrara, A.E.; Lehmann, H.; Joysey, K.A.; and Friday, A.E.
1973 Molecular evolution of myoglobin and the fossil record: a phylogenetic synthesis. *Nature* 246:389–395.

Roonwal, M.L., and Mohnot, S.M.
1977 *Primates of South Asia.* Cambridge: Harvard University Press.

Rosenberger, Alfred L.
1981 Systematics: the higher taxa. In *Ecology and Behavior of Neotropical Primates, vol. 1,* eds. A.F. Coimbra-Filho and R.A. Mittermeier, pp. 9–27. Rio de Janeiro: Academia Brasileira de Ciências.

Rosenberger, Alfred L., and Kinzey, Warren G.
1976 Functional patterns of molar occlusion in platyrrhine primates. *Am. J. Phys. Anth.* 45(2):281–298.

Rotenberry, J.T.
  1980 Dietary relationships among shrubsteppe passerine birds: competition or opportunism in a variable environment? *Ecological Monographs* 50:93–110.
Rowell, T.E.
  1966a Hierarchy in the organization of a captive baboon group. *Anim. Behav.* 14:430–443.
  1966b Forest-living baboons in Uganda. *J. Zool. Lond.,* 149:344–364.
  1969a Long-term changes in a population of Ugandan baboons. *Folia primatol.* 11:241–254.
  1969b Variability in the social organization of primates. In *Primate Ecology,* ed. D. Morris, pp. 283–305. Garden City: Anchor Books.
Rubio-Goday, A.; Caballín. M.; Garcia Caldés, M.; and Egozcue, J.
  1976 Comparative study of the banding patterns of the chromosomes of Cercopithecidae (sic). I. Subfamily Papinae (sic): *Macaca fascicularis* and *Papio sphinx. Folia Primatol.* 26:306–309.
Rumpler, Y., and Dutrillaux, B.
  1976 Chromosomal evolution in Malagasy lemurs. I. Chromosomal banding in the genuses (sic) *Lemur* and *Microcebus. Cytogenet. Cell Genet.* 17:268–282.
  1978 Chromosomal evolution in Malagasy lemurs. III. Chromosome banding studies in the genus *Hapalemur* and the species *Lemur catta. Cytogenet. Cell Genet.* 21:201–211.
  1980 Chromosomal evolution in Malagasy lemurs. VI. Chromosomal banding studies of *Lemur fulvus albifrons, Lemur rubriventer* and its hybrids with *Lemur fulvus fulvus. Folia primatol.* 33:253–261.
Rylands, A.B.
  1981 Preliminary field observations on the marmoset, *Callithrix humeralifer intermedius* (Hershkovitz, 1977) at Dardanelos, Rio Aripuanã, Mato Grosso. *Primates* 22:46–59.
Sahlins, M.D.
  1976 *The Use and Abuse of Biology: An Anthropological Critique of Sociobiology.* Ann Arbor: University of Michigan Press.
Sarich, Vincent M.
  1977 Rates, sample sizes, and the neutrality hypothesis for electrophoresis in evolutionary studies. *Nature* 265(5589):24–28.
  1980 Molecular clocks and hominid evolution after 12 years. Ms.
  1983 Appendix: Retrospective on hominoid macromolecular systematics. *New Interpretations of Ape and Human Ancestry.* eds. Russell L. Ciochon and Robert S. Corruccini. New York and London: Plenum Press.
  1984 Pygmy chimpanzee systematics: a molecular perspective. *The Pygmy Chimpanzee, Evolutionary Biology and Behavior,* ed. Randall L. Susman, pp. 43–48. New York: Plenum Press.
Sarich, Vincent M. and Cronin, John E.
  1976 Molecular systematics of the primates. *Molecular Anthropology,* eds. Morris Goodman and Richard Tashian, pp. 141–170. New York: Plenum.

Sarich, Vincent M.; and Wilson, Allan C.
1967 Immunological time scale for hominid evolution. *Science* 158(3805):1200–1203.

Savage-Rumbaugh, E.S., and Rumbaugh, D.M.
1982 Ape language research is alive and well: a reply. *Anthropos* 77(3–4):568–573.

Savage-Rumbaugh, E.S.; Rumbaugh, D.M.; and Boysen, S.
1978 Symbolic communication between two chimpanzees (*Pan troglodytes*). *Science* 201:641–644.

Savage-Rumbaugh, E.S. and Wilkerson, B.J.
1978 Socio-sexual behavior in *Pan paniscus* and *Pan troglodytes:* a comparative study. *J. Hum. Evol.* 1:327–344.

Savage-Rumbaugh, E.S.; Wilkerson, B.J.; and Bakeman, R.
1977 Spontaneous gestural communication among conspecifics in the pygmy chimpanzee (*Pan paniscus*). *Progress in Ape Research,* ed. G.H. Bourne, pp. 97–116. New York: Academic Press.

Schaller, G.B.
1972 *The Serengeti Lion.* Chicago: University Chicago Press.
1976 *The Mountain Gorilla: Ecology and Behavior.* Chicago: University of Chicago Press.

Schaller, G.B., and Lowther, G.
1969 The relevance of carnivore behavior to the study of early hominids. *Southwest J. Anthro.* 25:307–341.

Schlichte, H.-J.
1978 A preliminary report on the habitat utilization of a group of howler monkeys (*Alouatta villosa pigra*) in the national Park of Tikal, Guatemala. In *The Ecology of Arboreal Folivores,* ed. G.G. Montgomery, pp. 551–559. Washington D.C.: Smithsonian Institution.

Schwartz, J.H.
1984a The evolutionary relationships of man and orangutans. *Nature* 308:501–505.
1984b Hominoid evolution: a review and a reassessment. *Current Anthropology* 25:655–672.

Sekulic, Ranka
1981 "The Significance of Howling in the Red Howler Monkeys (*Alouatta seniculus*)." Ph.D. dissertation, University of Maryland.
1982a Daily and seasonal patterns of roaring and spacing in four red howler *Alouatta seniculus* troops. *Folia Primatol.* 39:22–48.
1982b The function of howling in red howler monkeys (*Alouatta seniculus*). *Behaviour* 81:38–54.

Senut, B.
1978 Contribution a l'étude de l'humerus et de ses articulations chez les hominides du Plio-Peistocene; thèse doct. 3e cycle, Paris.

1980   New data on the humerus and its joints in Plio-Pleistocene hominids. *Collegium Anthropologicum* 4:87–93.

Senut, B., and LeFloch, P.
1981   Divergence des piliers de la palette humerale chez les primates hominoides. *C.R. Acad. Sci. Paris, Ser. II* 292:757–760.

Senut, B., and Tardieu, C.
1985   Functional aspects of Plio-Pleistocene hominid limb bones: implications for taxonomy and phylogeny. In *Ancestors: The Hard Evidence,* ed. E. Delson, pp. 193–201. New York: A.R. Liss.

Service, E.R.
1966   *The Hunters.* Englewood Cliffs, NJ: Prentice-Hall.
1967   War and our contemporary ancestors. In *War: The Anthropology of Armed Conflict and Aggression,* eds. M. Fried, M. Harris, and R. Murphy, pp. 160–167. New York: Natural History Press.

Scuánez, Héctor N.
1980   Chromosomes and spermatozoa of the African Great Apes. *J. Reproduction and Fertility* 28:91–104.

Seuánez, Héctor N.; Robinson, J.; Martin, D.E.; and Short, R.V.
1976   Fluorescent (F) bodies in the spermatozoa of man and the great apes. *Cytogenet. Cell. Genet.* 17:317–326.

Shackleton, N.
1967   Oxygen isotope analyses and Pleistocene temperatures re-assessed. *Nature* 215:15–17.

Shapiro, D.
1978   The aggressive strategy of individual vervets during long fights. In *Recent Advances in Primatology,* vol. 1, eds. D. Chivers and J. Herbert, pp. 593–596. London: Academic Press.

Shea, Brian T.
1983   Paedomorphosis and neoteny in the pgymy chimpanzee. *Science* 222:521–522.
1984   An allometric perspective on the morphological and evolutionary relationships between pygmy (*Pan paniscus*) and common (*Pan troglodytes*) chimpanzees. In *The Pygmy Chimpanzee: Evolutionary Biology and Behavior,* ed. R.L. Susman, pp. 89–130. New York: Plenum.

Shipman, P.
1981   *Life History of a Fossil.* Cambridge: Harvard University Press.
1983   Early hominid lifestyle: hunting and gathering or foraging and scavenging? In *Animals and Archaeology* vol. 1, eds. J. Clutton-Brock and C. Grigson, pp. 31–49, Brit. Arch. Rep.
1985   The ancestor that wasn't. *The Sciences* 25(2):43–48.

Shipman, Pat
1986   Scavenging or hunting in early hominids: Theoretical framework and tests. *Amer. Anthropol.* 88:27–43.

Shipman, P., and Rose, J.
1983   Early hominid hunting, butchering, and carcass-processing behaviors: approaches to the fossil record. *J. Anthrop. Arch.* 2:57–98.

Shoemaker, A.H.
  1978 Observations on howler monkeys, *Alouatta caraya,* in captivity. *Der Zoologishe Garten* 48:225–234.
Sibley, Charles G., and Ahlquist, Jon E.
  1984 The phylogeny of the hominoid primates, as indicated by DNA-DNA hybridization. *J. Mol. Evolution* 20:2–15.
  1986 Reconstructing bird phylogeny by comparing DNA's. *Sci. Amer.* 254(2):82–92.
Sicher, H.
  1944 Masticatory apparatus in the giant panda and the bears. *Field Mus. of Natural History* Series, Zoology 21:61–73.
Siegel, S.
  1956 *Nonparametric Statistics for the Behavioral Sciences.* New York: McGraw-Hill.
Silberbauer, G.
  1981 Hunter-gatherers of the Central Kalahari. In *Omnivorous Primates,* eds. R. S. O. Harding and G. Teleki, pp. 455–498. New York: Columbia University Press.
Silk, Joan B.
  1978 Patterns of food-sharing among mother and infant chimpanzees at Gombe National Park, Tanzania. *Folia Primatologia* 29:129–141.
Simonds, P. E.
  1965 The bonnet macaque in South India. In *Primate Behavior: Field Studies of Monkeys and Apes,* ed. I. DeVore, pp. 175–196. New York: Holt, Rinehart, and Winston.
Simpson, G. G.
  1944 *Tempo and Mode in Evolution.* New York: Columbia University Press.
  1945 The principles of classification and a classification of mammals. *Bull. Am. Mus. Nat. Hist.* 85:1–350.
Skelton, Randall R.; McHenry, Henry M.; and Drawhorn, Gerrell M.
  1973b Social organization of wild chimpanzees. *Behavioral regulators of behavior in primates.* C.R. Carpenter, ed., pp. 68–80. Lewisburg, Pa.: Bucknell University Press.
  1986 Phylogenetic analysis of early hominids. *Current Anthropology* 27(1):21–43.
Slatkin, M., and Hausfater, G.
  1976 A note on the activities of a solitary male baboon. *Primates* 9:225–258.
Smith, J. D.
  1970 The systematic status of the black howler monkey, *Alouatta pigra* Lawrence. *J. Mammal.* 51:358–369.
Smuts, B. B.
  1983 Special relationships between adult male and female olive baboons: selective advantages. In *Primate Social Relationships: An Integrated Approach,* ed. R. A. Hinde, pp. 262–266. Sunderland, MA: Sinauer Associates.

Socha, W. W., and Moor-Jankowski, J.
1979 Blood groups of Anthropoid apes and their relationships to human blood groups. *J. Human Evolution* 8:453–465.
1980 Chimpanzee R-C-E-F blood group system: a counterpart of the human Rh-Hr blood groups. *Folia Primat.* 33:172–188.

Soma, H.; Benirschke, K.; and Robinson, P.
1974 The chromosomes of the proboscis monkey (*Nasalis larvatus*). *Chromosome Information Service* 17:24–26.

Soulie, J., and de Grouchy, J.
1981 A cytogenetic survey of 110 baboons (*Papio cynocephalus*) *Am. J. Phys. Anthro.* 56:107–113.

Southwick, C. H.; Beg, M. A.; and Siddiqi, M. R.
1965 Rhesus monkeys in northern India. In *Primate Behavior: Field Studies of Monkeys and Apes,* ed. I. DeVore, pp. 111–159. New York: Holt, Rinehart and Winston.

Spuhler, J. N.
1959 Somatic paths to culture. In *The Evolution of Man's Capacity for Culture,* ed. J. Spuhler, pp. 1–13. Detroit: Wayne State Univ. Press.

Stacey, Peter
1986 Group size and foraging efficiency in yellow baboons. *Behav. Ecol. Sociobiol.,* 18:175–187.

Stander, J. M.
1970 "Diversity and similarity of benthic fauna off Oregon." Ph.D. dissertation, Oregon State University.

Stanyon, R.
1982 "Chromosome evolution in the primates: *Macaca* to *Homo.*" Ph. D. dissertation, Pennsylvania State University.

Stanyon, R., and Chiarelli, B.
1982 Phylogeny of the hominoidea: the chromosome evidence. *J. Hum. Evol.* 11:493–504.
1983 Mode and tempo in primate chromosome evolution: implications for hylobatid phylogeny. *J. Hum. Evol.* 12:305–315.

Stanyon, R.; Patton, W. H.; Kurland, J. A.; and Taub, D. M.
1980 G-banding in the Barbary macaque (*Macaca sylvanus,* Linnaeus, 1758) of Morocco. *J. Hum. Evol.* 9:147–152.

Stearns, S. C.
1976 Life-history tactics: a review of the ideas. *Qrt. Rev. Biol.* 51:3–47.

Stern, J., and Susman, R.
1981 Electromyography of the gluteal muscles in *Hylobates, Pongo,* and *Pan:* implications for the evolution of hominid bipedalism. *Am. J. Phys. Anth.* 55:153–166.
1983 The locomotor anatomy of *Australopithecus afarensis. Am. J. Phys. Anth.* 60:279–317.

Steudel, K.
1980 New estimates of early hominid body size. *Am. J. Phys. Anth.* 52:63–70.
1981 Body size estimators in primate skeletal material. *Int. J. Primat.* 2:81–90.

1982a Patterns of intraspecific allometry in Old World primates. *Am. J. Phys. Anth.* 59:419–430.

1982b Allometry and adaptation in the catarrhine postcranial skeleton. *Am. J. Phys. Anth.* 59:431–441.

Stockholm Conference

1978 An international system for human cytogenetic nomenclature. *Birth Defects: Original Article Series* vol. 14 no. 8. Basel: S. Karger, for The National Foundation—March of Dimes.

Struhsaker, T. T.

1969 Correlates of ecology and social organization among African cercopithecines. *Folia Primatol.* 9:123–134.

1975 *The Red Colobus Monkey.* Chicago: University Chicago Press.

1978 Food habits of five monkey species in the Kibale Forest, Uganda. In *Recent Advances in Primatology* vol. 1. Behaviour, eds. D. J. Chivers and J. Herbert, pp. 225–248. London: Academic Press.

Strum, Shirley C.

1975 Primate predation: interim report on the development of a tradition in a troop of olive baboons. *Science* 187:755–757.

1976a "Predatory behavior of olive baboons (*Papio anubis*) at Gilgil, Kenya." Ph.D. dissertation, University of California, Berkeley.

1976b Primate predation and bioenergetics: a reply. *Science* 191:314–317.

1978 Dominance hierarchy and social organization: strong or weak inference. Paper presented at Wenner-Gren conference, "Baboon Field Research: Myths and Models" New York, June, 1978.

1981 Processes and products of change: baboon predatory behavior at Gilgil, Kenya. In *Omnivorous Primates,* eds. R. Harding and G. Teleki, pp. 255–302. New York: Columbia University Press.

1982 Agonistic dominance in male baboons: an alternative view. *Intl. J. Primatol.* 3:175–202.

1983a Use of females by male olive baboons. *Am. J. Primatol.* 5:93–109.

1983b Baboon cues for eating meat. *J. Hum. Evol.* 12:327–336.

1984 Why males use infants. In *Primate Paternalism,* ed. D. Taub, pp. 146–185. New York: Van Nostrand Reinhold.

(in press) Aggression, social skill and strategy in daily life: a baboon case history. In *Melford Spiro Festschrift,* eds. M. Swartz and D. Jordan. Univ. Alabama Press

Sugiyama, Yukimaru

1968 Social organization of chimpanzees in the Budongo Forest, Uganda. *Primates* 9:225–258.

1969 Social behavior of chimpanzees in the Budonga Forest, Uganda. *Primates* 10:197–225.

1973 The social structure of wild chimpanzees. In *Comparative Ecology and Behavior of Primates,* eds. R. P. Michael and J. H. Crook, pp. 376–410. New York: Academic Press.

1976 Life history of male Japanese monkeys. *Adv. Study Behav.* 7:255–284.

1981 Observations on the population dynamics and behavior of wild chimpanzees at Bossou, Guinea, in 1979–1980. *Primates* 22:435–444.

Sugiyama, Yukimaru, and Koman, Jeremy

1979a Social structure and dynamics of wild chimpanzees of Bossou, Guinea. *Primates* 20:323–339.

1979b Tool-using and making behavior in wild chimpanzees at Bossou, Guinea. *Primates* 20:513–524.

Susman, R. L.
1984 *The Pygmy Chimpanzee.* New York: Plenum.

Susman, R. L., and Creel, N.
1979 Functional and morphological affinities of the subadult hand (OH 7) from Olduvai Gorge. *Am. J. Phys. Anth.* 51:311–332.

Susman, R. L., and Jungers, W. L.
1981 Comment on bonobos: generalized hominid prototypes of specialized insular dwarfs? *Curr. Anthro.* 22:369–370.

Susman, R. L., and Stern, J.
1982 Functional morphology of *Homo habilis. Science* 217:931–933.

Susman, R. L.; Stern, J. T.; and Jungers, W. L.
1984 Arboreality and bipedality in the Hadar hominids. *Folia primatol.* 43:113–156.

1985 Locomotor adaptations in the Hadar Hominids. In *Ancestors: The Hard Evidence,* ed. E. Delson, pp. 184–192. New York: A. R. Liss.

Sussman, Robert W.
1972 "An ecological study of two Madagascan primates: *Lemur fulvus rufus* and *Lemur catta.*" Ph.D. dissertation, Duke University.

1974 Ecological distinctions in sympatric species of *Lemur.* In *Prosimian Biology,* eds. R. D. Martin, G. A. Doyle and A. C. Walker, pp. 75–108. London: Duckworth.

1977 Feeding behavior in *Lemur catta* and *Lemur fulvus.* In *Primate Ecology: Studies in Feeding and Ranging Behavior in Lemurs, Monkeys and Apes,* ed. T. H. Clutton-Brock, pp. 1–36. London: Academic Press.

1978 Foraging patterns of nonhuman primates and the nature of food preferences in man. *Fed. Proc. Fed. Am. Soc. Exp. Biol.* 37:55–60.

Sussman, Robert W., and Kinzey, Warren G.
1984 The ecological role of the Callitrichidae: a review. *Am. J. Phys. Anthro.* 64:419–449.

Sussman, Robert W., and Raven, P. H.
1978 Pollination by lemurs and marsupials: an archaic coevolutionary system. *Science* 200:731–736.

Sussman, Robert W., and Tattersall, I.
1981 The ecology and behavior of *Macaca fascicularis* in Mauritius. *Primates* 22:192–205.

Suzuki, A.
1969 An ecological study of chimpanzees in a savanna woodland. *Primates* 10:103–148.

1975 The origin of hominid hunting: a primatological perspective. In *Socioecology and Psychology of Primates,* ed. R. H. Tuttle, pp. 259–278. The Hague: Mouton.

1977 Society and adaptation of chimpanzees. In *The Chimpanzees,* ed. J. Itani, pp. 251–336. Tokyo: Kodensha.

Symons, D.
1979 *The Evolution of Human Sexuality.* Oxford: Oxford University Press.

Szalay, Frederick S., and Delson, Eric
1979 *Evolutionary History of the Primates.* New York: Academic Press.
Tanaka, J.
1976 Subsistence ecology of Central Kalahari San. In *Kalahari Hunter-Gatherers: Studies of the !King San and Their Neighbors,* eds. R. B. Lee and I. DeVore, pp. 98–119. Cambridge: Harvard University Press.
1980 *The San Hunters-Gatherers of the Kalahari: A Study in Ecological Anthropology.* Tokyo: University of Tokyo Press.
Tanner, Nancy M.
1981 *On Becoming Human: A Model of the Transition from Ape to Human and the Reconstruction of Early Human Social Life.* New York and London: Cambridge University Press.
1983 Hunters, gatherers, and sex roles in space and time. *Am. Anthrop.* 85(2):335–341.
Tanner, Nancy M., and Zihlman, Adrienne
1976a Women in evolution part 1: innovation and selection in human origins. *Signs: J. Women, Culture, and Society* 1:585–608.
1976b The evolution of human communication: what can primates tell us? In *Origins and Evolution of Language and Speech,* eds. S. R. Harnad, H. D. Steklis, and J. Lancaster. Annals, New York Academy of Sciences 280:467–480.
1985a Interstellar migration: the beginning of a familiar process in a new context. *Interstellar Migration and the Human Experience,* eds. Ben R. Finney and Eric M. Jones. Berkeley, Los Angeles, and London: University of California Press.
1985b *Madri, Utensili Ed Evoluzione Umana.* Bologna: Nicola Zanichelli, S.p.A.
Tanno, T.
1981 Plant utilization of the Mbuti Pygmies with special reference to their material culture and use of wild vegetable foods. *African Study Monographs,* Vol. 1.
Tantravahi, R.; Dev, V. G.; Firschein, I. L.; Miller, D. A.; and Miller, O. J.
1975 Karyotype of the gibbons *Hylobates lar* and *H. moloch.* Inversion in chromosome 7. *Cytogent. Cell Genet.* 15:92–102.
Tardieu, C.
1981 Morpho-functional analysis of the articular surfaces of the knee joint in primates. In *Primate Evolutionary Biology,* eds. B. Chiarelli and R. S. Corruccini, pp. 68–80. Berlin: Springer.
1983 Analyse morpho-fonctionnelle de l'articulation du genou chez les primates et les Hominides fossiles. *Cah. Paleoanthropol.* Paris: C.N.R.S.
Teaford, Mark F., and Walker, Alan
1984 Quantitative differences in dental microwear between primate species with different diets and a comment on presumed diet of *Sivapithecus. Am. J. Phys. Anth.* 64(2):191–200.
Teleki, Geza
1973 *The Predatory Behavior of Wild Chimpanzees.* Lewisburg: Bucknell University Press.

1981　The omnivorous diet and eclectic feeding habits of chimpanzees in Gombe National Park, Tanzania. In *Omnivorous Primates: Gathering and Hunting in Human Evolution,* eds. R. S. O. Harding and G. Teleki, pp. 303–343. New York: Columbia University Press.

Terborgh, J.
1983　*Five New World Primates: A Study in Comparative Ecology.* Princeton: Princeton University Press.

Terborgh, J., and Goldizen, Anne Wilson
1985　On the mating system of the cooperatively breeding saddle-backed tamarin (*Saguinus fuscicollis*). *Behav. Ecol. Sociobiol* 16(4):293–299.

Thompson, P. R.
1975　A cross-species analysis of carnivore, primate, and hominid behavior. *J. Hum. Evol.* 4:113–124.
1976　A behavioral model for *Australopithecus africanus. J. Hum. Evol.* 5:547–558.

Thompson-Handler, N.; Malenky, R. K.; and Badrian, N.
1984　Sexual behavior of *Pan paniscus* under natural conditions in the Lomako Forest, Equateur, Zaire. In *The Pygmy Chimpanzee: Evolutionary Biology and Behavior,* ed. R. L. Susman, pp. 347–368. New York: Plenum.

Thorington, R. W. Jr.; Rudran, R.; and Mack, D.
1979　Sexual dimorphism of *Alouatta seniculus* and observations on capture techniques. In *Vertebrate Ecology in the Northern Neotropics,* ed. J. F. Eisenberg, pp. 97–106. Washington DC: Smithsonian Institution Press.

Thorington, R. W. Jr.; Ruiz, J. C.; and Eisenberg, J. F.
1984　A study of a black howling monkey (*Alouatta caraya*) population in northern Argentina. *Am. J. Primatol.* 6:357:366.

Thorington, R. W. Jr.; Tannenbaum, B.; Tarak, A.; and Rudran, R.
1982　Distribution of trees on Barro Colorado Island. In *The Ecology of a Tropical Forest: Seasonal Rhythms and Long-term Changes,* eds. E. G. Leigh, Jr., A. S. Rand and D. M. Windsor, pp. 83–94. Washington, DC: Smithsonian Institution Press.

Tiger, L.
1969　*Men in Groups.* New York: Random House.

Tiger, L., and Fox, R.
1971　*The Imperial Animal.* New York: Dell.

Tilson, R. L.
1977　Social organization of simakobu monkeys (*Nasalis concolor*) in Siberut Island, Indonesia. *J. Mammal.* 58:202–212.
1981　Family formation strategies of Kloss's gibbon. *Folia Primatol.* 35:259–287.

Tilson, R. L., and Tenaza, R. R.
1976　Monogamy and duetting in an Old World monkey. *Nature* 263:320–321.

Tindale, N. B.
1974　*Aboriginal Tribes of Australia.* Berkeley: University of California Press.

Tooby, John
1982 Pathogens, polymorphism and the evolution of sex. *J. Theor. Biol.* 97:557–576.
1985 The emergence of evolutionary psychology. In *Emerging Syntheses in Science*, pp. 106–122. Santa Fe: Santa Fe Institute.

Toth, N.
1982 "The stone technologies of early hominids at Koobi Fora, Kenya." Ph.D. dissertation, University California, Berkeley.

Trinkaus, E.
1980 Sexual differences in Neanderthal limb bones. *J. Hum.Evol.* 9:377–397.

Trivers, Robert L.
1971 The evolution of reciprocal altruism. *Quart. Rev. Biol.* 46:35–57.
1972 Parental investment and sexual selection. In *Sexual Selection and the Descent of Man. 1871–1971*, ed. B. Campbell, pp. 136–179. Chicago: Aldine Press.

Troth, R. G.
1979 Vegetational types on a ranch in the central llanos of Venezuela. In *Vertebrate Ecology in the Northern Neotropics*, ed. J. F. Eisenberg, pp. 17–30. Washington, DC: Smithsonian Institution.

Turleau, C., and de Grouchy, J.
1972 Caryotypes de l'homme et du chimpanzé. Comparaison de la topographie des bandes. Mécanismes évolutifs possibles. *C.R. hebd. Séanc. Acad. Sci., Paris* (Séries D) 274(16):2355–2358.

Turleau, C.; de Grouchy, J.; and Klein, M.
1972 Phylogénie chromosomique de l'homme et des primates hominiens (*Pan troglodytes, Gorilla gorilla*, et *Pongo pygmaeus*). Essai de reconstitution du caryotype de l'ancetre commun. *Ann. Génét.* 15:225–240.

Turnbull, C. M.
1965 The Mbuti pygmies: an ethnographic survey. *Anth. Pap. Am. Mus. Nat. Hist.* 50:138–282.

Tutin, Caroline E. G.
1975 Exceptions to promiscuity in a feral chimpanzee community. In *Contemporary Primatology*, eds. S. Kondo, M. Kawai, and A. Ehara, pp. 445–449. Basel: Karger.
1979 Mating patterns and reproductive strategies in a community of wild chimpanzees. *Behav. Ecol. Sociobiol.* 6:29–38.

Tuttle, R. H.
1981 Evolution of hominid bipedalism and prehensile capabilities. *Phil. Trans. Roy. Sci. London*, Series B, 292:89–94.

Udea, Shintaroh; Takenaka, Osamu; and Honjo, Tasuku
1985 A truncated immunoglobulin E pseudogene is found in gorilla and man but not chimpanzee. *Proc. Natl. Acad. Sci.* USA Vol. 82 pp. 3712–3715.

Uehara, S.
1981 The social unit of wild chimpanzees: a reconstruction based on the diachronic data accumulated at Kasoje in the Mahale Mountains, Tanzania. *African Kenkyu (J. African Studies)* 20:15–32.

Van Couvering, J. A. H.
1980 Community evolution in East Africa during the late Cenozoic. In *Fossils in the Making,* eds. A. K. Behrensmeyer and A. Hill, pp. 272–298. Chicago: University Chicago Press.

van den Berghe, P. L.
1979 *Human Family Systems: An Evolutionary View.* New York: Elsevier.

van Schaik, C. P., and van Hooff, J.A.R.A.M.
1983 On the ultimate causes of primate social sysstems. *Behaviour* 85:91–117.

van Tuinen, P., and Ledbetter, D.
1983 Cytogenetic comparison and phylogeny of three species of Hylobatidae. *Am. J. Phys. Anthro.* 61:453–466.

van Valen, L.
1973 A new evolutionary law. *Evolutionary Theory* 1:1–30.

Vessey, S. H.; Mortenson, B. K.; and Muckenhirn, N. A.
1978 Size and characteristics of primate groups in Guyana. In *Recent Advances in Primatology, vol. 1: Behaviour,* eds. D.J. Chivers and J. Herbert, pp. 187–188. London: Academic Press.

Vine, D. T.; Yarkoni, S.; and Cohen, M. N.
1976 Inversion homozygosity of chromosome number 9 in a highly inbred kindred. *Am. J. Hum. Genet.* 28:203–207.

Vrba, E.
1980 The significance of bovid remains as indicators of environmental and predation patterns. In *Fossils in the Making,* eds. A. K. Behrensmeyer and A. Hill. pp. 247–271. Chicago: University Chicago Press.

Walker, Alan
1973 New *Australopithecus* femora from East Rudolf, Kenya. *J. Hum. Evol.* 2:529–536.
1981 Dietary hypothesis and human evolution. In *The Emergence of Man.* London: Royal Society and British Academy pp. 57–64.

Walsburg, G. E.; Campbell, G. S.; and King, J. R.
1978 Animal coat color and radiative heat gain: a reevaluation. *J. Comp. Physio.* 126:211–222.

Washburn, Sherwood L.
1957 Australopithecines: the hunters or the hunted? *Am. Anth.* 59:612–614.
1961 *Social Life of Early Man.* Viking Fund Publications in Anthropology, No. 31. New York: Wenner-Gren Foundation for Anthropological Research, Inc.
1963 *Classification in Human Evolution.* Viking Fund Publications in Anthropology, Number 37. New York: Wenner-Gren Foundation for Anthropological Research, Inc.

Washburn, Sherwood L., and Avis, Virginia
1958 Evolution of human behavior. In *Behavior and Evolution,* eds., Anne Roe and G. G. Simpsom, pp. 421–435. New Haven: Yale University Press.

Washburn, Sherwood L., and DeVore, I.
1961a The social life of baboons. *Sci. Am.* 204:(6)62–71.

1961b Social behavior of baboons and early man. In *Social Life of Early Man,* ed. S. Washburn, pp. 91–105. Chicago: Aldine-Atherton.

Washburn, Sherwood L., and Hamburg, D. A.
1968 Aggressive behavior in old world monkeys and apes. In *Primates: Studies in Adaptation and Variability,* ed. P. Jay, pp. 458–478. New York: Holt, Rinehart and Winston.

Washburn, Sherwood L., and Lancaster, C.
1968 The evolution of hunting. In *Man the Hunter,* eds. R. Lee and I. DeVore. pp. 293–303. Chicago: Aldine.

Weidenreich, F.
1947 The trend of human evolution. *Evolution* 1:221–236.

Western, D., and Strum, S. C.
1983 Sex, kinship and the evolution of social manipulation. *Ethol. Sociobio.* 4:19–28.

White, M. J. D.
1973 *Animal Cytology and Evolution,* 3rd edition. London: Cambridge University Press.

Wickler, W., and Seibt, U.
1983 Monogamy: an ambiguous concept. In *Mate Choice,* ed. P. Bateson, pp. 33–50. Cambridge: University Press.

Wiessner, P.
1982 Risk, reciprocity, and social influences on !Kung San economics. In *Politics and History in Band Societies,* ed. E. Leacock and R. Lee, pp. 61–84. Cambridge: Cambridge University Press.

Williams, G. C.
1966 *Adaptation and Natural Selection.* Princeton: Princeton University Press.

Williams, G. C., and Williams, D. C.
1957 Natural selection of individually harmful social adaptations among sibs with special reference to social insects. *Evolution* 11:32–39.

Wilson, Allan C.; Bush, G.L.; Case, S.M.; and King, M.-C.
1975 Social structuring of mammalian populations and rate of chromosomal evolution. *Proc. Nat. Acad. Sci.* 72:5061–5065.

Wilson, Allan C.; Carlson, Steven S.; and White, Thomas J.
1977 Biochemical Evolution. *Annual Review of Biochemistry* 46:573–639.

Wilson, E. O.
1975 *Sociobiology: The New Synthesis.* Cambridge: Harvard University Press.

Wilson, Golder N., Knoller, Mechthilde; Szura, L. Lynne; and Schmickel, Roy D.
1984 Individual and evolutionary variation of primate ribosomal DNA transcription initiation regions. *Mol. Biol. Evol.* 1(3):221–237.

Wilson, V.; Jeffreys, A.J.; Barrie, P.A.; Boseley, P.G.; Slocombe, P.M.; Easton, A.; and Burke, D.C.
1983 A comparison of vertebrate interferon gene families detected by hybridization with human interferon DNA. *Journal of Molecular Biology* 166(4):456–475.

Winter, J. S. D.; Faiman, C.; Hobson, W. C.; and Reyes, F. I.
1980 The endocrine basis of sexual development in the chimpanzee. *J. Reproduction and Fertility,* Supplement 28:131–138.
Wittenberger, J. F., and Tilson R. L.
1980 The evolution of monogamy: hypotheses and evidence. *Ann. Rev. Ecol. Sys.* 11:197–232.
Wolfheim, J. H.
1983 *Primates of the World: Distribution, Abundance, and Conservation.* Seattle: University of Washington Press.
Wolpoff, M.
1976 Some aspects of the evolution of early hominid sexual dimorphism. *Curr. Anthro.* 17:579–606.
1982 *Ramapithecus* and hominoid origins. *Curr. Anthro.* 23:501–522.
1983 Lucy's little legs. *J. Hum. Evol.* 12:443–453. Supplement 28:131–138.
Wood, Bernard
1978 An analysis of early hominid fossil postcranial material: principles and methods. In *Early Hominids of Africa,* ed. C. J. Jolly, pp. 347–360. New York: St. Martin's Press.
1979 Relationship between body size and long bone lengths in *Pan* and *Gorilla. Am. J. Phys. Anth.* 50:23–26.
Woodburn, J.
1968 An introduction to Hazda ecology. In *Man the Hunter,* eds. R. B. Lee and I. DeVore, pp. 49–55. Chicago: Aldine.
Wrangham, Richard W.
1975 "The behavioral ecology of chimpanzees in Gombe National Park, Tanzania." Ph.D. dissertation, University of Cambridge.
1979a On the evolution of ape social systems. *Soc. Sci. Info.* 18:335–368.
1979b Sex differences in chimpanzee dispersion. In *The Great Apes.* Perspectives on Human Evolution, vol. 5, eds. David A. Hamburg and Elizabeth R. McCown, pp. 481–489. Menlo Park, CA: Benjamin/ Cummings.
1980 An ecological model of female-bonded primate groups. *Behaviour* 75:262–300.
1982 Mutualism, kinship and social evolution. In *Current Problems in Sociobiology,* eds. King's College Sociobiology Group, pp. 269–289. Cambridge: Cambridge University Press.
1983a Ultimate factors determining social structure. In *Primate Social Relationships,* ed. R. Hinde, pp. 255–261. Sunderland: Sinauer.
1983b Social relationships in comparative perspective. In *Primate Social Relationships,* ed. R. Hinde, pp. 325–333. Sunderland: Sinauer.
1986 Ecology and social relationships in two species of chimpanzee. In *Ecological Aspects of Social Evolution,* eds. D. I. Rubenstein and R. W. Wrangham, in press. Princeton: Princeton University Press.
Wrangham, Richard W., and Ross, E. A. M.
1983 Individual differences in activities, family size, and food production among Lese horticulturalists of Northeast Zaire. Paper presented at American Anthropological Association meeting, Chicago, IL, Nov. 19, 1983.

Wrangham, Richard W., and Smuts, B. B.
1980 Sex differences in the behavioral ecology of chimpanzees in the Gombe National Park, Tanzania. *J. Repro. Fert.,* Supplement 28:13–31.
Wright, P. C.
1982 Adaptive advantages of nocturality in *Aotus. Am. J. phys. Anthrop.* 57:242.
1985a What do monogamous primates have in common? *Am. J. phys. Anthrop.* 66:244.
1985b "The Costs and Benefits of Nocturnality for *Aotus trivirgatus* (The Night Monkey)." Ph.D. dissertation, City University of New York.
Wright, Q.
1965 *A Study of War.* Chicago: University of Chicago Press.
Wright, S.
1951 Fisher and Ford on "the Sewall Wright effect". *American Scientist* 39:452–458.
Yamagiwa, J.
1983 Diachronic changes in two eastern lowland gorilla groups (*Gorilla gorilla graueri*) in the Mt. Kahuzi region, Zaire. *Primates* 24:174–183.
Yellen, J.
1977 *Archaeological Approaches to the Present.* New York: Academic Press.
Yerkes, R.
1940 Social behavior of chimpanzees: dominance between mates in relation to sexual status. *J. Comp. Psychol.* 30:147–186.
Yunis, Jorge J., and Prakash, Om
1982 The origin of man: a chromosomal pictorial legacy. *Science* 215:1525—1530.
Yunis, Jorge J.; Sawyer, Jeffrey R.; and Dunham, Kelly
1980 The striking resemblance of high resolution G-banded chromosomes of man and chimpanzee. *Science* 208:1145–1148.
Zihlman, Adrienne L.
1978 Interpretations of early hominid locomotion. In *Early Hominids of Africa,* ed. C. Jolly, pp. 361–377. New York: St. Martin's Press.
1979 Pygmy chimpanzee morphology and the interpretation of early hominids. *So. African J. Sci.* 75:165–168.
1981 Women as shapers of the human adaption. In *Woman the Gatherer,* ed. F. Dahlberg, pp. 77–120. New Haven: Yale University Press.
1983 A behavioral reconstructiuon of *Australopithecus.* In *Hominid Origins,* ed. K. J. Reichs, pp. 207–238. Washington, DC: University Press of America.
1984 Body build and tissue composition in *Pan paniscus* and *Pan troglodytes,* with comparison to other hominoids. In *The Pygmy Chimpanzee,* ed. R. L. Susman, pp. 179–200. New York: Plenum.
Zihlman, Adrienne L., and Brunker, L.
1979 Hominid bipedalism: then and now. *Yrbk. Phys. Anthro.* 22:132–162.
Zihlman, Adrienne L., and Cramer, Douglas L.
1978 Skeletal differences between pygmy (*Pan paniscus*) and common chimpanzees (*Pan troglodytes*). *Folia Primatol.* 29:86–94.

Zihlman, Adrienne L.; Cronin, John E.; Cramer, Douglas L.; and Sarich, Vincent M.

1978 Pygmy chimpanzee as a possible prototype for the common ancestor of humans, chimpanzees and gorilla. *Nature* 275:744–746.

Zihlman, Adrienne L., and Lowenstein, J. M.

1983 *Ramapithecus* and *Pan paniscus;* significance for human origins. In *New Interpretations of Ape and Human Ancestry,* eds. R. L. Ciochon and R. S. Corruccini, pp. 677–694. New York: Plenum.

Zihlman, Adrienne L.; and Tanner, Nancy M.

1978 Gathering and the hominid adaptation. *Female Hierarchies,* ed. Lionel Tiger and Heather M. Fowler, pp. 163–194.

Zneimer, S.; Kumamoto, A.T.; and Benirschke, K.

1979 Banding patterns of the chromosome of two langur species. *Pygathrix nemaeus* and *Presbytis entellus:* a comparative study. *Chromosome Inform. Serv.* 26:19–22.

Zuckerkandle, E.; Jones, R.T.; and Pauling, L.

1960 A comparison of animal hemoglobins by tryptic peptide pattern analysis. *Proc. Natl. Acad. Sci.,* USA 46:1349–1360.

List of Contributors

Carolyn M. Crockett, National Zoological Park, Smithsonian Institution, Washington, DC 20560, and Departments of Anthropology and Psychology, University of Washington, Seattle, WA 98195

Irven B. DeVore, Department of Anthropology, Peabody Museum, Harvard University, Cambridge, MA 02138

Warren G. Kinzey, Department of Anthropology, City College and The Graduate Center, The City University of New York, Convent Avenue and 138 Street, New York, NY 10031

Jon Marks, Department of Genetics, University of California, Davis, CA 95616

William R. Mitchell, 3720 Valencia Hill Drive, Riverside, CA 92507

Richard Potts, Department of Anthropology, National Museum of Natural History, Smithsonian Institution, Washington, DC 20560

Shirley C. Strum, Department of Anthropology, University of California, San Diego, La Jolla, CA 92093

Randall L. Susman, Department of Anatomical Sciences, School of Medicine, State University of New York at Stony Brook, Long Island, NY 11794-8081

Robert W. Sussman, Department of Anthropology, Washington University, St. Louis, MO 63130

Nancy Makepeace Tanner, Department of Anthropology, University of California, Santa Cruz, CA 95064

John Tooby, Department of Anthropology, Peabody Museum, Harvard University, Cambridge, MA 02138

Richard W. Wrangham, Department of Anthropology, University of Michigan, 1054 L.S.A. Building, Ann Arbor, MI 48109

Author Index

Abrahamson, D., 107
Ahlquist, Jon E., xii, 6, 7, 8t, 10t, 13, 25, 26n, 54
Aldrich-Blake, F.P.G., 160, 163t
Alexander, R.D., 69
Allen, L.L., 52
Altmann, Jeanne, 71
Altmann, Stuart A., 71, 173
Amerasinghe, F.P., 174
Andrews, P., ix
Angst, W., 99
Ardrey, R., ix, 35, 71, 75, 87, 90, 97, 99, 102, 222
Arnason, U., 142, 143
Avis, V., 91
Axelrod, R.T., 190, 196
Ayala, F.J., 8t
Azen, E.A., 8t

Badrian, A., 55t, 57, 62, 63, 66, 67, 78, 81
Badrian, N., 55t, 57, 62, 63, 66, 67, 78, 79, 81, 84
Baer, D., 52, 60t, 69
Baldwin, P.J., 55t, 67, 71
Barnard, A., 55, 61
Bartholomew, G.A., xii, 52
Baumgartel, W., 66
Becker, M., 148
Beckerman, S.J., 195
Beer, F.A., 67
Behrensmeyer, A.K., 31
Benveniste, R.E., 8t
Bengtsson, B.O., 143
Benirschke, K., 147
Bernstein, I., 40
Bernstein, R., 140, 145
Binford, L.R., 32, 35, 38, 222
Birdsell, J.B., xii, 52, 90, 97
Bodmer, W.F., 140
Boesch, C., 20, 20t, 21, 22, 23, 25, 44
Boesch, H., 20, 20t, 21, 22, 23, 25, 44

Bonnefille, R., 31
Bourliere, F., vii
Brace, C.L., 33, 34, 35
Brain, C.K., 75, 76, 85
Broom, R., 73
Brown, Wesley M., 8t
Bruce, Elizabeth J., 8t
Brunker, L., 85
Buchanan, D.B., 108
Buettner-Janusch, J., 147
Bunn, H.T., 32, 38
Bush, G.L., 142
Busse, C.D., 16
Butenandt, E., 67
Bygott, J.D., 63, 99, 102

Caballin, M.R., 148
Cachel, S.M., 74, 90
Callow, M.H., 141
Cambefort, Y., 145
Campbell, B., 36, 38, 90, 91, 110
Carpenter, C.R., 88, 89, 105, 115, 144, 232
Casimir, M.J., 67
Cates, R.G., 206
Cerling, T.E., 31
Chagnon, N.A., 63, 65
Chang, L.Y., 8t
Charles-Dominique, P., 168
Charnov, E.L., 190
Cheney, D.L., 63, 67
Chevalier-Skolnikoff, Suzanne, 11, 17
Chiarelli, A.B., 140, 142, 144, 145, 147, 148, 149
Chitolina, O.P., 122
Chivers, David J., 12, 108, 144, 160, 174, 175, 176f, 177
Ciochon, R.L., 54
Clarke, M.R., 118, 131
Clutton-Brock, T.H., 33, 52, 69, 120, 148, 163, 164t, 169t, 173
Comings, D.E., 140

Coolidge, H.J., 85
Coon, C.S., 106
Cooper, R.W., 117t
Coppens, Y., 203
Corruccini, R.S., 85
Cosmides, L., 189, 194, 196
Coult, A.D., 111
Couturier, J., 145
Crader, D., 32, 37
Cramer, D.L., 85
Crawford, M., 225
Crawford, S., 225
Creel, N., 29
Crespo, J.A., 117t
Crockett, C.M., x, xiv, xv, 89, 116, 118,
    119t, 120, 121, 122, 122t, 123, 124,
    125, 126, 131, 132, 133, 217, 232
Cronin, John E., ix, 8t, 12, 26n, 54
Crook, J.H., 33, 144, 173
Crozier, R.H., 142
Curio, E., 190

Dahlberg, Francis, x, 18, 19
Dalton, John, 186
Dart, R.A., 35, 72, 73, 74, 75, 76, 91,
    222
Darwin, Charles, viii, 4, 5, 26, 72, 73,
    76, 184, 186, 199, 203, 222
Davies, N.B., 36, 52
Dawkins, R., 189, 194
Dawson, G.A., 110, 148
de Bonis, L., 54
de Grouchy, J., 142, 145
de Vries, G.F., 145
de Waal, Francis, 16, 62, 102
Deblock, R., 85
Delson, Eric, 144, 148
Dene, H.T., 144
Denham, W.W., 173
DeVore, I., viii, ix, xi, xiv, xv, 38, 39t,
    67, 73, 74, 75, 88, 89, 99, 102, 144,
    187, 190, 212, 221
Dickemann, M., 130
Dittus, W.P.J., 169t
Dobzhansky, T., 113
Dodson, P., 31
Dolhinow, Phyllis, xvi
Doolittle, Russel F., 8t
Dover, B., 141
Draper, P., 226
Dresser, M.E., 147
Dugoujon, J.M., 148
Dunbar, E., 46t
Dunbar, R., 45, 46t
Dunnette, J.H., 8t
Durham, W.H., 67, 71
Dutrillaux, B., 7, 8t, 145, 147, 148
Dyson-Hudson, R., 67

Edey, M., 77, 85, 215
Einstein, Albert, 184, 189
Eisenberg, J.F., 33, 106, 107, 110, 116,
    119t, 120, 121, 123, 134, 223
Ellefson, J.D., 144
Ember, C.R., 61, 63, 67
Emlen, S.T., 52, 190
Estioko-Griffin, A., 25, 213
Estrada, A., 121, 122t, 123, 124
Euclid, 186
Ewel, J.J., 123

Fagan, B., 38
Falk, D., 22
Fenart, R., 85
Ferguson, Walter F., 12
Ferris, S.D., 8t, 54
Finney, Ben R., 6
Fisher, Helen E., 114
FitzGerald, R.W., 109
Flinn, M., 65
Forde, C.D., 62
Fossey, Dian, 55t, 56, 58, 64, 66, 67
Fox, R., 90, 99
Fragaszy, D.M., 109
Frisch, J.E., 44

Galdikas, Birute M.F., 11, 58, 82, 134
Gale, Fay, 18, 25
Gallup, Gordon G. Jr., 17
Gantt, D.G., 54
Gardner, Beatrice T., 17
Gardner, R. Allan, 17
Gartlan, J.S., 33, 89, 144
Gaulin, C.K., 121, 122t, 123, 124, 129
Gaulin, S.J.C., 109, 121, 122t, 123, 124,
    129, 134
Gautier, J.P., 108
Gautier-Hion, A., 108
Geertz, C., 19, 24, 235
Gentry, A.H., 109
Ghiglieri, M.P., 52, 54, 55t, 61, 63
Gillespie, David, 8t
Gittins, S.P., 144
Glander, K.E., 118, 121, 122, 122t, 124,
    125
Goetz, W., 99
Goldizen, A., 107, 110
Goodall, A.G., 55
Goodall, Jane, 14, 16, 42, 51, 55, 55t,
    57, 60, 61, 62, 63, 66, 67, 75, 81, 82,
    84, 90, 91, 99, 102
Goodman, Morris, 7, 8t, 54
Goss-Custard, J., 99
Gould, S.J., 235
Gregory, W.K., xvi
Griffin, P.B., 25, 213
Grine, F., xiv, 29
Groves, C.P., ix, 55t

Habenstein, R.W., 111
Haeckel, E., 72, 73, 85
Hall, K.R.L., 88, 89, 144, 221
Halperin, Stewart, 17
Hamburg, D.A., 51, 100
Hamilton, A.E., 147
Hamilton, W.D., 183, 189, 190, 192, 196
Hamilton, W.J. III, 71
Hanif, G., 118
Haraway, Donna, 89, 104
Harcourt, A.H., 42, 45, 52, 56, 58, 61, 63, 64, 65, 66, 67
Harding, R.S.O., 33, 166, 225
Harrington, J.E., 118, 119t
Harris, J.W.K., 37
Harris, M., 52, 235
Harris, Stephen, 8t
Harrison, M.J.S., 169t
Hart, Jon, 108
Harvey, P., 33, 52, 69, 120, 148, 173
Hasegawa, M., 7, 8t, 26n
Hasegawa, T., 64, 65
Hausfater, G., 58, 130
Hay, R., 12, 31, 32, 38, 41
Heisenberg, W., 184
Hernandez-Camacho, J., 117t
Hershkovitz, P., 118, 119t
Hewes, Gordon W., xi, 18
Hiatt, Betty, 19
Hill, A., 31
Hill, K., 222, 225
Hill, W.C.O., 174
Hinde, R.A., 36, 61, 62
Hiraiwa-Hasegawa, M., 64, 65
Hladik, A., 169t
Hladik, C.-M., 12, 160, 168, 169t, 173, 174, 175, 176f, 177
Hoebel, E.A., ix
Holdridge, L.R., 123
Holloway, Ralph, 22
Holmquist, G.P., 141
Homewood, K., 163, 164, 165f
Horn, A., 78
Hoyer, B.H., 8t
Hrdy, S.B., 103, 107, 108, 109, 111, 112, 130, 132, 196
Hubrecht, R.C., 110
Huxley, T.H., 72
Hylander, W.L., 173, 174, 177

Imai, H.T., 142
Irons, W., 52, 62
Isaac, G., xi, 32, 33, 37, 38, 39t, 44, 52, 85, 217, 218, 222, 224
Itani, J., 15, 84, 144

Janzen, D.H., 221
Jarmon, P.J., 173

Jay, Phyllis C., 44, 88, 89
Jerison, H.J., 225
Johanson, D.C., 7, 12, 37, 77, 85, 203, 215
Johnson, Steven C., 12, 70
Jolly, A., 33, 36, 40, 147
Jolly, C.J., ix, 43
Jones, C., 11
Jones, Eric M., 6
Jones, K.C., 147
Jones, K.W., 140
Jungers, W.L., 7, 13, 30, 77, 84, 85

Kano, T., 55t, 57, 58, 61, 63, 64, 66, 78, 79, 81, 82, 84
Kavanaugh, M., 163
Kawanaka, K., 16, 57, 67
Kay, Richard F., ix, 29, 43, 160, 168, 173, 174, 175, 177
Keeley, L., 32
Kepler, Johannes, 184
King, G.E., 35, 74, 90, 130
Kinzey, Warren G., ix, xiii, 14, 81, 85, 107, 108, 109, 110, 113, 116, 117t, 119t, 148, 173, 217, 230, 231
Kitamura, Koji, 16, 57, 62
Kleiman, D.G., 107, 109, 114, 134
Klein, R., 32
Klinger, Harold P., 8t
Kluge, A.G., 54
Kohne, D.E., 8t
Koman, J., 16, 42, 61, 62, 63
Konner, Melvin, 27n
Koop, Ben F., 8t
Krantz, G., 91
Krebs, J.R., 36, 52, 194
Kruuk, H., 74
Kummer, H., 44, 46t, 69, 99, 100, 144
Kurland, J.A., 109, 195
Kuroda, S., 42, 56, 62, 63, 64, 78, 79, 82

Lack, D., 173
Lancaster, C., 35, 73, 91, 97, 222
Lancaster, Jane, 33, 44, 85, 90, 100
Landau, M., 70
Laporte, L.F., 7, 30, 77, 85
Latimer, B.M., 12, 14
Latour, Bruno, 103, 104
Leakey, M.D., 12, 37
Leakey, R.E., 71
Ledbetter, D., 141, 142, 145
Lee, Richard B., x, 18, 67, 171, 212, 213, 226
LeFloch, P., 84
Leibowitz, Lila, 112, 113
Leutenegger, Walter, 109
Levins, R., 153
Lewin, Roger, 71

Lewontin, R.C., 192, 195
Lindburg, Donald G., 144
Linton, Sally, x, 18
Lorenz, K., 71
Lovejoy, C. Owen, ix, xiii, 27n, 29, 30, 52, 60t, 68, 69, 77, 85, 97, 103, 106, 133, 134, 197, 200, 215, 216, 217, 222, 236
Lowenstein, J.M., 53
Lowther, G., 35, 52, 74, 75, 90

MacArthur, R.H., 215
Macdonald, D., 119t
MacKinnon, J.R., 160, 163t, 166, 168f
MacKinnon, K.S., 160
Malenky, R.K., 78, 79, 81, 84
Marais, Eugene, 87, 89
Markowitz, J., 99
Marks, Jon, xiv, 109, 140, 145, 184, 233
Marshall, L., 226
Martin, D.E., 8t
Martin, M.K., 89
Martin, R.D., 211, 147, 174, 175, 177, 225, 234
Mason, W.A., 108, 109
Maxwell, James C., 189
Maynard Smith, J., 189, 190, 192
Mayr, E., 205
McEachron, D.L., 52, 60t, 69
McGrew, W., 17, 20, 21, 25, 44, 51, 60t, 68, 70, 82, 84
McHenry, Henry M., 85
McKenna, J.J., 109
Mead, M., 112
Mech, D.L., 74
Menzel, Emil W. Jr., 17
Middleton, R., 111
Miller, Dorothy A., 140, 141
Milton, K., 121, 122, 122t, 123, 124, 125, 161, 164t, 217
Mintz, K.P., 7, 8t
Mitchell, W.R., viii, xi, xiii, 34, 44, 51, 63, 73, 75, 185, 215, 224, 225, 229, 230
Mittermeier, R.A., 119t, 121
Mohnot, S.M., 144
Moore, J., 219
Morgan, Elaine, ix
Morris, D., 99, 102
Mulavwa, M., 78, 79, 82, 84
Murdock, George P., 111, 112
Myers, R.H., 145

Napier, J., 29
Newton, Isaac, 184, 186, 188, 189
Neyman, P.F., 110, 148
Nimkoff, M.F., 111
Nishida, Toshisada, 16, 55t, 57, 60, 61, 63, 66, 81

Noonan, K.M., 69

Oakley, K., 73, 75, 91
Ohno, S., 140
Oppenheimer, J.R., 169t
Oring, L.W., 52, 190
Orlove, B.S., 52
Otterbein, K.F., 63, 67
Oxnard, Charles E., 30, 77

Packer, C., 58, 63, 99, 131, 132, 144
Paris Conference, 148
Parker, C.A., 190
Petter, J.-J., 119, 119t
Pfeiffer, J.E., 99
Pianka, E.R., 153, 215, 216
Pilbeam, D.R., ix, 13, 31, 52
Pollock, J.I., 119, 119t, 161, 164t
Popp, J.L., 103, 190
Popper, K.R., 184
Potts, Richard, viii, xi, xii, xv, 5, 31, 32, 35, 37, 38, 39, 40, 41, 70, 85, 218, 219, 220
Prakash, O., 7, 8t, 140
Preuschoft, H., 29, 30
Price, G.R., 190, 192
Prouty, L.A., 145
Pusey, Anne, 82, 131, 132

Quris, R., 164

Raemaekers, J., 144
Ransom, T.W., 89
Raven, P.H., 168
Redican, William K., 109
Reynolds, F., 15, 81
Reynolds, P.C., 33, 43, 44, 89
Reynolds, V., 15, 51, 54, 81, 82
Rhoades, D.F., 206
Riccardi, V.M., 141
Richard, A., 33, 36, 40, 44, 45, 46t, 129
Ricklefs, R.E., 90
Rijksen, H.D., 58, 166, 168f
Ripley, S., 106, 111
Riss, David C., 16
Robinson, John G., 107, 108, 118, 119, 119t
Robinson, John T., 30
Robinson, P.A., 7, 8t
Rodman, Peter S., 13, 52, 58, 166, 168f
Romero-Herrara, A.E., 8t
Roonwal, M.L., 144
Rosenberger, Alfred L., 107, 173
Ross, E.A.M., 111
Rotenberry, J.T., 152
Rowell, T.E., 89, 144
Rubio-Goday, A., 145
Rumpler, Y., 147
Rylands, A.B., 117t

Sabater Pi, J., 11
Sahlins, M.D., 235
Sailer, L.D., 134
Sander, M., 122
Sarich, Vincent M., 8t, 12, 26n, 184, 205
Savage-Rumbaugh, E.S., 14, 17, 79
Schaller, G.B., 11, 35, 52, 74, 75, 90
Schlichte, H.-J., 118, 122
Schwartz, J.H., xii, 54
Seibt, U., 105, 112
Sekulic, Ranka, 120, 126, 129, 131, 132
Senut, B., 77, 84
Service, E.R., 55, 133
Seuanez, Hector, N., 8t
Seyfarth, R.M., 63
Shackleton, N., 31
Shafer, D.A., 145
Shapiro, D., 99
Shea, Brian T., 81, 85
Shipman, P., xi, 31, 32, 35, 38, 39, 220, 222
Shoemaker, A.H., 116, 118, 119t
Sibley, Charles, G., xii, 6, 7, 8t, 10t, 13, 25, 26n, 54
Sicher, H., ix
Siegel, S., 127
Silberbauer, G., 226
Silk, Joan B., 22
Simonds, P.E., 89
Simpson, G.G., 144, 145
Skelton, Randall R., 7
Slatkin, M., 58
Slightom, J.L., 8t
Smith, J.D., 40, 67, 117t
Smuts, B.B., 58, 61, 215
Soma, H., 148
Soulie, J., 145
Southwick, C.H., 88
Spuhler, J.N., 91
Stacey, Peter, 153, 165, 167t
Stander, J.M., 153
Stanyon, R., 143f, 145, 146f, 149
Stearns, S.C., 216
Stern, J., 12, 18, 29, 30, 77, 84
Steudel, K., 29
Stewart, K.J., 42, 45, 52
Stockholm Conference, 149
Struhsaker, T.T., 89, 163, 164t
Strum, Shirley C., viii, xi, xiii, 34, 44, 51, 63, 73, 75, 82, 91, 94, 96, 97, 98, 99, 100, 101, 102, 103, 185, 196, 215, 217, 221, 224, 225, 229, 230
Sugiyama, Yukimaru, 15, 16, 42, 55t, 61, 62, 63, 144
Susman, R.L., ix, xi, xii, xiii, xv, 11, 12, 13, 18, 29, 30, 34, 54, 77, 84, 85, 90, 130, 228

Sussman, R.W., xiv, xv, 11, 19, 107, 110, 113, 132, 145, 147, 148, 152, 154, 158, 168, 169t, 213, 231, 233, 234
Suzuki, A., 55t, 82, 169t
Symons, D., 103
Szalay, Frederick S., 144, 148

Tanaka, J., 169t, 171, 226
Tanner, Nancy M., x, xi, xv, 3, 5, 6, 7, 15, 16, 17, 18, 19, 26n, 34, 35, 44, 51, 53, 60t, 68, 97, 103, 185, 188, 197, 202, 203, 212, 215, 222, 236
Tanno, T., 171
Tantravahi, R., 145
Tardieu, C., 77, 84
Tattersall, I., 152, 158
Taub, D., 109
Teleki, Geza, 11, 19, 33, 75, 82, 102, 134, 185, 224, 225
Tenaza, R.R., 108
Terborgh, J., 107, 110, 168
Thompson, P.R., 35, 90
Thompson Handler, N., 78, 79
Thorington, R.W., 117, 118, 119t, 120, 122t, 124
Tiger, L., 63, 90, 99, 102
Tilson, R.L., 65, 69, 108, 110, 144
Tindale, N.B., 65
Todaro, G.J., 8t
Tooby, John, viii, ix, xi, xiv, xv, 189, 190, 194, 196, 197, 205, 215, 233
Toth, N., 32
Trinkhaus, E., 29
Trivers, Robert L., 5, 90, 190
Troth, R.G., 122t, 123, 125
Turleau, C., 142, 148
Turnbull, C.M., 57
Tutin, Caroline E.G., 14, 17, 64, 65
Tuttle, R.H., 77, 84

Udea, Shintaroh, 8t
Uehara, S., 55t, 57, 60

Van Couvering, J.A.H., 33
van den Berghe, P.L., 61, 63, 65
van Hooff, J.A.R.A.M., 52, 70
van Roosmalen, M., 119t, 121
van Schaik, C.P., 52, 70
van Tuinen, P., 141, 142, 145
van Valen, L., 209
Vine, D.T., 141
Voorhies, B., 89
Vrba, E.S., 31, 32, 235

Walker, Alan, 29, 30, 43
Walsberg, G.E., 118

Washburn, Sherwood L., vii, xv, 35, 38, 39t, 73, 74, 75, 82, 84, 88, 89, 91, 97, 99, 100, 102, 187, 222
Weaver, T., ix
Weidenreich, F., 73
Weinshilboum, R.M., 8t
Western, D., 98, 102
White, M.J.D., 7, 141, 203
Wickler, W., 105, 112
Wiessner, P., 57
Wilkerson, B.J., 79
Williams, D.C. 183
Williams, G.C., 183, 189, 192
Wilson, Allan C., 8t, 142
Wilson, E.O., 90, 108, 215
Wilson, Golder N., 8t
Wilson, V., 8t
Wittenberger, J.F., 65, 69, 108, 110
Wolfheim, J.H., 117t
Wolpoff, M., ix, 29, 30
Wood, Bernard, 29, 30

Woodburn, J., 171
Woolgar, S., 104
Wrangham, Richard W., xi, xii, 13, 40, 43, 52, 55, 57, 58, 61, 63, 69, 70, 82, 86, 102, 105, 111, 133, 197, 199, 214, 215, 227, 228, 229
Wright, P.C., 108, 109
Wright, Q., 67
Wright, Sewall, 206

Yamagiwa, J., 55t, 56, 58, 61, 66
Yano, T., 7
Yellen, J., 39
Yerkes, R., 99
Yunis, Jorge J., 7, 8t, 140

Zihlman, Adrienne L., x, 7, 12, 13, 17, 18, 30, 34, 35, 53, 77, 85, 97, 103, 185, 199, 212, 222, 229, 236
Zneimer, S., 148
Zuckerkandl, E., 8t
Zuckerman, S., 87, 88, 105

Subject Index

A.L. 129, 13
A.L. 288-1, 12, 13, 18
Acacia, 156, 157t, 158t, 162t
Acalypha, 162t
adaptive strategy, 110
African apes
shared features, 51-70, 227
aggression, 190
chimpanzee, 16
Agta, 25
Albizzia, 162t
Alchornea, 157t
Allenopithecus
chromosomes, 148
Alouatta, xiv, 89, 115-135, 227, 232
belzebul, 117f
caraya, 116, 117f, 119t, 120
fusca, 117f
fusca clamitans, 116, 118, 119t
palliata, 117f, 118, 120, 121, 121f,
122t, 161-163, 164t
pigra, 117f, 118, 120
seniculus, 117f, 118, 120, 121, 122t
altruism
reciprocal, 190
amino acid sequencing, 8t
Andaman Islanders, 111
Annona, 158t
Anonidium, 82
antelope
predation on, 92t
Antiaris, 78
Aotus, 107t, 108
arboreal habitat, 11, 84
Apes. *See* African apes; specific species
archeological evidence
to infer hominid behavior, 31-33
Arctocarpus, 162t
Arctocebus, 168
australopithecines, ix, xiv, 12, 18, 44,
73, 75, 76, 78
Australopithecus

afarensis, 7, 11f, 12, 13, 14, 18, 24,
77, 86, 134, 204
africanus, 11f, 13, 72, 77
robustus, 11f, 215
teeth, 34, 35
Avahi, 108

baboon. *See Papio*
behavior, chimpanzee, 15-17, 78-84
agonistic, 78
food sharing, 79-81, 82-84
behavior, hominid
diversity of, x
flexibility of, 210
uniqueness of, 36
bipedalism, 30, 72, 77, 199, 203, 205,
208, 211, 217
selection for, xi, 18
body size, 29
Brachyteles, 217
brain
evolution of, 22
size, 225

Callicebus, xiii, 107t, 108, 111
chromosomes, 148
Callitrichidae, 109-111
carnivores, 39, 41
social, 74
Cassia, 162t
Cebus, ix
capucinus, 169t
Celtis, 164t
Cercocebus, 144
chromosomes, 145
galeritus, 163-164, 165f
Cercopithecidae, 10
Cercopithecus
aethiops
chromosomes, 142, 148, 163
hamlyni, 108
neglectus, 107t

295

nigroviridis
  chromosomes, 148
sabaeus, 169t
Cetacea, 143
chimpanzee. 3–27, *See also Pan*
  common. *See Pan troglodytes*
  communities, 78
  mirror recognition, 17
  pygmy. *See Pan paniscus*
Chiropotes, 107
chromosome
  banding, 9t, 139
  homogeneity, xiv
Cissus, 162t
cognitive
  mapping, 17
  niche, 209–212
Colobus
  badius, 163, 164t, 169t
  guereza, 169t
concealed ovulation, 209
copulation
  Pan paniscus, 79, 81
culture, 5
  osteodontokeratic, 76
cytogenetic methods, 233

dental morphology, ix, 37, 173
Dialium, 78, 79, 82
dentition
  canines, 14
diet. *See also* Feeding; Food
  change, 19
  early hominid, 29, 205
  pattern, 169t, 173, 177–178
  primates, 11–12, 234–235
dikdik
  predation on, 92t
DNA hybridization, 6, 9t, 54
dominance, 190
  baboons, 97–100, 98t
duiker, 82

economy
  hunting and gathering, 151
Ehretia, 158t
Eichhormia, 162t
electrophoresis, 8t
Eleocharis, 162t
environmental variability
  effect on behavior, xiv, 123–129, 133
Erythrocebus, 35, 46t
  chromosomes, 148
Eskimos, 19, 111

faunal remains, 31
feeding
  adaptations, 173
  Alouatta, 120–123

chimpanzees, 82
  evolution of, 170f
female
  alliances, 61
  bonding, 201
  emigration, 133
  parental investment, 201
femur length, 29
Ficus, 121, 122, 156, 157t, 158t, 162t
field studies
  African ape sites, 55t
  cross-cultural, 24, 25
  long term, vii
  sites in Madagascar, 155f
fire, effect on
  predation, 40
  dietary adaptation, 177
Flacourtia, 156, 157t
food
  sharing, 25, 38, 79–81, 201, 217–222,
    223
  transport, 38
footprints, Laetoli, 12, 27n
foraging
  definition, 5
  strategies, 92
  theory, 190
Fucraea, 162t

Galago
  demidovii, 168
gallery forest habitat, 33
gathering. *See also* Hunter-gatherer;
    Hypothesis, gathering; Model,
    woman the gatherer
  as innovation in hominid evolution,
    x, 5, 35
gene sequencing, 9t
genetic drift, xiv
genito-genital rubbing, 81
  Pan paniscus, 79
geochemical studies, 31
gibbon. *See Hylobates*
Gorilla, 6, 8t, 10f, 11, 12, 56f, 197
  g. beringei, 55t
  g. gorilla, 55t
  g. graueri, 55t
Grevia, 157t
grooming
  Pan paniscus, 63, 79
grouping patterns
  African apes, 56–58, 59f
  chimpanzees, 55

Hadza, 203
Haematoxylon, 162t
hand function, 29
hare
  predation on, 92t

hemoglobin analysis, 54
home base, 38, 39t, 217–222, 224
hominid
  adaptations, 37
  evolution, stages of, 5, 202–207
  fossils, to infer behavior, 29–30
  unique behaviors, 46, 207–208
Homo, 148–150
  erectus, 11f, 18, 203, 204, 215
  habilis, 11f, 204
howler monkey. *See Alouatta*
hunter-gatherer, 35, 37, 42, 63, 67, 112,
  133, 169t, 220, 222, 225
hunting, 5, 73, 74, 208, 222
  cooperative, 75
Hydrilla, 162t
hyena, 43
Hylobates, xiii, 6, 8t, 107t, 111, 118,
  144, 211, 217
  chromosomes, 142, 144
  concolor, 119t
  hoolock, 119t
  hybrid chromosomes, 143f
  lar, 10
  pileatus, 119t
  syndactylus, 10
hypothesis
  gathering, 3, 6, 12, 18–23
  hunting, ix, 222–223
  killer-ape, 75
  seed-eating, ix, 43

immuno-reaction, 8t
impala
  predation on, 92t
inbreeding avoidance, 190
index
  dietary diversity, 152, 167t
  dietary similarity, 153, 167t
Indri, 161, 164t
infanticide, 130–132, 196, 214

klipspringer
  predation on, 92t
knuckle-walking, 11
Kromdraai, 13
!Kung, 39, 111, 203, 217, 226

Laetoli, 12
language, 44
Lemur
  catta, 145, 147, 154, 158t, 159t, 169t
  fulvus, 145, 147, 154, 159t, 169t
  macaco, 118, 119t
  mongoz, 166
Lepilemur, 108
Leucaena, 162t
lions
  infanticide, 131

locomotion
  chimpanzee, 85
  hominid, 29
Lucy. *See A.L.* 288–1

macaca, 144, 227
  chromosomes, 145
  fascicularis, 158, 162t, 163t
    chromosomes, 146f
  mulatta
    chromosomes, 142
  sinica, 169t
Madagascar
  study sites, 155
male
  coalitions, 223
  parental investment (MPI), ix, 201,
    208, 214, 223, 231
  provisioning, 215–217
Mandrillus
  chromosomes, 145
Mangifera, 162t
mango, 162t
Mariscus, 162t
marmosets, xiii, 110
Melia, 158t
microfauna, 31
model
  adaptive, 33–34
  baboon, xii, 33, 35, 45, 73, 74, 87–91,
    229–230
  chimpanzee, xii, xiv, 3–27, 34, 35, 90
  conceptual, 184–186, 188–189
  dietary, 173f
  killer-ape, 75, 76
  man-the-hunter, 192, 222–223
  primate-derived, 33–36, 132, 226
  referential, 184–188, 203
  savanna, 85
  savanna-based, 74
  social carnivore, viii, 35, 74, 90,
    130–132
  species-specific, 34–36
  strategic, 189, 190–200, 235, 237
  woman-the-gatherer, x, 3, 6, 12, 18,
    192, 197, 200, 212–215
monogamy, xiii–xiv, 69, 105–113, 114n,
  134, 215, 217, 230–232
  chimpanzees, 64
  humans, 65
morphology
  differences between common &
    pygmy chimpanzee, 12, 85
  of digestive tract, 172–177

Nasilis
  concolor, 107t
Neanderthal, 204
Newtonia, 164t

nuclear family, 112

O.H., 8, 13
Olduvai Gorge, 13, 37–43, 47, 219
omnivory, 19, 166, 168, 172t, 225
orangutan. See Pongo

pair-bonding, ix, 106, 144, 215–217
paleoenvironment
  evidence to inter hominid behavior,
    30–31
Pan
  paniscus, 8t, 10f, 12–15, 24, 53, 55t,
    56f, 78–84, 228–229
  troglodytes, vii, 8t, 10f, 42, 51, 56f,
    81–84, 134, 169t
  chromosomes, 142
  schweinfurthii, 55t
  troglodytes, 55t
  verus, 55t
Papio, xiii, 34, 35, 42, 51, 111, 144, 227
  anubis, 91
  chromosomes, 145, 146f
  cynocephalus, 165, 167t
  hamadryas, 42, 45, 46t, 69, 87
Paranthropus, 76
patas monkey. See Erythrocebus
patch size, 201
Phyllanthus, 158t
Pithecellobium, 158t
Pithecia, 107t
  pithecia, 118, 119t
plains habitat, 33
pollen
  fossil, 31
Pongo, 6, 8t, 10f, 11, 54, 56f, 134, 166,
    168f, 211
  close relationship to humans, xii
porcupine, 43
Poupartia, 157t
preadaptations, 211
predation, 75, 220
  by baboons, 74, 91–97
  competition from carnivores, 40, 42
  defense against, 190
  definition, 5
  pressure, 201
Presbytis
  entellus, 132, 169t
  potenziani, 107t
  senex, 169t
process
  distinction from result, 44
Proconsul
  africanus, 13
Propithecus, 129
provisioning
  chimpanzees, 55

pygmies
  Efe, 111
  Mbuti, 203

Quivisianthe, 157t, 158t

r & K selection, 215–216
rainfall, Hato Masaguaral, 124t
Ramapithecus, ix, 7, 13
range size, 15
Red Queen, 209
relationships
  among females, 16, 55, 58–62, 59f
  among males, 55, 59f, 62–64
  intergroup, 55, 60t, 66–67
  sexual, 55, 59f, 64–66, 69
resources
  transportation of, xi, 47
Rinorea, 158t
Rodentia, 143

Saccarum, 162t
safety
  feature of home base, 38
saki monkey. See Chiropotes; Pithecia
Samenea, 162t
San, 169t, 171, 212
savanna, 34, 45
scavenging
  by early hominids, xi, 32, 76,
    217–222
  by carnivores, 76
Schinus, 162t
secondary compounds, 206
sedimentological studies, 31
sexual
  choice, female, 14, 64, 133, 215
  dimorphism, 12–15, 29, 81, 85,
    116–120, 134, 199, 201, 223
  division of labor, 103–104, 213, 224
  segregation in food exploitation, 134
  selection, 4, 14, 118, 130–132, 134
siamang. See Hylobates
SK 54,76
Sivapithecus, 7, 13
skull length, 29
social life
  early hominid, 33
social strategies
  baboons, 100–102
socionomic sex ratio, 81
steenbok
  predation on, 92t
Sterkfontein, 13
stone cache, 40, 41f
Sts 7, 13
Sts 14, 13
Sts 34, 13
Sts 1513, 13

supraorbital torus, 35

Tamarindus, 156, 157t, 158t, 162t
tamarins, xiii, 110
taphonomy, 31, 37, 38
Tarsius, 108, 168
teeth. *See* Dental; Dentition
Terminalia, 156, 157t
territoriality, 67
theory
  game, 192, 196
  of evolutionarily stable strategies, 190,
    192
Theropithecus, 35, 45, 46t, 166
  chromosomes, 145
Thomson's gazelle
  predation on, 92t
titi monkey. *See Callicebus*
TM 1517, 13, 76
tool-making

by chimpanzees, 44
tools, 199
  bone, 73
  stone, 5, 32, 224
tool use
  by chimpanzees, 17, 19–23, 20t, 25,
    42, 75
  by orangutans, 17
  by humans, 203

Uapaca, 78

variation
  intraspecific, 71
  seasonal, xiv, 123–129, 133–134
vertical climbing, 77
Vitex, 157t, 158t

woodland habitat, 33